THE ARCHETYPE OF SHADOW IN A SPLIT WORLD

Proceedings of
The Tenth International Congress
For Analytical Psychology,
Berlin, 1986

Mary Ann Mattoon, Editor

DAIMON
VERLAG
ZÜRICH

The Archetype of Shadow in a Split World,
edited by Mary Ann Mattoon

Cover by Joel Miskin, assisted by Adrienne Pearson.

Composition by Stanton Publication Services, Inc.,
Minneapolis, Minnesota, U.S.A.

Paperback: ISBN 3–85630–506–8
Hardbound: ISBN 3–85630–514–9

Contents

Editor's Preface

The theme of the Tenth International Congress for Analytical Psychology, held in West Berlin September 2–9, 1987, was "The Archetype of Shadow in a Split World." This theme has a special meaning for the times in which we live, especially for a Congress set in the divided city of Berlin. In that city, awareness of the Wall between West Berlin and East Berlin is inescapable. The Wall is a vivid reminder of East-West divisions, which are prototypical of the countless divisions among humans.

Many of these divisions are reflected in this book. Some of the authors see them as resulting from collective shadow projections which, in turn, affect the psyches of individuals. Other authors focus more on intra-psychic and inter-personal divisions: inner conflicts, self-destructive attitudes, and projection of the individual shadow in personal relationships. All the papers bear on the multi-dimensional shadow: the individual and the collective, the inner and the outer, the archetypal and the personal.

In Jungian psychology the shadow is a major concept; it is both individual and collective. The personal shadow is composed of qualities that an individual prefers to hide—to keep in the dark. The specific contents vary with the person but are always undifferentiated: undeveloped, awkward, and even crude. In the eyes of their owners, these contents are undesirable and often wicked. Many contents, however, would be constructive if developed. Thus, they have a creative potential.

The collective shadow is more consistently destructive. It is sometimes described as including "absolute" evil. I prefer to say that the evil of the collective shadow is as absolute as is possible in human life; for example, the atrocities of war. Other examples of the collective shadow's manifestations are the offenses of racial, economic, and social groups against each other.

Projection of the shadow is a dynamic phenomenon in which all of us engage. On a personal level, when these projections are negative, they are likely to result in inter-personal conflicts; we oppose in others what we dislike and repress in ourselves. Or the projections are positive and produce strong attachments.

Projection of the collective shadow occurs through generalization. We make undesirable attributions to other neighborhoods, cities, sections of our own countries, religions, ethnic and racial groups, friendly nations, and adversary nations. Many societal and political problems ensue.

One set of such problems is inter-group prejudice and discrimination. Caucasians project their shadows onto the darker races who, in turn, attribute undesirable qualities to lower-status members of their own groups and to alien groups. "Liberal" whites become hostile to people who discriminate against minorities. A similar process occurs in almost any group in relation to another group that is considered different: projections of respectable middle-class people onto street people, political dissidents, religious sects, and those with a counterculture life style, and projections from those groups onto people different from them.

In war and other adversarial relations, dehumanization becomes an instrument of public policy, thus encouraging negative projections onto adversaries. With such an attitude, citizens who are normally nonaggressive can bear arms or willingly support war by their money, labor, and votes.

The feminist movement begins with the goal of equality of women with men. But, like all movements, it has a shadow side. Women discover the projections they receive from men. In turn, women may depreciate men. They also depreciate women with different life-styles; for example, housewives against career women, or heterosexuals against lesbians. (Men can be equally hostile in their attitudes toward women and toward men who are perceived as different.)

If the contents of this book are indicative, a shift is occurring in the thinking of Jungians. Most of Jung's own students accepted and retained his emphasis on inner solutions to outer problems. For example, in the era of the Cold War—following World War II—Jung held that the avoidance of a Third World War depends on the number of individuals who can bear within themselves the tension of opposites. That is, when we cannot accept the dark side of ourselves, we project it onto other individuals, groups, and nations. Then we do battle with the shadow "out there" and war is likely to result. If we acknowledge the negative qualities and forces in ourselves, we can live at peace with our neighbors. Jung seemed to believe that, if enough people can achieve such a state, their influence will hold in check the forces that bring war.

As world affairs have continued to increase in complexity, however, many psychologically developed individuals are convinced that inner development alone is not enough for individuation. Some of their energy must be devoted to influencing collective structures and policies – that is, participating in political decisions.

This conviction is supported by aspects of Jung's thinking, complementary to those already mentioned. Despite his focus on the inner world, he held that the desire for power is instinctual. Since the embodiment of the use of power is found in the political realm – from Jungian organizations to confrontations between great nations – political concerns must be expressed in order that they not be repressed and therefore become destructive. Moreover, Jungian psychology's focus on the individuation process does not preclude deep concern for the rights and needs of others. Indeed, individual development is deficient unless it includes grappling with collective shadow contents.

The efforts invested in psychotherapy – the healing of the soul – are futile if therapists do not recognize that many modern persons are burdened emotionally with societal problems: fear of nuclear arms and war, economic depressions, discrimination on the basis of race, gender, religion, or ethnic origin. Indeed, some of our terms for psychological states are identical with those for collective conditions: depression, inflation, integration.

Many Jungians see the world as a totality, not divided into inner and outer, personal and archetypal. With such a view, they feel impelled to take some responsibility for alleviating the collective conditions that produce pathology in themselves and other people. Their psychological knowledge and strengths make their active participation in the world community both possible and imperative.

This book demonstrates that the shadow is omnipresent in

personal and communal life. Therefore, as psychologists—students of the psyche (a term applicable to each reader)—we have a responsibility to recognize and confront the shadow in ourselves, in other individuals and groups, in our nation, and in the world.

* * * * *

The chapters in this book are arranged so as to reflect the authors' various emphases. Each of the first 14 is composed of a longer paper and a briefer commentary or "discussion." The first six deal with the collective background against which the Congress was held and in which its participants live. The next six present clinical manifestations of the shadow, individual and collective. The last two also are clinical but they focus on pathological states that reflect problems with the shadow. Chapters 15–21 discuss a similar varity of concerns: Three focus on collective manifestations of the shadow and four offer clinically-applicable resources. The last four chapters, which include three "workshops," describe specific methods of Jungian psychological work.

A book comprising papers by many individuals inevitably includes disparate writing styles, contents, and points of view. The goal of the editing has been to maintain the disparities, while clarifying and enhancing each author's contribution.

Jung's works are indicated in the text, wherever possible, by CW (Collected Works) and the volume number, MDR (*Memories, Dreams, Reflections*), Let-1 and Let-2 (Jung's *Letters*, Vols. 1 & 2), and FJ (Freud-Jung letters). Freud's works are indicated in the text as SE (Standard Edition) or GW (Gesammelte Werke) and the volume number. To save space, these works of Jung and Freud are not listed in the end-of-chapter references.

Other textual citations indicate author and date; they are keyed to the reference list at the end of each paper. Each reference is in the language cited by the author. A book published long ago and re-issued may carry both dates.

Non-English words in the text have been translated into English, unless their definitions are available in a standard English dictionary. American spelling has been used. Punctuation follows the University of Chicago *Manual of Style*. Names of archetypes are capitalized only when specified by an author or when necessary to distinguish them from often-used words, such as

Self, Great Mother, and Other. Dream texts are in italics. Gender-biased language, such as the generic "he," has been avoided.

The type style in this book is Palatino. It is characterized by such unusual features as an angular serif design notable especially on commas, semi-colons and quotation marks; uni-directional quotation marks; and an un-dotted "i" in the "fi" ligature.

All authors and the editor are Jungian analysts, members of the International Association for Analytical Psychology. They are identified only by the major city in or near which they work.

The name of each translator appears at the end of the appropriate paper. Katherine Bradway and Helen Johnson provided able help in editing; I thank them. My assistant editor, Bonnie Marsh, worked with me through the entire process of gathering the papers, editing them, incorporating authors' corrections, and reading proofs. I am indebted to her for her dedication.

Mary Ann Mattoon
Minneapolis, Minnesota
July 1987

Opening Address

Thomas Kirsch (San Francisco)

I have many personal reactions to being in Berlin and to the theme of the Congress. Both of my parents grew up in Berlin and lived here until they were in their early 30s. They were Jewish and with the rise of Nazism, they left this city in 1933. Eventually they settled in California. My mother never returned here because it was too painful for her. My father, along with Erich Neumann and Gerhard Adler, was one of the few Jungian analysts in Germany before World War II. He has returned several times. Unfortunately, because of advancing age, he is not able to be here now. I had not visited Berlin until planning for this Congress brought me here.

Moving away from the personal, what are some general associations to this city? Before World War II it was a city of cosmopolitan tastes, one of the great cultural centers of Europe – world renowned for its art, music, theater, intellectual life, and night life. And, yes, freedom and liberal traditions. Under the Nazis, Berlin became the center of Hitler's Third Reich. For many of us, that association lingers, along with the infamous Olympic Games of 1936, whose fiftieth anniversary was observed shortly before our meeting here.

Connected with the rise of Nazism is the specter of World War II itself, which conjures up many different emotions. I remember, as a small boy in California, seeing the newsreels of the bombing of Germany and especially the almost total destruction of Berlin. One still feels the after-effects of the war in a number of ways: the various sectors of the city, the Gedächtniskirche, for example. In East Germany the physical destruction of the war is still in evidence.

Now Berlin is a divided city, divided by a wall that symbolizes many of the tensions between East and West. The anniversary of the building of that wall was commemorated recently. The Berlin Wall is pictured in Jung's essay in *Man and His Symbols*. About the Iron Curtain Jung said, on the page opposite the picture of the Wall: "Our world is, so to speak, dissociated like a neurotic, with the Iron Curtain marking the symbolic line of division. Western man, becoming aware of the aggressive will to power of the East, sees himself forced to take extraordinary measures of defense, at the same time as he prides himself on his virtue and good intentions. . . . It is the face of his own evil shadow that grins at western man from the other side of the Iron Curtain" (p. 85).

Jung went on to describe how both East and West are in the grips of an image of paradise where everything is provided in abundance for everyone. To end this section he stated: "The sad truth is that man's real life consists of a complex of inexorable opposites—day and night, birth and death, happiness and misery, good and evil. We are not even sure that one will prevail against the other, that good will overcome evil or joy defeat pain. Life is a battleground. It always has been and always will be; and if it were not so existence would come to an end" (p. 85).

Thus, Berlin has become a potent modern symbol of our divided world, both on an inner and outer level. I am reminded of a dream of my first patient after I finished my psychiatric training. He was a middle-aged physicist who had made a severe suicide attempt and was in the midst of a deep psychotic depression for which he had been hospitalized. He remained in a deeply retarded state for weeks, and I was quite concerned that he might not come out of it. He reported the following dream: *He was in Berlin. The city was completely devastated, except that he saw the Wall dividing the city. He was watching construction going on as new buildings were being built.* This dream was the first sign I had that he might come out of his depression, which he eventually did. One can only hope that this may be possible on a collective level.

Let us now move from the subject of Berlin to the Congress itself. It offers each of us, in addition to the papers, opportunities to meet people from other groups and many countries. I encourage you all to do this; it will make the Congress much more valuable for everyone. Most of us see each other only every three years, at these Congresses, and yet the resulting friendships and collegial contacts are very meaningful. This cross-fertilization promotes the gossip that is one of the most important but least talked-about aspects of such a Congress. I do not know whether gossip is archetypal, but it certainly is a legitimate undertaking, and it enriches every Congress. Therefore, gossip! And I urge you to move away from the prevailing introversion of Jungians so as to meet the world in the form of this gathering.

I wish us all a sense of fun and participation, along with the serious business of delving into the contradictory nature of Psyche.

An Undivided World Includes the Shadow

Alfred Plaut (London)

The aim of this paper is to introduce a world-view that takes the shadow so for granted that it is no longer a separate archetype. I hope that my argument contributes in some minute measure to a world less split than present. Immediately, I find myself in a double bind; in order to reach an integrated world-view, I must presuppose the shadow—which is precisely what I want to avoid. I must take this risk in order to continue.

We all know that the shadow not only divides but also proliferates. It promotes strife under the cover of temporary unification. This tendency is noticeable not only among nations and political parties, but in small institutions such as families. Institutes of training in Analytical Psychology are not immune. Yet there is no use beating our chests; taking back projections is of little avail. Knowing about the reality of evil is not, in my view, helpful. Homilies and exorcisms equally have no lasting effect. The situation remains unchanged; called or uncalled the shadow will be with us. Jung knew this better than most. An apocryphal story has it that he left a chair free in his consulting room for the devil. Perhaps that is the most any of us can do. But before resigning myself to the apparent hopelessness of the situation, I want to look into the detailed ways by which the shadow archetype operates and the dynamics by which it receives constant sustenance. In order to do that I need to draw an artificial distinction between the archetype as such—the pure crystalline structure, on the one hand—and the phenomenology, its functions and our reactions, on the other.

The archetype of the shadow does not exist in pure form, as an isolated determinant of our behavior. It is characteristically multifaceted and appears as an amalgamate in nature. This statement is so even more in the case of the shadow than of other archetypes. Therefore, to isolate the shadow for the purpose of research constitutes not only an artifact; it also makes it, like a fissionable element, more dangerous than the amalgamate. For the shadow acts like the distorting mirror in Andersen's fairy tale "The Snow Queen," which showed nothing but the repulsive features of everybody. It had been made by the devil. When dropped, it splintered into countless fragments so minute that the people whose eyes the fragments penetrated did not even notice. What a poetic way of denoting the isolating and paranoid-driving effect of the shadow!

The shadow at work is illustrated by a few selected personal encounters. One of these occurred when I was a very small boy at the end of the First World War. I went with my nurse to welcome back some German cavalry; they were uhlans riding proudly on very tall horses. There was jubilation among the people who received the troops smilingly with cigarettes and flowers. Everybody seemed happy, and church bells rang. They had rung on several occasions when victories were celebrated, my mother explained. Shortly afterwards the Rhineland was occupied by French troops. My friend and I went to watch their military ceremonies. Utterly fascinated, we found ourselves imitating their martial music and the way they marched and presented arms. This did not prevent me from having a fantasy of possessing a gigantic broom with which I would sweep their whole army into the Rhine. These reminiscences illustrate how easily the idealization of power overpowers us, and how seductive it is to identify with it in perfect innocence, until we are forced to have second thoughts.

Here is another example: A Rumanian writer, Petru Dumetriu, in his great novel *Incognito*, described examples of changes of loyalty in the story of the hero who was swayed by the varying fortunes of the Second World War. He watched as a man suspected of being a spy was marched by his German captors through the town to be put against a wall and shot. But what really horrified the onlooker was that the wretched prisoner marched in perfect step with his execution squad. It is the very rhythm of power which can reduce an apparently rational human being to becoming identified with the robot that kills him. Whether we call such phenomena *participation mystique* or "identification with the aggressor" or "introjective identification," makes no difference; we are rendered powerless at the time. Only on recollection can we feel a little ashamed or at least humble.

My third example also dates back to childhood and illustrates the seductive power of language, both in the literal and metaphorical sense. It happened on the return journey from a Dutch seaside resort. We went there, so I was told, because of the anti-Semitism at the more popular German seaside resorts of the early twenties. We had had language difficulties in playing with the Dutch- and English-speaking children. Then the engine and crew of the train were changed for a German crew and I remember the joy I felt that everybody was speaking my native tongue again. Ten years later I crossed the same border point, alone this time, on my way to South Africa via England. I had known the danger I was in when walking the streets in Germany. After crossing the border I heard only Dutch and English spoken. "Good," I thought. "I won't be beaten up or arrested in the street." My identification with English and the English-speaking world had begun.

In Johannesburg I had been offered a place at the medical school to continue my studies; I could make a new start in life. But if I thought that I had escaped anti-Semitism, racial prejudice and hierarchical segregation, I could not have chosen a better place to be disillusioned.

There was very little fraternization among the three competing sections of the whites who were mainly of Dutch, English, and Jewish backgrounds. All three were united only in their unquestioned belief in superiority over blacks, who were considered to belong to a different species. I also remember the first time one of the native servants—called a "boy" although he was a man twice my age—asked me for a piece of paper called a pass so that he could go to town without being arrested.

The black population was also split. According to tribal factions they bashed each others' skulls in on Saturday nights.

Very soon I was pulled into the social system. Of course, skin color had not mattered in Germany as long as it was not black. Now I discovered that Asiatics were colored and thereby tainted, too. I wanted to visit the relative of an Indian friend of mine who had been a fellow student in Germany. My own relative expressed some horror and told me that I could not be on social terms with a colored person. To my shame I bowed to her superior knowledge and judgment.

I hope I have shown that I have some personal knowledge regarding the divisive and persuasive qualities of the shadow and the primitive as well as subtle ways in which it operates. But in order to present the phenomenal power of the shadow and its wily ways I have to borrow illustrations from literature.

The repetitive and cyclical nature by which power corrupts has often led to dictatorial regimes. The cycle becomes blatant among poverty-stricken and desperate populations but is also seen among prosperous and overtly democratic administrations. As I do not propose to launch into politics I can do no better than to remind you of George Orwell's classic *Animal Farm*. In this book the cycle leads from oppression and decadence to revolution and the institution of an egalitarian animals' republic. There is as yet no authoritarian principle; each animal works according to its capacity for the common good. But it soon transpires that the animals' endowment differs and a ruling caste—the pigs— emerges. The lower creatures have to work harder but are mollified by reminders that they are now free. When that is not enough and the new regime fails to prosper, a witch hunt is instituted by the leadership and the scapegoat must flee. When discontent over reduced rations and increased working hours threatens the leadership, a few of the "guilty" animals are made to confess their "sins" and are viciously executed by the rulers' bodyguard. To the original commandment "No animal shall kill another animal" the words "without cause" are added overnight. The book ends with the tragic realization that the animals are back where they started. Their ideals have been destroyed, their future is hopeless, their rulers have become tyrants.

What do we know about the dynamics of this familar archetypal pattern that we are compelled to repeat? Why can we not learn from experience? My brief answer is that we shall be walking around in circles for as long as we regard God and the Devil as opposites, as antagonists. If the indivisible, albeit paradoxical unity of good and evil spirits that both dominate and reflect human nature is not fully acknowledged, we have no alternative other than to react by worshiping idols and destroying disbelievers first, then our fallen idols, and finally ourselves. This answer is so brief that I shall devote the rest of the paper to elucidating it.

I am aware of two handicaps: First, I may be asking for trouble, because I have not followed closely the existing debate about the reality of evil. Second I am no theologian; therefore I shall omit the question of sin and I am not concerned with the origin of evil. With these provisos I offer the following observations: Most people in our profession agree with Jung that the traditional explanation of evil as privatio boni (deprivation of good) is inadequate. But where does that leave us?

Jung in *Aion* (CW9–II) mentioned relative and absolute evil. "To gaze into the face of absolute evil" Jung called a "shattering experience" (par. 19). True. But I doubt whether the relative and the absolute, like the personal and the collective unconscious, can always be distinguished, since it depends both on the circumstances and the sensitivity of a person's conscience. Nor am I certain of Jung's position as regards dualism in its Manichean form. On the one hand, he wrote that Christianity was terrified of it and preserved monotheism by main force. But as darkness and evil could not be denied, there was no alternative but to hold humanity responsible for it (CW9–I, par. 89). Jung made it clear in his *Answer to Job* (CW11, pars. 553–758) that he was in profound disagreement with this view as well. Was he a Manichean then? The Manicheans represented Satan as eternal and coexistent with God and regarded evil as something within us. (St. Augustine felt drawn to this view before his conversion but later regarded it as heresy.)

Jung once said in conversation, with a twinkle in his eye, that he was a Manichean. He also wrote that the gnostic system with their dualism make sense because they "at least try to do justice to the real meaning of evil" (CW11, par. 249). Yet elsewhere he defended himself against Victor White's suggestion that he had a Manichean streak in him. In his defense he adduced his emphasis on the unity of the Self, which is a combination of opposites, and added that "my leanings are therefore towards the very reverse of dualism" (CW9–II, par. 112n). I shall return to this apparent contradiction.

In addition to the two handicaps I mentioned, I must add that

I am aware of the well-nigh impossible task of changing a deeply ingrained pattern of behavior on which our culture and civilization are based, that is, the certitude with which we distinguish between good and evil. On the other hand, for as long as our survival depends on fear of retaliation, and as long as love of our neighbors and compassion are restricted to high days and holidays, I propose that we continue to seek change in our worldview, even if the chances of success are small.

If my view about the basic unalterability of human nature is regarded as pessimistic resignation, I shall offer no defense. Instead I shall console myself by considering that the drive for survival finds expression not only in eros, but also in specifically human curiosity and the pursuit of truth; this, too, continues despite our awareness that truth is ultimately unknowable. I shall quote no further illustration from my own life. Much of what I would have to say is covered by Guggenbühl's *Power in the Helping Professions*; nor shall I use case material on this occasion. Instead I shall resort to poetry, a device that is not unknown to analysts. Winnicott, for example, wrote in one of his late papers (1974) that if there was any truth in what he had to say, it would already have been said by the world's poets. "But flashes of insight," he continued, "that come in poetry cannot absolve us from our painful task of getting step by step away from ignorance towards our goal" (p. 103). For the moment, I shall stick to poetry.

Oscar Wilde, in "The Ballad of Reading Gaol," written while he was imprisoned there for two years because of a homosexual relationship, described in gruesome and compelling detail the atmosphere surrounding an execution by hanging. He dedicated the ballad to the memory of a trooper of the Royal Horse Guards who was sentenced to death for killing the woman he loved. The ballad ends with these words:

> And all men kill the thing they love,
> By all let this be heard,
> Some do it with a bitter look,
> Some with a flattering word.
> The coward does it with a kiss,
> The brave man with a sword.

The ballad helps me to grasp a crucially important term

Winnicott (1971) employed for the understanding of borderline patients when he differentiated between object relations and object usage. By this he seemed to mean that the formerly inner object, let us say the analyst, has survived all the patients' attacks. In the end, the analyst is granted the right to exist outside the patient. The patient's unspoken feeling is: "You have value for me because of my destruction of you." Alas, the poor trooper of the ballad could make no distinction between killing his inner object and killing in external reality. Can we be sure that we are able to make the distinction at all times? Do wars retain their dreadful appeal because they give us license to simplify and thereby to slaughter our own kind without any more discrimination than who appears to be friend and who enemy?

Here is another example from literature. In James Hogg's *Memoirs & Confessions of a Justified Sinner* the hero is a minister in a fundamentalist church. He perceives the folly and inconsistency of ministers' remonstrating with sinners whom the Maker had doomed to destruction. "How much more wise it would be, thought I, to begin and cut sinners off with the sword!" He continued: "Should I be honoured as an instrument to begin this great work of purification, I should rejoice in it."

We see that the moment we lose our capacity to be conscious of fantasy, which then becomes a conviction, inner and outer reality merge; much killing has been done in the name of a deity. We can call it religious fanaticism but is it not also possession by that superpower vested in the unity of a God-Devil? And how can we rely on being conscious? Surely, when the war drums are beating and killing beomes a pious duty, that paradoxical unity is far more powerful than our compassion with the fellow creature. I prefer "paradoxical unity" to our well-worn conflict of opposites or union of opposites.

General Gordon of Khartoum, a devout Christian, in a letter to his sister, described the incongruous quality of the paradox very simply:

> Soudan 16 July 1879: I feel so strongly that death is not an evil that, if I thought that the shooting of any number of slave dealers would be of avail in stopping the slave trade, I would shoot them without the least compunction. Though if a slave trader was sick and it was in my power to cure him, I would do my best to do so.

Gordon was just, but barely sane enough not to believe that the only good slave trader was a dead slave trader and so desisted from doing a "pious deed." Ironically, Gordon himself became the victim of a fanatical religious murder.

I now want to add some points in support of my thesis, that is, the paradoxical unity of God and Devil. Kluger (1967), in her *Satan in the Old Testament*, came close to it. She presented a theological view. I want to be pragmatic.

By offering us the simplicity of black or white solutions to all conflict, the shadow appeals to our wish to act and take short cuts rather than to reflect. This is tremendously effective in its popular appeal. Churchill, for example, who was a master of rhetoric and remains eminently quotable, stated: "In war – resolution. In defeat – defiance. In victory – magnaminity. In peace – good will." The stirring words sound like a recipe for success. And it is true that people are rarely more resolved than in war. Having few if any options, they need not think much. But Churchill gave no indication how to implement the goodwill of peace-time. Nor is there any hint why it happens that we return from the bliss of peace to the bloody conditions of war.

Simplifications, then, however regrettable in themselves, come also as a welcome relief. You are simply told what to do. One is reminded of the soldiers' "ours is not to reason why, ours is but to do and die." But although simplistic solutions appeal to our primitive and sheep-like condition and will continue to do so, we have become aware of the shadow's capacity to appear in many guises. "You have the chameleon art of changing your appearance," says the hero in James Hogg's story to the seemingly pleasant and serious young scholar, who is in fact no other than the Prince of Darkness. The scholar's reply is: "If I contemplate a man's features seriously, mine own assume the very same appearance and character." It is of secondary importance whether we explain these phenomena as intro- and pro-jective identification, as Klein (1955) does (in her interpretation of Julian Green's novel *If I Were You*), or with Jung as participation mystique connected with dissociation, as in cases of multiple personality. What matters is the loss of soul and identity or, expressed in slightly more animistic terms, possession by a demon who has invaded the person. What is of even greater relevance to my theme, is that this unrecognized and disowned invasion by the archetypal God/Devil unity causes a Jekyll and Hyde type of split in the afflicted person. According to Jung, the shadow's capacity to amalgamate with other archetypal images resembles Mercurius, who can appear (like other gods) in many guises—for example, as devil or trickster, or in animal form. As guiding savior he seems to have a Lucifer quality. Jung (CW11, par. 254n) referred to Christ and Satan as both being sons of God, therefore brothers. Albeit hostile antagonists, they are also the offspring of one and the same deity. We separate them at our peril.

For Neumann (1964) too, the shadow is more than a hostile brother. It is a companion and friend, the twin of the Self, also the doorkeeper: The way to the Self must lead through the gate of the shadow. Neumann here is concerned with a systematized outline of personality development. I agree with him that friendship with the shadow can lead to friendship with the Self. However, these abstractions are also idealizations. I am less optimistic and fear ideals. Certainly I have not observed in patients, colleagues, or myself, that pinnacle of development, individuation. I know that it is not to be realized within a lifetime; one gets glimpses of it but it seems to go wrong very often. I fear that this term too, lends itself to idealization. It is nevertheless striking that a type of super-egoism commonly may be the result of a combination of shadow and super-ego (as in superman or superwoman). I refer to that state in which power fantasies lead to narcissistic inflations, preserving what Melanie Klein called the paranoid-schizoid position with its isolating and destructive outcome.

I should at least mention the combination of shadow with anima and animus. But sexuality is so popularly known to be the instrument by which the shadow achieves dominance by seduction that I feel I need not dwell on it. When the disguise is dropped and sex combines with aggression to result in rape and murder, we are justly horrified. But is this an example of the absolute evil Jung wrote about; does this confirm the reality of evil?

When trying to answer this question I was reminded of St. Augustine and his pear tree. We know from his *Confessions* that as a boy accompanied by others of the same age he despoiled a neighbor's pear tree. This would not have been so terrible if he had been hungry and if his parents had not had better trees at home. But he was inspired by wickedness for its own sake and it was this that made the deed so unspeakably bad. Although most of us would shrug off this bit of mischief, in principle it is the wickedness for its own sake that matters. It does not help to attribute St. Augustine's exaggerated conscience to his psychopathology. The example demonstrates the relativity of evil and makes me question the "reality of evil" as if it were a separate thing.

If looking for a comprehensive unitarian view of the world includes gods and devils, which is the only way to avoid opposites and to replace them with paradoxes, it is important not to jump from the frying pan into the fire. In worshipping Satan instead of God, for example, we would be no better off.

In my search for a symbolic representation of paradoxical unity, the old Roman god Janus occurred to me. The two heads, facing in opposite directions, would lead us no further than the familiar positive and negative aspects of any archetype. The door of his gateway which was open in war and closed in peace represents a paradox, because we are used to thinking of war as a barricaded state. Adverse weather, too, forces people to "stay indoors." "To keep the door open" means hospitality. Historians of antiquity are not agreed on the meaning of the open or shut gate. In fact, the majority deny that there was a symbolic aspect to it at all.

In these circumstances I take the liberty to interpret the ritual to suit my own purpose. We are, after all, dealing with an ancient god of creation—his former name was chaos—of new beginnings, to whom the first day of the first month was dedicated. In war, as we saw, matters are simple. So simple that even in England strangers could talk to each other in the street. Except in civil wars, the nation is united. The ordinary citizen has no decisions to make. In Churchill's word, there is "resolution." All do their duty. In peace, on the other hand, there are divisions; there is open hostility within the nation; all are trying to feather their own nests. The shut gate of peacetime is called "good will."

What I want to express by the paradox of the gate is that war and peace are inseparable, as inseparable as God and Satan, good and evil. These are not dualities, not opposites, although our senses alone would persuade us that they are. True that each thing is known to us by what it is not. But the paradox is a true reflection of the human condition. I feel supported in this statement by Jung who wrote in *Aion* (CW9–II, par. 124): "Naturally the conjunctio can only be understood as a paradox, since a union of opposites can only be thought of as their annihilation" (par. 124). Jung did not go quite as far as to call the monistic God a paradox. But the question is whether the demonic and mysterious aspect of evil must also be considered as an aspect of that God. It is a practical and not just a theological question if one holds, as I do, that we conduct our lives according to the gods we actually worship, often without knowing it. Donald Meltzer (1984) wrote that every person has to have a "religion" in which the gods, like parental figures, perform functions. He adds that if a person does not put trust in internal gods, that person must live in a state that Kierkegaard described as "despair."

As for the paradox, it is not the contradictory quality so much as its shocking nature that makes it overpowering. The terror of violence and mutual annihilation is inherent in the child's experience of the primal scene of parents locked in intercourse. We may posit that the experience is partly anticipated by archetypal disposition, partly guessed at by observations and elaborated by fantasy. That image of union of opposites, threatening destruction and foreshadowing creation cannot ever be fully and directly assimilated into consciousness. To what degree it is dealt with by repression, denial or symbol formation—including fiction and legend—influences the development and fate of each person quite decisively. In other words, the primal scene resembles Jung's concept of the Self.

All this is easier to digest if we bear in mind Plato's story about the original round and highly mobile hermaphroditic human being. That species had become so powerful and arrogant that the gods themselves felt threatened and Zeus had to bisect it into male and female halves. Each half tried to restore its original shape and unity whenever they met. They asked for nothing better than to be rolled into one again. It is in such allegoric guises that the primal scene, like other symbols of the Self, can be accepted—even with a smile.

To sum up: An undivided world must include the shadow. If the opposite qualities of our perceptions blind us to the unity of our god-devil image we isolate the shadow and split the world as it really is. In short, it might be better neither to speak of the devil nor of the shadow, without remembering the unified mysterious deity with its varying faces.

REFERENCES

Guggenbühl-Craig, A. (1971). *Power in the helping professions*. Dallas: Spring Publications.

Klein, M. (1955). *New directions*. London: Tavistock.

Meltzer, D. (1984). *Dream life*. Reading: Clunie.

Kluger, R. (1967). *Satan in the Old Testament*. Evanston, IL: Northwestern University Press.

Neumann, E. (1964). *The origins and history of consciousness*. (R. F. C. Hull, trans.). New York: Pantheon.

Winnicott, D. W. (1971). *Playing and reality*. London: Tavistock.

Winnicott, D. W. (1974). Fear of breakdown. *International Review of Psychoanalysis, 1*.

Discussion: John Talley (Sante Fe)

Of Plaut I say what he wrote (Plaut, 1972) about D. W. Winnicott: "He is such an artist with words. . . that he tempts one to imitate or repeat before one has, by hard work, found a way of fully comprehending his thoughts" (p. 86).

Plaut's paper is intensely personal. It was presented by a man of Jewish heritage, German-born, in the homeland from which he fled, to a professional family whose patriarch was Swiss-German.

In another article, Plaut (1977) asked the question, "What of Jung is most in need of rebirth today?" (p. 142). I imagine that he is answering in this paper. He stated his aim: "To introduce a Weltanschauung that takes the shadow for granted to such an extent that we do not have to refer to it anymore as a separate archetype." We are asked to re-examine the crucial role which the shadow plays in the human condition and in the individuation process.

Jungians have written endlessly on the subject of the shadow, perhaps too much. One can intellectually tick off its aspects glibly. As Plaut reminds us, "Taking back projections is of no avail. Knowing about the reality of evil is not helpful. Homilies and exorcism equally have no lasting effect."

Perhaps we too easily fall into what Yandell (1978) has called "the imitation of Jung," forgetting that what he was experiencing in those years described in his memoirs (MDR) as "Confrontation with the Unconscious" was not called individuation then. A man, torn by his two natures, was alone, confronting a near-overwhelming threat of disintegration. He was not fighting a monolithic shadow archetype. Rather, he was wrestling with countless diverse pieces of instinct, emotion, terror, outer calamity, as if his eyes and heart had been pierced by those shattered fragments from the devil's mirror.

Plaut reminds us of the reality of the human condition and of the psyche. Although we experience ourselves and the world as dual in nature and made up of conflicting opposites we are, like nature, just what we are: each a whole with many parts. While I may project my own less than savory dimensions onto another person and experience myself as good and the other as bad, I am only seeing my own ugly nature outside myself where it is more tolerable to my self-image. That bad, greedy, angry, envious, lustful killer is me. As the comic strip character Pogo said, "we have met the enemy and he is us."

Plaut is asking us to abandon our idealizing and romanticizing about the concept "individuation," and instead do the work, accept the suffering and the sacrificing which coming to terms with the reality of the shadow demands.

This paper and the others in this book deal with perhaps the most difficult problem we have to face as individuals and as cultures. The theme touches the very heart of our everyday work as analysts.

Jung's structural description of the psyche, without intention certainly, can lend itself to misunderstanding. One speaks of the persona and of the shadow, as if each were a single entity. Yet, just as there are many personas, many social roles which an individual calls upon, so Plaut is reminding us that there is not one shadow. There are many, probably as many shadows as there are entities or affects. Jung said this again and again.

In considering shadow phenomena, then, it is necessary to keep in mind that we are talking about shadows—plural, the many. I offer my definition of these shadows.

1. *Personal Shadow.* Jung's simplest definition called the personal shadow "the thing a person has no wish to be" (CW16, par. 470). In view of what I've just said, one might rather say, "the *things* a person has no wish to be." These are all those experiences which have occurred from conception onward which are not acceptable to one's view of oneself and are either repressed, suppressed or not yet known. These personal shadows are in part determined by personal relationships with the parents and family and also by the collective shadow(s).

2. *Collective Shadow.* Gordon (1968) quoted Frey-Rohn who defined the collective shadow as "a cultural product deriving from the rejection and denigration of certain traits by a socially significant group of people." It is comprised of what a cultural group rejects as part of its Weltanschauung. Frey-Rohn stated that "the collective shadow may more frequently personify ethical or moral evil."

3. *Archetypal Shadow.* The archetypal shadow carries "those

characteristics whose condemnation appears to be universal and beyond the frontier of individual culture" (Gordon, 1968). It is neither individual nor cultural but, as archetypal, affects both.

The three categories describe phenomena which one experiences first as belonging to another person and later, if one has become aware enough, as being parts of oneself.

Perhaps underlying all shadow phenomena is the instinct for survival. We see it, for example, in a group of gorillas where the males instinctively mark out their territory by urinating on its boundaries. Everything within is safe and familiar, while everything outside is the enemy, dangerous, the collective shadow.

Plaut describes these collective shadow phenomena which he experienced as a boy. He visited a foreign country where he encountered people speaking different languages. He was relieved to reach the frontier where his own familiar language was spoken by everyone once again. Later, he tells us, the opposite occurred. Times and regimes changed at home. The collective shadow shifted. Confusion multiplied. What had been safe became dangerous. As Plaut so poignantly describes, what was once his own home and language became part of another collective shadow, an enemy to his survival.

In his discussion of Wilde's "The Ballad of Reading Gaol," Plaut is addressing the problem of the personal shadow. The personal shadow is composed of those unconscious complexes which, derived from personal experience, become activated and projected onto another person. While we don't know from this paper exactly why the soldier killed the woman he loved, we can surmise that he killed some negative aspect of a personal complex projected onto his beloved.

This is an example of what comprises a great deal of our everyday analytic work. A patient talks about a negative part of a friend or of the analyst; if projection can be separated from reality, and if the patient can understand and integrate those negatives which are truly his or her own, the personality is enlarged. Parenthetically, this can only occur if the analyst is constantly mindful of the capacity for projection onto the patient.

The archetypal shadow has been seen traditionally as evil per se. And although Jung repeatedly included evil as part of the Self, the general tendency in speaking of it is to split it off. Plaut underscores Jung's view that evil is not a separate archetype. Rather, we are asked to remember — to see — the paradoxical unity of a Self-image which includes as much darkness as light, as much power as eros, as much evil as good. It follows that an encounter with an image or an emotion which presents itself as archetypal shadow is an encounter with the Self and is basically a religious phenomenon.

Like Athanasius in *The Golem*, one may become committed to a deeper and more spiritual life as a result of encountering but not accepting anything that the murderer-rapist archetypal shadow presents. From this encounter Athanasius became aware of his own spiritual qualities.

Another, true story (Russack, 1986) expresses another dynamic. A man had been captured by a German soldier under conditions where prisoners were not to be taken. The man was going to be shot at close range by his captor. Before the soldier could fire the man had a heart-felt, intuitive flash and cried out to his enemy, "Ich liebe dich!" ("I love you!") The German lowered his gun and embraced him. At that moment, the man's life was transformed. He saw his future life as one dedicated to a helping profession, which he has pursued to this day with devotion.

This experience was an encounter with the Self as a paradoxical unity. It was deeply religious and transformative. In the extremity of crisis, the man's soul cried out and the near tragedy was inverted, turned into its opposite. Both men were redeemed at that moment.

Plaut is reminding us that all encounters with the inevitably myriad shadows, each of which is a living part of that which contains and reflects it, whether personal, collective or archetypal, has within it the potential for making us aware of our own limitations, responsibilities and creative capacities.

If ignored or worse, caged, our shadows, like Rilke's panther, may mutely rage and pace and do God knows what when unleashed.

> His vision, from the constantly passing bars,
> has grown so weary that it cannot hold anything
> else. It seems to him there are a thousand
> bars; and behind the bars, no world.

As he paces in cramped circles, over and over,
the movement of his powerful soft strides is
like a ritual dance around a center in which
a mighty will stands paralyzed.

Only at times, the curtain of the pupils lifts
quietly –, An image enters in, rushes down
through the tensed arrested muscles, plunges
into the heart and is gone.

As Plaut (1974) wrote earlier, "man's greatest need is to distinguish what is within and without his powers. He must choose a master – or rather, recognize the limits of his mastery and pay tribute to what lies beyond" (p. 180).

REFERENCES

Gordon, R. (1968). Book review: R. Kluger, Satan in the Old Testament; Curatorium, C. G. Jung Inst., Zurich (Eds.). Evil. *Journal of Analytical Psychology*, 13-2, 173.

Plaut, A. (1972). Critical notice: D. W. Winnicott, Playing and reality; Therapeutic consultations in child psychiatry. *Journal of Analytical Psychology*, 17-1. 86–89.

Plaut, A. (1974). Part-object relations and Jung's "luminosities." *Journal of Analytical Psychology*, 19-2, 165–181.

Plaut, A. (1977). Jung and rebirth. *Journal of Analytical Psychology*, 22-2, 142–157.

Russack, N. (1986). Personal communication.

Yandell, J. (1978). The imitation of Jung. *Spring*, 54–76.

Where There Is Danger Salvation Is Also On The Increase

Uwe Langendorf (Berlin)

The Berlin Wall, which encircles West Berlin like a ring of death, represents the deadly front between East and West. Today everyone knows that the conflict between East and West can become fatal for humanity. Both military blocs have accumulated so many nuclear weapons that they threaten human life with extermination. The situation becomes especially dangerous because of the mutual distrust and fear. A nuclear duel is assumed to be inevitable in the long run. This could become a self-fulfilling prophecy.

Humanity's world-wide expenses for arms are higher than those against hunger, and they are increasing continuously. Whereas, according to a United Nations (1982) report, in 1980 more than 500 billions of dollars were spent on armament; estimates for 1985 were 663 billions of dollars. An increasing number of weapons causes an increasing fear of war. Indeed, nuclear war is seen today as suicidal insanity.

Political leaders affirm time and again that, by continuing to arm, they only want to preserve peace. Both world powers have committed themselves to create a peaceful world; the East wants a peaceful communist, the West a peaceful capitalist world. Each side considers itself peaceful but experiences the other as hostile and untrustworthy. The 1985 Soviet military encyclopedia, for example, stated: "The aggressive nature of imperialism has not changed, and as long as it continues to exist there will also be the danger of wars" (Cited by Frei, 1985, p. 30). American Secretary of Defense Weinberger stated on the other hand: "We are facing the danger that one day Soviet leaders could draw the conclusion that they can blackmail us with the threat of a nuclear war" (Cited by Frei, 1985, p. 81).

Both sides follow a "worst-case-thinking." They perceive only the negative traits of the other side and consider the positive traits to be deceptions. Consequently, a vicious circle of distrust intensifies the hostility on both sides; one day a confrontation must come. Peace on earth, which is desired so desperately, seems to be a utopian dream that cannot be realized.

Eternal peace seems suitable only for a "satirical heading like the one on the shield of that Dutch restaurant on which there was painted a graveyard," as Kant (1954, p. 15) put it in his treatise on peace. Must we follow Kant's "practical man," who "bases his hopeless denial of our benevolent hope on: that he believes to see in advance from the nature of Man, that Man will never want what is needed, in order to realize that which leads to eternal peace" (p. 53)? What does the consciously desired peace mean for the unconscious side of the individual, for the shadow? I ask polemically: Is peace actually beautiful?

Heraclitus said, "War is the father of all things." And Freud: "It is obviously not easy for Man to do without the satisfaction of his tendency to aggression; he then does not feel at ease" (GWXIV, p. 473). Children play war with enthusiasm. But peace? They might play a ring-around-the-rosy when they are asked to do so but they will soon get tired of it and start to fight. Does human nature then conflict with peace? Eternal peace is seen as paradise on earth but again I ask polemically: Is paradise actually beautiful?

Pictures of paradise or of the heavenly kingdom as we find them on medieval altars or in naive art communicate peace and harmony but also monotony. Zacharias (1982) quoted early Christian texts of mysteries where the abolition of all dark and Dionysian elements leads to a radiant monotony. The Christian image of paradise is so one-sidedly light, harmonious, and unsensuously monotonous that a counter-image of hell is necessary to balance it. Is our image of peace one-sided, also, needing war as a balance? If we consider peace to be "feminine," we must also ask for the "masculine" war. But with the power of destruction modern war has we can no longer accept its being unavoidable.

Here an important distinction must be made. Heraclitus did not mean war in our sense. His *polemos* actually means "tumult of battle." It does not refer to organized extermination as in modern wars, but to the human capability to fight, to argue violently. This necessary element of fight and battle is expressed by the poet Matthias Claudius:

> God, let us be hungry now and then
> As to be full makes us dull and lazy,
> And send us enemies man by man.
> As fight keeps us strong and busy.

Since civilized societies offer fewer possibilities for fighting, the repressed and undeveloped pugnacity explodes periodically in wars. Modern war satisfies an already perverted need to fight. On the other hand modern civilization intensifies intra-psychic and social tensions. The diversion of these tensions into organized war is an instrument of the power of the ruling classes. The king rules his subjects mainly by two reins: a carrot and a stick, hope and the enemy. He repays them for their loyalty with the hope for peace, for utopia. He keeps them under control with fear of the enemy.

I have described here three vicious circles which are at work today and which aggravate the hostility between East and West:

1. Mutual distrust and hostility;
2. A deficiency of aggression in civilization and the urge for a warlike release;
3. The technique of ruling by means of the utopia of peace and the enemy image.

In modern empires, the two power blocs, utopias also play an important part; they conserve the power and intensify the tension. The "carrot" of the eastern empire is the utopia of the communist society. War and strife, misery and poverty will have vanished. There will be enough for everyone. There will be an oral-passive paradise. The "carrot" of the western empire is the utopia of the affluent society. There will be enough for everyone and free competition will automatically provide for the common benefit and for social harmony. There will be an oral-active paradise.

Both utopias go back to religious hopes for redemption. Both want to create paradise on earth by human power. Youthfulness and optimism take the place of religious immortality and salvation. Both utopias help to maintain an immature stage of development.

The "stick" of the East is the viciousness of the capitalists and the fear of the American nuclear bomb. The "stick" of the West is the fear of infiltration by communism and of the Russian nuclear bomb. With a demonic image and the phantom of nuclear war both power systems keep their populations in a state of anxiety in order to make them rally around their leaders like a herd in danger. In this way all criticism of their own leaders can be blocked or diverted to the outside.

Of the three claims of the French Revolution, "Liberty, Equality, Fraternity," the East promises to realize equality. But in exchange it condemns liberty, denouncing it as western poison. The West promises liberty. But in exchange it condemns equality, which it lacks, as eastern slavery. Even the faults of their own ideal are projected onto the adversary. In the East, displeasure at the privileges of the functionaries is projected on the West; in the West, displeasure at the manipulation of opinion and at the state's patronizing attitude toward its citizens is attributed to the East. Both sides postpone the ideal of fraternity to a utopian future.

The eastern enemy image seems to be characterized by oral greed. According to some sources, the Russians see western people as a bunch of Wall Street gangsters and bloodsuckers who exploit their own people and want to raid the whole world. They see them as cunning cheaters, lurking to attack the peaceful Soviet empire, as Hitler did.

A power complex characterizes the western enemy image: the Russians wanting to blackmail, rule, and enslave western people—a danger from the East which has always existed. Westerners think that the peace-loving West has always been threatened by attacks from the primitive, greedy hordes of barbarians from the East: first the Persians, then the Huns, the Mongolians, the Turks, and today the Soviets.

With every enemy image there is the tendency to aggravate and to demonize. The enemy becomes a brute, a subhuman creature, then an animal and finally the devil. What on our side is the "empire of the evil" is on the other side the "devilish imperialism." The devil is the archetypal core of the enemy image. Today enemy images are worked out and used by political propaganda with scientific precision. But their manipulators are themselves prisoners of their "product." Hitler, for example, manipulated the complex of anti-Semitism cleverly and consciously but he also was its victim. The identified devil is at the same time servant and master.

Today these images are more dangerous than ever. Since the two power blocs threaten each other with weapons which could bring extermination, their enemy image, too, has to become increasingly devilish. As an example of demonization I would like to report an episode from my childhood, by which I experienced a "conflict between East and West."

As a small boy growing up in a western country, I heard from the adults that our country was to be devoured by a big and powerful country of the East. The eastern people were not as goodnatured and friendly as we were. They were said to crave power. They wanted to rule us and to take everything from us, even our most precious possession, our identity. It was said that we would not be allowed any more to be "western people" but we would be made second class eastern people. We would not be ourselves any more. We must fight to the very end against the superior eastern might.

What I have just described, and as a child experienced, is the formation of the state of Baden-Württemberg in the early fifties, when two smaller German states were joined. The mutual fears which the western people from Baden and the eastern Swabians had of each other provoked the same demonic anxieties as today's conflict between East and West. Although east and west only indicated the geographical location of the little countries, the emotionally loaded image of the enemy of the East (or the West) had developed out of it.

Because part of my family was Swabian I felt that it was my task to mediate. Baden and Swabia appeared as two Great Mothers, one protecting, the other devouring. As a go-between, which meant to be a traitor of both at the same time, I tried to unify the two poles of the split mother image.

Don't we have the same situation today? West and East appear as estranged mothers with protecting and devouring aspects. Today, too, it is necessary to reunify the diverging poles of the Great Mother in order to prevent the tension between them from exploding in the deadly short circuit of a nuclear war. Today, too, we need the go-betweens, the "traitors."

The prototype of the traitor is Judas. Seduced by the devil, he actually was the devil. Now the devil appears as a healing image in the East-West split. Here we can apply the principle "like cures like." The devil is the archetypal core of the enemy image. Rather than go into detail about the enemy images of East and West I refer to the papers of Dieckmann (1986) and of Frei (1985), while stressing only a few points here.

Behind the Russian enemy image of the greedy western gangster there is an envy complex based on the Russians' repressed greed. Behind it there is the negative Great Mother who is gluttonous and devouring. In the western enemy image of the bestial Russian I see envy of the Russians' being closer to nature and therefore closer to the nourishing Great Mother. A negative father complex underlies the enemy image of the Communist who destroys everything. The destroyer and rabble-rouser is the rebellious son who protests against the father but who remains dependent on him and therefore is stuck in negation. Thus, the Communist represents the repressed rebellious impulses of the West. The envy of the Communist community, the cozy nest, of something maternal, comes only second.

When the West projects the rebel onto the East, the image of the devil reappears. The devil is the prototype of the rebel; through his rebellion against God, Lucifer becomes Satan. Although the devil as rebel is a potentially healing image, it is a conflicting and tragic one because the devil is sad. Mourning Satan longs for paradise which he still has to fight against. He cannot sacrifice himself for the father as Christ did and return to paradise because, if he did so, he would be devil no longer. Satan has to go on being evil so that the father in heaven can remain good. He has to represent God's dark side, God's shadow. Consequently, he stays attached to God in his protest; he is a rebel and never a revolutionary. The rebel is always a tragic figure. He fights against the king but hopes for the king's promises, for his utopia. Thus he dare not be successful with his rebellion; if he were, he would destroy his own utopian hope.

Here we have the fourth vicious circle of threat. Both empires, East and West, produce rebels: in western countries leftists, in the East dissidents. Fear of rebels leads to an intensified oppression, which strengthens the empires and cements the split.

This vicious circle of the authority complex is especially dangerous for peace because it sets the soldiers marching. It can be overcome only by autonomous disobedience. Antigone obeyed the gods—her own inner law. That made her autonomous enough to disobey Creon, the state. Berthold Brecht posed the question, "What if there were a war and nobody went?" Unfortunately, it is utopian to hope for nations to refuse to obey their leaders when they order war and extermination. Perhaps for us Germans it is especially hard to practice autonomous disobedience. We are afraid of our rebels or even hate them but our revolutionaries, who embody much more autonomy, are forgotten by us.

In Martin Luther, who strongly influenced German development, the conflict between rebellion and submission became especially obvious. He rebelled against his father by going into a monastery. But then he rebelled against the pope (papa) and in doing so, he obeyed his father, after all. He meant to obey God and not his father. His God, however, had assumed the characteristics of the severe father Hans Luder. Martin Luther preached the freedom of a Christian but when the peasants took him at his word and started the biggest German revolution, the Peasants' War of 1525, he wrote "against the thievish and murderous bands of peasants. . . . Whoever can might strike dead, strangle and stab, and be aware that there can be nothing more venomous, harmful and devilish than a rebellious man" (Fromm, 1985, p. 15).

Luther's authority complex becomes even more obvious in a letter about the defeated peasants: "If there are any innocents among them, God will save them. . . . If he does not do it, they are surely not innocent" (Zimmerman, 1982, p. 632). God was seen as the ally of the punishing sovereign. The ecclesiastical uprising against the pope ended in the secular submission of the churches under the sovereign.

The vicious circle of powerless rebellion and self-denying sub-mission has continued to the present. The German spirit submitted to Hitler with a certain pleasure. The euphoria of new departures of 1933 shows in the historical documents of that time. After 1945 the German inability to mourn showed that not much had changed. The Germans faithfully served the Emperor, Hitler, and West German Chancellor Adenauer or East German Communist leader Ulbricht. The ruler's portrait in a clip-on picture frame kept its place in the soul, the place of a dominating introject which hinders autonomy. Today's portrait of the ruler is identified as America in West Germany and the glorious Soviet Union in East Germany.

Those who step out of line and hold diverging views in public may arouse great anger. Today the symbols of the peace movement make people furious. The anger is aimed at the "traitor" who "secretly works for Moscow." But the anger also comes from a legitimate envy.

Many people cannot grow up in harmony with themselves and cannot experience their conscience as right. They are forced to adapt to that which is conventionally accepted. These broken people, alienated from themselves, have to hate and envy everyone who can stand by personal convictions. This is why autonomous disobeidence unleashes so much hate.

Out of this anger come excesses of violence and destruction as if adversaries and minorities were not only to be fought against but to be exterminated. In the pandemonium of street fights an orgiastic element appears. From there it is only a small step to the ecstasy of blood of the pogroms and plunders, of mass persecution and mass torture. The frenzy of blood seems to be the wildest and strongest ecstasy of which people are capable. This is also a face of the devil as master of the witches' sabbath and as prince of darkness. The Greek myth of Pelias' dismemberment describes the ecstasy of blood as the climax of the Dionysian-maenadic orgy.

The history of the twentieth century offers more than enough examples of such blood orgies. In order to explain the terrible fascination with this aspect of the devil, I choose a description of events which happened 80 years ago. On March 17, 1906, a reporter of the Petersburg newspaper *Daily Review* wrote about Russian punitive expeditions against revolutionaries:

They have forgotten for a long time the political purpose of their mission, they kill and burn out of an innate bloodthirst. . . . The black bunches. . . started to vandalize and plunder in the Jewish city (Kiev). The masses seemed to be fanaticized by the rattling of the windows and the crashing of the broken displays. . . . Finally some Jews were found. . . . They were pushed into the street. People hit them with everything they could find until the Jews were completely unrecognizable. . . . Then the mob really started to thirst for blood. . . . Everyone started to kill according to his individual manner. A nursing mother's breast was cut off; some girls' clothes were torn off and the girls were whipped through the streets. A Jewish woman was undressed and tied up; she was bound by her hair to a carriage and it went on at a gallop to drag her to death. The street urchins ran behind, hitting her. But why describe these scenes which make the heart ache and which at the same time make you want to shout out with joy? (Weitbrecht, 1963, p. 143)

That the reporter was overwhelmed by the fascination with evil seems obvious. I personally owe it to favorable circumstances and not to the strength of my ego that up to now I have not been overwhelmed. Can I be sure not to shout out with joy? I have kept in memory an episode from my childhood. For a time boys performed real acts of hunting and beating girls. Today I think with mixed feelings of the pleasure I had when, as a hunter in the group, I hounded and caught the screaming prey.

Today it may be crucial for our survival to recognize this orgiastic side in us. We live in an especially rational, controlled Apollonian culture. In our cities and on our planet it has become more and more light; the night has been driven away. But couldn't this lead to the appearance from behind of a secret desire for darkness, ecstasy and something Dionysian in an especially terrible manner? Today this dark element is concretized in the nuclear bomb. Like the strategists with their complicated logic, we speak in a calculating manner about megatons and megadeath, first and second blows.

But this practice indicates a splitting off of emotions. The unconscious sees nuclear war as a cosmic blood frenzy, an infernal celebration of extermination, a doomsday ecstasy. We are unconsciously ready to prepare this infernal celebration and to perform it one day, just because this devilish fascination is such a taboo. This is the last and most dangerous vicious circle of threat, the conflict between the rational mania for control and the longing for the great ecstasy of destruction.

Thus it is our duty as analysts to express in public our opinion on the present situation. For who, if not we, could render conscious this side of the individual and, though with an aching heart, bear it?

The five vicious circles of threat:
- mutual distrust and hostility.
- deficiency of aggression and release of tensions.
- split between utopia and enemy image.
- authority complex, rebellion and submission.
- need for control and longing for ecstasy.

The five complement and intensify each other. As a result hostility periodically increases and presses to be released in a war. Today these wars are waged as if along with extermination of the enemy, the evil were to be exorcized. Since the gas war of World War I, we fight not only for victory but for extermination. The nuclear bomb is only the climax, not the cause or the only expression of the war of extermination.

In each of the vicious circles however, there is also a good element which is usually missed. In distrust there is careful protection; in the deficit of aggression there is a warlike element; in utopia and enemy image the principle of hope; in the authority complex, autonomy; and in ecstasy there is religious devotion. Thus, the devil of each vicious circle also represents a potentially healing image.

In former times the devil was worshipped as the dark side of God or the gods, or as a dark demon with its own dignity. In this way the devil's healing aspect could become effective. Still in the sixteenth and seventeenth centuries the witches' sabbath was a healing ceremony. The reason that today we are at the mercy of the danger of extermination may be that we are no longer able to worship the dark – the dark side of God, for example – and to comprehend it in a religious emotion. Only in a hidden and often completely unconscious manner may an individual be able to approach the dark, acting against the ruling consciousness.

One of my patients dreamed that *I had locked her up in a psychiatric concentration camp in Siberia. I was a mad dictator, like Stalin.* I did not like to be compared with Stalin; according to Fromm's

(1977) pathography Stalin was a sadist of satanic cruelty. With this initial dream the negative father transference became obvious. The patient's father was a paranoid tyrant. With the dream dictator the patient built up a counter-tyrant against her very severe super-ego, a tyrant whom she therefore took from the opposing side. Despite its horrors the concentration camp in Siberia also represented a protected place of healing, a temenos.

Another patient dreamed that *she was travelling by train through Russia, among strangers. At the final station she got out of the train and continued on foot. The country became increasingly deserted. Finally she reached a frontier. From that point on all outlines blurred as in a fog. She could not go on because here, she felt, began the kingdom of death.* All her life this woman had been torn between her Russian emigrant father who disapproved of everything German and her German mother who hated everything Russian. The patient herself had denied her Russian origin. But it was the Russian element of her personality which included the parts she needed in order to become sane – her emotional side. She had to go to the edge of death to find her roots. But those lay in the despised region on the other side.

When I was a child I liked to play at conquering Russia. With my finger on the map I went tirelessly east. An uncle of mine was in World War II as an officer of a tank division. Having been missing in Russia, he must have served as example for that game. What on earth was I looking for in this huge land of Russia? On that map Russia was green and the farther you got into it, the more it spread out. This makes one think of something maternal and of nature. For me Russia was the terrible country of cold, of death, and of the cruel camps of silence, but also the land of fertility, of vodka, and of warm tiled stoves. It was Mother Russia. Thus I was actually looking for the good and the terrible Great Mother.

In this way, from the dark and terrible shadow image of the East, contents come to the fore which might help us to balance our one-sidedness. On the arduous road to shadow integration individuals approach the repressed contents which are projected onto the enemy. But meanwhile the threat of doom endures because of the split between East and West. Can individuals still unite on the long road to individuation in order to prevent the worst?

But isn't that another utopia? Can we still count on the slow processes of becoming conscious, while at the same time political and technical development seems to race toward extermination like an infernal machine? Must we come to terms with the fact that earth has become a planet of death, that it is all over with us? After the death of Goethe's Faust, the devil says:

> A foolish word, bygone.
> How so then, gone?
> Gone, to sheer Nothing, past with null made one! . . .
> It is by-gone! How shall this riddle run?
> As good as if things never had begun,
> Yet circle back, existence to possess:
> I'd rather have Eternal Emptiness.

Mephistopheles appears here as devil of Nothing. The idea of divine Nothing is represented even more clearly in the Tantric Kali. Shiva says: "As you Kala devour [time], you are Kali, the beginning and the end of all things. After the destruction you take your own form, black and without features, and indescribable and not recognizable you alone stay as the one" (Kinsley, 1979, p. 128). Could there be also a healing image in the Nothing?

Because the nuclear bomb will continue to exist at least as a knowledge and as a possibility, extermination will never cease to threaten us. This disastrous situation conveys a message, however, that we can find some sense in the situation. But what?

In answer to Albert Einstein, Freud wrote in "Why War?" (GWXVI, p. 23), "If willingness to war is an effect of the destructive instinct, it suggests itself to call on the antagonist of this instinct, the Eros." Thus, he expressed the hope for our understanding the message that now we should learn to love the threatened life on earth. Another message refers to the utopias. As it has become doubtful whether and how long there will be a future for humankind, all the hopes for the future and all the utopias have become doubtful, too. Utopias have lost their value and their suggestive power. They are dead.

But the clearest message is the following: After a nuclear war, even after a "limited" one, life on earth will become hell for those who survive. The accident of Chernobyl has given us a foretaste of what radioactive contamination can mean. With a nuclear war humanity would drive itself out of paradise; afterward—if there is an afterward—our present time will be a lost paradise. There-fore the paradoxical message is: Paradise is now. That seems con-tradictory; how can we call a life "paradisiacal" which is constantly threatened? Furthermore, we know paradise only as lost, gone, or in the future.

Jacoby (1980) suggested that the state of paradise as integral reality represents a regression into preconsciousness that, only afterwards, is recognizable as lost. But if we do not imagine para-dise as infantile happiness or as a land of milk and honey but as a state of harmony with our own nature and the world, with our self, a harmony which can be achieved for moments or even longer, then the concept of *Kairos* suggests itself to describe something paradisiacal which is not in contradiction with con-sciousness.

In the passage from the Bible where Jesus says to the thief: "To-day you will be with me in paradise" (Luke 23:43), he did not re-fer to a state or place after death but to the Kairos, to the possibility of harmony in the here and now even on the cross, to the right way of dying which is to be accepted and fulfilled. But this conception contradicts western thinking. Even the structure of our language leads us to focus our field of consciousness rather than to let it spread. We more easily learn how to plan the future than how to expand in the here and now. Hence, we are in an especially hopeless situation in the face of the nuclear threat. We are at our wit's end.

I shall attempt to use far eastern thinking in order to become detached from our own confirmed logic and to find a different point of view for our problems. It is difficult to transfer far esastern thinking to western culture because thinking remains bound to the structure of each language. But this difficulty can be helpful in questioning what for us is self-evident.

In a Zen story, a man who is pursued by a tiger hangs over a precipice, holding on to a branch. Above the man the tiger is standing, and down in the abyss a second tiger waits. Two mice nibble at the roots of the branch. Suddenly the man sees that a strawberry hangs close to his mouth. He eats it. How sweet it is!

This story could be misunderstood easily if it were about enjoy-ing what is offered, the strawberry, our prosperity, our private life without worrying about the threat which will only come tomorrow: the tiger, the nuclear bomb, ecological dangers. But this would be to narrow consciousness to the pleasant sides of the here and now, and it would not mean Kairos, which comprehends the wholeness of the here and now. Even while the man tastes the sweet strawberry, his hands remain painfully clinging to the branch and he can smell the tiger. Can we find here an answer to our most urgent problem?

The eastern principle of acceptance is expressed by the Chinese "wu wei," which means "not doing," but is often translated wrongly as "doing nothing." Wu wei does not mean motionlessness or passivity; it describes the mutual penetration of doing and not doing. Lao Tzu's *Tao Te Ching* (1978) is full of descriptions of the wu wei: "It accomplishes its task yet lays claim to no merit" (II). "Do that which consists in taking no action, and order will prevail" (III). "In action it is timeliness that matters" (VIII). "To retire when the task is accomplished. . . ." (IX). "Thirty spokes share one hub. Adapt the nothing therein to the purpose in hand" (XI). The nothing therein is the empty and unmoving space in the middle of the moving wheel. Wu wei points to a greater third which embraces the contrast between acting and non-acting.

We as western people like to think in alternatives: "Better red than dead." "Better to have a terrible end than to live through a terror without end." "We either do away with the nuclear bomb or it does away with us." We think in a Cartesian way, following a logic which excludes a third. Is that what makes our situation so hopeless?

The atom bomb itself is the last and most terrible child of western logic. It was supposed to make the political and military situation unambiguous and, following the principle that only one can be the strongest, to establish definite predominance. "That gives me a big stick against the boys in Moscow," Truman is supposed to have said. The promised unambiguous situation would be the unambiguousness of death; the bomb would do away with life and humankind. Because we do not want to be done away with, we do not know how to go on. The principle of mutual deterrence adds something mad to the logic, which is based on the desire of each side to overcome the other. Therefore it is rightly called "MAD" (Mutually Assured Destruction). With the newest principles of a "rational nuclear war" which "can be won" and with the Strategic Defense Initiative project, reason and humanity's will to survive seem to have vanished from the political-military planning. This is only the logical consequence of an unsolvable situation.

Can we find a greater third? Could East and West be understood as two poles of a whole, like yin and yang which are unified in a circle where the prevailing of the one initiates the change into the other? This third, embracing element would be a non-place, a utopia of a new kind. The question of the right behavior or of an attitude which we can still permit ourselves to adopt often leads to the dilemma of whether we as analysts should become politically active or not. We are said to be obliged to abstain from such activity but we, too, are affected by the threat. We cannot stay out of it by abstinence. Whatever we do or not do, whether we talk or are silent, whether we go out on the street or stay at home, we give our answer to the situation. Someone who swims in a river and gets into a whirl can either fight against the vortex or dive with the current and emerge with the next current, but abstinence is not an option.

The issue is less about the right behavior which could help us along than about the right attitude for our situation. A new attitude, if there is one, expresses itself through the body, the posture and the gestures. There are healing gestures and disastrous ones, including those relating to today's great political and spiritual movements.

The political attitude which now seems to prevail is the one of pointing away from oneself. This is a psychological projection. If the hand opens, we have the Hitler salute, a gesture of projection. And the Red front salute shows the clenched fist which pushes away, which projects. These gestures mean a forcing into line and into conformity. One sees oneself as a particle of the mass, forced into line. The energy of these particles can be concentrated in a political power which corresponds to the sum of its particles, as the power of a magnetic pole corresponds to the sum of its rectified molecules. If the particles give up their rectification, there is inertia. Thus, active participation means partisanship.

In a posture of Tai Chi meditation the arms are bent into a circle. This circle represents the microcosm of the individual and at the same time the macrocosm of the world. With this image of wholeness the number does not matter. A circle can be formed by many persons but each individual can represent the circle of wholeness. This expresses one's taking part in the whole, being responsible for the whole, and at the same time being supported by the whole. One seizes and is seized. The two arms can also be understood as the two poles of East and West which close to a circle. This results in a new interpretation of the Berlin Wall. In the beginning I understood it as a symbol of the deadly conflict between East and West. It now represents also the circle of death, which embraces the living and in which the Kairos wants to be fulfilled.

Is there a salvation which increases in times of danger? It cannot be something that comes to us from outside, like a deus ex machina. What can increase is our willingness and ability to see the salvation which is already here, which is real. Kairos could actually be understood as the fulfillment of existence. Hölderlin says it better in his poem "Patmos" from which I took the question of my title. Patmos is the place where the apostle John wrote the "Apocalypse." Here again we have a close relation to our subject:

> Near is
> And hard to grasp the God
> But where there is danger,
> Salvation is also on the increase.

Translated from German by
Dagmar Henle-Dieckmann
and Sabine Osvatič

REFERENCES

Dieckmann, H. (1986). Gedanken über den Begriff des "Feindbildes." *Analytische Psychologie, 17*–1.

Erikson, E. (1970). *Der junge Mann Luther*. Hamburg: Rowohlt.

Frei, D. (1985). Feinbilder und Abrüstung: Die gegenseitige Einschätzung der USSR und der USA. München: Beck.

Fromm, E. (1977). *Anatomie der menschlichen Destructivität*. Hamburg: Rowohlt.

Fromm, E. (1985). *Über den Ungehorsam*. München: Deutscher Taschenbuch.

Goethe, J. (1963). *Faust*. London: Penguin Books.

Jacoby, M. (1980). *Sehnsucht nach dem Paradies: Tiefenpsychologische Umkreisung eines Urbildes*. Fellbach, West Germany: Bonz.

Kant, I. (1954). *Zum ewigen Frieden*. Stuttgart: Reclam.

Kinsley, D. (1979). *Flote und Schwert, Krishna und Kali: Visionen des Schönen und des Schrecklichen in der altindischen Mythologie*. Bern: Scherz.

Lao Tse (1978). *Tae Te King*. Gia-Fu-Feng und Jane English (Hrsgs.). München: Hugendubel.

United Nations (1982). *Studie Kernwaffen*. München: Beck.

Weitbrecht, H. (1963). *Psychiatrie im Grundriss*. Berlin: Springer.

Zacharias, G. (1982). *Der dunkle Gott: Die Ueberwindung der Spaltung von Gut und Böse; Satanskult und schwarze Messe*. Wiesbaden: Limes.

Zimmermann, W. (1982). *Der grosse deutsche Bauernkrieg*. Berlin: Verlag das europaische Buch.

Discussion: Bou-Yong Rhi (Seoul)

In a systematic and detailed contribution Langendorf describes the vicious circle which, in his opinion, intensifies the enemy image. It is understandable that he points out the danger of a nuclear war and the dismal future of humankind. I feel that there should be a voice which expresses hopes for the future in order to complete the picture.

I will put three questions which should be taken into consideration. First is the question of the concept which underlies the political terms: eastern bloc, western bloc, and the split between East and West. The physical separation of the city of Berlin, the separation of a country by barriers and political restrictions, can never be denied. But the split in the psyche of a people is of a quite different intensity and value. One could even doubt whether the split between East and West exists at all in the psyche. We ask ourselves whether the ordinary citizens of the countries of the so-called eastern and western blocs always project their terrible shadows onto each other as their leaders want them to do. We must conclude that political terms such as "split between East and West" actually represent a concept with very unreal, abstract and one-sided meanings.

It is misleading to use such political terminology uncritically as something that does not need further demonstration. If, from a depth psychological point of view, we emphasize the exclusively negative shadow-side of the political problem, we sometimes even support – without being aware of it – the suggestive power of the illusory and fatal opinion that the vicious circle will go on and on until it finally leads us into war.

Humans suffer because they cling to something which does not really exist, as we can learn from Mahayana Buddhism. When we realize that what we eagerly wanted to take possession of was nothing, we will be able to free ourselves from the vice. Therefore in psychotherapy it is always more important how things are looked at than what is said about them.

The second question which should be taken into consideration is: How does the human unconscious react when confronted with the danger of the world's destruction? It is the great merit of Jungian psychology to have discovered that the unconscious, following its own principle, compensates the one-sidedness of consciousness. The aim is to achieve psychic wholeness. I therefore suggest that we go beyond the causal interpretation of the vicious circle as regards the enemy image and direct our attention toward the unconscious process of transformation.

In my Korean patients I have often noticed that the motif of psychic opposites appears in their dreams in the form of the conflict between North and South. It always has had a healing effect on them when these dreams are interpreted on the subjective level, that is, as their own problem. Some mentally ill persons have claimed in their dissociation that they would or could reunify the separated country. The more severe our own psychic splitting is, the more sensitive we are to the external splitting. Especially when we should examine our own problem we tend to focus only on the external. Therefore I find it important that such politically determined dream motifs and inner anxieties are seen not only as referring to objective facts but are realized and worked through as personal shadow problems.

Shadow is not at all static, but dynamic and capable of transformation. It is like a legitimate messenger of the Self and not an angel fallen from heaven, as Christianity says. When we look at the slow but certain transformation of the socio-economic system in Russia and, even more, in China and also at the transformation of the Christian West which has adopted a socialistic-materialistic orientation, we discover the invisible effect the compensatory unconscious has in the world's history.

The third and last question is: But where is the solution of such a global crisis? Nobody can give a generally valid prescription. The solution can be found only on the individual level. Jung repeatedly emphasized that only the individual is able to renew the world by renewing one's own psychic attitude.

> The great events of world history are, at bottom, profoundly unimportant. In the last analysis, the essential thing is the life of the individual. This alone makes history, here alone do the great transformations first take place, and the whole future, the whole history of the world, ultimately spring as a gigantic summation from these hidden sources in individuals. In our most private and most subjective lives we are not only the passive witnesses of our age, and its sufferers, but also its makers. We make our own epoch. (CW10, par. 315)

A renewal of the world could come about through the self-knowledge of the individual, as Jung said, but it would take a very long time and need an enormous amount of persistence and perseverance. Too much is expected nowadays from politics and from the social system, as if those alone could bring the promised paradise on earth.

Politics and the social system have become gods of the modern time, and the western image of utopia remains one-sided. The clear, the good, and the bright which make the image of western utopia must be dealt with first. In the boredom of such a paradise one hopes for some sensational event. Out of such a dangerous attitude one secretly applauds the orgiastic rage.

The split in the world will continue to exist in one form or another as long as we have the task of beocming one with ourselves—to realize wholeness. We cannot abolish the opposites but must accept them as an archetypal condition. One must follow one's own fate, this inner voice which we in the East call Tao (Rhi, 1981) and which in the West may be called *vox Dei*, the voice of God, the original conscience which comes into being by moral collision. This inner voice, the unifying power, is a matter of insight and intelligence rather than of so-called eastern wisdom.

An eastern example of the Self appears in the following description of the nature of the Tao. These lines may contribute to scientific discussion.

> Between yea and nay
> How much difference is there?
> Between good and evil
> How great is the distance?
> What others fear
> One must also fear.
> And wax without having reached the limit.
> The multitude are joyous
> As if partaking of the t'ai lao offering
> Or going up to a terrace in spring.
> I alone am inactive and reveal no signs,
> Like a baby that has not yet learned to smile,
> Listless as though with no home to go back to.
> The multitude all have more than enough.
> I alone seem to be in want.

My mind is that of a fool—how blank!
Vulgar people are clear.
I alone am drowsy.
Vulgar people are alert.
I alone am muddled.
Calm like the sea;
Like a high wind that never ceases.
The multitude all have a purpose.
I alone am foolish and uncouth.
I alone am different from others
And value being fed by the mother.

Lao Tzu, 1963, pp. 76–79.

Translated from German by
Dagmar Henle-Dieckmann
and Sabine Osvatič

REFERENCES

Lao Tzu (1963). *Tao Te Ching*. Translated by D. C. Lau. New York: Penguin Books.
Rhi, B.-Y. (1981). C. G. Jung's conception of Tao with reference to Tao Te Ching. In *Tao and human science: Collected papers in commemoration of the sixtieth birthday of D. S. Rhee* (pp. 223–41). Seoul: Sam Il Dang.

The Sacred Significance of Democratic Pluralism in an Endangered World

Charles Taylor (New York)

Reflecting on our split world, I find myself drawing inferences which are not all easy to accept. Our situation is dangerous and I am moved to lay out my concerns.

Three years ago I made my first visit to Israel, to Palestine, to the Holy Land; these disparate names for the small area where so much western culture took root reflect the tensions of religious and national fervor which are woven into its landscape. In Jerusalem I felt that paradoxical mix of exultation and agony, of awe in the landscape of sacred passion that is peculiar to the place. The city seems to reveal God's passionate involvement, but it bears scars of hatred as much as memorials of sacred devotion. Holding an international meeting there evoked latent divisions among its participants, despite our commitment as Jungians to hold the conflict of opposites in consciousness rather than project it in paranoid hostility.

Visiting Jerusalem was a powerful reminder of the price humanity has paid, and continues to pay, for religious dedication. Sacred passion has striven to impose the convictions of one group on another by force during most of the years of human history. There is no magic boundary which limits this aggressive acting out to the Middle East, or to religious convictions only, as the many sites of religious, ethnic, and national conflict throughout the world vividly attest. We see news reports nearly every day in which Hindus are pitted against Moslems, Catholics against Protestants, Arabs against Jews and, most dangerously, West against East. Closer to home, we find overt or latent violence in racial tensions in every major American city, in psychoanalytic infighting in New York, and in the distrust of one Jungian group by another across the United States and Europe.

These projections of the hostility of one tribe, nation, faith, or even professional group, upon another are nothing new; aggression in the name of deeply felt conviction is recurrent human behavior. I propose to focus on the dangers of these projections, both the macrocosmic risks of religious and political fanaticism and the microcosmic example of the beam in our own eyes as Jungians. We, perhaps above all others, should grasp the sacred importance of a symbolic rather than a fanatical attitude, but we too have difficulty bearing the conflict of the opposites.

The more we care, the more certain we are that we see into the heart of reality, and the more we wish to make others see it, value it, and live within its frame. But, as a species, we are now at a time when we should be doing all we can to alleviate the danger of fanatical attitudes, rather than falling into them.

I want first to consider the larger peril in which we live, the destructive power which has never been given to humankind before, to explore what kind of regard for the sacred is crucial to our survival, and then to ground this view in some observations about how we as Jungians relate to each other. It is easy to see the shadow problem of others, but harder to face it in our own work and relationships.

Returning from Jerusalem with a heightened awareness of how close to flashpoint religious fervor and national feeling can bring us, I described (Taylor, 1984) in common language just what the appalling capabilty of modern weaponry really is. Noting that we frequently refer to the threat of nuclear annihilation as the possibility of "apocalypse," I pointed out that this at first seems an anomaly, as "apocalypse is an image of what will be done by God, and we are referring to the catastrophe man himself may bring about." But the point, as Jung makes clear with passion in *Answer to Job* (CW11), is precisely that humankind must accept responsibility for having the dark power that hitherto we imagined as belonging only to God. We do not know precisely the risk that we may now terminate all human life, that we cannot only kill hundreds of millions of persons but even, as Jonathan

Schell (1982) puts it, bring about the "death of death" in the extinction of the species. But we do know from many studies that there is a real possibility of that extinction, and that, at the least, we can destroy viable civilization on most of our planet. I will not review evidence of this potential, but trust that we are able to imagine this reality, despite our deep psychological resistance to admitting its horror.

What I wish to emphasize is this: We, as human beings, command power to end the world in an apocalyptic way, power that we have imagined only gods, or perhaps a malicious fate, to possess in all previous times. In our capacity to destroy, we now *are* gods.

In the past, we damned ourselves for hubris if we claimed any part of the power of gods. Paradoxically, in the nuclear era we evade reality if we deny the hard fact that the scale of our destructive power, whether we call it demonic or divine, is of godlike dimensions.

Ironically, the gods, being immortal, do not have the power to destroy themselves, whereas we, being mortal, certainly do. We cannot, like Homer's gods, throw thunderbolts about with the assurance that we will not suffer personally, and we must fear our power at every moment, using it only with the utmost restraint and caution.

In *Answer to Job* (CW11), Jung wrote with "passionate intensity" of how much we must fear the awe-ful power we now possess. He wrote also of hope that we can be helped to contain our vast destructive power by a new and deeper incarnation of the loving, nurturing and forgiving aspect of God that has been associated for millenia with the largely hidden feminine element in Judeo-Christian mythology. If we are to save ourselves from ourselves, we must invite ascent from the depths of that part of the goddess that affirms life for its own sake and hope that the flow of the collective unconscious is with this part of her rather than its opposite. But in reality, though we may not like it, we must continue to rely on fear to keep us vigilant and focused on survival. We must fear and respect our neighbors, as we do our own shadow, even if we are not yet ready to love them.

What do we as Jungians know that would enable us to make a particular contribution to the increase of the consciousness that we require? We are under unprecedented pressure of time and have almost no room for experiment, compared to the centuries of trial and error which historically have been required for significant reorientations of collective consciousness. Perhaps we can derive hope from the fact that, in the paradoxical way of the opposites, the unprecedented knowledge of physical nature that has brought us to this precipice in the twentieth century has been accompanied by a deepened understanding of psyche which may help forestall our self-destruction. All depth psychologists now understand the processes of projection and how they distort our awareness of reality in delusional and dangerous ways. The larger collective is gradually coming also to grasp something of how these processes work, though few of us — and I include analysts — know when we are actively in the grip of a projection.

Beyond our understanding of projection as a psychic phenomenon, I believe that students of Jung have a particular contribution to make just at the point where projections operate most powerfully. This is the point where sacred passion and religious fanaticism come together. It is, as we can see, the very juncture where many of the world's flashpoints wait only for a match. Just because religious convictions run so deep, and touch the Self, they arouse the energy of sacrifice, both creative and destructive.

Few depth psychologies of other schools are able to take religious truths seriously; their epistemologies do not permit the transpersonal dimension of psychic experience to be real, and they do not perceive that the great symbol systems of religion and mythology point to actualities of psychic life. Traditional Psychoanalysis reduces the manifestations of the transpersonal realm to no more than delusional defense mechanisms of individual or collective pathology. In contrast, Jung's work has demonstrated that every great mythological and religious tradition is full of images which reflect, as no denotative language can, the psychic realities which give meaning to human life and suffering.

Yet many of these sacred systems have been used energetically and repeatedly to persecute and oppress unbelievers and heretics. For many modern persons, the intolerance and cruelty of convinced believers makes all religion suspect, and almost all western democracies deal firmly with any attempt by one religion to impose its will on others. One of the glories of democracy is its generally high level of religious tolerance. In the United States, this is not at present a result of indifference, but rather of constitutional guarantees of freedom of worship and the separation of church and state born of the founders' determination to prevent religious violence. Building on the experience of persecution in the Old World and the values of the Enlightenment, Americans avowed that, however certain they were personally that only they would be saved, it was self-destructive to try to impose their views on citizens of other faiths.

In the democratic West, with only scattered exceptions for special reasons, as in Ireland, the traditions of human rights enable the collective ego of the body politic to endure doctrinal conflicts without forced conformity. This secular tradition of freedom of worship and separation of church and state is spiritually wiser than those religions which claim exact insight into the divine order. In a manner largely unconscious, the western heritage of constitutional democracy actualized a symbolic attitude toward religious truth before that attitude could be described as such. By undertaking to communicate the psychological foundation of these democratic rights and their symbolic attitude toward sacred truth, we can contribute significantly to the awareness necessary for our survival.

The gradual separation of sacred and secular in western political tradition has profound psychological parallels in the development of personality. As the individual ego grows away from the initial certainties of parental, collective or religious ideals, it moves toward a mature ability to hold in conscious tension the conflicting claims of diverse instincts and needs. Similarly, a democratic government controls conflict by allowing its free expression. It provides for majority rule, with protections for minority views, which later may become majority opinion and rule in their time.

Constitutional systems assure that no ideology becomes predominant in a way that represses the possibility of change, just as the mature ego will not foreclose the possibility that something new may come up from the unconscious to be incorporated in a larger, even if inconveniently different, personality structure. Much of what Jung sees as an adult ego's capacity to endure the conflict of the opposites in conscious reflection is incarnated in the group processes institutionalized in a working democracy.

Its members are able to accept frustration of narcissistic grandiosity because relativization of the individual's claims is required by the social contract.

The separation of sacred from secular power is not a new idea. The Romans were careful not to impose their religious system on newly-conquered peoples, for the sake of efficient conquest. In other situations the separation protected church or state. Dante railed against the imperial ambitions of the Church after Constantine's conversion, because he could see how worldly wealth and power distracted the papacy from its religious mission. Our forebears established pluralist rather than sacral political systems, because they could see that religious states were against the commonweal.

Today there is more to this separation than just the prevention of corruption or unnecessary conflict. As Jungians, we perceive that religious states do not serve the sacred needs of modern peoples. We do not know what God or the Goddess looks like objectively. We do know that the gods are real subjectively, that each religious tradition renders profound sacred and psychological truths in its own images, and that each of us must be free to find his or her own connection to the sacred realities of psychic life. Passionate fanaticism on behalf of particular religious faiths (or political ideologies) brings us to the edge of disaster in the world as it is today—and as it will always be, for we have the means of our destruction forever in mind if not at hand. But passionate assertion of the sacredness of all religious truth, symbolically understood, is one of the necessities of our survival. This we need to perceive and to communicate to those who are open to hear.

Jung is the foremost proponent of a view of life that is at once empirically founded and spiritually centered. It is important, in my view, that in our proper concern for clinical excellence we do not abdicate our perception of the religious, and ultimately lifesaving, heart of Jung's work. Indeed, to be good clinicians we must assist the teleological drive in our patients' psyches. We are being joined gradually in this by many of the newer therapeutic orientations, though few of them are yet consciously and overtly religious in their thrust. There is much they can teach us about grounded clinical work, sharpening especially our sensitivity to the transference as it is manifest in the session. Nevertheless, we must continue to assert our awareness of the sacred realities of psychic life.

Returning to my experience in Jerusalem, let me describe the difference it makes to look at a religious image symbolically rather than literally. As a visitor, I was stunned by the power of the Temple Mount, seeing the reality of the Second Temple exposed in the excavation of the Western (Wailing) Wall. And passing the Israeli guards to the upper level, I was awed again by the beauty of the Dome of the Rock, and also of the simpler El Aksa Mosque. As you know, the rock over which the Dome of the Rock is constructed is the one sacred to Judaism as the site on which Abraham was prepared to sacrifice Isaac, and additionally sacred to Islam as the point from which Muhammad ascended to talk with Allah.

From a traditional Jewish point of view, the conquest of the Temple by the Moslems in the seventh century was a disaster; the location of Islamic mosques on its ground is a sacrilege which is still deeply resented and even the target of occasional violent assaults. One of these was attempted one night when I was there, but prevented by the Israeli police who provide security for the Temple Mount. One can only imagine what the consequences might be if such an attack were successful. Given the distrust and fanatical hatred that is never far from being acted out, the provocation was understood by the Israelis to be extremely dangerous, and they strive diligently to keep the sacred sites open to the faithful of each tradition. In this, the principles of pluralism take precedence over religious fanaticism, but the loss of the Temple heights is nevertheless mourned by believers.

To a sympathetic visitor taking a symbolic view, however, the image of the sacred foundations capped by splendors of Moslem architecture feels strangely compelling. The physical site itself expresses the syncretism of the Islamic tradition, which honors Abraham among its ancient prophets. For an outsider it seems natural to be moved by a common spiritual energy, and the feeling of paradoxical truth is very strong. To a convinced believer, however, the Temple Mount evokes understandable grief and longing.

In a response to Erich Neumann's appreciation of *Answer to Job*, Jung (Let-2) addressed the inevitable subjectivity of genuine religious involvement. "God is always specific and always locally valid," he wrote, "otherwise he would be ineffectual. . . . Only my intellect has anything to do with *purusha-atman* or Tao, but not my living thralldom. This is local, barbaric, infantile, and abysmally unscientific" (p. 33). In another letter, he observed, "God may be everywhere, but this in no way absolves believers from the duty of offering him a place that is declared holy, otherwise one could just as well get together for religious purposes in the third class waiting-room of a railway station" (p. 128). He then deplored the profanation of using a sacred space for secular functions.

The Temple Mount is different in that the sacred space has been dedicated successively to two separate religious traditions, as a very sacred place for each. Here, particularly, the believer's passion is specific and even "barbaric," making it almost impossible to take a symbolic attitude toward one's own cherished place.

"Profane" and "fanatical" have the same root, the Latin word "fanum" for "temple," and the two words together illustrate the vexing paradox of genuine religious feeling. To violate a sacred space is profane, but to care too concretely for one's temple is fanaticism, a passionate craziness that is supremely perilous in the modern world. This paradox must be borne in consciousness if we are to survive, and the Temple Mount remains touchy ground indeed.

Touchier yet is another implication of taking a truly symbolic attitude toward sacred truth and freedom of worship. From a psychological point of view, any religious state is suspect. This becomes obvious in totalitarian states, where claims of exclusive truth justify the pursuit of Islamic Jihads, fundamentalist crusades, Marxist supremacy, or Aryan purity.

But subtler forms of oppression also arise in states which are otherwise modern in their democratic ideals. Calls for the eradication of an "evil empire" smack of religious fanaticism. More overtly, when adherence to or birth within one particular religious tradition is required as a condition of full citizenship, one sacred truth is used to aggress against others. The very idea of a religious state literalizes what needs to be symbolic.

Thus, I feel that a Jewish democratic state is ultimately a contradiction in terms, for some of those within its borders are unlikely ever to be fully equal citizens. From a point of view which acknowledges the existence of the collective unconscious, it is hard to see how any state that asserts its authority in the name of a particular religion conforms to psychic reality as we know it.

Any state which purports to be both devoted to a particular religious tradition and genuinely democratic in its concern for the rights of all its citizens must attempt to bear this contradiction in daylit consciousness. If it can do so, it may perform a crucial service for us all, finding new ways to express a passionate commitment to the particular symbols of one tradition while allowing each citizen full secular rights and complete religious freedom. For this to be possible, no rights can be infringed in the name of the dominant mythos of the state.

Knowing that some of the observations I have just made are not informed by a Jewish perspective, I shared a draft of this paper with Jerome Bernstein, a friend and colleague on whom I knew our meeting in Jerusalem had made a profound impression. With his permission, I am sharing a few of his responses.

He reminded me that so far no nearby Arab state, "with the notable exception of Egypt, has yet renounced its commitment to the obliteration of Israel as a state or of the Jewish people. Nothing is or can be equal or reasonable when that kind of threat hangs psychologically over the heads of one group or another. It is very hard, I feel, for anyone not having had the experience, to comprehend the profound wound it leaves on a collective psyche to have been the object of genocide.

"This wound is to the collective Jewish psyche. No Jew, I believe, can escape its import. Some of us do better than others in wrestling with it. None of us are not affected by it. Some become genocidal advocates themselves. . . , others deny their Jewishness in a hope to escape the cruel and angry hand of God. Some of us manage to consciously struggle with the horrors, rages, ambivalences and impossibilities of that mark, but all of us are affected. You, other Christians, Arabs, and others do not know this wound or this struggle. This is not an accusation; just a statement of emotional fact."

Enlarging my perspective, he observed that Israel is not only a democratic religious state, but also was "founded to take in and protect the refugees from genocide which the rest of the western world condoned more than it resisted." This emotionally-laden fact is inextricably bound up with Israel's problematic existence in the Middle East. These realities, he pointed out, set the stage for the emotional meetings between Germans and Jews during our conference in Jerusalem. For him, the most powerful of those meetings evoked "the tragedy that we shared as victims. Not that we were victims equally. . . but that it was our mutual feelings as victims that brought us together that night. I believed then and still do that it is through the sharing of our sense of suffering as victims that we can meet and heal each other's wounds" (Bernstein, 1986). Out of that meeting he made a German friend, which he had not expected to do ever, who has allowed him to share with him the depths of his anger and grief in an intensely healing, humanly caring way.

A similar theme is struck in Richard von Weizsäcker's (1985) remarks on the fortieth anniversary of the end of the war in Germany. He spoke movingly of the suffering of all those caught up in the consequences of Hitler's reign, and accepted with great forthrightness the particular responsibility of Germany for the unparalleled suffering of millions of Jews. He said, for example, "Whoever criticizes the situation in the Middle East should think of the fate to which Germans condemned their fellow human beings, a fate that led to the establishment of the State of Israel under conditions which continue to burden people in that region even today."

Reading the German President's observations, I was reminded of Dante's visionary perception in his *Commedia* that the great difference between those in Hell and those in Purgatory is the latter's conscious awareness and acceptance of the burden of their own evil. We all know from our work on ourselves and with others how healing conscious suffering of one's own shadow and one's responsibility for wounding others can be; in approaching others with such an attitude, reconciliation can be born. I hope that this meeting can play its part in this process.

For the projections which Jews have endured over the centuries most non-Jews share collective responsibility, including in particular the citizens of western nations who refused to see what was happening in the 1930s and 1940s, or even saw it and declined to help when asked. As Nazi Germany was a religious state of the most Satanic kind, it serves as a reminder of what can happen to any of us, individually and collectively, if we allow fanatical convictions to repress awareness of our own evil.

I want now to turn from the risks of projecting sacred devotion

in the larger world to parallel issues in our professional community. Jung observed that "It may reasonably be doubted whether
man has made any marked or even perceptible progress in
morality during the known five thousand years of human civilization" (CW16, par. 393). In terms of individual human nature,
Jung is surely right, as we can attest from our own and our patients' struggles with the shadow, as well as eruptions of so-
ciopathic acting out wherever they occur. Yet it is also true that
persons living in modern western democracies are not as much
the victims of immoral behavior as in the past. Constitutional as-
surances of individual liberties protect much more than religious
freedoms, for they constrain the other aggressions of primitive
human nature—of greed, lust, hatred and power, for example.
The strongest do not impose their rule on us at will.

Most of us live in Europe and North America where we have
rights that limit the destructive effects of the shadow-side of human nature. A major achievement of social and political institutions in the western world, these rights are an accretion of
consciousness which is quite recent, relatively secure in only a
modest number of nation-states, and by no means enjoyed by
the majority of persons on most of the continents of the earth.
These democratic traditions expose, contain, and resolve social
conflict without large-scale violence, in much the same manner
that the mature ego of an individual is able to do.

As analysts, we do not appreciate sufficiently our opportunity
to practice our rather bizarre profession without collective persecution of what we do. Essentially, we work only in societies
where Anglo-European political values are dominant. These
values do not have an exclusively European flavor, for example,
in Japan or India, but the guarantees which permit openly expressed conflict and protect minority rights in those derive from
the colonial dominion or victory of western powers. When
democracy has been grafted onto a collective psychology not yet
able to carry consciously the more vehement oppositions of the
indigenous culture, the collective ego of the body politic loses its
capacity to suffer conflict peaceably. The social structure breaks
down and minorities are persecuted and abused, as can be seen
in occasional outbursts of religious and ethnic violence in various
parts of India.

Protected as we are, it is easy to take our democratic culture for granted, and to fail to see how important it is in our own collective life as analysts. Jung said relatively little about democratic values in his writings, though he made passing references to the character of true democracy as "a conditional fight among ourselves" and as a "highly psychological institution which takes account of human nature as it is and makes allowances for the necessity of conflict within its own national boundaries" (CW10, par. 456). As a good Swiss, he certainly understood how democratic confederation functioned, but he had little more than this to say about its psychological meaning.

From my experience of Jungian behavior within groups and among groups, I have been surprised to find how primitive our ways of governing ourselves have been, how much unease and distrust we have about the ideas, intentions and presumed power-drives of our co-workers. I know that questioning human motivations is always appropriate and I am not arguing for naiveté about the shadow, which operates in all of us below the threshold of consciousness most of the time. But what has surprised me is our reluctance to trust democratic process as a means of controlling aggression, of exposing and then working through the conflicts of opinion and desires for power which are active in group life. All too often, we seem to prefer a throwback to dominion of the strongest, some form of oligarchy, or the continuing rule of those already in power.

It is notable, further, that in the United States at least, there is considerable mistrust among our several professional groups of the ideals and standards of other groups. We seem to be as subject as any others to "in-group, out-group" feelings, verging on paranoid unease. This finds expression in suspicions of manipulation behind efforts to provide increased communication and cooperation among our several groups. We lack confidence that worthwhile proposals can be distinguished from dubious ones, or that procedures can be adopted which provide adequate protections against abuse. Observing the splits among societies in some other countries and doubts among analysts in one place of the quality of training in another, the situation internationally appears not much freer of shadow projections than it is in America.

As Jungians, we have a bias against collective consciousness, knowing how much individual development is a struggle to free the true Self from the unauthentic influences of parental, societal, churchly or other outer dominants. We know that the ego's dialogue with the Self requires disidentification from the collective particulars of personal history, place and time so that we may follow our individual Way and contribute our own drop to the reservoir of consciousness which is gradually drawn up from the primeval sea. In return for the sacrifice of an idealized self-image, we hope for an increased awareness of our bond to all humanity and a deeper relationship to ancestral human nature as we experience it in the archetypal images of psychic life.

Accordingly, we are skeptical about the applicability of collective standards to what we do and how we live. Our touchstone becomes instead the call of the Self, as we understand it, in our individual lives. We may claim that we know better than others how to evaluate what is right and wrong, valid and invalid, in our relation to the world. We behave individually as if we had the certitude claimed by religious zealots.

In rare cases, we may even allow the inflation of our "special" connection to the Self to lead us into unethical and psychologically cruel abuse of our patients. Analytic training and professional expertise increase our ability to help our patients, but they also enlarge our capacity to manipulate them in hurtful ways. The transference of a patient's Self images to the person of the analyst, making him or her larger than life, carries authority which can be used both for healing and for injury. We may indulge urges for desirous, greedy or aggressive ego-gratification which we justify to ourselves with rationalizations asserting obedience to inner authority. Our presumed awareness of shadow motivations subtly deceives us when we are blinded by our own complexes.

Fortunately, serious ethical abuse occurs infrequently. What is not so rare, however, is our reluctance to take advantage of the well-defined and highly conscious procedures which have been developed within democratic cultures to deal with those occasional cases that do arise and need to be resolved. Deriving from the long evolution of British and Continental law, there are elaborated traditions for discovering and evaluating fairly the facts of a case, and for exposing them to a qualified judge or a jury of one's peers. When adapted to dealing with questions of professional ethics, these traditions offer us much more conscious guidance than we can find on our own under the pressure of an actual charge.

There is reason for some skepticism of our quasi-legal processes as we see them in action. We read and hear daily of how these can be corrupted by manipulation and dishonesty, and so we approach a formal test of our own rights at court or City Hall or before the bar of professional opinion with trepidation. Nevertheless, as refugees and exiles passionately attest, the judicial and constitutional traditions of the West are precious beacons to those who have experienced the alternatives in closed societies elsewhere in the world.

I do not wish to exaggerate the difficulties within our own community. The efforts we have been making in the United States to communicate among ourselves and with representatives of the European groups significantly involved in training American analysts have been fruitful and encouraging. The increased trust that conversations among ourselves have fostered is one of the clearest evidences that some degree of regular and structured interaction is the best antidote to negative projections as our groups become more numerous and separated from each other. I would hope before too long for some kind of federation in the United States, in which local and minority rights are well-protected, in keeping with our traditions. I expect that this would enable us to lessen our differences and fears, and to work together effectively where we have common interests. At the least, it should help us to distinguish more clearly our real and substantive disagreements from repetitious tilting at windmills of our paranoia.

Even more encouraging, in recent years women have assumed increased responsibility for our professional life. Women now lead a number of our societies and, certainly in New York, carry a fully proportionate share of the burdens of governing, evaluating, and teaching in our training program. The movement of women toward full equality in social and political life is the natural consequence of the rights espoused by the democratic tradition. Given the strong patriarchal bias of virtually every culture as it develops, it is not surprising that the full psychological implications for the quality of the feminine, as for the rights of races on whom the shadow has long been projected, have taken time to unfold. But now the inner logic of the traditions that flow from the Enlightenment has inexorably brought feminine power up from the unconscious, where it hides and works behind the scenes in patriarchal systems, into the daylight where it takes its rightful place.

This movement too has its roots in the imagery of the sacred. Over the millennia of human history, the centering of human authority derivative from God has gradually moved from the god-man power of the Pharaoh or the hero, through the extension of authority to the nobles under the King in the Great Chain of Being, to the equality of freemen in the early democracies and into the sharing of power by all persons in modern times. The transition is not complete, but it is under way. Correspondingly, the inner imagos of the Great Mother and the goddess have joined the Great Father and the god within as carriers of sacred authority for individual psyches. It is a shame that this movement of the feminine into conscious parallel with the masculine is still resisted in the most traditional or fundamentalist strongholds of western religion, whether Roman Catholic, Protestant, Jewish or Moslem, but if we survive as a species there is no question that in open societies equality will become the norm.

Whether we look at our obligations in a divided world microcosmically or macrocosmically, we arrive at a similar place. Among ourselves, we need to be respectful of each other's, and each group's, right to seek the truth in its own way, to incarnate its particular vision of psychic wholeness or centeredness in terms of its own balance between the clinical and the archetypal, the reductive and the teleological, the personal and the transpersonal. Jung remarked that theories are the very devil, for while they clarify understanding they can never depict the complex reality of the psyche. In our own community as in the world at large we need to shun the doctrinaire and welcome representations of psychological truth in many forms.

We may also seek to develop truly democratic processes with which to govern ourselves, and recognize the psychological wisdom inherent in the protection of minority views and the right to change. Knowing that the deepest truths are always paradoxical, that in some measure the opposite of any given choice is partly valid, we can make the judgments that need to be made without fearing that they will require self-destructive revolution in order to be altered in the light of later experience. We can in-

carnate in our immediate community the attitudes that are necessary for collective survival.

In the larger world, we have a sacred duty to protect and es-
pouse the separation of church and state and the unholiness of
holy wars. Only so can we embody in political reality the awareness that there is no exclusive and literal religious truth applicable to all humanity. Rather, we must make it as clear as we can
that religious statements, mythologems and rituals are truly, as
Jung so often insisted, symbols – the paradoxical "throwing together" of images and ideas which are logically incommensura-
ble, but psychologically true.

I believe that we must sacrifice some of our interiority and attempt to communicate these truths in every appropriate forum,
ranging from dialogue with thoughtful religious friends to more
public discussion of how a symbolic attitude is implicit in the
democratic traditions of the West, which are gradually gaining
ground around the world. In an era in which the existence of the
archetypal psyche is not yet widely recognized, we will have to
search for language and images in which to convey these realities
effectively.

At present, it appears that only the Soviet Union and the
United States possess the power to annihilate each other and
perhaps the rest of humankind. But we each have some part of
the trusteeship of one trigger point or another, be it Berlin or
Jerusalem or some other sore spot around the world. We all share
in the risk that our godlike powers may be exercised to effect
some apocalyptic vision, from which there may be no saving
remnant. To prevent this, we have a sacred duty to defend with
our whole hearts the symbolic rather than the literal nature of religious truth, and to honor rather than lament the many ways in
which sacred reality expresses itself.

REFERENCES

Bernstein, J. (1986). Personal letter.
Schell, J. (1982). *The fate of the earth*. New York: Knopf.
Taylor, C. (1984). Apocalyptic power and human care.
     Yale Review, 73-4, 491–502. (Also in *Quadrant, 18-2*,

35-44 as Imagining apocalypse: Godlike power and human care.)

von Weizsäcker, R. (1985). Commemorative address. In *Remembrance, sorrow, and reconciliation: Speeches in connection with the end of the Second World War in Europe* (pp. 57-72). Bonn: Press & Information Office, Federal Republic of Germany.

Discussion: Kurt Höhfeld (Berlin)

Preparations for this discussion have confronted me with facts and points of view, to which I have reacted with fear, depression and desperation. I have been familiar with this reaction since 1979 when I began to consider questions of ecology and nuclear armament. Through this confrontation I have gained new insights. One result is that I have become a member of the International Physicians for the Prevention of Nuclear War (IPPNW). From this standpoint I offer my critique of Taylor's paper.

Taylor intends to represent no dogmatic or extreme positions and not to force his position on anyone. He sees a great danger coming from religiously dogmatic and politically authoritarian groups. Modern democracy appears to him as the only viable option in the western world. Taylor describes how a democratic state handles conflicts, and suggests that smaller groups – for example, our professional circles – should follow similar processes. His view is that only democracy creates the preconditions for the development of the individual personality and actually permits us, as analysts, to practice our profession.

It is easy for us in Berlin to agree with Taylor's statements, especially when one sees the Wall or passes the control points at the border into East Germany (the German Democratic Republic or GDR). And if one reviews the origin of this regimented situation, one encounters the National Socialist dictatorship and its reign of terror. Only after 40 years can we recognize clearly how that regime not only threatened and persecuted the individual analyst, but also had a deforming effect on the thinking and concepts of all analysts, even those who were not threatened directly. Lockot (1985) described the special historical background which plays a major role in Berlin.

With regard to nuclear armament and the arms race, as well as the problem of ecology, however, it seems to me that we need more than mere knowledge and recognition of opposites in the world, more than the principle of democracy as "treatment."

I see Taylor's main recommendation as that of keeping the conflict of opposites in consciousness, in order for a person not to lapse into a reality-repressing picture of the enemy via projections. My question is: How can I reach this consciousness; how do I get there? My contention is that before a unity of opposites is possible there must be a phase of polarization. The unification of opposites—my understanding of Taylor's request for a "symbolic attitude"—is a process and not a result. The prerequisite for this process seems to be the struggle between the opposites, which must unfold within me. More exactly, it may be necessary for me to take an extreme position, then to subject myself to the ensuing tension. Thus, I cannot avoid the struggle, the defeat, the coercion of the unaccepted side. I doubt that this experience of the opposites has been reached in me or in most other people. There is danger that the idea of the coniunctio could become a recommended ideal, then ideology and finally a dogma—a dogma of the middle.

If a condition of polarization and thus dissociation must appear, then it seems an essential prerequisite that, on the one hand, I obtain facts and, on the other hand, begin an analysis of collective and individual forms of defense against fears toward the threats named.

With regard to facts, I think of the areas of politics, economics, sociology, public communications and their laws, ethnology, history, philosophy, and religion—just to name those I consider the most important. Obviously, I do not have sufficient knowledge at my disposal. However, I have begun to inform myself and am amazed and shocked.

I cite one example. In order for a nuclear power plant to work economically, it must have a large capacity, about 600 megawatts. Even more is necessary because of a legally specified reserve capacity. Thus, nuclear power plants are built with capacities of 900 to 1300 megawatts. The amount of energy available greatly exceeds the present need. Consequently, the state institutes economic measures to increase the demand for energy through the encouraging of corresponding industries and developments such as robotization. The indirect influence on unemployment is only one result. (This example is taken from the book by Traube, 1975, who evolved, like so many others, from being an earlier advocate of nuclear energy into being its opponent.)

Regarding the analysis of indirect and collective forms of defense against fear, I must begin this alone as well as with colleagues. In doing this I feel myself merely on the way toward the polarization I described, far from the uniting of opposites. I am not sufficiently in a position, either, to lead the political confrontation made possible by democratic rights. My main experience consists of continuing to keep track of material aspects. In this way I hope to avoid psychologizing an outer conflict if I consider the theme only at a psychological level, minimizing it if I rely on insufficient information.

Just how effective the acquisition of factual information can be is shown in the example of the inhabitants of Wyhl, a town in Baden (Germany). Merely by reading a book (Strohm, 1981), they acquired enough specialized knowledge that they were able, at the community level, to prevent the construction of a planned nuclear power plant.

Richter (1979) and Mumford (1977) have described additional connections. Over our heads is evolving, seemingly without any action on our part, Mumford's so-called mega-machine, whose laws we obey without noticing. Instead, we have the deceptive impression that we control this machine. Actually, the principle of technological feasibility controls us. Instead of wisely wielding control of production, we are dominated by the laws of growth and expansion. The result is exploitation and the tendency to think aggressively of security and property-ownership. This domination has military consequences. It led very early to political threats of the atomic bomb being drawn into the everyday calculation of all nations. The essential thought, however, is that the western, democratic form of government does not protect us from the consequences of the development of such a mega-machine, but conceals the development and makes it largely unrecognizable.

A recent document of the IPPNW (1986) illustrates the threat:

> It is reported that, in the nineteen fifties, military advisers had suggested to President Eisenhower that the atomic arsenal be enlarged. The advisers demanded that the nuclear potential of the United States be increased to 500 atomic warheads. Eisenhower, shocked at this, supposedly answered, "And why don't we go completely crazy and build 5000 warheads?" Now, the world has gone insane: not 500, not even 5000, but 50,000 warheads exist world-wide. This corresponds to an explosive force equal to a million Hiroshima-type bombs. That is enough to annihilate the world population twenty-five times, enough to inflict all the destruction of the Second World War every hour for 165 days and nights.

Kennan (1982) wrote, "The atomic bomb is, for me, the most useless weapon that has ever been invented. It cannot be applied for any reasonable purpose. It is not even an effective means of protection against itself. It is nothing more than an object with which one, in a moment of anger or panic, can strike such destructive blows that no person who is in his right mind would ever want to have this on his conscience" (p. 261). He wrote also, "What proof of spiritual poverty, what illustration of bankruptcy of intellectual statesmanship if we have to admit that this keystone of our military strength, as we have come to look upon it, can be used best in such blind, senseless acts of destruction" (p. 260).

For me, two questions now surface as to the origin and background of this present development. The date of origin seems to be the start of the Middle Ages with its crisis of belief; one thinks of the papacy and the religious wars between Catholics and Protestants on the one hand, and the discovery of the natural sciences and new lands on the other. Through these events, various dominating ideas have survived. Earlier generations were occupied with the construction of churches, such as the gothic cathedrals, which expressed a striving for the hereafter. Later, there was increasing development of a more worldly conception regarding feasibility and power. What stands in the place of these dominating ideas today? Can the belief in democracy offer a substitute? Is perhaps the confrontation between the democratic west and communist east our present version of religious struggle?

We need to consider what further shadows western democracy has. What percentage of the population actually supports it? As I understand it, 31 percent of the eligible voters (53 percent of those voting) re-elected Reagan president of the United States in 1984. What are the other reasons for the weak protest of the population against multiple dangers? Have the goals of democracy and personal freedom been reached at all? As early as 1956, Anders spoke of "apocalypse blindness" (p. 267), placing the same guilt upon the potential victims as upon the perpetrators. But what does the perpetrators' reality, especially their psychic reality, look like? The experiences of many people in the western democracies are characterized by indifference, a feeling of powerlessness, perplexity, fear, or withdrawal. No one feels strong, and only a few take a stand of protest; these few are likely to be ostracized by the representatives of power. As compensation, a world-wide identification with power or the powerful develops and is communicated by western television even deep into the GDR.

All over the world irrational, megalomaniac fantasies compensate for actual impotence. At the same time, the individual becomes more alienated. This state of affairs helps us to understand the conflicts in Lebanon as well as those in Ireland, Laos, and other crisis areas. Because of the threat of nuclear destruction, it is equally important to analyze the conditions in parts of the world that are influenced by the western democracies. Before we recommend the symbolic attitude psychologically and democracy politically, we should consider multiple factors. But this can mean that, where Taylor (1983–84) recommended an "as well as" attitude, the elaboration and stressing of the conflict of opposites may be necessary before one can concern oneself with the suspension of the conflict.

For me as an analyst, the result is twofold. On the one hand, I understand the "neurotic misery" in this collective content better; thus, there is a direct influence of my "exterior" experiences on my "interior" analytic work. In no way do I mean that analytic work should be politicized, but I can avoid the psychologizing of outer conflicts better than before. On the other hand, I am of the opinion that we, as analysts, are forced more than ever to orient ourselves politically and thus, as I call it, polarize ourselves. We owe it to ourselves and other people.

Translated from German by
Richard Mann

REFERENCES

Anders, G. (1956). Die Antiquiertheit des Menschen: Ungekurzte Sonderausgabe. München: C. H. Beck.
International Physicians for the Prevention of Nuclear War (1986). Stoppt die Atombombentests. *Flugblatt der Sektion Bundesrepublik Deutschland der IPPNW.*

Kennan, G. (1982). *Im Schatten der Atombombe*. München: Deutscher Taschenbuch Verlag.

Lockot, R. (1985). *Erinnern und Durcharbeiten: Zur Geschichte der Psychoanalyse und Psychotherapie im Nationalsozialismus*. Frankfurt: Fischer.

Mumford, L. (1977). *Mythos der Maschine: Kultur, Technik und Macht; Die umfassende Darstellung der Entdeckung und Entwicklung der Technik*. Frankfurt: Fischer.

Richter, H. (1979). *Der Gotteskomplex: Die Geburt und die Krise des Glaubens an die Allmacht des Menschen*. Reinbek bei Hamburg: Rowohlt.

Strohm, H. (1981). *Friedlich in die Katastrophe: Eine Dokumentation über Atomkraftwerke*. Frankfurt: Zweitausenseins.

Taylor, C. (1983–84). Apocalyptic power and human care. *The Yale Review, 73*, 491–502.

Traube, C. (1978). *Müssen Wir Umschalten? Von den politischen Grenzen der Machbarkeit*. Reinbek bei Hamburg: Rowohlt.

Original Morality in a Depressed Culture[*]

Andrew Samuels (London)

Women and men are moral creatures. Psychology, ethology and the arts all attest to this. Yet our fundamental sense of morality does not guarantee ethical behavior either in relation to ourselves, to others or to the general human landscape. On its own this moral sense just isn't enough; there has to be some dialogue and interplay with a different kind of morality. This second morality—equally inborn, easy to recognize but hard to define accurately—generates tolerance, forgiveness, openness and an ingenious approach to problems. I want to call it "moral imagination" and to distinguish it from the first, fundamental, ineluctable morality which I designate "original morality." The reference to original sin is deliberate.

While these two moralities differ, there is a crucial link between them. Original morality employed on its own has a tragic outcome. Yet it is the home base to which prodigal moral imagination constantly returns. Without the grounding in certitude which original morality supplies, moral imagination is too slippery by far.

We need not judge between the two moralities, branding one as schizoid and the other as mature and concerned, for original morality is not all crazy blood and bone. Nor does one kind of morality adhere to the ego and the other to soul, for both subsist in each of these. Original morality does not develop into moral imagination. Hence, I shall not suggest a need to make individual

---

[*]Part of a larger work-in-progress.

a collective moral code or render personal an archetypal super-ego. Original morality and moral imagination are equally arche-typal; both have to become personal and express themselves in human relationships at all stages of life. I do not want to play favorites between original morality and moral imagination. Nei-ther is divine; if it lies anywhere, divinity lies in their conclave.

What will emerge, I hope, is an anatomy of morality in its own terms rather than in the languages of myth or of the psychology of the individual. Then some communication among all of these may be fostered. My intention is to do more than aim toward a synthesis that would simply set two moral viewpoints side by side and then transcend their differences in a calm and superior manner. The tension within morality between certainty and im-provisation cannot be resolved as easily as that.

Positing these two moralities may illuminate some of those perennial conundrums about destructiveness, wickedness and the shadow. These may be re-cast so that such dark riddles are seen as reflecting a clash of moralities rather than a struggle be-tween morality and immorality or between conscience and evil or between ego and shadow. Morality itself is a paradox, a conflicted ideogram; the split resides in humankind's moral per-ception, not between our moral side and our baser aspects. That women and men have shadows is an obvious truth; of course they do, and they know it far better than analysts concede.

If we could allow original morality its dialogue with moral ima-gination, maintaining the contact between them, and do this eas-ily and reliably, there would be no need for this paper. But what often happens is that we get caught on one or the other, original morality or moral imagination. If the former, then our approach to problems which cry out for choices to be made will be "by the book"—correct, stolid, safe, reliable—but missing out on the nu-ances of the situation. If we are hooked on moral imagination, our one-sidedness will have a different tone—bags of ingenuity and so-called flexibility, responsiveness to the uniqueness of the situation—but with no grounding, conviction or moral muscle. To make any headway when things are tough and complicated, we need the blend of certainty and improvisation that I have been describing. Moral imagination enables us effectively to use original morality; original morality guarantees the depth and authenticity of moral imagination. I will show how it is depression functioning on a personal basis and on a cultural level, which is one of the main obstacles to the development of morality in its fullest sense. Depressive dynamics align with and support those of original morality. I will present depression as a kind of philosophy whose ideological stance is set against the reciprocity of original morality and moral imagination. But first we should look at what is involved in a term such as original morality.

Original Morality

Jung pointed out that morality emanates from within; it is a daimon, a voice which we have in us from the start. He was referring to our "moral nature" (CW7, par. 30) and not to precise moral formulations. Jung's focus was on the split which may develop between deeply personal ethics and the collective moral code. To Jung's recognition that morality has its own force and drive, I add an attempt to go further into its dynamics without presupposing the kind of conflict he described.

In contemporary psychoanalysis, we see similar claims for some kind of innate moral sense. One of Melanie Klein's contributions was to raise the possibility of the super-ego's being an innate factor. This idea forms one theoretical base for D. W. Winnicott's insistence that children have an innate sense of guilt and hence are not born amoral (Davis & Wallbridge, 1981). Milner (1977) also suggested that we stop seeing morality as something implanted in children by parents and society. After all, the Oedipus complex is as much about inter-generational cooperation and lineage as it is about competitive rivalry and father-murder. Further, what ethologists tell us about animal behavior suggests that cooperation has always existed alongside competition. Both are equally archetypal.

In spite of all this, original morality is insufficient for the leading of a moral life; it can be experienced as harsh, vengeful, primitive and cold. In an adult, original morality can take the form of a profound suspiciousness of others, a tendency to jump to the worst possible conclusions, to rejoice in the other's misery when it seems deserved, and, ultimately, to retreat into the wilderness to feed on locusts and honey. Occasionally, such a psychology may buttress social order but somewhere there will always be an inferior element in it.

The fatal flaw in original morality is its vertical perspective, its obsession with the superior-inferior dynamic. The need to maintain this split, which is central to original morality, fuels the horizontal split (America/Russia) which threatens the world so pressingly just now. The vertical split is shifted onto the horizontal plane: them and us. If we ask ourselves what it is that enables such shadow projections to occur, we have to posit some hypothetical force such as original morality. For something enables me to take the superior position in relation to you, leaving you smelling of my shit. The judgmental flavor of shadow projections may be laid at the door of original morality. In this form, original morality has helped to create our divided world, slouching toward apocalypse.

Nonetheless, it remains vital to see beyond the developmental aspects of original morality, to value it as a lifelong capacity, as well as concentrating on what has to be achieved to overcome it. Even if original morality dominates a certain phase of development, it contributes a potential richness of texture and quality to all phases, not merely as an anti-libidinal ego.

Original morality casts things in black and white, but black and white are genuine colors. In them, images of perfection and perfectability are kept alive. They are body-less, humorless, careless; nevertheless, are reassuringly perfect. Original morality is essentially a morality of narcissism, of the uroboros, of once-and-for-all redemption. But it is precisely these problematic features that we often need. Original morality saturates behavior, serving us as a well into which we can dip, regenerating ourselves, overcoming cynicism, recapturing enthusiasm, relieving pain. Original morality keeps alive our dreams of getting things done as planned. In pathological form, this may be an "addiction to perfection" but original morality also stands as a prefiguring of its partner, moral imagination.

Original morality has a function, then. As Jung noted, striving after moral perfection is "not only legitimate but is inborn in man as a peculiarity which provides civilisation with one of its strongest roots" (CW9–I, par. 123). Original morality is a broad-horizon reality for all its oversimplification and certainty. "Insight [exists] along with obtuseness, loving-kindness along with cruelty, creative power with destructiveness" (CW11, par. 560). Original morality is present in the experience of being in love, when the loved one can do no wrong and in the experience of hate when the hated one can do nothing right. A picture emerges in which the task of the one confronted with original morality – parent, friend, or analyst – is to defuse, moderate, mediate such morality, tenderize it, round it out, render it fruitful, de-idealize it, shake it up a bit – but not to do away with it altogether.

Moral Imagination

By now you probably are asking, what is this "moral imagina-tion?" Broadly speaking, it is moral imagination that we use when confronted with a pressing, problematic, and especially a conflict-laden situation. Moral imagination is the means by which we consider complex social and political issues. "Moral" because a choice may have to be made. "Imagination" because that choice may have to be ingenious, less than clear-cut, a com-promise or a creatively improvised adaptation. Let us now look in detail at what is involved; at first, my approach is going to be an oblique one.

At the start of the Jewish Day of Atonement service (Yom Kip-pur), there is a short prayer that is of fundamental importance. So central is this prayer that, in some congregations, it is not recited by the reader alone but together with two members of the congregation. In all versions of the ritual, the prayer is recited three times and therefore may be assumed to be of supreme sig-nificance. This is the prayer:

> All vows, bonds, oaths, devotions, promises, penalties and obliga-tions: wherewith we have vowed, sworn, devoted and bound our-selves: from this Day of Atonement unto the next Day of Atonement; lo, all these, we repent us in them. They shall be ab-solved, released, annulled, made void, and of none effect: they shall not be binding nor shall they have any power. Our vows shall not be vows: our bonds shall not be bonds: and our oaths shall not be oaths.

Our vows shall not be vows. What are we to make of this extra-ordinary pronouncement, the equivalent of cancelling all resolutions at the very moment of making them? Remember, this is *the* high, holy day. There are three possible understandings of the prayer. First, we must be careful not to aim too high, making promises for the future which we cannot keep because of our human limitations. Given the massive sanctions laid down in the Old Testament against those who break their vows, it is crucial to state, right at the start of the process of repentance and atonement, the possibility that it will not work out as intended. Thus, reference is made to the period between this Day of Atonement and the one next year. The second interpretation of this Kol Nidrei prayer is exactly the opposite: that the vows, bonds, promises which are being annulled refer to those made last year which experience has shown to be unfulfilled or unfilfillable. It is urgently necessary to cancel these promises for we are even now in breach of them. Finally, a third reading, by cancelling all human moral contracts, we are free to contract with God.

I have introduced these reflections on the Yom Kippur ritual to show that a recognition of the unlivable nature of original morality on its own lies at the heart even of Judaism, which is so often unfairly castigated by Jung before and after the War as the source of repressive and legalistic moralism. Judaism, perhaps like all religions, enjoys and suffers the tension between original morality and moral imagination. It is not a case of contrasting absolute moral principle with relative quasi-moral behavior. Both original morality and moral imagination have principles. What follows is an attempt to outline some of the principles of moral imagination.

Moral imagination contains an intuitive and psychological understanding of what a moral principle really is. Moral principle differs from etiquette or good manners in that moral rules are not rigid rules; it is sometimes right to ignore them. For example, it is sometimes morally permissible to tell lies (we call these social lies or white lies); sometimes it is morally permissible to break promises (as when ill on the day of an appointment) and sometimes it is morally permissible to refuse help (when the cost of giving it would be disproportionate). Thus, we tend to accommodate the exceptions within morality.

Accommodating the exceptions within morality suggests that forgiveness, and not blame, characterizes moral imagination. Forgiveness of one part of the self by another part, forgiveness of another person, or by another person, forgiveness of one group by another. Forgiveness is important because it can bring a new element into a situation. It is therefore creative and, to a degree, an autonomous force in pysche and culture. The value of forgiveness can be seen in analysis when the patient explores the alarming possibility of forgiving the parents for having been damaged by them. The patient drops armor and displays hospitality toward images of the past. This process is the justification of reductive analysis.

Continuing to discuss moral imagination, we come to the question of moral pluralism. Though I intend to develop a different set of ideas here, I am thinking also of a morality of transition, liminal morality, differing moralities attached to the erotogenic zones, to specific images, to the various gods or to the stages of life. (See Samuels, 1985.)

If one looks at the multifarious moral commandments and prohibitions that exist, it is difficult to state one general principle, or even a few general principles, which connect all of them. They are unavoidably plural; it is their essence to discriminate numberless kinds of approved and disapproved behavior. An example is the Day of Atonement ritual, in which enormous lists of specific sins are confessed aloud; general confession seems inadequate even though it is general absolution that is sought. The specific, the nitty-gritty, the plural images of sin are put forward. These images are necessary because human beings have no single dominating concern or goal, no one supreme interest; the concerns, goals and interests which may be observed are, again, numberless. It is not a question of moral perception but of moral perceptions. There is a need to reconcile, to downplay, or to accentuate very different concerns—for individual and society alike. One person's meat is another person's poison. One person's meat may be poisoning another person's meat. One person's poison may meet another person's needs. What we admire and value in ourselves and others need not follow any logical format: warmth and openness together with careful attention to detail, driving ambition with pervasive self-doubt. Societal conflicts and political pluralism are model and mirror for the moral conflicts of the soul.

It follows that moral imagination typically requires a weighing of conflicting claims; for example, should I support my friend whom I know to be in the wrong? My response to this kind of question, coupled with my responses to myriad others of equal difficulty, inform the dynamics of social *communitas* and of moral imagination. Here, in the weighing of claims in conflict, original morality comes into its own, vital for the workings of moral imagination. We must endeavor to use the moral knowledge that we have always had.

Thus far, I have been pitting moral imagination against the adoption of single-criterion ethics. I have been arguing that there is a psychological value in facing a conflict of claims, something more than a mere acceptance of practical realities. Such acceptance would be moral relativism or situation ethics. It is important not to see moral imagination as just the daily version of original morality, or as the relative outcome of absolute principle. Pluralism is not the same as relativism. Perceiving a conflict of moral principles is not the same as accepting the fact that, in life, principle has to be watered down. Moral relativism implies a hierarchy in which principle is placed above and distinct from praxis. Moral pluralism sees no value in unlivable principle, nor takes such a pat-on-the-head, there-there, attitude to moral failure, based on unavoidable concessions to human appetites. There is a name for that attitude: casuistry. The principles involved in moral pluralism embrace their own tricksterish failure in the world. We accommodate the exceptions within morality; the exceptions make the rules.

When we reflect upon moral pluralism, as an experience and in emotional terms, aggression cannot be avoided. Without aggression, "conflict" remains a word and not a living and coruscating process. Aggression fuels moral imagination. These remarks on moral principle, forgiveness and moral pluralism bring to an end my brief account of moral imagination. Now it is time to consider how depression drives a wedge between original morality and moral imagination, castrating their dialogue and crushing their mutual fertilization.

Depression

I want to present depression as a philosophy of our day, dedicated to the condemnation and suppression of aggression. As such, depression may be seen as a moral disorder and injurious to moral imagination. Depressed patients tell us of being over-whelmed by feelings of badness and, above all, of destructive-ness. For some, the issue is one of having destroyed (in fantasy) the loved person who was necessary for emotional survival; ambivalence was not a possibility. For others, depression is a means of guaranteeing parental love and acceptance by gainsay-ing the aggression which is felt not to be permitted by the par-ents. One of the many consequences of depression is that the psychological value of aggressive fantasy is lost. Depression, functioning as a moral philosophy, promotes two seemingly in-tractable conflations or mix-ups: of aggressive fantasy and de-structive fantasy, and then of fantasy and action. Let us consider these in turn.

Aggressive fantasy has its own *telos*. In saying this, I do not in-tend to minimize the damaging, negative, painful, perverted, controlling aspects of aggressive fantasy. However, aggressive behavior, in the form of healthy self-assertion, is a necessity for survival in both an absolute and a social sense. My concern is more with aggressive images and images of aggression: images of tearing things up, dissecting them, controlling them, playing with them, making use of them. Aggressive fantasy has much to do with our desire to know. Thus, it promotes one style of con-sciousness; it is not, in itself, completely bloodstained and un-reflective.

Aggressive fantasy can bring into play that interpersonal sepa-ration without which the word relationship would have no meaning. In this sense, aggressive fantasy may want to make contact, get in touch, relate. The same is true for internal units and processes: Aggressive fantasy enables separate images of the parents to emerge, and other imagos and inner discriminations; for example, what theory refers to as the ego-Self axis. At one moment a violent urge may express a striving to be free and at the next a desire to relate. Aggressive fantasy forces an individu-al to consider the conduct of personal relations. When one fanta-sizes an aggressive response to one's desires on the part of the other, one is learning something about that other as a being with a different but similar existence to one's own. Without aggressive fantasy, there would simply be no cause for concern about other people; thus aggressive fantasy points beyond ruthlessness to discover the reality and mystery of persons. It is only when intense aggressiveness exists between two individuals that love can arise. Aggressive fantasy is playful at times, even humorous, a continuous cartoon of ejaculatory, exploratory enjoyment.

Since it is composed of images as much as impulses, aggressive fantasy can be approached via its specifics. An example appears in Freud's "A Child Is Being Beaten" (SE17). And Jung writing about the treatment of depression, suggested that getting to the inherent fantasies leads to "enrichment and clarification of the affect" (CW8, par. 167). But it is clarification of the image that is needed in relation to aggression: Biting is not tearing, nor smearing, nor cutting, nor punching, nor shooting, nor beating.

Aggressive fantasy, like incest fantasy, has a refueling and regenerating function which is accentuated in more extreme fantasy. For aggressive fantasy returns us to basics, to evolutionary dangers just as much as to the mother's body or the father who bars our path. What Jung pioneered for fantasies of incestuous sexuality in *Symbols of Transformation* (CW5) should be attempted for aggressive fantasy. This would mean, for example, that aggression between persons, or the aggressive fantasy of one about the other, may not be about only those two persons; its symbolic meaning as well as its literal potential engages our interest. The perversity and horror of aggressive fantasy may give it its creative capacity to nourish the soul. Just as with sexuality and spirituality, the transformation of aggressive fantasy tends to be in the general direction of its opposite: creativity and moral imagination—toward forgiveness and the new departure which that can bring, toward moral pluralism, and toward an acceptance of the body's irreducibly aggressive motions. We should not forget the thrill and excitement of aggressive fantasy, its action in and upon sexuality and feeding. Then there is the bliss of the calm after the storm. Aggressive fantasy, breaking taboos as it does, proposes an image of human moral creativity, shorn of idealizations and full or eros—Jacob wrestling with his angel. Transformation is never easy, sometimes destructive, and impossible to order up on room service. Renewal and aggression are twins. Finally, in this survey, there is the part played by aggressive fantasy in the formation of an esthetic sense—the gut response, that free play of imagination which permits one to react outside of the rules.

In myth, when Kronos turns on Uranos, one of the imaginal birth moments of western culture, he cuts off his father's genitalia with a sickle, casting them into the sea. From them Aphrodite is born, the goddess of love. Out of the despair and violence steps the epitome of beauty. Here, too, the imago of child as phallus has its archaic roots. It seems to be no accident that so many contemporary depth psychologists have needed to make of the aggression-depression dynamic a central part of their theorizing. Nor is it coincidence that Herman Hesse's counterpart to Narcissus, the one who leads a life of mind and spirit, is Goldmund, as often killer as fornicator.

I mentioned that depression promotes two conflations and we have just been at one of them, between aggressive fantasy and destructiveness. The other mix-up was between fantasy and action. Here the designation of depression as a moral philosophy makes sense. In depression we can see a distorted application of what, in philosophy, is referred to as intentionality. Any emotion (and that includes fantasy) will construct an object toward which it is directed, toward which it has intention. For example, I cannot be aggressive save in relation to an object of aggression or believe without an object of belief. For most of us, most of the time, when the intentional object intrudes into our perceptual field, we can track it, relate to it, converse with it; it becomes a component of imagination. But in depression the strength of fantasy, and the consequences ascribed to it by the ego, make for intentional objects of immense power. While the value of intentional objects is that they facilitate emotional expression, their coming to psychic dominance — as they do in the omnipotent, destructive fantasies of the depressed person — has absolutely the opposite effect: a paralysis of the imagination and a landslide victory for original morality. Instead of imagination and intentionality, we are confronted with an appallingly literal portrayal of the outcome of fantasy. In the language of philosophy intentional objects become material objects and a depressed person cannot dance the inner-outer tango.

I have been working up these ideas about depression at some length because they have particular relevance to our reactions and responses to the nuclear threat. This is my case illustration, so to speak. Consider: In almost every respect, the emotional dynamics of our confrontation with the nuclear situation replicate and simulate those of depression. There is a confusion between inner and outer; inner fantasies of world destruction which have always existed are now literal fact. There is an enormous fear attached to the expression of aggression today; total war might result. The imagination is overwhelmed and the ego searches for something to blame: history, the system, patriarchy, the enemy, the scientific ego itself.

The pressing issue is our powerlessness in the face of the nuclear problem. We need to distinguish between the psychological dynamics of the world political situation and the specific psychological dynamics of our inertia and impotence. Not what is felt about the Russians, nor why it is felt, but how we feel about a world in which Russians, Americans and others are locked into a certain kind of confrontation. If we look at things from this standpoint, the critically disabling anxiety from which we suffer is not paranoid anxiety, hence not characterized primarily by splitting, projective identification, projection of the shadow, and so forth. In the nuclear age such concepts, often promoted by depth psychologists, do not illuminate our paralysis when what used to be regarded as an over-literal apperception of aggressive fantasy has become the plain fact. We can destroy our adversaries. From that, depression will follow, silencing the articulation between original morality and moral imagination. There is no principle, no forgiveness, no pluralism—only the control of arms.

Like depression, the nuclear situation forces us to stay locked into original morality. For whether we anticipate with certainty total nuclear destruction, or a peaceful balance based on the fear of retaliation, it is such certainty itself which keys us into original morality. When depression and original morality collude, one's sense of responsibility becomes the victim; integration of the shadow becomes a pious nonsense. If nuclear weapons have injured our capacity for moral imagination, they certainly show our need for it. But cultural depression will prevent the need from being met. Hopelessness has become global; there is no space for good and compassionate thoughts about ourselves.

In our culture, depressive fear of our own destructiveness, and the corresponding paucity of moral imagination in relation to that, have reached epidemic proportions. Our culture suffers from a collective depressive delusion that it is all-bad, all-destructive. We are therefore alienated from the possibility of forgiveness. Moreover the process is circular; depression and original morality feed into one another so that we cannot extract the value from our aggressive fantasies. When we talk of the positive side of the shadow or of healthy aggression, we should take care not to neglect the depressive block in us which prevents such gold from being mined.

Women in our culture experience particular difficulties in expressing aggression; the result may be their statistically greater tendency to become depressed. For women have much to feel aggressive about: They have to be nice, adopt a passive social stance, and worry about their appearance; they are said to be "maternal"; their eroticism is limited by male preconceptions. And yet it is women who have led the way in protesting against nuclear proliferation. Perhaps their anger at what is required of them by society has freed their imaginations and enabled them to take action. However, for men *and* women, the depressive fear of losing parental love makes it hard to say no to the political parent figures. This problem is not usually addressed by those who want the "people" to act.

Recapitulation

It may be useful to recapitulate the argument. I proposed a tension and an articulation within human morality between original morality and moral imagination. In our day, cultural depression has driven a wedge between the two types of morality, depriving the flower of its nourishment. Depression has this effect by suppressing aggressive fantasy, which is a crucial element in moral imagination. Understood in the broadest sense, depression is an ideology that is opposed to moral imagination. Our powerlessness and inability to cope with the specter of nuclear destruction could be attributed to the damaging effects of depression upon the capacity of moral imagination to make use of aggressive fantasy. We are forced to fall back on our reserves of original morality, leaving no alternatives except to dream of a planetary culture or perish in a nuclear war.

Coda

I had thought to stop the paper here, with depression as the problem, so to speak. But, conscious of the fact that there are many positive aspects to depression, I gradually became aware that depression, the problem, could also be visioned as a kind of solution, or at least as an ambience in which solutions could be worked upon (because there is no obvious solution).

Overcoming depression involves a reconstruction and reconstitution of the internal world so that losses are somehow made good or accommodated to, imagos of others (particularly parents) allowed fruitful life, and personal responsibility for disaster reassessed. All of these involve entering fantasy, owning the aggressive images and hence one's potential for aggressive, even warlike discharge. An alternative to discharge, though, is to be forgiven for one's aggression; by oneself or by its recipient, whether friend, enemy or analyst.

Described in this way, depression may be seen as lying at the heart of moral imagination and, especially, of forgiveness. Paradoxically, depression may then actually constitute a link between original morality and moral imagination as well as being the prime attack on that link. Maybe we can see in depression something of a stimulant to moral imagination. For depression forces us to take fantasy seriously, if not literally. This means facing the potential outer reality of aggressive fantasy alongside its inner creativity. When that happens, depression becomes the forum for an integration of the instinctual body and the imaginative soul and our aggressive dreams show us the meaning of our despair.

Finally, I want to introduce the metaphor of depression as a search. For the individual, such a search may be a search of collective memory — mother of the Muses and hence of creativity generally. The work of memory is the work of mourning. In the nuclear age, we have to search in our memory for the archaic fascination with death which spawned civilization and from which we have turned our faces. Depression may be seen as a piecing together, over time, of a solution. That is partly why the writer has to get depressed when the book isn't going well, the mother when the baby won't feed, the worker when faced with unemployment, each of us when threatened by the bomb. Each must search for a solution. The depressive process, static on the surface, is a flow of information, intuitions and images leading to a reorganization of these. For that is all that is meant by solution; it is not cure or getting rid of depression. The misery of depression comes in part from the awful slowness of the search and its apparent futility.

REFERENCES

Davis, M.; Wallbridge, D. (1981). *Boundary and space: An introduction to the work of D. W. Winnicott*. London: Karnac.

Milner, M. (1977). *On not being able to paint*. London: Heinemann.

Samuels, A. (1985). The image of the parents in bed. In A. Samuels (Ed.), *The father: Contemporary Jungian perspectives*. London: Free Association Books.

Discussion: John Beebe
(San Francisco)

The moral area has always been central to Analytical Psychology, and Samuels' flawlessly argued, deeply-felt paper is a breakthrough in clarifying our birthright. Jungian analysts, after all,
have paid considered attention to morality. After the break with
Freud, Jung pointed us in a moral direction by making his subject
the analysis of attitudes, where Freud's had been the analysis of
impulses. Jung recognized that the complexes were more than
drive derivatives; they were unconscious moral positions. To the
scorn of the early Freudians, Jung made it the analyst's duty to
bring patients to examine their morality. Jung's focus, however,
was on the moral content of the complexes, and he did not look
hard at the intra-psychic process of morality itself. Moral process
is the neglected area that Samuels considers in this paper.

This is hardly to gainsay Jung's moral achievement. We all
know how hard Jung worked on the moral problem he inherited
from his father. Paul Jung, a Protestant minister, lost his faith at
exactly the moment in history that Friedrich Nietzsche was writing in his Zarathustra notebook, "Don't they know that God is
dead?" The elder Jung continued to go about his pastoral duties
but his dead spirit cast a pall over Carl's childhood. His father
was physically dead when Carl was barely twenty-one. Jung
took it as his own moral duty to solve his father's unsolved problem with belief, and he gave it the full benefit of his historical approach. He mastered patristics, the study of the vicissitudes of
faith in the fathers of the Christian church; he discovered and explored the interesting heresies, such as gnosticism; he compared
Christianity to its rival mystery religion, Mithraism—and so on.
I feel sure he questioned deeply those para-Christian authorities
he found within his own psyche—Philemon, Salome, and Elijah.
He even met with tribal fathers of surviving aboriginal religions
in his effort to uncover the root of the impulse to believe.

My conviction is that Jung took on this work to atone for his
father's moral weakness in continuing to serve a religion in
which he no longer believed. The moral payoff for Jung came
when the BBC interviewer asked him the question his father

could not have dealt with: "Do you believe in God?" There was an unmistakable look of satisfaction on Jung's face when he replied, "I don't need to believe, I know." His scholarship had secured for him the gnostic position against the tradition of authority that had left his father spiritually bankrupt.

Jung's attention to his own morality is impressive, but it can blind us to the fact that on the psychology of morality itself, Jung's work leaves a great deal to be desired. In comparison to Samuels' paper, Jung's major essay on moral process, "A Psychological View of Conscience,"(CW10, pars. 825–57) seems thin. In that late essay, Jung set up a distinction between morality — the code of the collective — and ethics, which he saw as the standpoint of the Self. This distinction is seductive but does not hold up, etymologically or psychologically. Samuels is right to complain.

When Cicero coined the Latin word *moralis*, he meant it to stand for the Greek *ethikos* (Weekley, 1967). I believe he meant to convey that what is naturally right is also in accord with the deep customs of the community, its mores. To squeeze all of ethics into the voice of the Self is only to voice a proud elitism, not to explicate the process by which the Self remains morally related to a situation even as it defines an individual standpoint.

Nor is this made significantly clearer when one turns for help to Erich Neumann's *Depth Psychology and a New Ethic* (1969). In that work, moral process is confused with the psychology of individuation. Neumann took as his point of departure the new culture of psychologically developing individuals. He pointed out that individuals who have faced the shadow in accord with the findings of depth psychology will realize that scapegoating, a basis for morality in former times, is no longer acceptable. Their new ethic is based on the Self, seen as the wider standpoint that emerges with the development of consciousness. Neumann's reasoning is fascinating, but is it really true (as he implies) that those who have grasped the shadow will have a wiser moral process? Neumann realized that their next step, to avoid inflation, must be to discriminate and develop the Self that emerges as fictions give way. But, like Jung, he had too little to tell us about the psychology of moral differentiation at this level. Instead, we get a cautionary either/or. Either the Self is omniscient and to be trusted above all other authorities in moral matters; or it is showing its dark side and humanity has to try to resist its own greatest Evil. When the Self becomes a structure, a capitalized entity, its process aspect is lost. Earlier, Jung spoke of the Self as a "sensing" that will appear when the individual has had enough experience with the unconscious (CW7, par. 405). "Sensing" can develop into sensibility; Self rules by divine right. By opening the door to a theology of the Self, Neumann and late Jung foreclose a psychology of Self's moral development.

The effect of this foreclosure on our morality in the practice of analysis has not been good. At its worst, Jungian analysis has been distinguishable from the other psychotherapies in the community by being the one that one may conduct arrogantly, without much attention to community standards. Our most painful examples are sexual relationships with patients in the name of Self. Within a few institutes that have dealt with this problem, a sad but understandable compensation has been the move to draw up for Jungian analysts codes of ethics modelled on those of other psychotherapeutic collectives. The cult of Self has threatened, paradoxically, the hard-won spontaneity of Jungian practice.

This is dirty linen, and I bring it out only to make clear that our moral base is insecure, that we really need Samuels' contribution. To have a better morality in our practice we must have a better Jungian understanding of moral process. Relying on either/or won't do. Is this id or superego? Voice of the Self or dark side of the Self? Individuated ego or inflated ego? Asking these questions does not help us to connect our alternatives with our standards.

As Samuels recognizes, moral process is more than a conflict of opposites. We need room for the whole middle ground of complexity, the muddles that facilitate moral development. Samuels' model gives us such room. His terms, original morality and moral imagination, are rooted in an English tradition and they are not designed with the opposites of German Romantic philosophy in mind, even though they permit a dialectic. Rather, he sets them up like goal posts for the football game of morality, allowing plenty of space between for the scrimmages of moral thinking.

Samuels' frame can contain all the moral behaviors — the obsessing, the insomnia, the consulting of the I Ching, the big dream, the little dream that follows to contradict the big dream, the unexpected piece of information, the analyst's opinion, the spouse's opinion of the analyst's opinion, and so on. These are the behaviors on the surface of morality, not the conflict in depth. If you let their surface interest attract you, you will find the esthetic level of morality, where a great deal of moral process occurs. As Thurn (1986) discerned, this was the level that Jung too often left out.

In 1928, the city of Berlin saw thrown upon its theatrical stage a work which could teach analysts much about the esthetic handling of morality. This was "The Threepenny Opera," a musical morality play that was a strange hybrid of eighteenth century British drama, American ragtime, German expressionism, and leftist proletarian theater. The production boasted the strident crooning of Lotte Lenya, who belted Bertolt Brecht's hard lyrics against a tin pan alley cacophany of catchy staccato rhythms. Her voice would suddenly leave its raucous background and break into the tender melodies and eerie nostalgic harmonies that Kurt Weill's music could offer. And her song was of revenge. Thus Brecht and Weill got a Berlin audience on the eve of world depression to imagine the seductiveness of envy and greed — and its own temptation to immorality. The work sets free the moral imagination.

How might analysts imagine their morality in the conduct of analysis? Can we take a tip from the irreverence of Brecht and Weill? Their irreverence lets the bloody fantasies of Pirate Jenny and of Mack the Knife work on an audience's souls. Good analysts too must be irreverent, playful, toying with the idea of being bad analysts, to accept the aggressive fantasies that sometimes surface in the midst of their efforts to heal.

The sexual transgressions that occur in analysis often may be traced to the analyst's fear of aggressive fantasy. When such fantasy is interpreted literally (and, as Samuels says, the job of deliteralizing aggression in Jungian analysis has not been done), it gets walled off in a paranoid way by the original morality. The Jungian analyst's own conflict with inner aggression may seek expiation in erotic behavior because at least, after *Symbols of Transformation* (CW5), the erotic part of the moral imagination can conceive itself symbolically and avoid the most ruthless self-judgments, even when literal enactment takes place. This technique does not lead to a moral result.

Can we imagine a moral technique that could handle our aggressive fantasies toward our patients? Let us use the tools Samuels has given us. We can start by enjoying the comic aspect of angry fantasies' emerging in the midst of our efforts to help people. We could be more playful about acknowledging to patients that we know what we are sometimes like for them. We could let them in on some of the negativity that we are experiencing, especially when they sense it is there, but not in a grim confessional way. To achieve the moral imagination Samuels is talking about, there must be, I think, a befriending of the aggressive fantasy. Sometimes the patient is the friend who can help us to see it symbolically. What can be talked about is less likely to be literalized and then warded off.

Then we must attempt the reconciling of aggressive fantasy and original morality, with the patient watching. This is pioneer work, a chemical marriage we know next to nothing about. We could let the patients in on the secret that this is pioneer work. After all, this reconciliation is their goal too; they also want to survive as moral creatures in the midst of their own fantasies of envy, greed, and revenge.

The bit of original morality that I think needs to be married to aggressive fantasy is the wish to remain virgin in the analytic endeavor. This too could be talked about rather than enacted or repressed. Some Jungians have identified with their wish to keep analysis pure by becoming fierce guardians of the container, by reviving a Freudian technique, or by working non-stop on their shadows to avoid the potential for contamination. Other analysts have been ashamed of their desires for purity within the analytic field and have adopted counterphobic mad analytic personas, but they are virgins in the hairy hides of wild analysts.

Perhaps when our compulsions start to guide our responses, we could tell the patient about our struggles with technique. Then the wish for purity might recover its symbolic nature and be recognized as part of original morality.

Getting the elements — aggressive fantasy (the tough part of the moral imagination) and our wish to stay pure (the shameful part of original morality) — out of hiding and out of literal enactment is only the preliminary to their conclave. The conclave of moral imagination and original morality is, as Samuels says, the divine part of moral development. I believe that, in analysis, that conclave will occur only when the irony of the situation of one human being's trying to better the lot of another is accepted. Those times when I have found the heart fully to explore that irony with a patient, I have discovered that both of us have been led to a profound acceptance of our smallness before the mystery of transformation, a smallness that makes conventionally ethical behavior and our modest roles within the enterprise easier.

A longtime patient of mine with whom I have recently been experiencing this enabling smallness dreamed, as I was struggling to find words to convey to you what this moral level is like, that *an older man she trusts was saying in her presence, "Every good relationship has a childlike quality about it."* The patient's dream was referring, I believe, to her discovery within the analytic relationship of the openness children can have in their play in discussing with each other what they should and should not do. This is an openness that appears to adults, too, when they are not demoralized, an openness to moral process that becomes the basis for the development of character. I feel indebted to Andrew Samuels for making clearer what this openness consists of and suggesting a theoretical basis for its therapeutic facilitation by analysts.

REFERENCES

Neumann, E. (1969). *Depth psychology and a new ethic*. New York: Putnam's.

Thurn, R. (1986). Review of Friedrich Schiller's *On the aesthetic education of man in a series of letters*. *The San Francisco Jung Institute Library Journal*, 6–4, 27–33.

Weekley, E. (1967). *An etymological dictionary of modern English*: Vol. 2. New York: Dover.

Planning Without Shadow

Theodor Abt (Zurich)

The Quest for an Integral Approach

The way we recognize problems today, the way we analyze them and tackle them, developed in an age when it was possible to have an overall view of life. The purposeful application of reason was an effective method of redressing individual grievances. An example that springs to mind is the progress in agriculture, thanks to a specific search for the causes of bad harvests. By resorting to causal logic and the statistical laws of cause and effect, humans were able to extricate themselves from all sorts of difficult situations and deal with their fears and dependence on Nature.

Today it is commonly acknowledged that we are living in an age of transition. Material progress, which we owe to this rational approach, has grown alarmingly, in a very short time. Distances are getting shorter and spheres of life that were once separate now overlap. Money economy, industrialization, liberalization of the economic situation and a growth in freedom of movement for the individual have eaten away at the framework of a way of life over which we once had an overview. A consequence of this is that it is no longer possible to keep track of the complexity with which so many aspects of our life are mutually interdependent.

Given this complexity, one feels increasingly out of one's depth and concentrates on a special field. But, once individual operations and innovations are the product of a limited and specialized point of view, the ensuing side- and long-term effects on other spheres can lead to serious disturbances. The increasingly rapid pollution of our environment and the innumerable examples of inequality in social politics are the consequence of such indirect effects of well-meant measures. Thus, the urgent cry goes out for a solution to contemporary problems that is not just patching-up. No longer can we tackle individual abuses as they crop up; we must learn to think in a more coherent and integral manner. The fundamental change in our overall situation calls for a new approach.

On the political level, this transformation has been reflected in the movement away from individual decision-making. A corresponding increase in overall planning and concepts gives the impression that the collective problems of today are mainly of a material nature. In the hectic pace of everyday political life there is thus more and more talk of the fact that external basic factors, which apparently cannot be altered, demand a certain course of action.

Despite all these harsh facts, and the way they are applied to the working out of concepts, there is no denying the central role of humans, for ultimately it is people who see and analyze problems and make the final decisions. Yet it is precisely here that there seems to be growing uncertainty. For the question at stake here is: Under what conditions is it at all possible for humans to pass adequate judgment on a complex sphere of reality and to make the right decision for the future, in the light of the overwhelming dimensions of the overall situation? And what sort of *image* have humans of this overall situation considering that they are being called upon to think in an integral manner?

Among experts there is a belief that the best way to deal with complex spheres of reality is cybernetic thinking: trying to get a grip on problems with the aid of a computerized assessment of all relevant control areas and threshold values. Such a representation of an external system is by no means doomed to failure. "For as soon as the links *between* the parts of a system emerge more clearly—which is precisely the case with very complex systems—and an analysis is built up on these links, the significance of the *parts* of the system then fades. They can be brought together in groups and the links can be reduced to a few reciprocal effects between such principal nodal points, without the actual statement getting lost" (Vester, nd, p. 74).

We can perceive only the basic pattern or the overall picture of a problem when we concentrate less on the details and look more closely at the links between the parts. Despite this important realization, we must concede that there are limits to this way of thinking; it is based exclusively on the law of causality. One hopes that with the assistance of successful models from the world of reality, it will be possible one day to get a grip on our problems. But to think on these lines would be to have a false estimation of the possibilities of cybernetics. Even if we are able to perceive the external basic patterns of social and ecological problems, we must see that we can apprehend statistically only a one-sided reflection of life (Dahl, 1982).

The problem is that no computer system will ever be able to handle the unique, the irrelevant and the unpredictable. Moreover, there will always be a limit to our ability to understand the potential effects of any interference with a living system. For any system, from the smallest organism to the most complicated ecological or social system, breaks down into a "visible outside margin" and an "invisible kernel" (Dorner, 1983, p. 28). This means that the observer cannot establish directly the states of many elements in a system because they are located in the shadow of what is perceivable.

How is it possible for people to work with that shadow area beyond the knowable? In theory, knowledge always can be extended, but, because of the human basic structure, our capacity for knowledge is limited to the conscious. (The unconscious archetypal patterns are not incorporated through the perceptions of biological patterns.) Consequently, model perception is always incomplete unless it includes the unconscious shadow area. This leads us to the question of how humans can relate to this shadow in the area of knowledge when they draw up their plans. Is there a way to have access to the integral perception of a sphere of reality? Or must it be conceded that those people are right who claim that modern planning is ultimately just a question of replacing chance by error?

Collective Problems and Collective Unconsciousness

Questions of this nature arose for me when I was given the task of running the project for working out two regional development concepts dealing with an integral economy. The first one was for the Canton of Uri, commissioned by the cantonal government. That was in 1973. Three years later I was given a similar commission for the mountain region of the Canton of Zurich. Of course the very doubts I have mentioned, about the viability of modern planning methods, made me embarrassingly uncertain of myself. Not exactly the perfect qualification for a young, inexperienced project leader! But there was no avoiding the issue, for I was pursuing two courses of study at the same time. I was studying in the Department of Agriculture at the Federal Institute of Technology (ETH) in Zurich, specializing in agrarian and regional economics. I was also training as an Analytical Psychologist at the C. G. Jung Institute. What I learned at the ETH were the rational methods of the natural sciences, and the laws applying to the *homo okonomikus*. It was a matter of objective science; the only interesting feature about the researching subject was the intellect. In contrast, my studies at the C. G. Jung Institute showed me the effect that complexes, archetypes and symbols have on our thinking. I was made vividly aware of the reality of our general human instinct structure, and the images that are part and parcel of that.

These two methods of acquiring experience led to a growing conflict between two different images of humanity. This conflict was based on a different image of wholeness. At the university and in development planning the criteria, in judging a problem from an integral point of view, are almost exclusively the measuring, weighing and analyzing of efficiency factors that are externally determinable. Every operation is played out on the level of consciousness. The result is presented in clear concepts and statistics. A sound clarification of the individual and the interwoven cause and effect relationships are the bases for perceiving the external patterns of reality. (Dorner, 1983, goes to great lengths to show by means of his Lohhausen experiment that the emotional background of a person is very relevant to the way one goes about solving complex problems. Dorner seems to have been unaware of the results of Jung's research.)

In the course of my training as an Analytical Psychologist, I learned how to look at reality in a totally different way. In addition to the external factors involved in defining a person's problem, the psychotherapist must recognize and understand those factors which come into consciousness from the spiritual interior. In this respect I was impressed by the interpretation of images. I saw how, in the images or symbols of a dream, a fantasy or a symptom, something can be expressed out of this unconscious mental background. Even an outsider, after lengthy patient observation of such images, can be put gradually into the picture. Only when there has been recognition of both the external and internal (archetypal) basic patterns is it possible to reach a proper understanding of the meaning of a problem and then of a person's development potential.

From this tension there arose for me the question of whether the discovery of an unconscious mental reality, and the interpretation of imagery based on this background, could be transferred to the treatment of collective problems. I felt that Jung's proof that there was such a thing as the collective unconscious was extremely important. What are the implications of this discovery in dealing with collective problems? In my search for a link between these two worlds, I was struck by my own dreams, which clearly related to my planning work. Encouraged and guided by my training analyst, Dr. Marie-Louise von Franz, I worked on a series of nine such dreams as part of my thesis at the C. G. Jung Institute.

I started from the hypothesis that, if there is one-sidedness in the conscious attitude, collective external problems will probably lead to compensatory reactions from the collective area of the unconscious. Hence, dreams relating to my external treatment of collective problems should contain guidelines or suggestions for improvement in the way I approached this task (just as dreams provide guidelines in psychotherapy). Together with the results of the external development planning, these nine dreams, with my attempts to interpret them, were accepted as a doctoral thesis at the ETH in Zurich. This empirical investigation, which took place over a period of three years, shows clearly that a valuable contribution is to be made by bringing in dreams when handling complex problem areas. In the meantime, almost 15 years of empirical research seem to show clearly that it is not only in psychotherapy that dreams can be useful guides; they also have some contribution to make to the treatment of the pathology of our day and age.

Subsequent to my research, the results of comprehensive brain and sleep research, with people and with a large number of animals, have produced very informative insights into the meaning and significance of the brain's activity. Measuring brain waves in mammals, during the dream phase and during phases of heightened stages of alertness, have shown clearly that, during sleep, when only limited information reaches the brain from the sensory organs, apparently a "very special kind of information processing is going on" (Winson, 1985, p. 85). In terms of theta waves and the activated brain sections (especially hippocampus and frontal lobes), this processing is the same as in heightened stages of alertness (Winson, 1985, chs. 7 & 8).

These results have been confirmed by the research team of Prof. Wolf-Dieter Heiss of the Max Planck Institute for Neurological Research in Cologne, with the assistance of the PET (Positrone Emissions Tomography), a new method of measuring cerebral glucose metabolism. Heiss and his team reported that, during the dream phase—in contrast to the deep sleep phase—it was possible to see an increase in energy consumption that was on average 16.4 percent higher than in the waking state. Thus, our brain is more active in the dream phase than during the waking state. A further remarkable finding was that there is not only a higher consumption of glucose in the brain in general, but that in certain sections it was possible to see significantly higher activity. The conclusion was that these sections of the brain are particularly involved in the dream work. Tallying with the findings announced by Winson, the frontal lobes, the hippocampus and other sections are more active in the REM phase. The frontal lobe is the most advanced and most highly developed part of the human cerebrum. It organizes language and thinking and enables people to plan for the future. The hippocampus is an older section of the brain and forms the bridge to long-term memory and to the biogenetically oldest sections of the brain, the limbic system and the brain stem. During the dream phase there seems to be a process going on that is vitally important for warm-blooded animals; a processing of external impressions with the specific knowledge stored in the gene material. We have only to look at the process of evolution to find support for this theory.

Winson (1985) also showed, on the basis of many experiments, that the new daily impressions are linked with the experience patterns of the basic instinctual structure. This process was decisive for the survival of warm-blooded animals and for their constant adaptation to changes in their circumstances. It was also a crucial factor in the further evolution of this branch of creation. For it has not been possible to discover REM phases with reptiles. Oddly enough, this is also true of the spiny echidna family, a type of oviparous mammal to be found in Australia. Although these animals have no REM phase, they do have an overlarge frontal lobe; in relation to the whole brain it is the same size as in humans.

The things that go on with warm-blooded animals during the REM phase occur with the spiny echidna in the frontal lobe during the waking state. As the branch of oviparous warm-blooded animals did not evolve any further, perhaps because any further stages of development would have called for an enormous head to accommodate the corresponding growth in the frontal lobe, the development in the REM phase seems to have been the right solution. In the dream phase, the brain has the full capacity at its disposal and so it can easily process the impressions of the day and work out new behavior strategies, being able to accomplish more with a smaller brain. Summing this up, we can state that the REM or dream phase performs a function that must not be underestimated. When our dreams are so vivid that we remember them, it is reasonable to assume that they derive from a maximum performance of our brain.

In order to give insight into my empirical research on the inclusion of the REM phase in working out collective problem situations, I can illustrate a possible combining of the internal and the external world, with the aid of a selection of previously unpublished dreams.

The Significance of Our Reflex Faculty

After completing my work on the development concept of the overall economy of the Canton of Uri, I had the following dream just one week before being asked to work on a similar concept for the Zürcher Berggebiet, an area of about the same population as Canton Uri: *I am with Mr. X just before taking off for Riyadh to work out a development concept for Saudi Arabia. We want to take a look at the area beforehand. The globe we are looking at shows Saudi Arabia as*

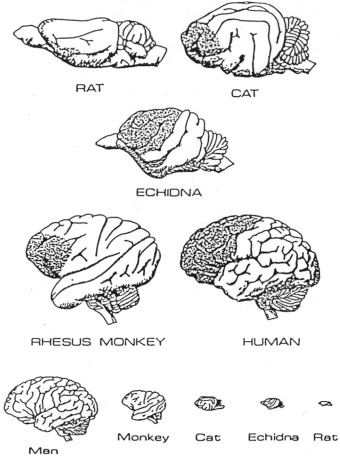

Figure 4-1. The prefrontal cortex in each species is shown as a shaded area. For clarity, all brains are drawn to the same size with the relative sizes illustrated below. In placental and marsupial mammals, the amount of prefrontal cortex increases as the animal advances in the mammalian order. In the rat, prefrontal cortex is very small. It grows progressively larger in the cat and monkey, and finally reaches its greatest development in humans. The growth of prefrontal cortex is even more pronounced than is shown by the shaded areas, for in higher species the neocortex becomes more and more convoluted, indicating that a greater mass of neural tissue is squeezed together and folded upon itself in a given brain surface area. The brain of the echidna is a remarkable anomaly. Although its behavior and capabilities are no more advanced than those of a rat, it possesses a very large, convoluted prefrontal cortex, greater in size relative to the rest of its brain than any mammal including humans.

a globe of its own. The whole globe is taken up by the country, the development area. We realize that no matter how we turn the globe, we always lose one side of the country; it goes to the back, out of sight. It is as if the dimension of depth is lost through the way we look at it, as if reality is "flattened out" by our consciousness. Somehow I manage to lay hands on a mirror. This enables us to look at both the front and the back of the globe. This means that we can keep track of what was out of sight before and can look at it closely whenever we want to. We are very pleased about this unexpected but nonetheless convincing possibility that is opened up. Then we leave.

Before I try to interpret this dream, we need the personal associations. Mr. X worked with me on the development concept for the Zürcher Berggebiet. During my work for the Canton of Uri I was able to talk to him openly about my sense of conflict between the internal and external worlds. As in the situation in the external world, Mr. X and I are also about to leave in the dream, to embark on a new task. In the dream, however, it is not to the Zürcher Oberland that we are going, but to Saudi Arabia. More than most other countries, the desert kingdom of Saudi Arabia is exposed to a dangerous conflict between progress and tradition. It is also a peninsula that is of great strategic significance.

To compensate for my attitude on a conscious level, the dream image can be understood as an indication of the fact that this new project may present me with a far greater field of tension than I had hitherto supposed. Before we get down to work, Mr. X and I get a picture of the geographical structure of the country. But in the dream we see Saudi Arabia not as part of a normal map, but as a globe of its own. The sphere is known in many cultures as a symbol of wholeness or of God. Thus, the country as a globe is an indication of its relationship to wholeness. The dream image of the region as a globe compensates for our usual conception in view of the fact that, in any such development planning, we would be able to deal with only a section of the complex world. Instead of this flat, one-sided picture of a region, I apparently must come to a view that will incorporate the dimension of depth in the whole area behind it. But the wholeness of this country consists of two sides, one half that is tangible and one that is not. The sphere as a rounded whole also indicates a global view, something we strive for in development planning. But the dream shows vividly how this global view is not possible with the method of apprehension adopted by the conscious. No matter how we turn the globe, there is always one side that we cannot see. Hence, our view of a region is always one-sided. We have the same experience in our analyses of situations in the different regions: When we find out anything about a region, we must ignore certain aspects of it. Similarly, in the dream, the conscious is only able to describe a partial view. Scientific circles, too, have the resigned attitude that an overall view of planning problems is just not possible; in dealing with complex assignments one must be contented with being a "patchwork technocrat."

Now comes the turning point in the dream. Somehow I manage to acquire a mirror, in which I can see things that otherwise cannot be seen. In psychological terms, the mirror makes possible perceptions that are beyond the level of consciousness. Our unconscious soul, with its symbolic statements, provides access to the shadow area of our conscious mind, and in the same way the image of the mirror points to the significance of understanding the images from the unconscious. In the practice of psychotherapy we never cease to be amazed at how often dream images provide information, sometimes in a most unusual way; thus it is possible to arrive at a full picture, one that has a healing effect. As the bridge from the conscious to the unconscious is made up of reflection of the symbolic statements from the unconscious, the mirror is the very symbol of the language of symbols. This makes possible the compensatory completion of the approach on the conscious level. The dream says that, with the aid of an instrument of reflection, the other side of reality can be kept in sight, thus making it possible to have an overall view.

About the forthcoming assignment, the unconscious pinpoints a specific danger of development planning, one that arises from the necessity for conceptualization in abstract terms. Today's large-scale planning projects, with their use of statistics and maps, are divorced from external reality. It is important to realize the limits of this one-sided, flattening approach. This realization leads to a compensatory disposition toward reflection, heeding and observing what cannot be seen. In Zen Buddhist meditation the master tries to teach the disciple how to keep the internal mirror free from dust. We can see in ourselves and in the practice of psychology just how much attention the inner world needs if the soul's capacity for reflection is to become visible or remain visible.

The Roots of Our Lack of Equilibrium

A dream that I had in June, 1974, in the initial stages of working out the development concept for Uri, is an indication of the central importance of turning inwards, away from external activity, to the depths of the soul. *I am in San Francisco, at the river, and I can see a bridge which has a pillar on an island in the middle of the river. The bridge is rather medieval in construction. People live on the island and are playing the trumpet. The water is rough. On the side where I am standing, which is somehow also part of San Francisco, it is all covered with trees and behind me there is a steep slope. The city itself is on the other side of the river. Then an unknown voice says: "Cain goes into the mountain instead of into all the hustle and bustle and there he meets Abel and his family." I ask myself: "Am I Cain?"*

The link to the development concept for Uri comes from the people playing the trumpet on the island. One of my colleagues at the time played the trumpet. Later he became the Cantonal Planner for Uri. He had received additional training as a planner at the Institute for Local, Regional and National Planning (ORL), and thanks to this, was able to bring to our team his specialized knowledge of cybernetic thinking and planning technology.

The starting point for the dream is an American city on one side of a river, with a wooded mountain on the other. Between them is a bridge with a pillar on an island in the middle. In the dream I am on the bank that has the mountain. The contrast between the wooded mountain and the city of San Francisco is very marked. On the one hand there is the peaceful mountain, with its trees deeply rooted in the soil; on the other hand there is the hectic, rootless city. As a metropolis of California, in the land of unlimited possibilities, we can see this city as an encapsulation of our western culture, that of the individual. The wooded mountain is solid and enduring. With clearly defined outlines, the mountain rises from the plain, all the more striking because

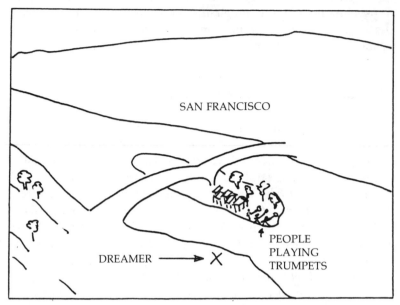

Figure 4-2. First drawing of dream after waking.

so much of California is fairly flat. The wooded mountain has long served as an area of retreat, not only for endangered species of animals, but also for people who are persecuted, partisans, wise people and those seeking God.

In the center of the dream picture stands a bridge, medieval in construction, linking the two worlds. Its central pillar stands on a small island where people are playing the trumpet. The colleague who played this instrument was a trained planner and a committed exponent of thinking of how things link up together. He used his professional skills to elucidate connections and continuity. Laudably, he also applied this approach to his own life style which, like the island in the dream, could be a model "eco-center." The rows of houses, the gardens and trees symbolize a communal working together of humanity and nature. From the point of view of the inner soul, these island people, encouraged by planning and ecological circles, embody the attempt to create a world picture which combines civilization and nature. It was on these lines that I saw my own external activity: to blow into the trumpet, together with kindred spirits, and somehow, to help make the world a better place.

But then the dream changes in an unusual way: Cain and Abel are mentioned. The transformation from San Francisco to the tranquility of the wooded mountain is already unusual, but the sudden intervention of Biblical figures is even more so. An unknown voice says: "Cain leaves the hustle and bustle"— apparently the extraverted society of the trumpet players, too— in order to go into the mountain. There Cain meets his brother Abel and his family. It seems that the way the dream presents the problem of opposites of nature and civilization and bridges them from the viewpoint of the unconscious is not enough. The problem demands to be seen and treated on a deeper level, namely in the sphere of the early history of western consciousness, at the origin of the split into good and evil.

In this day and age there is no lack of experts, planners and environmental organizations to join forces and tell us what we should do to get the world sorted out again. And there has been a noticeable improvement in the way people lead their lives. But, in the dream, the bridge is a medieval one. A central feature of the Middle Ages in the West is the search for realization of the Christian ideal, to help good to prevail. The one-sided tendency away from evil has been thwarted in modern times. Since the Renaissance, the earthly and Satanic elements blocked out by Christianity have struck back with all the force of the repressed and, via the Age of Enlightenment, have brought us to the materialism and lack of equilibrium so familiar today. The medieval bridge, a bridging of the opposites of progress by means of "good" planning and working or by means of world-improvers is, according to the dream, only half the journey. Cain has to leave the hustle and bustle on this island in order to meet Abel by submerging himself in the heart of the mountain. To understand this section of the dream, we need to look at the motif of the hostile brothers.

Compared to the shepherd Abel, the farmer Cain is more settled and progressive. With the produce from his progress in agriculture, the Lord is dissatisfied, rather unfairly. For where there are innovations, the devil always has a finger in the pie. Out of envy and resentment, Cain murdered his brother. As a punishment he was cursed from the land by God. Consequently,

Cain became the first man to found a city. As I have shown (Abt, 1987), founding a city is connected directly with the development of an established consciousness. The curse on Cain, and his expulsion from his home country, meant that the whole sphere that has to do with innovation and progress was separated from the religious sphere. The origin of this split is to be found in the Christian divine image itself. The Lord did not wish to see the offering of the progressive farmer because everything that has to do with progress and insight is the work of Satan. Thus, the Christian church has never taken seriously the whole field of modern science and planning.

Back to the dream picture: My assignment is (a) to become aware of the Cainitic-rootless nature of my scientifically-formed consciousness and (b) to lead it toward introversion. There, in the mysterious depths of the inner soul, the homeless Cain finds the brother he thought was dead; there the consciousness that is isolated, separated and cursed by God or by a superordinate whole, a consciousness that questions everything can be reunited with the other side, which has a naive, childlike faith in God.

This uniting of opposites can be described also with the aid of modern concepts such as the coming together of modern, purposeful planning approaches, and a way of thinking that is bound by tradition and simply goes around in circles. In the light of modern brain research, the myth of the hostile brothers can be seen as an intuitive, internal view of a situation that can be proved from an external, scientific point of view. The development of greater consciousness generally leads to a dominance of the left over the right hemisphere of the brain; the left hemisphere can even largely eliminate the right one. The latter is then hidden "in the mountain" and can be seen as a living reality only by means of a voluntary going into oneself. The right half of the brain is connected with the spatial, visual processing of information, and the non-verbal form of expression of the symbol builds a bridge to the older brain structures. Thus, this coming together of Cain and Abel in the mountain can be seen as a possibility of uniting consciousness and unconsciousness in deep introversion. A further mystery inside the mountain can be inferred from Abel's being in the mountain with his family; the feminine element (the wife) and the renewal of Abel (the children). This image contrasts with the Abel in the Bible, who is unmarried.

An examination of publications and speeches by people involved in planning and ecology reveals that they almost always end by saying that this or that should be done to make something better. For example, even as I write, the Central Office for Regional Economic Advancement in Berne is considering having new development concepts drawn up for the mountain regions in Switzerland, for the so-called "second generation." Faithful to the motto that "The good is replaced by the better," those involved in the science of planning and regional economics are always trying to help good things to be developed. Apparently they do not realize that the constant suggestions for improvement lead to a throw-away mentality in this field, as in others. But the problem goes even further. At the end of the dream the question comes: "Am I Cain?" As a planner I have to ask myself whether my efforts to help to improve the external world come from a Cainitic "feeling of incompleteness." Again and again we see that innovations and plans of the second, third and nth generation are supposed to do away with shortcomings. And for these improvements to make the final breakthrough we need the media (the trumpets). The disappointment comes later.

The dream was a compensatory one, leading me away from my well-meant extraversion, and concentrating my attention on the reality of the inner soul. In becoming aware of this inner split into a Cain and an Abel, and in the search for a synopsis of these two halves, a genuine uniting of opposites comes about. There is more to this than a medieval bridge, whose central pillar rests on doing good in the hope of chasing evil out of the world.

In conclusion I am using an image "from inside the mountain" to illustrate how new insights can be gained in dealing with collective problems by bringing in the dream world.

Searching for the Uniting of Opposites

At the end of 1976 the development concept for Uri was approved by the federal government. As part of working out the cantonal guidelines to ensure that all area planning projects are coordinated, the Uri government decided that it made sense to work on the development concept beforehand. I was invited to join in the work involved, and I readily accepted, in order to pursue my investigations more deeply. On the surface, the work consisted of examining a network of interconnecting features. This time I was more aware than in 1973 of the need to bring in the reality of the soul. But how to formulate the problem in such a way as to be generally understood?

As the time drew nigh for me to submit a proposal to my employers, I was in serious trouble. I set off, in the spring of 1983, to spend a couple of weeks in my remote house in the mountains. The isolation there made me even more painfully aware of my ignorance. One morning, after spending the previous day deep in thought on the development concept, I awoke with the following dream: *I am in the room of my little daughter Doris, holding the problem "Development concept Uri" in my hands on a sheet of paper. There is a line down the middle. On the left-hand side there is a piece of bacon, and a flower on the other side. I don't know what to do so I play with it in Doris' room.*

Figure 4-3.

I concentrated in the following weeks on trying to understand the dream iamge in a playful way, as I had played with my three-year-old daughter in her room. In accordance with the laws of dream interpretation, I tried to embellish the bacon and the flower with generally familiar experiences. Why bacon? A side of bacon hanging in the fireplace used to be a sign of prosperity. Today one thinks of bacon more in terms of being unhealthily overweight. Thus the word symbolizes material prosperity, a major factor in all our political programs. By way of contrast, the flower has always been a symbol for intangible values. We offer flowers to express our feelings on the important occasions in life. And we plant flowers on graves as a sign of the resurrection of the immortal soul from the tomb. Thus we can look at the meaning of the two images by placing the following key words alongside each other:

BACON	FLOWER
Life quantity	Life quality
Biological needs	Mental-spiritual needs
• Prosperity	• Meaning
• "Functions"	• Love, fantasy
• Movement	• "Having time"

According to the dream, the problem of the "development concept Uri" is basically that the material aspect might be cut off from the mental and spiritual dimension as if by a wall. A one-sided view of development, only in the form of improving material conditions, could indeed make us lose sight of the needs of the other side and thus cause the flower to wither. Thus, the problem of the Uri development concept is that, with a one-sided concentration on material goods, and an ensuing neglect of the world of flowers, the variety and wealth of the spiritual life will become stunted.

In November 1983 my work was finished. The results of the newly-revised concepts could be put to the cantonal government. I had decided to risk using the image from my dream to illustrate the problems involved in incorporating the mental and spiritual dimension in concrete development planning. I had serious misgivings that I could be criticized as a scientist for working with vague pictures instead of with facts and figures. Consequently, to avoid once again falling into the trap of one-sidedness against plans that were too rational, I included tangible figures in the first part of my remarks, together with an appropriate commentary. When I had finished my address, the first one to speak was the Uri Finance Director, who was known for being very critical. He said that he was satisfied with the first part of my speech, with the analysis of the situation and revised objectives worked out at the ETH, but he said he had just one criticism to make of the second part, with the image of the bacon and the flower: "It was much too short!" The gratifying outcome of this response was that the picture of the bacon and the flower was moved from the chapter on quality of life to its rightful place at the beginning, in the introduction.

May this dream image serve as a model to remind us of the basic problems involved in contemporary development. What we must do is to remain aware of this split whenever we make decisions, so that development or progress will not lead to loss of soul. In the dream a symbol was born, one that illustrates the problem of united opposites. To compensate for the veritable deluge of printed pages, the image that occurred in this dream indicates a remarkable focusing on what is essential.

We must be aware of the problem of the wall's separating the two worlds of the bacon and the flower. The sufferings caused by the tension between the two apparently irreconcilable opposites of concrete politics and spiritual reality are ultimately necessary to give birth to a new spirit, which is able to unite progress and soul. The essence of this concept seemed to be understood by the Uri government. Included in the highest official's report was the following:

"Anyone involved with the development concept and the basic plan for the Canton of Uri—and that was an agreeably large number of our citizens—must have become aware of the numerous conflicts. In my opinion, that alone is a valuable experience, one that should keep us from unrealistic over-simplifications and make us adopt well-considered and balanced compromises."

This dream image serves to illustrate how, in the dream phase, the older brain structures that are activated accomplish a crucially valuable processing of information. The brain structure that has developed over thousands of years—the "two-million-year-old man" in us, as Jung called it—has an empirical knowledge that is processed in the dream phase along with the impressions of the day.

Since first postulating in my thesis at the Jung Institute that dreams can make a vital contribution to the treatment of collective problems, I have built up quite a collection of examples from other researchers, experts and politicians. But there is nothing new about my working hypothesis; it is merely an applied formulation of a supposition made by Jung. He was actually writing about modern art at the time; his views are nonetheless valid for modern planning and construction:

> The negative aspects of modern art show the intensity of our prejudice against the future, which we obstinately want to be as we expect it. We decide, as if we knew. We only know what we know, but there is plenty more of which we might know if only we could give up insisting upon what we do know. But the Dream would tell us more, therefore we despise the Dream and we are going on to dissolve *ad infinitum*.
>
> What is the great Dream? It consists of the many small dreams and the many acts of humility and submission to their hints. It is the future and the picture of the new world, which we do not understand yet. We cannot know better than the unconscious and its intimations. *There* is a fair chance of finding what we seek in vain in our conscious world. Where else could it be?
>
> I am afraid I never find the language which would convey such simple arguments to my contemporaries. (Let-2, pp. 591–92)

These words are among the last written by Jung on the problem of our times. Our investigation has shown how dreams related to the subject of development planning can illuminate certain aspects that have remained unconscious. As long as the contents of such dreams are archetypal, what they have to say is not hopelessly subjective, for their origin lies in a sphere of reality that is common to all humankind, the collective unconscious. In order to understand the orientation guidelines from the unconscious, careful attention must be given to the symbols from the spiritual interior. Every effort must be made to understand this language of imagery; this is a task that cannot be taken over by the collective. This work can result in an enormous increase in the meaning of the life of the individual. It also enhances development and progress without losing sight of the reality of the soul.

Translated from German by
David Roscoe

REFERENCES

Abt, T. (1987). *Progress without loss of soul*. Chicago: Chiron.
Dahl, J. (1982). Oekologie. *Natur, 12*.
Dorner, D. (1983). *Vom Umgang mit Unbestimmtheit und Komplexität*. Bern: Huber.
Vester, F. et al. (nd). *Man and biosphere*. Ravensburger.
Winson, J. (1985). *Brain and psyche*. New York: Anchor.

Discussion: Jean-Marie Spriet (Brussels)

I am uneasy at the thought of working on projects for the development of society for two reasons. As a therapist, I have no concrete experience in matters of social perspectives and, as an individual and a citizen, I notice each day the stupid moves, the alienations, and the crimes caused by ideologies and their programs. What right do certain ideologists have to impose, in the name of God and Truth, their fantasies about the infinite complexities of human situations and the contradictions in each person? I have great uneasiness in the face of the violence and intolerance created by putting ideologies into practice.

Having thus expressed the gut feeling that the idea of such programs brings to me, I am going to discuss briefly some disadvantages—some shadows—that could be occasioned by putting into practice Abt's hypothesis.

He believes that dreams can bring essential contributions to the explanation of collective problems, especially in the domain of projects for developing society. The hypothesis appears to me to be fully defensible and can be illustrated with many historical examples. However, we should not lose sight of the dangers of the ideological use of the dream. What brings light can also create shadow when it becomes a revealed truth, an ideology. Many founders of religions or of socio-political movements got from a dream a new perception of the situations of their time. They developed doctrines, favoring certain aspects of society and rejecting others. In the long run, this process becomes alienating.

It is important for the therapist or the seeker to examine to what degree the use of dreams hides a desire to remodel reality by exaggerating it. Plans for the building of a better society have always been the basis for blessing a utopia. Thus, the personal dreams of each of us, and their interpretation, are subject to cultural influences in our conception of a new society. By telling each other our big dream, we can confront associations and interpretations and correct, in part, a view of things that may have been too personal.

To believe in a spirit of the time specific to our age seems to me not to take into consideration the various points of view and the interpretations that one could have concerning our era. Such a conception of things is an underlying ideology in itself. The recourse to dreams, to productions of the inside world, is used by some people in an unrealistic manner as a panacea. Thus they deny the necessity of taking into consideration the economic and social adaptations.

I do not believe that the benefit from the contributions of dreams is self-evident. It presupposes that one is attentive to the inner life, and is able to dream; this means that one has an inner world sufficiently rich and precise. Some personalities, with too narcissistic a nature, using their imagination to fill a void, do not have this ability, because they do not feel comfortable in their bodies, in their own centers. They tend to develop technological projects where their inclinations to dominate and to fragment ignore the complexity of human realities. Persons resorting to defense mechanisms of a psychosomatic nature probably will build up a model society based on an anxious search for security.

How is it possible to put into practice the contributions of the dreams? It is difficult to offer spiritual next to purely economic measures. Such a combination would be a polarization, a death-carrying split. I consider the contribution of the dreams to be that of bringing light to the heart and mind of the searcher, who can then offer innovative measures to other people.

If the important point is to give to Caesar what belongs to Caesar, and to God what belongs to God, it is becoming urgent to reconcile God and Caesar in a domain where dissociation brings about disastrous consequences for humanity and for the planet. Most important, however, is to remain realistic. There is no fundamental approach to any problem, but there is a dialectical contest between divergent points of view.

It is not easy for us to let go of our illusion of dominance and of our desire for perfection, and to allow contradictions to coexist in the discomfort of an open wound. This seems to me to be what Abt tries to do, bringing our society face to face with its shadow.

Translated from French by
Paula Kondrick

The Structure of Collective Shadows: Why They Endure

James A. Hall (Dallas)

The personal shadow constellates a practical and moral problem in the psychology of individuals. Similarly, in the world of collective consciousness, the phenomena of collective shadow projection pose moral, ethical, and practical problems for humankind as a whole. Indeed, failure to understand and contain collective shadows could unleash forces that would annihilate the civilized world if not disrupt the delicate biological balance of our planet.

Collective shadows may arise between and among national, ethnic, tribal, or other groups, or even cause splits within existing collectives, as evidenced by the histories of all major religions. The shifting images of collective shadows during World War II are another example. I recall my confusion after the end of the conflict when the stereotypes began to change. It was a shock to learn that the wartime Stalin, "Good old Uncle Joe" in the stereotypes, had been responsible for liquidation of many people in Russia, including the Kulak class of peasants.

My first psychoanalyst, Bingham Dai, was not Jungian but was trained by Harry Stack Sullivan in what has been known in the United States as the "cultural" school of psychoanalysis. Dai was a Chinese sociologist before becoming an American psychotherapist, so he had a wide opportunity to observe the dreams of several cultural groups. He told me that in his experience the shadow in dreams of Chinese was often represented by the Japanese, while the shadow in Japanese dreams was often represented by the Chinese. Even with less cross-cultural experience

I can confirm that racial and cultural stereotypes may appear in dreams as a representation of the personal shadow. This observation suggests linkage between the personal shadow and stereotypic collective shadows.

The Personal Shadow

In the personal sphere of the psyche, the ego and the shadow may be considered identity structures, while the anima/animus and the persona are relational structures that interface between the personal part of the psyche and, respectively, the collective unconscious within and collective consciousness outside. (See Hall, 1983b, pp. 14–18.) As shown in Figure 6-1, the ego and shadow are contained within a personal sphere of the psyche, while the persona and anima/animus form the boundaries of that personal area.

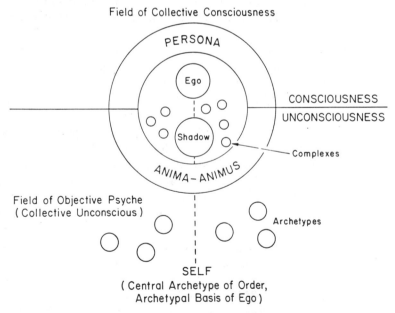

Figure 6-1. Structure of the Psyche

Contextual Nature of the Shadow

Some complexes and their attendant identity structures are dissociated into the shadow in the course of early development. Any complex may have both positive and negative forms, as seen from the point of view of a particular ego-identity. A child's natural assertiveness, for example, may be dissociated into the shadow because that particular family equates assertiveness with unacceptable aggressiveness. Such a child may reach physical maturity without easy access to the needed assertiveness, which has been assigned to the shadow while its opposite, passivity, may be well integrated into the structure of both the child's ego and persona.

While the existence of a shadow is a normal part of the human personality, the specific contents of the shadow are dependent upon variables in early environment and experience including, as Martine Drahon Gallard shows elsewhere in this volume, the "white shadow" or void of hidden family secrets. The re-working of the contents of the shadow is a major part of most psychotherapeutic activity.

Shadow as Preliminary Integration

In its formation, then, the shadow is only a preliminary integration. It allows the developing ego to achieve only a relative stability that is necessary for a later and more complete integration of the opposites that were originally split between ego/persona and shadow. This later, more complete integration focuses on the unification of opposites (Hall, 1983a, discusses this more fully.) and the archetypal image of the coniunctio. (See Nathan Schwartz-Salant's discussion of the *Rosarium* pictures in this volume.) This deeper integration requires a reliable ego and an adequate analytical *vas* or *temenos*. And it requires the moral courage necessary to face the dark shadow side of oneself, of one's parents, of one's culture.

Shadow Formation in a Field of Moral Tension

Although the presence of a content in the shadow, rather than in other structures of the psyche, does not imply an actual negative form (from the viewpoint of the present ego), it does imply that the content was originally assigned to the shadow under the tension of an original field of moral differentiation. This field's being childish, premature, or incongruent with more adult standards does not detract from its moral tone. It is perhaps what Andrew Samuels called original morality. Later I will suggest where this field may arise in one structural form of the archetype of the Self.

Shadows and Relational Patterns

Complexes are natural building blocks of the psyche. Our usual structural terms for the personal psyche (ego, persona, anima/animus, shadow) designate relatively enduring structures of complexes and a relatively stable identification of the ego with certain of those structures. The moral tension between ego/persona and shadow, however, as well as the sex-role tension between these three structures and the contrasexual anima/animus, suggest that each of these structures has at least two poles. This bipolarity, as reflected in the shadow, is emphasized in Donald Sandner's paper in this volume.

A bipolar structure of complexes, as for example, the ego/shadow relationship, offers two poles with which the ego can identify: its usual ego-image or the shadow of that usual ego-image. The shadow pole of the bipolar structure is often projected onto another person in the environment. This process makes the shadow easy to identify; one looks for a person of the same sex whom one does not like, usually for very justifiable conscious reasons.

Therapy Groups as Small Collectives

An intermediate stage between individual and collective psychology may be observed in the interaction of small (8 to 12 person) psychotherapy groups. Jung (Let-2, pp. 217–221) distrusted group psychotherapy. The British analyst Bion, a pioneer in group psychotherapy, stated a similar concern: In order to avoid their official conscious goal of work, psychotherapy groups tend to move among three different "cultures" of basic assumptions about their purpose (Bion, 1961). The three basic-assumption cultures according to Bion are fight-flight, dependency, and pairing.

My own experience of psychotherapy groups as well as that of some other Jungian analysts (e.g., Whitmont, 1974) has been quite positive, although most of my patients who are in group psychotherapy are concurrently in individual analysis. In my experience, psychotherapy groups are supportive of individual differences, aiding their members to find personal expression rather than conformity to the group.

Therapy groups are a distinct aid in the individuation processes of their members. They have in fact seemed to be a form of what Polanyi (1966) called "a society of explorers" (pp. 83–84), where each person, as well as the society, is devoted to exploring the deeper nature of reality. Needless to say, this reality includes the shadow, both personal and collective. How can psychotherapy groups be a collective that furthers individuation, while the collective in general may actually work against it?

One obvious answer is size. A psychotherapy group seldom exceeds 12; the traditional size was eight. And in functional terms, the psychotherapy group has something that most larger cultural collectives lack: a container, a boundary, a vas or temenos. Without a secure and safe boundary individuals often function, as Jung observed, with less consciousness than they are capable of in private. Thus, even if individual consciousness is maintained in a collective situation, the individuals may act as if they are unconscious. A parallel phenomenon occurs in group psychotherapy when something is known consciously to each individual member, but has not come into the group discussion and is therefore functionally unconscious to the group process.

The Shadow of Individual and Collective Guilt

While our clinical experience is largely with the personal shadow, our world is particularly threatened by collective shadow projections. Although our western Christian heritage has established guilt and redemption as modalities for the transformation of an individual's consciousness, there are no such established categories for collective consciousness. The concept of reparations is an attempt toward such a form, as is the current American legal concept euphemistically called "affirmative action"—having a hiring quota for minority groups to redress discriminatory inequalities of the past. Clearly, such collective attempts at restitution and repair may be unfair to particular individuals. In most instances, neither those who receive the restitution nor those who give it are the actual persons who were injured or did injury. Reverse discrimination to atone for past discriminations constitutes a tacit commitment to a principle of collective discrimination that is opposed to the judgment of individuals on their unique merits.

Collective guilt based upon judgments of historical guilt is psychologically similar to the unearned guilt that a neurotic individual suffers. It also contains an innate tendency to engender reaction formation and so perpetuate a cycle of collective inflation and deflation over an extended period of time. Politically-sponsored terrorism against individuals who only represent collective groups is a current example.

It is not relevant here to discuss the pros and cons of collective rituals of restitution, but merely to suggest that, like most collective concepts, they ride roughly over individual persons, who may seem to be only insignificant units in the collective world. However, seen subjectively, each person is a unique universe. This perspective is perhaps the most valuable component of our Jungian heritage.

Preliminary Integration and Lack of Temenos

The existence of excessive collective shadows represents for the collective, as it does for the personal, a state of having attained only preliminary integration. Like the individual shadow, the shadow of a group represents unintegrated aspects of the collective and is both dangerous and alluring.

The modern history of blacks in America may serve as an example. During my childhood in eastern Texas prior to World War II, my grandmother called blacks by other, less neutral names, and there were separate restaurants, drinking fountains, and toilet facilities for blacks and whites. At that time, black persons carried the shadow of the white community as being lazy and intellectually inferior, but also possessing a childlike joy in living and having none of the white society's conflicts about sexual expression.

That has all changed. Blacks now are judged largely as individuals, and as a group are considered just as neurotic, unhappy, and sexually conflicted as everyone else. As to the sexuality that had been lodged in the black collective shadow, it has perhaps been overly integrated into the culture, with attendant benefits and disabilities. All this major change in public attitude has taken place quite rapidly and with relatively little overt conflict. It gives one hope for other integrations.

But note that the integration of blacks into American society took place within a container, a structure which officially favored the integration. It is precisely the lack of such a container that constitutes a major danger in the actions of collective shadows in the world today.

The terms in which the collective shadow appears are similar, then, to the terms of the personal shadow. The principal similarities are continuing pressure toward integration of the shadow coupled with a tendency to subvert true integration of the shadow into a preliminary, premature, and incomplete integration. This premature integration involves a splitting of contents into positive and negative. The negative pole belongs to "them" and the positive opposite, of course, to "us."

The Collective Shadow Problems of the Modern World

Collective shadows, like personal ones, arise in a field of moral valuation, involving judgments of what is good and desirable and what is not. There are two major problems associated with the collective shadows of the modern world. The first, already mentioned, is the problem of shadow projection by one cultural group on another, complicated by the absence of a conscious world container for integration of the collective shadows.

The second problem, which I will discuss below, is best articulated by Polanyi's (1958) concept of dynamo-objective coupling, which, earlier, he called moral inversion. Both problems touch upon Jung's concern with the shadow in the model of the archetypal Self that he presents in *Aion* (CW9-II).

Science and Shadows

When groups become large enough, as in the present era of nation-states, the container must be larger still—a world culture; such a culture is still in the embryo stage of development. The archetype of the *anthropos*, a higher form of humankind, would appear in collective consciousness as a sense of the *humanum*, a sense of the unity and destiny of humanity as a whole.

In contrast to the present early and fragmented beginnings of the humanum, science is already universal because it is based upon the unavoidable unity of the physical universe. But science achieves this unity across the boundaries of nation-states only at a substantial price: Science intentionally excludes the moral tensions that are part of the innate mechanism for the establishment of consciousness.

This preliminary integration in terms of moral differentiation, which produces the shadow, is precursor to a more complete integration involving the archetype of coniunctio, the alchemical image for the *hieros gamos*—the unification of the opposites. On the physical plane, the unity of science foreshadows the potential unity of the humanum on the plane of world culture.

Need for a Collective World Temenos

The personal shadow constellates a problem of moral courage for the individual. One must confront one's shadow in the innate process of individuation, a confrontation that may take place consciously (with the help of the ego's moral courage) or unconsciously (if the ego attempts to side-step the problem of shadow integration).

While the integrity of the individual psyche withstands the pressure of shadow integration, there is no such ready-made container for the integration of most collective shadows. In a profound sense, the problem of our present world is to find a container for integration of collective shadows while there is still a world to integrate.

In a physical sense, the container for collective shadows is the physical boundary of the planet earth, already unified in the studies of science. The earth is not an absolute container, for technological escape from the earth is a possibility, at least for a seed of humanity. But in practical terms, the earth is a spaceship that must sustain itself and its inhabitants and requires the integration of collective shadows for its continued existence.

There is no established world culture at present, although we need the overarching images of shared collective values that a coherent world culture could bring. At present there are competing images of such a world unity, and the crucial difference among them may well be the place of individual initiative and freedom – in psychological terms, the freedom for individuation.

The humanum is an appropriate term to represent for the collective sphere what the concept of individuation represents for the individual psyche, the microcosmic component of the macrocosmic humanum. The image of God is a link between the external collective and the collective psyche within. In the external world it informs the image of the humanum, while in the psyche within it constitutes the *imago Dei*, an image of the archetypal Self. The image of the archetypal Self is clearly concerned with the unification of opposites, which may be seen in dreams. The archetypal Self is in much less danger of reification as only "good" than is its representation in cultural forms of God.

The Shadow Quaternio in the Aionic Self

We have discussed the current lack of a reliable and sufficient world container for the integration of collective shadows. Let us now relate the field of moral tension in which both individual and collective shadows arise to Jung's three-dimensional model of the archetypal Self as discussed in his essay "The Structure and Dynamics of the Self" in the concluding section of *Aion* (CW9-II, pars. 347–421). To distinguish clearly Jung's diagramatic representation of the Self from other, more discursive presentations, I will refer to his model as the Aionic Self.

The image of a transcending, higher collective unity, the humanum, is related to an archetypal image of humanity, the anthropos. Jung placed this image in a crucial position in his hierchical model of the Self in *Aion*.

Originally I considered calling this hierarchical model of the archetypal Self the *de-integrate form of the Self* to distinguish it from Jung's non-hierarchical "Self in uroboric form." However, the term de-integrate seems best reserved for discussing the primordial contents of the infant mind. Therefore, I have chosen the designation "hierarchical form of the archetypal Self," leaving undiscussed (for the present) its relation to the developmental concept of de-integration.

HIERARCHICAL FORM OF THE ARCHETYPAL SELF

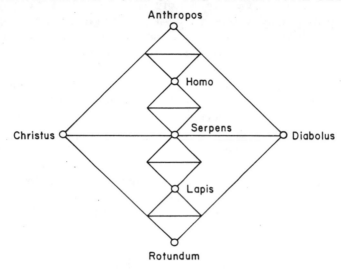

Figure 6-2. The Hierarchical Form of the Archetypal Self

ANTHROPOS QUATERNIO

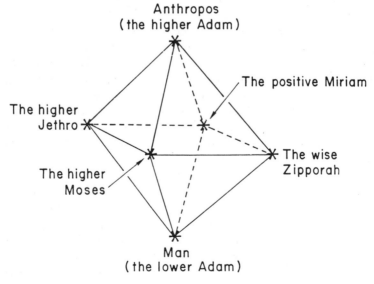

Figure 6-3. Anthropos (Moses) Quaternio

The hierarchical form of the archetypal Self (Figure 6-2) is based on the model of the cross-cousin marriage which can be seen clearly in the double pyramid that Jung (CW9–II, par. 363) labeled "The Moses Quaternio" because he used part of the story of Moses to illustrate its structure. Jung also called this "The Anthropos Quaternio" (Figure 6-3) for the highest figure of the double pyramid.

From the ego standpoint of the ordinary person, the "lower Adam," situated in this figure at the lower apex of the double pyramids, Moses appears as culture hero. To this ordinary person Moses is also the father. Zipporah, the wife of Moses, is the daughter of a king and Midianite priest, Jethro, "the great wise one." From this same viewpoint of lower Adam Zipporah is the "higher mother." Thus from this viewpoint of lower Adam, Moses and Zipporah together represent the "royal pair" that Jung discussed in "The Psychology of the Transference" (CW16).

But the ego may be identified also with the figure of Moses. From the ego-identity of Moses, Jethro is the "higher man" and his sister/anima is Miriam, while Moses' wife Zipporah concerns coniunctio. Jethro and Miriam introduce the incest tensions that are an innate part of the marriage quaternio.

This situation is complicated when Moses marries the Ethopian woman, who is unacceptable apparently because she falls into the collective shadow projected onto a different ethnic and cultural group. From this part of the Moses material Jung (CW9–II, par. 361) developed the shadow quaternio in which Moses appears as "carnal man." Jethro becomes a "heathen priest" who "did not serve Yahweh and did not belong to the chosen people, but departed from them to his own country" (Exodus 18:27). Zipporah is replaced by the shadowy Ethopian woman. In response to this situation, Miriam becomes leprous and speaks against Moses. These altered, shadow relationships are shown in this diagram (Figure 6-4).

Jung's exposition is quite complicated, and extends downward below the shadow quaternio to the paradise quaternio (Figure 6-5) and even lower to the Lapis Quaternio (Figure 6-6).

The range that Jung attributed to the hierarchical Self, then, extends from the inorganic world with its nadir in the *rotundum*, an archetypal image of the original wholeness, which may relate to the atomic world (CW9–II, par. 391) to the zenith above

SHADOW QUATERNIO

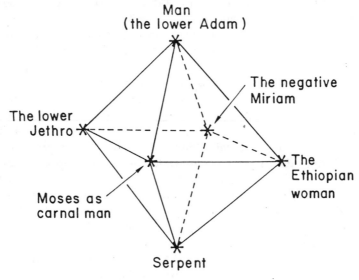

Figure 6-4. The Shadow Quaternio

PARADISE QUATERNIO

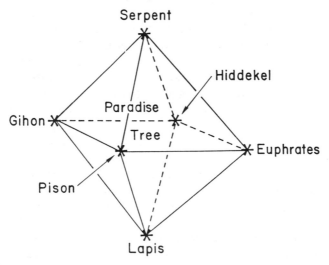

Figure 6-5. Paradise Quaternio

humankind, symbolized by the anthropos, an archetypal image of the human potentiality. Jung described the *serpens*, an ambivalent image compressing the opposites of good and evil, as the point of maximum tension in this chain of four double pyramids. The serpens compresses within itself the extreme opposites of *Christus* and *Diabolus* (Figure 6-7).

I will not explore here all the implications of Jung's thought regarding this model of the hierarchical Self, but several observations are pertinent to our discussion of collective shadows:

(1). It is clear that the ego-identity, as in a fairy tale, can be assigned to various figures within the structure of the hierarchical Self—to Moses or to lower Adam, for example. Thus the hierarchical patterns of the Self may serve as models of ego-identity and the structural relationships of the figures vary according to whether the ego is identified with one or another of what might be called an archetypal complex in the structure of the Self.

(2). It is not simply the ego of Moses that falls into the shadow identity, symbolized by his marriage to the Ethopian Woman. Rather, the entire quaternio of relationships falls into the shadow state.

(3). In the hierarchical form of the archetypal Self there are clear possibilities for movement upward toward the higher goal of the anthropos, and corresponding dangers of falling downward in a regressive direction toward the sub-personal paradise and lapis quaternios. Indeed, it would not be too much to say that the field of moral tension in which the personal shadow arises is based on the structure of the hierarchical form of the archetypal Self. But Jung did not stop at this point in his description of the Self; he asked how the situation would look if "higher" and "lower" were collapsed and the rotundum and the anthropos were placed side by side (Figure 6-8).

This configuration Jung clearly labeled as "the arrangement in the uroboros" (CW9–II, par. 391), justifying the convenience of calling it the uroboric form of the archetypal Self in distinction to the hierarchical form. Although the image retains the greater tension between the anthropos-rotundum and the serpens (as compared to the lesser tension between homo and lapis) it is clear that the hierarchical stresses and the tension implicit in the serpens have lessened greatly.

Jung clearly stated that the quaternio structures he chose were

LAPIS QUATERNIO

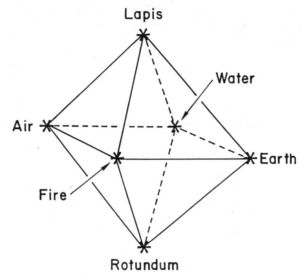

Figure 6-6. Lapis Quaternio

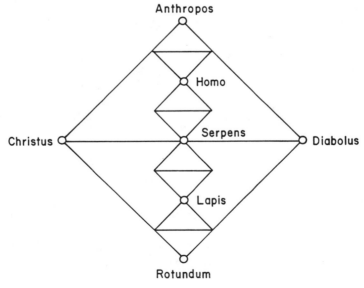

Figure 6-7. Christus and Diabolus

OUROBORIC FORM OF THE SELF

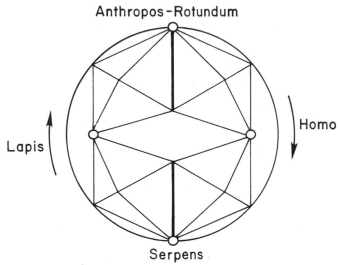

Figure 6-8. The Ouroboric Form of the Self

for explanatory purposes only and could be replaced with other examples (CW9–II, par. 363). He intended to emphasize the underlying structure, which he did even more diagramatically by showing the quaternio series in the form of an equation (CW9–II, pars. 408–411) that emphasizes the innate dynamic processes of the Self (Figure 6-9). This process returns to its beginning, but at a higher level, through a process of enantiodromia. It is equivalent to a rotating mandala image.

The uroboric form of the archetypal Self is analogous to the center of a mandala—that which is symbolically circumambulated but never reached—while the pathways of the hierarchical form of the archetypal Self, set in the circular formula of figure 9, are the processes of circumambulation of that center in the time-bound world. It would appear from the equation model of the Self that this circumambulation is sometimes experienced in an enantiodromia movement that only seems to move against (in a-b-c-d, for example) the larger spiral process (A-B-C-D-A, etc.) that actually has as its goal the continual achievement of a "higher plane" (CW9–II, par. 410).

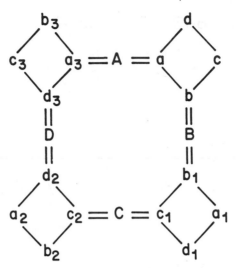

Figure 6-9. The Self as an Equation

These forms of the archetypal Self (hierarchical uroboric) would appear to be complementary. This is what I understand Alfred Plaut, elsewhere in this volume, to mean by "paradoxical unity." Emphasis on the hierarchical form constellates the moral tensions that are innate in the empirical personality and its development, with the attendant problems of personal and collective shadows. But an emphasis on the uroboric form almost collapses the moral tension and makes all gods relatively equal. It is no stretch of the imagination (at least for Jungians) to see in these two forms of the archetypal Self analogs to the three schools of Jungian analysis defined by Samuels (1985).

I wish to draw from this brief discussion of Jung's Aionic Self one major conclusion: Jung's model of the hierarchical form of the archetypal Self includes an inevitable moral tension in both individual and group shadows. I conclude with a brief elaboration of Polanyi's moral inversion, more formally described as dynamo-objective coupling.

Polanyi

Michael Polanyi was a post-critical philosopher of science, a fellow of the Royal Society for his work in physical chemistry. He grew up in Budapest only a few years earlier than Jolande Jacobi. My Zurich thesis was based on applying his epistemology to the problem of the dream-ego and the waking-ego, and I have found his work fruitful in other contexts as well (Hall, 1981; 1982; 1984).

The Modern Problem of Collective Shadows: Polanyi's Dynamo-Objective Coupling (moral inversion)

One of Polanyi's (1958, pp. 227–245) questions was why many western democratic intellectuals were attracted to Marxism in the early decades of this century. A lesser concern was the untestable nature of Freudian Psychoanalysis, despite its claims to scientific status. Both Marxism and Psychoanalysis were allegedly based upon scientific principles, and yet each had the quality of a religion whose basic assumptions were insulated from falsifiability.

From these considerations, Polanyi came to understand the psychological structure of what he called dynamo-objective coupling: a linkage in which a system of beliefs that are consciously and overtly held for allegedly objective reasons are actually and covertly held because of strong moral commitment. Such a coupling is difficult to alter. Why is this so?

If attacked on moral grounds, the dynamo-objective coupling is defended as being objective, and, like science, having nothing at all to do with morality. If attacked on ground of its supposed objective nature, the dynamo-objective coupling is defended with moral fervor, although the moral basis is simultaneously denied. Thus if one pole of the dynamo-objective coupling is attacked, it is defended from the other pole. This produces an extremely stable structure, but one not open to ordinary forms of evidence and persuasion. I have discussed elsewhere (Hall, 1984) how the structure of dynamo-objective coupling underlies the structure of neurotic defense mechanisms. In that context, I have referred to the dynamo-objective coupling structure as an attitude of pseudo-objectivity.

The Allure of Pseudo-Objectivity

Polanyi described an innate moral commitment in the human mind, one that is present even in scientific investigation, although it is inconsistent with the official collective view of the dispassionate nature of science. Jung postulated a similar innate moral tension in humanity, as illustrated in our previous discussion of how personal and collective shadows are grounded in the hierarchical form of the archetypal Self.

A dynamo-objective coupling occurs when the moral nature of one's position is denied consciously, while continuing to be expressed unconsciously. This was Polanyi's answer to why so many intellectuals in democratic countries were attracted to Marxism in its early years. Through an over-identification with the official objectivity of science, they had lost the grounding for their moral values. Their innate need for moral differentiation was denied and remained unsatisfied.

The dynamo-objective coupling structure of Marxism (and early Freudian psychoanalytic theory) permitted an unconscious pseudo-solution for the non-integration of scientific values of objectivity with religious values of meaning. While continuing to deny consciously that they were working on moral assumptions, and whle proclaiming their service to a supposedly objective process, adherents of Marxism had free reign to express moral judgments while denying that they were doing so. Thus, through a form of neurotic compromise, they fulfilled the proverbial state of "having one's cake and eating it too." Or perhaps eating the cake of someone else would be more precise—perhaps Lithuanian cake, Latvian cake, Estonian cake.

Religious persecutions of the past had an overt moral basis, even if mistaken in application. Much of the current Middle East conflict has this form, with mutual shadow projections among collective groups. This represents the classic form of the collective shadow. Given a sufficient collective container for the values of the humanum, such conflicts are resolvable in the name of universally applied moral principles, a resolution denied by the existence of collective dynamo-objective couplings.

Albert Camus (1956) in his book *The Rebel* made an important distinction between rebellion and revolution. Both are resistances to oppression, but in revolution the power struggle to overthrow an oppressor often miscarries because the successful revolutionary becomes the new oppressor, taking the place of the former foe without any change in the underlying power structures. Camus defined rebellion, however, as a resistance to an oppressor in the name of common human values that embrace both the rebel and the oppressor. Revolution has the tendency to continue divisions; rebellion carries the potential of healing. These are crucial practical differences in our current world. I suggest that what Camus called "revolution" is based upon a dynamo-objective coupling that inhibits it from realizing the unconscious moral principles that are its actual motive force. In Camus' description of rebellion the moral claims are conscious and therefore realizable in the collective world.

The presence in the modern world of collective ideologies that appear to be based upon the structure of dynamo-objective coupling, something rare in the world hitherto, constitutes the second and more serious difficulty in the resolution of collective shadows today. Undoing the moral inversion of a dynamo-objective coupling is equivalent to the treatment of a collective neurosis. I do not at present know of an analytic couch of sufficient dimensions for this high purpose.

In closing this essay on the persistence of collective shadows, I quote Jung's concluding sentence from *The Undiscovered Self* (CW10):

> I am neither spurred on by excessive optimism nor in love with high ideals, but am merely concerned with the fate of the individual human being—that infinitesimal unit on whom a world depends and in whom, if we read the meaning of the Christian message aright, even God seeks his goal. (par. 588)

Summary

Collective shadows, like personal shadows, seem to originate in the hierarchical structure of the archetypal Self. Their excessive presence indicates that only a preliminary integration has been achieved, as a precursor, one hopes, to a more complete integration based upon the archetypal form of the coniunctio. If expressed in a collective conscious image of the *humanum*, the archetypal image of the *anthropos*, which Jung located within the archetypal Self, may be a sufficient container (*temenos*) for the integration of these ordinary collective shadows.

The image of a higher collective unity, the humanum, can be traced to the archetypal image of the anthropos, or higher person. The collective image of the humanum, humanity as a higher unity, is greater than the collective shadow images, and offers a possible psychological container commensurate with the physical container of the planet earth. It may be only the image of the archetypal Self, projected into a traditional image or God or into an Aquarian image of the humanum, that is capable of containing the tension implied in the integration of the collective shadow.

A greater problem in the persistence of collective shadows is what Polanyi has called dynamo-objective coupling or moral inversion. In this structure, equivalent to a neurotic defense in an individual, moral considerations are repressed and actions are justified on a pseudo-objective basis. Shadow projections based on moral judgments continue to be acted out, but the moral basis of the action is denied. The undoing of dynamo-objective coupling requires a willingness of the collective to tolerate self-reflection in the light of potential common universal values of humankind.

REFERENCES

Bion, W. (1961). *Experiences in groups*. London: Tavistock.

Hall, J. (1981). Psychiatry and religion: A review and a projection of future needs. *Anglican Theological Review* LXIII–4, 422–35.

Hall, J. (1982). Polanyi and Jungian psychology: Dream-ego and waking-ego. *Journal of Analytical Psychology, 27,* 239–54.

Hall, J. (1983a). Enantiodromania and the unification of opposites: Spontaneous dream images. In D. Young (Ed.), *The arms of the windmill: Essays in Analytical Psychology in honor of Werner H. Engel*. New York: C. G. Jung Institute.

Hall, J. (1983b). *Jungian dream interpretation: A handbook of theory and practice*. Toronto: Inner City Books.

Hall J. (1984). Pseudo-objectivity as a defense mechanism: Polanyi's concept of dynamo-objective coupling. *Journal of the American Academy of Psychoanalysis, 12–2,* 199–201.

Polanyi, M. (1958). *Personal knowledge: Towards a post-critical philosophy*. Chicago: University of Chicago Press.

Polanyi, M. (1966). *The tacit dimension*. New York: Doubleday.

Samuels, A. (1985). *Jung and the post-Jungians*. London: Routledge & Kegan Paul.

Whitmont, E. (1974). Analysis in a group setting. *Quadrant*, *16*, 5–25.

Discussion: Henri Duplaix (Paris)

As I was considering my response to Hall's paper, the case of "Pascal" emerged from my memory. This contemporary Ulysses came to see me 10 years ago, with his wife. Their relationship was going poorly. The two of them came naively, to find out which one should go into psychotherapy with me. Pascal threw himself at me with such guilt-laden energy that I decided to work with him; I referred his wife to a colleague of mine. Years went by and the couple officially separated. He accomplished an important piece of work—Freudian, I would say—on his quasi-incestuous relationship with his mother and with his sister who is a few years older than he. He had lived a pampered life with them, after his father's death when Pascal was 12, until he was married at the age of 25.

Three brief dreams led up to his encounter with the shadow. The first dramatizes his encounter with an image of a paternal archetype.

> *He was walking through a hospital ward, mocking the patients. His gaze fell upon the dust-covered soles of the feet of a patient who had just died. As he was laughing insolently, shrugging his shoulders, an indignant nurse said to him: "Have you no shame? It is King Louis XIV who just died." He then left, running to seek refuge in a hut in the woods.*

He realized in this dream that he was finally becoming conscious of the importance of his father in his life. The latter, a humble taxi driver, became, in his eyes, a king—the Sun King.

In reality, his father had taken four years to die of stomach cancer when Pascal was eight through 12 years old. The boy was in and out of school during that time and spent much of his time in the woods, where he had become a solitary wolf-child. He had defended himself against the absence of his father and the degradation of his father's physical image by ridding it of all value. He understood in this dream that this reviled Sun King surpassed the image of his father. It allowed him to become painfully conscious of a paternal archetype, the motivational value of which he had been, until that day, neither willing nor able to recognize in himself. He had been able to survive this period in which he was almost orphaned of both mother and father only through the animal part of his shadow (the wolf-child).

The second dream and its association with objective social reality offers the scenario of the rebel who thought that he had found, in a revolutionary ideology, an answer to the anguished questions raised by the shadow rising within himself:

> He saw himself on the steps of a railroad car, calling joyously to numerous comrades and helping them climb aboard. This car was part of a very long train pulled by a steam engine that was bristling with red flags. The enthusiasm of this revolutionary train began to die down once it got under way, and Pascal found himself in the caboose, talking with some friends. He heard behind the train a terrifying noise. Rushing toward the door, he saw that his car was being pursued and was going to be overtaken and crushed by a locomotive still bristling with red flags, but spewing black smoke, furiously. In an intuitive flash, he realized that it was on a circular track and going around faster and faster. Without hesitating, he jumped off and woke up out of breath.

He had told me early in the analysis that he was a member of the Communist Party; he had even insisted on bringing me a booklet justifying Psychoanalysis that was compiled by a group of Communist Freudian analysts. I knew that he had joined the Party with a quasi-religious fervor, and that an old friend of his from work—a generous, energetic man—had taken him under his wing and had become a father figure for him. Pascal told me that this man had taught him the political language and had encouraged him to read, which he had never done before.

For more than a year, I had noticed that he no longer made reference to his revolutionary ideology, and that he seemed to be distancing himself from it. In this dream, this dynamic ideology had become a devouring, crushing machine, Cronos devouring his children. The interpretation of this dream was a painful, awkward task. For several months, he mourned this ideology which had allowed him to project on the collective conscience his personal unconscious shadow.

Farewell Comrade Pascal; hello, Ulysses. Yes, Ulysses, the eternal, universal Ulysses in each of us.

Pascal had concretized this Ulysses over the course of several years, by spending his week-ends building, with his own hands, a seven-meter sailboat. It was a task of several years, after which he learned to sail and then to navigate the Atlantic coast. He had even imposed on his family, a wife and children, vacations under the sign of the implacable gods of the sea and the wind. Indeed, with his long coppery hair and his Flemish heritage, he had the look of a Viking. Since his divorce, since he had stepped back from, indeed jumped off the train of the revolution, he had undertaken, single-handedly, the construction of a ten-meter metal-hulled boat, anticipating that, in six or seven years, when his children would be grown up, he would sail alone the seas of our planet. I felt that he had given himself a new ideal goal, that he was trapped again in the fascination of a false self.

Pascal had numerous dreams in which he envisioned sunken ships, ships that had been rolled over and broken apart by a tidal wave. Then he had the following dream:

> I came to a dock where I knew my boat should be. I didn't find it. Leaning over the edge of the dock, by the ring where I knew I had tied my boat, I looked into the depth of the sea. I could hardly make out the outline of my boat, which was barely visible at that depth where the water was very dark. It was resting on the bottom and seemed intact. A line was attached to the boat's stern and came up to the surface. I followed it with my eyes and then walked to where it reached the dock. At the end of this veritable Ariadne's thread, I arrived in front of a house built at the edge of the dock. The thread rose slightly to where it was tied to a small door that closed a small nook built into the facade of the house. The door was finely crafted, made out of a precious wood. It seemed to be the door of a holy tabernacle on an altar. The decorations on the door were shaped like the rose in a cathedral's stained glass window. The end of the thread was attached to a very delicate key, that was gold-colored, perhaps even made of gold. I was feeling very meditative and did not dare touch this key that would open this tabernacle, for this tabernacle surely contained an essential, sacred object. I was filled with the certainty that this object, that was attached in this fashion to my sunken but intact boat, would permit me, when the moment arrived, to raise my boat.

Through this thread, which Pascal himself called his Ariadne's thread, is there not, for this Ulysses whose boat had been "de-Icarized," an apparent link between his boat drowned in his shadow, in the deepest layer of his psyche, and the most authentic expression of a Self in its sacred representation as a mandala?

What had happened to Ulysses, over the course of this long journey? At the age of eight, and for four years thereafter, he felt abandoned by his dying father and by his mother who gave herself entirely to the care of her ailing husband. Pascal shunned them and lived his shadow in the most animal part of himself. He had made himself a lair deep in the woods, where he sprawled out by himself. There he crawled in the grass and actually lived this saurian tail of his personal shadow.

After his father's death, Pascal fell back into line and repressed the animal part of himself. He went back to school and learned the ways of civilization. Several years later, the father figure he admired offered him a structured space by integrating him into the collective of an ideology. Pascal felt that he had integrated his own shadow into this collective shadow where he would find a path of light.

Later, when he built his first boat, he thought he had found for himself and for the family he had created, a strong enough support to go toward alluring horizons. When everything came apart, he left his family and tried to recreate his childhood lair in a small, squalid apartment. At that time he began psychotherapy.

It was only after several years, when he encountered the archetype of the father in the second dream, that he de-integrated his shadow from a collective shadow. The work of "owning his shadow" by coming to consciousness about it had begun.

The last dream indicated that, in a representation of the fundamental shadow, the boat which represented his ego was directly related to a Self that he had yet to discover. From the "nigredo" to the "albedo," the path is a long one, but Ulysses can return to himself. His Penelope-anima awaits him to continue her tapestry.

Translated from French by
Colette Hyman

The Shadow: Drive and Representation

Susanne Kacirek (Paris)

My purpose here is to discuss the shadow archetype from within analytic practice. From this perspective, it is difficult to escape this archetype's power to engender identification. When choosing clinical cases, as a woman I can speak only about women. However, the problems I am dealing with do not concern only women.

Through my analytic practice I meet with shadow problems posed in terms of splitting. The splitting I mean is not that between good and bad objects, nor in a too general sense. The splitting I am speaking of, a frequent phenomenon in clinical cases, occurs between the representation side of the archetype, the shadow images, and the impulse side: the oral, anal, and auto-erotic drives. The activation of the shadow brings about a regression that affects dynamic imagination without touching the impulse sphere and object the relations. Thus, the splitting is between the archetypal world of imagery and the impulse.

Despite the problems connected with definitions, I feel that I must define my terms.

1) By "the impulse sphere and object relations" I mean aspects of the body and the relation to the other that are connected in the subject's personal story.

2) In addition, by "impulse sphere" I mean aspects of the body and the relation to the other that reflect the primary mother-child relationship.

3) The implulse sphere, so defined, directs in practice a special

kind of transference dynamics. An analysis that avoids this form of splitting in working with the shadow, while taking the shadow sufficiently into account, leads to relived memories that affect the transference relationship in quite a different way from what would happen in working with the archetypal imagery alone.

4) I wish to underline the unbinding—dissociative, disintegrating—activity that characterizes the impulse when it is left to itself. In Jungian terms, the impulse "left to itself" means that it is not related to the shadow images or that we have not embodied the shadow. According to my observation, this unbinding activity takes place every time the impulse sphere remains split from archetypal dynamics.

5) The unbinding of the impulse is difficult to track, because the unbound impulse tends to evade representation. This unbinding activity seems well accounted for by the Freudian concept of death instinct: insidious disintegration, erosion of the impulse energy, return to an undifferentiated, inanimate world which cannot be represented because it is without meaning.

Activation of the shadow, through the mere fact of starting an analysis, may bring about a regression. This regression, which has every appearance of a process, develops spontaneously into an apparent transformation of archetypal images. If we look closer, however, no relating of the impulse to the shadow images, no embodiment of the shadow has taken place; the impulse has been excluded. This imaginary movement forms a kind of undifferentiated collective shadow, containing the ego and maintaining it in archaic identity. In such a psychic situation synchronicity, clairvoyance, or premonition phenomena often appear.

This splitting is likely to take place in persons who suffer from severe early narcissistic wounds. They are unable to face the impulse shadow right away. They seek to have value, or rather power, in that imaginary world, even when it contains horror visions. The analyst is placed in the position of the Great Mother Phallus, which protects the archetypal, imaginary world against invalidation by the impulse. Becoming aware of this impulse would create too much suffering. Fascination is then substituted for the feeling function, under the protection of a kind of narcissistic isolation.

A young German woman, suffering from successive losses and abandonments, undertakes her first analysis, with a man. She sees in her analyst all the qualities of the wise man. At the beginning of this work she has the following dream: *She is in bed with her lover. The analyst, in the form of an ugly dwarf, interposes himself between them, setting up a window pane that separates them.*

Wth this dream, the analyst was warned that the dreamer's transference to him was that of the Great Mother's phallus. He lends the screen (the window pane) which reflects, in this woman, a heroic narcissistic drama provided by the dwarf's imaginary power. The dreamer associates the dwarf with Mime, who is treasure keeper and blacksmith as well as the instructor and protector of Wagner's Siegfried; that is, the hero's abusive adoptive mother. The power of this transferential projection on the analyst is all the greater since a misleading transparence (one might say unconsciousness) keeps away the questioning about this woman's impulses and affective life. A window pane casts no shadow. It may be that the transference, when fed by the archetypal dynamics alone, maintains the splitting.

Subsequent events showed that once splitting was exposed, the lover received important oral and anal-sadistic projections he did not deserve. The impulse life, shut away behind the window pane, remained linked to non-value.

Nevertheless, this first stage of analysis—this heroic inflationary process—had been useful to this young woman inasmuch as her narcissism had been reinforced. In addition, she had been able to form a myth that, for some time, helped her to live and strengthen her beliefs and values, thus enabling her to exist.

Despite all this, two problems arise which encourage me to consider seriously this reflection about splitting in the work with the shadow. First, this myth, which excludes a large part of the subject's truth, can become drained of its meaning and cause the person's breakdown. In terms of dynamics, the gap between the opposed archetypal poles (positive and negative, light and shadow) increases. The impulse, void of symbolization, neglected and destructive, rushes in.

The other problem arises from an episode in the history of psychoanalysis which shows that the analyst's theoretical error in maintaining this splitting in the approach of the shadow may lead to an ethical error. The same conceptual insufficiency may have led Jung to write, in 1934, a certain paper (CW10, pars. 157–333) which he later wished he had not written, so many were its controversial interpretations. One can read in it that the young barbarian imagination is creative in a culture which is able to preserve ideals — "these so-called illusions" — and that it is opposed to the obscene and sterile poverty of the Freudian drive world. Once more, the world of images is split from the world of impulses, but also between value and non-value; mythical ideal on the one hand from obscenity on the other. The shadow, an insufficiently defined concept, has made use of a perverse effect.

In 1912, in *Transformations and Symbols of the Libido* (the original title of *Symbols of Transformation*, CW5), Jung had chosen quite a different starting point with regard to the relations between the impulse/drive and the archetype. Stated briefly: Jung thought then that an important drive regression occurs with the "return to the mother" — that is, to the archetypal matrix — and conditions it. This impulse regression, Jung wrote, goes through the "incest stage." In fact, it is the primary relation being relived. When it regresses still further, the impulse becomes auto-erotic with an important oral component. At this stage, the subject goes through severe suffering, due to a lack of the real external object — the personal mother. It is this lack that constellates the archetype.

For Jung, in 1912, archetypal dynamics were only an intuition, formulated in a chaotic way. But what strength there was in this suggestion of a link joining the impulse sphere with the archetypal processes! At that time, the term "incest" was to be understood on two levels which must complement each other in analytical process and transferential work:

1) The first level is that of reliving the primary, earliest mother-child relationship;

2) The other is that of the "return to the mother," which gives birth to the hero in the sense of activating the archetypal matrix. Thus, in 1912, there was not a trace of splitting in the Jungian theory.

Four years later Jung wrote "Instinct and the Unconscious"

(CW8, pars. 263–82). We notice that Jung said "instinct" and not "impulse/drive" (Trieb). We also notice that, from 1916 on, the word "Trieb," when used by Jung, lost all the specificity it had in the Freudian world. Jung came to define the archetypal image as the instinct self-portrait, the vision the instinct has of itself. The archetype thus was given its source of energy, the instinct. This archetypal energy, moreover, is above all a narcissistic energy; it is its own mirror. To recall these texts from Jung is to say that in 1916, while we gained the definition of the energetic foundations of the archetypal dynamics, we lost, it would seem, the specificity of the impulse.

From then on, some people in the Jungian world have formed the habit of thinking that the impulses are an integral part of archetypal dynamics, in some way the reverse side of the archetype; that it would be enough to work with the shadow archetype on the image level; and that the drive would become integrated with it at the same time. It is much more likely that the work will be done on the narcissistic value level of the ego, and that the impulse, being neglected, will finally escape. When it reappears as a symptom, it is often very late.

In order to avoid these splitting phenomena in clinical work with the shadow, it is necessary to maintain in theory that the archetypal instinct and the drive proceed from two distinct energetic sources and that they are not moved by the same laws of functioning. But, although archetypal representation and impulse representation do not occur in the same mode and do not imply the same kind of psychological work, impulse and archetype can be grasped by the same process. Later, I will cite clinical cases to support this statement.

The impulses' representations of themselves obey the complex mechanisms described by Freud, provided that unbinding has not made the impulses unconscious to the point where they cannot be represented. The archetypal image, on the contrary, offers itself so generously that we risk being misled. Thus, the appearance of an ogress with a bleeding mouth, for example, does not mean necessarily that the oral drive is at work. The image may be related to the negative pole of the archetype, filled with a numinous, terrible energy but devoid of personal emotions and recollections.

Sometimes, these archetypal images function as resistance, in the form of idealization, against a true confrontation with the shadow. "One idealizes whenever there is a secret fear to be exorcized," wrote Jung (CW9–I, par. 192). This idealization means that, paradoxically, the upsurge of the shadow may lead to a heroic response, to the will to fight the evil forces with light, or to cross hell in an initiatory ritual. To these topics archetypal dynamics provide an inexhaustible variety of mythic images.

Thus, one of the causes of splitting is the tendency to idealize, either in the patient or in the analyst. Misplaced idealization tends to paralyze the work. The Self then appears as an imaginary compensation. But in the analysis the Self, when it returns to the arena of the impulse shadow, finds its dynamics again.

As an example, I offer two dreams of a patient who is an engineer with an important position. Much admired, she nevertheless wears herself out in the practical organization of her life. In analysis, she is searching painfully for a new creativity. She is the devoted mother of two children and the daughter of a mother who sacrificed the other aspects of her femininity to motherhood with a bitterness that was dangerously unconscious.

This patient dreamed that *her little daughter wishes to celebrate her birthday with particular glamour. The child dresses in a princess gown and puts a crown on her head. She climbs on window ledges high on the house, eventually finding herself, with legs spread, in an unstable balance over the precipice. As a further touch of the supernatural she tries to rest a white dove on her hand. Seeing that the bird might upset the balance and throw the child to the ground, the dreamer intervenes and saves her daughter.*

This solid woman has phobic anxieties concerning feathered animals and unexplained chronic pains in her back. The little girl in the dream, thirsting after spiritual purity and elevation to the supernatural, is the shadow image of the dreamer, who sees herself as stuck in materiality. Her ego's capacity for realistic perception enables her to become conscious of the illusory aspect of this attempt to be borne to the heights against a background of emptiness. In analysis, at least, regression will not occur in free fall. But it is clear in this case that the saving Self, the creative power, is not on the side of the infantile idealistic innocence. The awareness of this fact made the woman feel deeply deprived.

In her analysis there followed an uneasy period for her, because of her confrontation with hero-son problems and because of a profound modification of the transference relation. Until then, I had received projections of harmony and kindness, no matter what happened. Now the slightest mistake on my part started strong aggressivity, which the patient herself connected with recollections of situations experienced with her mother. After a few months the patient, who was suffering from depression, dreamed: *She is getting ready to make her baby eat some minced meat. Having put it on the plate, she finds in the middle of it children's jaws with milk teeth, opened like a crown.* (She repeats twice that the teeth are set like a crown.) *Horrified, the dreamer then understands that the butcher sells children's flesh as meat intended for children. She runs out to the butcher's—who in the dream is confused with the dairyman—and asks him for an explanation. He does not let her speak, but asks her first to pay her debts; he has business commitments to meet at the end of the month.*

In our work it was possible to connect the dream elements to the personal story of the dreamer. But I wanted to show how, once the idealistic illusion had vanished, the Self appeared, revealing the scandal. This occurred in the middle of the destructive drive shadow (the minced meat) in the very place where the child was cut into pieces, where the unconscious creativity had been nullified, in a mouth opened with a primitive thirst scream. From the wide-open oral distress, a relived disorder of the primary relation, the Self dynamics appear, starting a true process. The mother's animus appears, exposed in its dreadful trade, in its blameful and perverse anality which blocks speech (the scream) and any deep creativity. The persona is questioned in that the dairyman, confused with the butcher, refers not only to the mother's milk but also to the "cream of society." Finally, the sacrificial pathology in relation to the hero-son is brought out into the open. A moral illusion drives this woman to sacrifice her creative life, a kind of subjective genuineness. The incestuous motivation of this illusion is dismantled.

The value is to be found on the side of the murdered royal child. But we are far from any idealistic compensation that such an image could constellate. When, as here, the Self presents itself under cover of an impulse regression, it acts as a formidable condenser of processes. Thus, it leaves no opportunity for splitting and, consequently, creates an overwhelming questioning of the subject's values. This example can illustrate how taking into account the impulse shadow favors the emergence of the archetypal organizer.

In reverse, we can see how the archetypal shadow image – the primitive shadow – manages to bind an impulse which is in a state of unbinding and thus saves the narcissistic integrity of the subject. For it is true that certain fragile subjects would be threatened with breaking up by a work which focuses unilaterally and explicitly on the analysis of impulses.

It is essential to be able to analyze the evolution of the shadow images in dreams and, in particular, in the relation they keep with the dream ego. Close observation enables us to follow, step by step, the process by which one becomes able to face the state of one's own impulses. We can thus adapt our interventions and the handling of the transference. Three examples will each illustrate a different aspect of the emergence of the primitive shadow.

The first is a woman patient for whom the slightest frustration, the merest impulse disturbance that one inflicted on her might provoke an acute inflammatory crisis in the disease from which she suffered, or throw her into delirium. Her dream ego never appeared otherwise than totally squashed, helpless, flayed alive, or as a distant witness of some drama. Finally, this ego appeared in an undifferentiated identification with a group of mad women; they were dressed in black and danced around a sun king who kept them at a distance with his stick.

One might think that the fascination this woman showed for a spiritual master, with whom she was practicing meditation, would enable her to maintain a certain splitting. That is, the idealization might have helped her to keep out the impulses which threatened to set her ablaze. But the strength of the splitting had not resisted a first psychotherapy during which a disabling inflammatory infection had appeared. Flayed alive as she was, this woman lacked the capacity to contain her energies, even if they were narcissistic. Thus, she was not able to manage a "good," undamaging inflation. In a dream *she finds herself on a height without any tree or shadow. She loses her head which she sees, without any emotion, rolling downward.*

For a long time my role as analyst consisted in the delicate task, like a mountain guide, of preventing a faltering roped climber from falling; that is, to preserve in a certain way this woman's myth which was bent toward an ascetic spiritual ideal, while letting her catch sight gradually of another possible reality, that of the green valley.

With this woman, the powerful appearance of a primitive shadow image came to me in the most unexpected way, at a moment when I found myself weary and impatient with her distress. She had just undergone surgery for attaching a hip prosthesis. The day I visited her in the hospital, she told me first about the death of someone very dear to her, a kind of spiritual hero to her. She told me this with a violence that she had never expressed. She had not been able to let her aggressivity come out, only crude anxiety and heartbreaking suffering. She then told me about the dream she had just dreamed: *The horizon is on fire, it is an oil slick burning, devastating the whole landscape. Helpless, the dreamer watches this fire. Then far away a beautiful brown, suntanned woman arrives, dressed only with an animal skin tied around her hips. She is walking toward the dreamer and crosses the fire without any damage.*

The emergence of this shadow figure with an invulnerable skin—like Siegfried—who does not fear the mad fire of an unbound energy, enabled us henceforth to work on the impulse sphere and object relations without endangering the ego complex. We must note that, in this dream, the archetypal image does not directly perform the integration of the flaming impulse energy; it merely offers the dreamer new capacities for facing it. Under the protection of the cohesive power of this shadow archetype, a dark but solid anality has been able to emerge. The ego, being less and less subject to fascination, has developed amid a rich feeling function, which gives it access to an authentic inner life.

The primitive shadow, in the form of a cold-blooded animal, provides my second example: a single woman who was a psychologist in a business firm. She consulted me about a phobia that she would feel induced to kill children. Her anxiety was tremendous.

From the start of the analysis, the problem for me was that of a most virulent negative transference in which operated a most corrosive animus that had never before appeared. At first, I thought that this violent projection on me of a negative mother could do some good to my patient. She could see very well that her destructivity had no hold over me and that she was not as dangerous as she felt. In short, I felt that I could diminish her aggressivity by accepting the transference. Nevertheless, this woman unceasingly made use of all her knowledge to provide me systematically with interpretations concerning her homosexual impulses and defenses. One could not say that her interpretations were actually wrong. But this violent game resulted in maintaining a vicious circle of aggressivity, guilt, and anxiety. Captive of the negative mother complex which fed on her impulses and in which she had managed to include me, this woman was absolutely unable to have a receptive attitude in the face of the unconscious matrix which would allow the archetypal process to happen. One can say that she was possessed by a shadow impulse which had never been integrated into the shadow. Thus, she maintained a negative, destructive activity, split from the archetype.

Eventually I pointed out to her with some insistence that she was perverse in using her knowledge against herself and that she was using the negative transference as a resistance against all positive emotion. In believing that she was protecting her fragility, she was sustaining an unconscious destructivity and preventing the forces of development from coming into existence. During this session I was full of wisdom and kind equanimity.

The following night she had this dream: *The dreamer is in her parents' apartment in a tall building. All around, the town is devastated to the point where only waste land is left, as far as the eye can see. A giant iguana or saurian emerges from the horizon and moves toward the tower. The dreamer rushes to collect her prettiest dresses, intending to run away—an eminently feminine gesture but ill-adapted to the situation. Too late. The saurian has opened a breach in the wall, then goes away. Then the dreamer's mother appears.* (I suppose I here make my first positive transference appearance.) *She tells her dumfounded daughter that she has noticed a gleam of humanity in the beast's eyes and that she even obtained its promise to write to her.*

As this woman's analysis continued the saurian kept his promise. Regarding the dream, one can see in it the damage due to impulse destruction: the ruined town, the wasteland where no shadow is to be found. The work of civilizing humanization is primed here by the archetypal symbolization process which obtrudes in a violent blow by the shadow, a breaking-in which evokes a primal scene. Everything happens as if this ugly iguana had introduced in the dreamer's parental house a new way of understanding, different from these rationalizations which only badly protected a deep narcissistic wound. It is true that the condition is that there be someone who knows how to receive and read the beast's letters. In the dream, it is the dreamer's personal mother. As a result, one may say that the saurian's message concerns what had remained excluded, not lived, not integrated in the mother-child relation. Let us suppose that it concerns the reference to father, as suggested by the dreamer's association.

My last example deals with a specific form of shadow embodiment. The shadow archetype here is linking with a death instinct in the most Freudian sense of the term; that is, an impulse which disintegrates into undifferentiated, unconscious components. This time, the archetype seizes the death instinct and converts it into a life process.

Here is the dream: *The dreamer runs the vacuum cleaner in her parents' house, more precisely in the bedroom she lived in herself as a child. This room is absolutely empty. At a certain moment, the vacuum cleaner throws on the wall, in a heap, the dust it has accumulated. From this heap is released a womanly figure made of stones and agglutinated dust. The figure comes to life, starts to breathe, becomes animated, then goes toward the dreamer and holds out its hand to her. In its turn, the vacuum cleaner starts breathing like a human being. In a panic, the dreamer rejects the shadow-woman's hand, pushes her out of the room and shuts the door after her. She can now unplug the vacuum cleaner, which then stops breathing.*

The dreamer's associations to the dust refer to the body's decay through death. At the time when the parental house was being built, several century-old graves were discovered. In the room where the dreamer comes back at last to do the cleaning, which should be filled with the joy and pain of childhood, she only finds this layer of dust, a dead deposit of the flight of time into insignificance. A whole side of the affective and the impulse life has disintegrated here into dead particles.

The archetype, in operating the passage from inanimate to life, produces a magical, anxious effect. The shadow-woman, however, is not a ghost. She does not walk through walls. She is shown out by the dreamer—the ultimate defense—through the door. The projection on the wall (by the vacuum cleaner) stops at this opaque limit, the wall, which clearly marks the boundary between inside and outside. (The effects of a splitting, paradoxically, would tend to abolish such a differentiation.) It is there that the projection takes shape, in the roughness of the wall that stops the particles from scattering into infinite space. Neither does the wall offer the smooth delusion of reflections in a window pane.

As an analyst, I made the acquaintance of this woman when she was at the end of a period of inflation, characterized by splitting. Her solar imagination finds here a salutary, healthy intensity in grasping the remains of childhood's unsatisfied desires under the influence of the death instinct. Indeed, the shadow archetype has reversed the direction of the impulse and transformed death into life, meaninglessness into story.

About the vacuum cleaner, the dreamer's associations are in the anal sphere. However, breathing in (aspiration) animated with life-giving breath, and with a centering effect, even if only to collect dust, probably refers to the action of the Self.

Yet this woman, who experiences strong death anxieties at the moment of the dream, says to me "I have lost my gods." An intense desire for relationship emerged later from these anxieties; this desire signed the end of her chronic depressive moods.

I have insisted throughout this paper that analytic work with the shadow, when it succeeds in avoiding splitting, opens one to the Self. Stated otherwise: The work with the shadow, when it takes place with a view to individuation—becoming whole—opens above all to a more substantial human feeling.

Translated from French by
Denise Zémor and
Philippe Sorensen

Discussion: Ute Dieckmann (Berlin)

My response to Kacirek's interesting and clear paper was at first to agree with her ideas to such an extent that I found it hard to contribute to the discussion. But eventually a question occurred to me: Why has that which is described here as a danger in dealing with the shadow image, not struck me much in my analyses? I refer to Kacirek's statement that, when we are fascinated by shadow images which appear in the dreams, narcissistic enhancement of the ego is likely to result. The instinctual side, which is hidden behind the shadow image, thus remains in the unconscious and therefore is negatively accentuated and destructive.

The activation of the shadow leads to a regression, but this regression does not always mean that instincts and object relations are worked through. In the beginning of an analysis, before a stable transference relationship is established, probably none of us would interpret the shadow dreams in a pronounced manner on the instinctual level. For the many patients whose anxieties restrict their activity, an ego-strengthening results from finding a grasping robber in their dreams. This image is too helpful to be destroyed through an interpretation of the underlying oral and aggressive instincts, or of an eagerness for personal importance.

I think, for example, of a 21-year-old student who started his analysis with considerable anxiety, accompanied by compulsive symptoms. In the initial phase, the following motif appeared time and again in his dreams: *I am going somewhere and meet a robber. I am not afraid at all, but I am happy to meet him.* In telling his dream and in his associations, the patient conveyed his pleasure in this encounter. The dream says nothing about whether the dream ego and the robber establish a relationship. In my dealing with the dream, I would let the patient keep the narcissistic feelings that may appear. Thus I would support the possibility, expressed in the dream, for the dreamer to be robberish.

Another patient, who also was very compulsive, had the following dream after 200 sessions of analysis: *I am a gangster and go, with a pistol in my hand, into the bank where I work in order to rob it.* This patient was a bank clerk and had to deal every day with large amounts of money, while his salary was comparatively small. He was very proud that in his whole working life he had felt neither envy nor desire for the money. He said that for him the money he had to deal with was simply printed paper, without any value. Here the situation is completely different from that of the dream mentioned above. The dream ego is identical with the shadow figure and experiences the impulses which here are aggressive. The problem of the shadow complex, "robber," is obviously close to the threshold of consciousness. In the course of the session, it was possible for the patient to experience his fear of his own impulses and his considerable feelings of guilt.

In both examples I reported very simple dreams. However, the considerations concerning these dreams can be applied also to archetypal dreams. Now I return to Kacirek's paper. She certainly did not mean what I wanted to express with my example but was rather referring to a getting lost in beautiful images, perhaps later in an analysis. Then one would fail to uncover the instincts and to link them with the patient's personal world, present or past.

This mistake may occur quite often among us Jungians. But I do not think that we can blame Jung and his theory. Remember the patient mentioned above who, in the beginning of his analysis, was so proud of the robber he had discovered in himself. I must add that robbers and similar shadow figures, which appeared later in his analysis, were of course dealt with on the object level. The question posed afterward, "Where and with whom have you ever experienced such a robberish behavior?" leads closer to reality, to the emotions the patient has experienced, and to his instinctual side.

In his works about dreams, Jung repeatedly said that before interpreting a dream on the subject level, one should look at the object level as thoroughly as possible. But amplification and application of myths and fairytales are so much more fascinating—for me, too—that in Jung's publications we can find this kind of approach much more often than a simple interpretation on the object level.

Although, as Jungians, all of us follow the same basic principle, there are still considerable differences of approach in different countries. In our Berlin institute we work with Freudians. During the first semesters our trainees attend many—perhaps too many—lectures about classical Psychoanalysis. Due to the necessity of working with health insurance, many lectures about clinical psychology are included. Therefore our difficulty is familiarizing our trainees with archetypes and with imagistic, holistic thinking.

When reading Kacirek's paper, I noticed that for me the Self came second. With the first dream reported in the paper, the birthday party and the crowned daughter on the windowsill who is in danger of falling, I would have asked spontaneously for associations to the patient's own daughter. I would have tended to bring home to the patient the exalted image she had of her children, and the aggressiveness hidden behind it. Kacirek proceeded in a slightly different manner. Nevertheless, the topics of the following sessions, and especially of the subsequent dream, brought to consciousness the personal side.

Another point is important: Kacirek said that in 1912, in his work *Transformations and Symbols of the Libido* (CW5), Jung still spoke of impulses. Later on he rarely used this word; he always spoke of instincts instead. I have never seen much difference between these two concepts. Impulses and instincts, of course, are not the same, but for me, the concept of instinct is the generic term which embraces the impulses.

After 1912, Jung increasingly developed his theories of wholeness and of complexes. Subhuman creatures clearly have an impulse for the survival of the species. Our patients' dreams of animals refer to the instinctual side and its inherent impulses. We do not have to go back to the Jung of 1912. When following him in his holistic thinking our constant effort must be to be aware of the many individual facets that are included, for example, the shadow complex or the instincts.

In fact, holistic thinking is used more and more in today's modern science and also in Freudian analysis, especially when working with the concept of narcissism. Such a way of thinking was preferred by Jung from the beginning.

Kacirek says that archetypes and instincts come from different sources—they only meet in lucky moments—and that they are subject to different rules of functioning. I also see different possibilities for functioning, but what different sources does she mean? Instincts and archetypes are both rooted in the collective unconscious, even if the instinctual world seems to be linked closer to the personal unconscious.

While thinking about the difference posed by Kacirek, I found a paper of Williams (1963). She, like Kacirek, wrote of the necessity for resolving the splitting in practical work. She did not mention the splitting between archetype and instinct, but of that between the personal and the collective unconscious. She often quoted Jung, who first had strictly separated the two concepts in theory, but who pointed out later that they cannot be separated in practical work. One statement she quoted was: "This distinction [between the personal and the collective psyche] is not at all easy to draw, because the personality arises out of the collective psyche and is intimately linked with it: hence it is very difficult to discern which are the collective and which are the personal elements." (CW7, par. 462). With some vivid examples from her analytic work, Williams showed that images which emerge from the collective unconscious can have a healing effect only when they can be linked to images from the patient's personal life — those that emerge from the personal unconscious. This example reveals that her approach is similar to Kacirek's; the instinctual side is more obvious in the personal unconscious even if it is also present in the archetypal images of the collective unconscious.

Williams stated that parts of the patient's personal life story stimulate the archetypal images to emerge. In order to demonstrate the close link between the two unconscious fields, Williams formulated the following theses:

1) Nothing in the personal experience needs to be repressed unless the ego feels threatened by its archetypal power.

2) The archetypal activity, which forms the individual's myth, is dependent upon material supplied by the personal unconscious.

My concluding thought is that shadow image and instinct appear simultaneously. In alteration of Kacirek's phrase, the "lucky moment," I maintain that it belongs to the lucky moments of an analytic session if we succeed in making possible the patient's experience of the instinctual dynamics which are behind the images.

Translated from German by
Dagmar Henle-Dieckmann
and Sabine Osvatič

REFERENCE

Williams, M. (1963). The indivisibility of the personal and collective unconscious. *Journal of Analytical Psychology,* *8*–1, 45-50.

Shame: An Overshadowed Emotion

Peer Hultberg (Hamburg)

Emotions, affects and feelings are essential parts of our daily work. We endeavor to bring our patients into contact with their true feelings and, when we talk about rendering unconscious elements conscious, we mean basically that unclear feelings should be made accessible to the ego by words. In theory, Freud stressed very early the crucial importance that the repressed, split-off and denied affects have for the etiology of neurosis, and it is the emotionally-toned complexes which are the foundation of Jungian psychology. Nevertheless, emotions have come off badly in the theoretical considerations of depth psychology, including Jungian. This may reflect a general situation of our modern Western culture. One need only compare the handful of words which, in depth psychology, express emotional states with the description of the 40 emotions given by Descartes in *Traité des passions de l'ame* (*The Passions of the Soul*), written in French and published in 1649, in order to realize how undifferentiated is our time in the perception and description of emotions.

For us Jungians this impoverishment becomes especially evident when we deal with feelings which are linked to shadow or persona. The concept of shadow provides us with an outstanding and refined image of the repressed and the denied. We work with expressions such as "appearance of the murderer shadow," "being overpowered by the traitor shadow," and "being defeated by the thief shadow." But when it comes to the description of the accompanying affects, we often seem to be amazingly undifferentiated and able to offer only a small range of possibilities.

This can make our patients feel misunderstood or even let down, and we rightly run the risk of being reproached for bloodless labeling.

In the following I discuss an emotion which has been considerably neglected not only by depth psychology but also by philosophy, by the humanities and by ethics, that is, the emotion of shame. It is linked closely not only to shadow and persona, that is to say, to the individual as social personality, but also to the Self, to a personal experiencing of the Self. Shame is a frequent human affect and a fundamental factor of human existence. It can be a violent feeling, lasting for a very long time and making one, even after 50 years, wish that the ground would open and swallow one. At the same time, shame is a taboo feeling, especially for us so-called modern persons. In analysis it can often be touched only when a very trusting transference relationship has been established. If one is attentive and allows shame, it may lead into the deepest layers of the psyche.

Many events from my practice helped to draw my attention to the subject of "shame." Two of these were especially helpful. The first began when I was consulted by a girl of about 16 years, rather plump but quite good-looking. She was in despair but was not able to give concrete reasons for it. Twice a week she sat before me, crying and repeating: "I'm so ashamed, I'm so ashamed." It would have been useless to question the girl; I could only stay with her, accompany her, inwardly avoid all kinds of false consolation, and take her seriously. I saw that the sessions were following a certain pattern: Shame was answered with shame of the shame until it became an almost global state which seemed to devour the girl's identity; its overwhelming power threatened to dissolve her psychically. Given the short time we had at our disposal it was impossible to get to the bottom of her state and she left me behind – as I felt – with the enigma of shame. I could only hope that she had felt accepted as an individual whose mode of being is shame, so to speak, and that I had respected her shame as a phenomenon which had an important function in her psyche.

The other event occurred during violent disturbances in Frankfurt because of a new intercontinental runway apparently designed to be easily convertible for military purposes. All my patients gave their views on it, many participated actively in a blockade, and several of them spent the night "out in the woods," as it was called. A 27-year-old man told me excitedly how a clash with the police was provoked by the fact that the crowd had shouted at the police officers, "Shame on you, shame on you." In his opinion these shouts made the police lose their self-control and attack the demonstrators. The man was almost trembling when he told me about it; I understood that he was experiencing strong projective and introjective processes based on a traumatizing situation from his childhood. This event had brought back an unclear parent-child relationship. The words "shame on you" had almost cast a spell on him. He considered them to be a provocation which had to lead to a violent answer because of the underlying, almost overpowering archaic aggressions and the corresponding archaic fears. Again I was confronted with questions about shame: Why can it cause violence at all? What does one actually want to say with the words "shame on you," a request all of us have heard in our lives and to which we reacted – with feelings of shame.

Shame in Depth Psychology: Historical Considerations.

In depth psychology shame is a phenomenon which is mostly ignored – an overshadowed emotion, indeed. The expression is often used, in connection with guilt, but purely rhetorically; it emphasizes the concept of guilt and is not considered to have a quality of its own.

The concept of shame is rarely found in Freud. In the *Interpretation of Dreams* (SE2), it is connected with embarrassment, as in dreams of being naked. Otherwise, shame is used almost exclusively in a specific function, along with "disgust" as expression of resistance or defense, against the instincts, especially against the sexual instinct. Later, Freud linked the concept of morality to these two terms so that after 1910 he operated with a triad of mechanisms of repression or defense: shame, disgust, and morality.

Jung, too, rarely mentioned shame, except in his early works where he propagated psychoanalytic thinking. It was typical for

Jung, however, that he did not consider morality as a form of defense but contented himself with shame and disgust.

Adler (1919) mentioned shame in the first of his main works *The Neurotic Constitution* in 1912. He connected it with "masculine protest," with "the feeling of inferiority," and with "the striving for security of the neurotic" but without discussing it in a more detailed manner. He emphasized that "some neurotics tend to feel ashamed in an exaggerated manner" (pp. 50–51), and he seems to have been the first to stress shamelessness as an important psychic phenomenon, considering it an expression of masculine protest. This led him close to considering shamelessness to be a form of defense against shame, a process Wurmser (1981) pointed out. Furthermore, Adler briefly discussed shame as a separate affect in *Understanding Human Nature* (1927) where he understood it not only as a separating affect but also as a connecting one. In an unambiguous manner he stated its importance for human society: "[Shame] is a construction of the sense of community and as such it is not to be banished from human psychic life. Human society would not be possible without this affect" (p. 225).

But it was especially Janet who examined the importance of shame as a psychic phenomenon. As an essential component, it influenced the work of Ludwig Binswanger in turn, especially his classic study (1958) of Ellen West. In his important work of 1903, *The Obsessions and Psychaschenia* Janet distinguished between two forms of shame: the shame of the body and the shame of oneself. Janet connected shame mainly with such terms as self-contempt and discontent with oneself. Furthermore, he described two forms of shame: "That which the subject despises in himself is his mind, his will power, his intelligence," and where "shame lies rather in the physical side of the individual, and the subject is discontented with his body or his bodily functions" (p. 23).

To discuss Janet's theories in detail would go beyond the scope of this paper. The most important point is that he seems to have been the first among the early depth psychologists to consider shame not only as a fundamental human affect but to connect it explicitly with self-contempt, that is, with a lack of self-esteem. Further, he distinguished between two forms of shame: one form which is directed at the environment (the object), and a second form which re'fers more to the subject. However, these two forms are not identical with those I am about to discuss.

Shame and Anthropology

It is not the depth psychologists but the modern anthropologists who have emphasized the importance of shame. Based on Benedict's (1946/1977) work 40 years ago about Japan, two forms of culture are often distinguished: guilt and shame. A culture of guilt is based on the individual's developing a conscience with firm ideas about right and wrong and, as a consequence, submitting to ethical and moral standards. In such a culture authority is based on concepts like offense and punishment, sin and remission of sins, eternal salvation and eternal damnation, a punishing God and a gracious God.

In a culture of shame, the highest authority is not a good conscience but a good reputation. Identification, not submission, is the most important factor of the socialization process. There are no definite concepts of good and evil in the metaphysical sense but absolute ideas of honor and disgrace, of glory and contempt, of respect and ridicule. In such societies ridicule often is the most severe punishment that can afflict an individual. In some Eskimo cultures, for example, differences are settled in so-called song duels where the opponents sing satirical songs about each other. A loser who can feel ridiculed to such a degree that life in the settlement becomes impossible, must withdraw into isolation. In Eskimo society, isolation practically means death. When a conflict arises between two individuals in a culture of shame, one wins and feels proud; the other loses and feels ashamed.

Typical cultures of shame are the Northern Viking culture, certain Eskimo societies and North American Indian cultures, the Japanese society before World War II, and the ancient Greek culture as it is reflected in the Homerian epics, especially the Iliad. Our Western European-North American society seems to be developing from a culture of guilt toward a culture of shame, or it may be on the way to a mixed form. Just as the conventional Christian religiosity is losing influence without a viable ideological alternative in religion or politics, the values of good and evil which used to be experienced as absolute seem to have almost faded away. What psychoanalysts call healthy superego values are more and more doubted. Thus, shame begins to dominate at the expense of guilt.

The boundaries between societies of guilt and of shame are floating, of course, according to contemporary anthropologists. As we can learn, for example, from the work of Dodds (1951) about the Greek culture, the theories of Benedict influenced other scholarly fields. Her theories are often questioned today, but the differentiation between the cultures was instrumental in the clarification of the concepts of shame and guilt.

My description should not be understood as a lament or an attempt to restore outdated values. It is always disquieting when established values dissolve, but it is even more disquieting when one desperately and fiercely tries to keep them after their basis has ceasd to exist. Furthermore, it is wrong to judge cultures hierarchically, assuming perhaps that a culture of guilt is to be rated higher than a culture of shame or that a culture of shame is only a stage in the development toward a culture of guilt. Nevertheless, such hierarchic thinking seems to be one of the reasons for the fact that, in general, shame has been given scarcely any attention by depth psychologists and other scholars.

Like such concepts as honor and pride, shame seems to be linked in our culture to particular forms of society. For example, the feudal system came into conflict with the bourgeois culture as it developed after the Reformation. Bourgeois culture, with its originally close connection with Protestantism and Puritanism, considered shame something irrelevant which hindered productiveness. Guilt, on the other hand, was considered useful because it not only stressed the conscience with its distinction between right and wrong but also bound the individual to the bourgeois society by accountability to it on the grounds of a divine command. The capacity to feel guilt was seen to be a true sign of nobility of a bourgeois nature, contrasted with the aristocrats who claimed to be above the ordinary social rules for good and evil. This attitude was probably reflected also in the work of the great classical depth psychologists who were rooted in the bourgeois form of culture and life. Thus, it is understandable that they fixed their attention more on guilt than on shame.

In addition to the socio-cultural factors and the hierarchical perception of shame and guilt, there was a personal reason for the focus on guilt. Shame touches deep layers of the psyche and the blushing and sweating show the link to the vegetative nervous system. The connection of shame with painful and fearful experiences resulted in an unconscious tendency for the pioneer depth psychologists to avoid shame in their self-analyses and their work with patients, and to replace it or identify it with guilt.

Shame and Guilt

The affects of shame and guilt are linked closely to each other; many people have great difficulty distinguishing between the two affects in themselves. But when we pay attention to our feelings we know that there is an essential difference. We all know the desperate and often mournful feeling of guilt on the one hand and on the other the burning, gnawing shame which makes one wish that the ground would open and swallow one.

This almost unspeakable element in shame probably finds its most brilliant expression in the English poet Keats (1958) who, referring to his embarrassment, wrote in a letter of 1818 that "the unhappiest hours in our life are those in which we remember the past blushing – if we are immortal this is what hell must be like" (p. 273). This idea that hell could be a permanent state of shame is an excellent statement on the torturing nature of shame. One seems to be on the verge of psychic annihilation and to be kept alive nevertheless.

In order to distinguish between shame and guilt one can maintain that guilt assumes that the subject offends the object, perhaps merely by existing. The subject has the feeling of having done something evil and wrong, and expects and fears that the object will react with punishment. But once the offense is atoned for, the matter can be considered as settled; subject and object are reconciled again. As regards shame, it is not the object that is offended but certain non-material norms are infringed. There is a much deeper fear than the one of punishment: fear of being cast out from human society. Shame means fear of complete desertion – not fear of physical death but of psychic annihilation.

From a societal point of view we can say that the one who is burdened with guilt is punished according to the laws of society. Even if sentenced to death the person is still subject to the laws of society and therefore remains its member with a social identity and some worth, albeit as a criminal. But burdening oneself with shame goes beyond the norms of society; one stops being a human being. This burden includes a feeling of humiliation and worthlessness which gives shame its torturing character.

Intra-psychically the fear that occurs when one is feeling guilt is based on inner figures, beginning with negative images of the parents. These images have been built up through introjective processes and threaten the ego with punishment up to the death penalty. Shame, too, is based on introjective figures which, however, are unconsciously idealized; they become threatening when the ego is not as it should be and they react by leaving, excluding, or emotionally starving the person. This reaction can go so far that psychic coherency is in danger and psyche is therefore threatened with disintegration. This is the almost undescribable fear which is imaged as the ground's opening and swallowing the individual. It is not the fear of physical death, which also holds the possibility of resurrection. It is the fear of psychic death, which is experienced as identical with annihilation or destruction of the personality without the possibility of a resurrection.

It becomes clear that guilt and shame are not opposites and are not to be classified in a hierarchical order. They are closely linked to each other and often exist side by side. Guilt can be understood as reaction to an action, shame as reaction to a mode of being. However, an action can be also the expression of a mode of being and a mode of being can be a product of an action. Guilt and fear of punishment result when the object is injured but, at the same time, a norm can be violated – the norm that this object should not be injured. Then shame is provoked, along with deep fears of abandonment. This subtle combination of guilt and shame may find expression in their being employed as defense mechanisms against each other.

An example is the experience of a patient who, after a promotion, unscrupulously pushed a colleague out of the company they worked for, thus causing serious financial trouble for the colleague and his family. In the analysis the patient continually circled the subject of guilt. He proved himself to be a person with delicate moral sensorium which had ceased to work in this single, clearly marked situation of conflict. His misdemeanor would not go out of his mind after his "confession," however, and he referred to it time and again. It became obvious that the feeling of guilt covered a very deep shame about the fact that, although he had organized his life according to high humanistic ideals, he experienced himself as an aggressive and envious person who was not worth being accepted as a member of human society. These feelings of shame were replaced unconsciously by feelings of guilt—much easier to endure—which were accompanied by fear of concrete punishment and retaliation and the hope of a possible expiation.

Two Forms of Shame

A closer consideration of the phenomenon of shame allows a distinction between two forms that are essentially different. One form serves one's social adaptation; the other protects one's integrity. Thus, these two forms actually have opposite functions. One guarantees—by conformity—the individual's belonging to the society; the other takes care that the collective does not penetrate too deeply into the personality. In other words, one function takes care that the subject and the object are in connection with each other; the other that the subject does not give up integrity because of the object. These two forms or functions of shame are so different that we can ask why our European languages do not have different terms for them. This lack may be due to the general ignorance about our emotional life.

To become aware of this difference we need not go to a famous European psychiatrist or philosopher; we can learn it from a New Guinea tribe member, who knows that shame is either "skin-shame" or "deep-shame." For example, a person who is observed when urinating or having sexual intercourse feels skin-shame, but the one who hurts the spirits of the forebears reacts with deep-shame (Heller, 1985). Shame here is the emotional response to a false social attitude as well as to a violation of the inner value system. In our culture a famous example of this second form of shame is the raped Lucretia whose integrity, physical and psychic, was so damaged that she could not go on living but had to kill herself out of shame. Another example is the betrayal of the disciple, Peter. He cried bitterly, not because he had done harm to Jesus and therefore had become guilty, but because he was utterly ashamed of the betrayal of his own integrity. When we speak about guilt in this case, it expresses less the emotional condition of Peter than our culture's tendency to avoid deep shame through guilt.

Now I return to the two examples I mentioned in the beginning. The example of the young man who told how he and his friends had shouted at the policemen, "Shame on you, shame on you," shows us shame as a factor in the formation of the social personality. In his childhood he had often heard the words "shame on you" and had been threatened with the fear of being excluded. Now he experienced, in identification with powerful inner figures, his own original fears and could ward them off at the same time. For him the words "shame on you" had the same meaning that they have always had in the individual's socialization process: "Be a human being, be like us!"

In the example of the young girl who could only utter the sentence "I am so ashamed," shame meant something different: "I am so injured; I am hurt in my innermost core. I was psychically violated so that I can hardly live any longer. I have been disdained but I do not dare to let you come close to me because I am afraid that you, too, will injure my integrity."

The being of the young girl had been wounded from her earliest childhood on, so that she could only draw attention to her wound by a feeling of shame which overwhelmed her. The young girl always thought of the past and was in the hell of shame: restless, uneasy, desperately fidgeting as if she were encircled by flames and constantly trying to avoid them. She was in a condition similar to agitated depression.

Shame and Depression

Out of the many aspects of shame I emphasize the connection between depression and chronic feelings of shame. Although guilt plays a part in the psychodynamics of depression, one has the impression that guilt functions as a defense against a profound shame.

I was consulted by a 76-year-old woman. She suffered from an inoperable tumor and came to get help to die; the doctors had

given her two more years and one had already passed. She was
the leader of an esoteric group of "healing" people. On the basis
of far eastern religious thought she had put together her own
eclectic philosophy of life, which she passed on in her pedagogi-
cal and therapeutic work. For her, cancer was the deepest humiliation she had ever experienced; she had withdrawn from all her
disciples and patients, living isolated, completely embittered and
ashamed. Her illness was a brutal reminder of her body, from
which she had wanted to escape. The disease had destroyed her
hope that, during a meditation exercise, she would be called to
a higher level of incarnation. Her life seemed to consist only of
shame which had thrown her into deep persisting depression. It
was not that she could die out of shame but that she could not
die because of her shame.

We discussed her biography briefly; very early she had felt her
life to be shameful. She was the second daughter of an officer;
her parents wanted a boy. The father was killed in World War I
without having a son and heir; the mother had a break-down and
gave this daughter to the rich and unloving grandparents where
she grew up all alone. Nevertheless, the patient claimed that she
had a beautiful childhood and, if anything went wrong at that
time, she alone was responsible for it. She could endure the guilt
of bad deeds more easily than the shame of having no right to
exist.

The woman had escaped into a belief in the purity of the human being, which she first thought to be realizable by political
means. Later she found belief in a vague, non-Christian ideology
which served her as a substitute for religion. Thus, as defense
against her existential shame, she built up an ego-ideal which
was so high that it could not provoke shame when she failed to
fulfill it. But while she strived to realize this ideal she neglected
to develop her true self and it was only closeness to death which
brought to the fore the striking discrepancy between her true and
her false self. Her whole life had been pervaded by depression
as a response to chronic feelings of shame. The depression was
warded off by ideology and, in a manic manner, by intensive
work. In a repetition compulsion, however, she brought herself
time and again into shameful situations.

The shame which lay behind the strong depression and hopelessness of this woman was mainly the form of shame which is

connected with the social personality and with inflated ego-ideals. In many creative persons, too, this shame comes to the fore. It seems to have influenced decisively the destiny of Virginia Woolf, for example; apparently she was often overwhelmed by acute shame as she awaited the reviews of her books and even when she was reading her own works, in which she had exposed so openly her personality and her ambitions. She committed suicide in 1941 shortly after having finished her novel *Between the Acts*. In her diary of March 1937, the time when she was awaiting the reviews of her novel *The Years*, she wrote:

> My sensations at this moment. . . are so peculiar and so unpleasant. . . . As if something cold and horrible – a roar of laughter at my expense – were about to happen. And I am powerless to ward it off: I have no protection. . . . I know that I must go on doing this dance on hot bricks till I die. . . . I'm going to be beaten, I'm going to be laughed at, I'm going to be held up to scorn and ridicule. (Bell, 1984, p. 63)

Woolf expressed clearly her burning fear of having turned herself to ridicule by her writing, going along with feelings of agitation and depressive emptiness. In this extract of her diary she showed two frequent defense strategies against the shame that is provoked by exposure through creative work. The first is further intensive creative work, an almost contraphobic maneuver of further exposure which is related to shamelessness as defense against shame. The second is analytic self-observation which enables the individual to build up a perceiving distance to the injured self. Through productive processes of defense, shame can lead to further self-knowledge.

But there is one group of people especially in whom shame as protector of the self can occur in a close connection to depression. We often meet this group in our practice; they are the children of psychologists. Without intending it, certain psychologists convey to their children, "I know you better than you know yourself." Expressed in the terminology of the theories of narcissism and of the new empathy research, an active, penetrating, intrusive empathy prevails at the expense of the passive, feeding, receptive one (Read, 1984). The child experiences a strong penetration into its being. In self-defense the child tries to block with chronic shame any access to the Self. But in the process the child's own access to the Self is blocked. The blockage is experienced as depression, often warded off through manic adaptation.

The disastrous consequences of an obtrusive observation of children and adolescents were noticed already by the pedagogues of the end of the eighteenth century. Maria and R. L. Edgeworth, for example, wrote in their *Essay on Practical Education* in 1798:

> Nothing hurts young people more than to be watched continually about their feelings, to have their countenances scrutinized, and the degrees of their sensibility measured by the surveying eye of the unmerciful spectator. Under the constraint of such examinations they can think of nothing but that they are looked at, and feel nothing but shame and apprehension.

Shame in Transference and Countertransference

In human relations there is hardly any situation that causes more of both forms of shame than the analytical one. The analysand may be a person who has great difficulty with social adaptation, who is in the throes of regression, who feels immature or even infantile, who is out of touch with the real Self, and therefore is suffering in a diffuse manner. Such a person encounters the analyst who is assumed to be calm, centered and having solved all personal problems. All elements of the analytic constellation hold the possibility of shame. I emphasize only two of these elements: the therapy, which may be experienced as a deep humiliation; and the shameful fear of being manipulated by the analyst. The shame of being in therapy may be found mainly in those patients who, as children, unconsciously felt that they were superior to their parents. They could not idealize their parents; they played the leading part in the parent-child relation or unconsciously believed that they should do it.

In therapy they feel inferior, often because they have come to know relations only as those of superiority and inferiority. Unconscious feelings of hate reactivate the original feelings of contempt for their parents and make them experience again uncertainty about their own worth. Thus, shame provokes unclear, irrational aggressions which are then warded off either by over-adaptation or by directing them against oneself, often in the form of worsening symptoms. These feelings of guilt can also be sexualized in a masochistic manner or acted out in a demonstrative, often idealizing clinging to the analyst. We often must deal with a mingled form of these defense mechanisms where patients are over-adapted, admire the therapist and his or her school and hide the fact that they feel worse and worse. In such cases the analyst, in countertransference, often experiences the aggressions and guilt feelings but less often the underlying shame and humiliation of the child who was ashamed of the parents and at the same time had to submit to them with shame.

Loss of control is one of the most profound causes for shame; it underlies the common human fear and shame of old age and illness as well as today's tendency to interpret all personal events as "psychically determined." When we are exposed to chance we feel that we are the playthings of destiny. The resultant shame is soothed when chance is explained as faulty action, as a consequence of one's own psychic events. This attitude can even lend a certain grandiosity to the individual. To be afraid that one is not in complete control of a situation can lead also to the fear of being manipulated, a fear that can take on almost paranoid traits. This fear seems to point to an injury of the psyche; a situation from childhood is repeated, where the parents tried—often in a violent manner—to penetrate the innermost core of their child's psyche.

In analysis such chronic feelings of shame give rise to anger that is felt to be irrational and therefore provokes strong feelings of guilt. The overadapted brooding in analysis (which is often called confrontation with the shadow) is a specific form of defense against these feelings of guilt. Aggressions are directed against oneself in a masochistic manner and combine with exhibitionism to produce persistent, noisy self-reproaches. Behind them there is a hidden grandiosity to which any access is blocked. A characteristic of shame which goes back to a deep early injury of the psyche is the almost shrill discrepancy between the shame which devours almost everything and its apparently minor outer cause. It is disastrous if this event, which seems to be unimportant and which in fact is of extremely great personal importance, is treated as irrelevant. This not only wastes the opportunity to acknowledge shame but it also constellates the whole arsenal of defense mechanisms against the dis-

guised feelings of shame. A conception of the psychic which includes the symbolic is of greatest importance here—the careful,
tactful and empathetic approach to the symbolic.

In countertransference the analyst experiences shame mainly
in an introjective identification with the patient's shame, unease
and humiliation. The analyst's guilty feelings give rise to a
masochistic sparing of the patient's feelings or to aggressions
against the patient. Many countertransference aggressions
which are rooted in the analyst's neurotic attitude are caused by
such feelings of guilt. This is especially true of those aggressions
which are expressed by technique of confrontation, which carries
the possiblity of a rationalized but serious hurting of the patient.

Final Remarks

Shame is one of the most important human affects. It is not a
regressive phenomenon which should be answered with shame
of the shame, but it plays a significant part in the socialization
process as well as in finding the Self. Thus, it takes on a status
which is often not noticed but may have a more important part
in the psychodynamics of neurotic disorders than guilt has. For
the individual's moral development, too, shame seems to play a
greater part than guilt; it actively promotes the adaptation to
moral norms, while feelings of guilt, in a more passive manner,
serve to avoid punishment. Shame points at the self as well as
at the other person and therefore at the vivid cooperation of inner
and outer world.

The role of the other may reveal a gap in the list of classical
Jungian archetypes; we lack an archetype of the Other. Even a
wide extension of the shadow archetype does not seem appropriate to cover the experiencing of another human as a biological,
social and ethical factor. If archetypes are genetically coded at all
and contribute to the survival of the species, we need a representative of the Other, sex-specific or not, which does not emphasize
only the repressed, as the shadow does. The need seems to be
one of survival—a genetic need of humans to be surrounded by
other humans. This idea was expressed in Kohut's (1984) last
work, where he extended his conception of the bipolar self in the
tension between basic ambition and basic idealization by adding

an intermediate stage of basic talents and skills. The bipolar self is tripartite, with elements of mirroring, alikeness and idealization; the need for alikeness is basic to the individual.

In our dreams we continually encounter figures which only by force can be labelled as shadow or as anima and animus figures, but which can be understood easily if a basic archetype of the Other is postulated. The experience of shame in its two forms seems to point at such an archetypal figure and, thus, emotionally connects the experience of the outer and the inner world.

Shame is closely connected with our being human, so closely that even biologists have considered it to be our main characteristic. For example, Burgess in his essay (1839) on blushing, emphasized that black people and North American Indians are able to blush and therefore have the moral instinct which is the essential human characteristic. Darwin (1872/1965) also adopted this concept.

The most beautiful example of the connection between shame and being human is found in Dostoevsky's novel *The Idiot*, where Duke Myshkin's great humaneness is revealed in his empathetically reacting with shame, proving that he is no idiot at all but a human being on the highest level of development. Dostoevsky, probably the greatest researcher of shame, showed how it can be an emotional expression of a person who lives in inner harmony and who at the same time is able to react very empathetically to others. Thus, shame is the expression of a person for whom individuation is not colorless individualism but a vivid confrontation with oneself and others.

Translated from German by
Sabine Osvatič and
Dagmar Henle-Dieckmann

REFERENCES

Adler, A. (1919). *Über den nervösen Charakter*. Wiesbaden: Bergman.
Adler, A. (1927). *Menschenkenntnis*. Leipzig: Bergman.
Bell, A. (Ed.). (1984). *The diary of Virginia Woolf* (Vol. 5). London: Hogarth.

Benedict, R. (1946/1977). *The chrysanthemum and the sword: Patterns of Japanese culture*. London: Routledge & Kegan Paul.

Binswanger, L. (1958). The case of Ellen West. In R. May, E. Angel, & H. Ellenberger (Eds.), *Existence*. New York: Basic Books.

Burgess, T. (1839). *The physiology or mechanism of blushing. . . .* London: John Churchill.

Darwin, C. (1872/1965). *The expression of the emotions in man and animals*. Chicago: University of Chicago Press.

Dodds, E. (1951). *The Greeks and the irrational*. Cambridge, MA: Harvard University Press.

Heller, A. (1985). *The power of shame: A rational perspective*. London: Routledge & Kegan Paul.

Janet, P. (1903). *Les obsessions et la psychasthénie*. Paris: Alcan.

Keats, J. (1958). *The letters of John Keats 1814–1821 (Vol. 1)*. Cambridge, MA: Harvard University Press.

Kohut, H. (1984). *How does analysis cure?* Chicago: University of Chicago Press.

Read, G. (1984). The antithetical meaning of the term "empathy" in psychoanalytic discourse. In J. Lichtenberger (Ed.), *Empathy*. London: Analytic Press.

Wurmser, L. (1981). *The mask of shame*. Baltimore: Johns Hopkins University Press.

Discussion: Gilda Frantz
(Los Angeles)

In the film, "Oh, God!" God is on earth as an "ordinary" person. At one point God, played by George Burns, says: "I made two mistakes when I created the world. The first mistake was inventing shame, and the second was that I made the avocado pit too big!" The avocado pit is an image for the seed that gives us the potential of becoming. It is the core of the ego-ideal/shadow/Self axis. Like the avocado pit, shame/shadow takes up a great deal of room.

From the moment I read the title of Hultberg's talk, I felt a deep sense of what it means to have shame stand between the idealized ego and the Self. While his paper touches upon many aspects of shame psychologically, socially and anthropologically, I will focus on shame as related to individuation. Thus I will elaborate rather than offer a critique of his paper.

One of Hultberg's examples that particularly caught my interest is that of the 76-year-old woman who found herself suffering from an inoperable tumor.

This story has certain parallels within our own Jungian community. We too practice a philosophy. Being exposed on a daily basis to the radiating effects of the unconscious is inflating. As receptors of the powerful archetypal energies of the transference, we analysts are prone to godlike projections and to hubris. Many of us are directed by our own individuation process, yet like Hultberg's patient we may have a misconception about the rewards of individuation. Do we have the notion that we will not have to suffer the humiliation and shame of a painful illness or death if we pay attention to our dreams and active imagination? Here I refer particularly to cancer, which seems to be the most stigmatized disease for those of us in the healing arts. Ironically, individuals who deal with pain and suffering often seem to have painful deaths or illnesses themselves. The notion that inner development can make one immune to such a fate is, indeed, a form of hubris.

Careful attention to one's dreams can guarantee the rewards of consciousness but not a so-called "good death." The idea that we will be saved from the shame of illness or suffering if we listen to the unconscious is something we might pass on, unconsciously, to our analysands, as though the unconscious were a benign and good god. Yet nothing could be further from the truth. While one needs to prepare for death by understanding one's own myth and by having a religious attitude toward the mysterious and wondrous experience of life itself, nothing can insure that we will die gloriously, or even painlessly. If there is such a thing as a good death, it is a conscious death, one without shame. Consciousness does not prevent pain or suffering; it can only help prevent meaningless suffering.

Shame belongs in the same category as terror and anxiety. Natural creatures, that is, unconscious ones, are spared such troubles. The consequence of shame is that it pulls one out of containment in nature; that is what happened to Hultberg's cancer patient. In spite of her spiritual practices she developed a serious illness and felt she would be deprived of her idealized image of death – that she should die while meditating and be sent to a higher incarnation.

The issue of shame belongs to human consciousness. The fairy tale of the ugly duckling is an illustration. It is only when the "ugly duckling" becomes aware of his true identity that he ceases to feel ashamed of his appearance. His consciousness is expanded to fit his true Self. This is what Jung called development of personality. The hardest task each of us has in life is to become aware of our higher personality. An important point Hultberg makes is that feeling shame produces the wish that the earth would open under our feet and swallow us. Being swallowed is the return to the mother, the desire to return to the womb, a hiding place of dark safety. It also signals the death of an ego-ideal. This ego consciousness has to die – be swallowed – in order for a new awareness of oneself to expand and include the shadow or the dark side of the Self. The danger of being swallowed is in having one's consciousness swallowed. If shame is to be understood as accompanying an experience of the Self, then being swallowed is the desire to re-enter Paradise and return to an unconscious state – to slip away from the consciousness of one's own dark shadow.

Jungian analytic practices are of a spiritual nature; they involve *spiritus and materia*, soul and body. We all have our analytic secrets about which we might feel shame if exposed. An example of such a case was presented by the late Kieffer Frantz (1971). A woman analysand was having difficulties in her analysis with him. He suggested that she consult another therapist in our Los Angeles Jungian community to discuss these difficulties. The patient asked, "Wouldn't you rather I go to a therapist outside of your own community?" She implied thus that there would be shame involved for him if their analytic relationship was exposed; she said she was trying to protect his reputation. This was not a concretized relationship, nor was there any physical contact. Their analytic relationship contained a great deal of heat nonetheless. This is a good example of the analyst's not trying to hide from exposure, of being in relationship to both ego ideal and Self. One of the definitions of shame has to do with being unclothed or exposed. Similarly, one of the definitions of the word bereft is to be naked, to have one's clothes taken away.

Shame is the gristle we must chew on in order to integrate our shadow complex. For some it is totally indigestible. In my own practice was a woman who carried a tremendous amount of guilt and shame from an early trauma: witnessing something within her family which was shameful to her. She dreamed of being back in the old neighborhood and having something unchewable in her mouth, and she couldn't find a place to spit it out. She simply wasn't able to swallow it. Finally she spit it into a public drinking fountain with a great sense of relief. The shadow complex could not be integrated in a personal sense but needed a more collective container.

Shame has to do with individuation. Shame results from a conflict between the ego-ideal and the shadow and theirs is related to the Self. Shame as an integral part of individuation is well illustrated by the story of Genesis, and in particular by The Fall. In the beginning there was chaos, then creation, and then Yahweh created Adam and Eve. He placed them in the Garden, provided them with all the good things of life, and warned them not to eat of the fruit of either the Tree of the Knowledge of Good and Evil or the Tree of Life, warning them that death would surely be the result of transgression. There is breath-taking abundance; this is Paradise. The two walk hand in hand, bodies touching at the hips, flesh to flesh. Their bareness is pleasant, unnoticed, neither cared about nor thought about. "Now both of them were naked, the man and his wife, but they felt no shame in front of each other" (Genesis 2:25; Jerusalem Bible).

The Serpent seduced Eve into tasting the fruit of the Tree of the Knowledge of Good and Evil, telling her that she would not die but rather would be like God in all respects. She, in turn, seduced Adam into eating the fruit, and then Yahweh appeared. When He approached, Adam and Eve saw that they were naked and felt shame and covered themselves. Yahweh knew by their shame that they had transgressed and disobeyed Him. He then cursed the Serpent, Adam, and Eve individually; aware that they would now be tempted to eat of the Tree of Life and become immortal, He cast them out of Paradise. Yahweh saw that Adam and Eve felt shame. It was the capacity to feel shame that told Yahweh that they were now conscious, for shame occurs only where there is consciousness, and consciousness involves the shadow. Their shame focused on their nakedness because the body is container of the soul, and the soul co-exists with the shadow. The body contains the seed and the egg from which life has its source.

The myth of Genesis involves the eternal problem of containing the opposites, Yahweh and the Serpent, within each of us. Each of us carries opposing energies, first urging us toward further growth and then warning us of the consequences if we listen. If we do not listen we avoid shame, but we remain unconscious. If we do listen we lose our attachment to the ego-ideal, our innocence, and try to cover ourselves and hide. Shame is the price we pay for becoming increasingly conscious human beings.

REFERENCE

Frantz, K. (1971). The analyst's own involvement with the process and the patient. In J. B. Wheelwright (Ed.), *The analytic process: Aims, analysis, training.* New York: Putnam's.

The Shadow Between Parents and Children

Mara Sidoli (London)

Webster's Dictionary defines shame as "the painful emotion excited by a consciousness of guilt, shortcomings and impropriety." In this paper I will discuss how the emotion of shame arises during childhood, and how it seems to occur out of the young child's recurrent experiences of shortcomings, inadequacy and dependency in youthful attempts to explore an increasingly wider world. Shame is linked to an individual experience which takes place in relation to a social context, whether to the mother, the father, siblings, school friends or, in adulthood, to society as a whole.

For shame to be experienced it seems necessary for a child to have developed sufficient ego to be able to experience being separate from parents and other people in the environment, and endowed with certain good or bad attributes. This differentiation occurs gradually but is established toward the end of the first year of life, reaching its peak in the various phases of toilet training and during the oedipal stage. In that stage, jealousy of and rivalry with the parent of the same sex are at their highest and are accompanied by feelings of shame about one's inadequacy. In the course of observing how much the rival parent and the desired one can offer each other, the child suffers great anguish and feels rejected, envying the couple but also feeling guilty and ashamed about the envy. Each child will deal with these painful emotions by adopting defense mechanisms, but most commonly two: regressing to the babe-in-arms stage in order to avoid the conflict; or becoming prematurely independent, that is, jumping ahead of the conflict. Both are unsatisfactory as they tend to lead to loss of ego and to pathological splitting rather than to integration, working through, and assimilation of the dark or shadow aspect.

Within the family the "bucket" of the shadow is passed on from the older siblings to the younger ones, often with merciless cruelty, as the young ones represent outwardly the messy stage over which the older ones have just managed to triumph. The same occurs when parents and other adults project their inadequacy, shame or guilt onto the children, contributing to the child's feeling of inadequacy because of being small. Since smallness is a fact children must live with, they suffer severe blows to their narcissism, feel ashamed of their smallness and try to compensate for inadequacies by over-identifying with grown-ups. Indeed, there is much praise for good children who never cry, are well-behaved and who act like little adults both at home and in social life. Smallness is equated with inadequacy and mess, and bigness with competence and perfection.

In moving out of the family into the wider world the child will be shamed at school by teachers and older students who evoke shame as an effective way to control behavior. The shaming and denigration of weakness and overpraising of strength and power are even more extreme in collective structures such as social institutions (political, religious, military and professional organizations) and tend to be experienced by the child via the parents' connection to the collective unconscious.

In the same way in which a very young baby can dispose of frustrating feelings onto the mother (in the form of her breast) who then becomes equated with badness, a group can become intolerant of its shameful and messy side, split it off and project it onto a weaker group nearby. It may then attack the group carrier of its shadow projections with the aim of doing away with its own shadow projected outside. Collective conflicts are caused by shadow projections leading in extreme cases to wars. In such cases the shadow archetype is activated but disowned because of the sense of shame and guilt that it engenders.

Having constructed the theoretical framework for the clinical part of my paper, I will now explore, with the support of clinical material, the links between the collective and personal shadow, the emotion of shame, and its reflection on the life of an individual, first in early infancy and then in relation to the case of a five-year-old child called Ricky.

Shame in Infancy

At the beginning of life dependency on a parent is total. Thus, frustration is unavoidable, for even at the best of times there is often a gap between the child's subjective needs and the parent's empathic understanding and satisfying of them.

This state of affairs from the start leads the infant totally unconsciously to experience the negative side of dependency. When frustrated, the infant is filled with feelings of impotence, helplessness, rage and despair. At this point omnipotent fantasies come about to help the child's survival. In them the frustrating object is pushed away and disposed of, while a fulfilling fantasy is hallucinated and retained in times of duress in order to make life bearable. However, in the process of growing up, and with the increase of the young child's sense of reality, omnipotent fantasies recede and the child is bound to face and come to terms with the facts of being separate from the parents and of the parents' greater autonomy.

As feelings of being separate increase in the child, a situation of trust must be established. To this end parents must be aware of the child's needs, dependency, and anxiety from feeling small, impotent, and vulnerable. Because the child is not aware that each developmental stage will be outgrown, shortcomings related to these stages tend to arouse anxiety, shame, guilt and envy of bigger and more powerful people. When all goes well, with the help of parental care, tolerance and support, the baby comes to accept such a painful state of affairs.

Between the first and third year of life, usually, the child has mastered great skills and is struggling to manage impotence and omnipotence; sensitivity to feelings of shame and guilt is at its highest. The parents must provide containment and support for the child to be able to manage and to integrate diverse elements: impotence and omnipotence, hopelessness and helplessness. This containment is most necessary while the child is struggling with growth and development in the outer world. At that time, the child's ego must cope also with a primitive super-ego in the inner world. The super-ego shames the ego to keep violent instinctual drives under control.

Thus, when the parents, instead of relating to their child at each stage of development, have unrealistic expectations, or overwhelm the baby with massive archetypal unconscious projections of their own, the child has to rely mainly on her or his own protection and containment with the result that these defenses encroach on the potential space for relationship.

Growing up means having to come to terms with and manage powerful instinctual drives and uncontrollable urges, and all kinds of extreme and opposing emotions. Because in the early stages of the infant's life the boundaries between internal and external are not differentiated clearly, parental help is extremely important in mitigating the archetypal quality of the child's experiences and allowing for flexibility in the defensive system. Flexibility will enable defenses built up as protection in times of distress and need to be dropped when the bad feelings go away; then the child need not erect rigid barriers between the opposites.

To give an example: By using splitting mechanisms, the child's ego can disown vulnerable and shameful bits, which cause bad feelings inside and push them outside (by projective mechanisms), while retaining good-feeling bits. When splitting is excessive the shadow thrives at the expense of ego consciousness. Development becomes one-sided; independence, thoroughness, and pseudo-competence are prematurely demonstrated by the child, who may achieve successful adaptation at severe cost to psychic health.

Weaning seems to stir up in the child feelings of shame, inasmuch as the child attributes the loss of the breast to personal inadequacy and badness; "there must be something wrong with me if mother pushes me away," seems to be the way the baby feels.

The example of Lilli shows how the realization of being separate from the parents—about at the time of weaning and beginning to walk—highlights feelings of both impotence and omnipotence at the same time.

Lilli was a normal and generally well-adapted baby, with a caring, "good enough" mother. At the age of 14 months Lilli was having a difficult time after weaning from the breast. It seemed that, in order not to feel rejected and a failure for having lost the breast, she was compensating by trying to behave in a way that was grown-up beyond her age.

I quote here extracts from observational reports, recorded by a student of infant observation seminars at The Society of Analytical Psychology. The student went to visit the mother and baby weekly for two years. One observation reports that Lilli seemed to be terribly intent on getting what she wanted, and appeared desperately upset if she or her mother did not get it right—quite minor things such as when she wanted tea rather than fruit juice, or when she asked for something and her mother could not guess what she wanted quickly enough. Her frustration was obvious.

Two weeks later, Lilli was observed trying to prove that she was a big girl by trying to steal her older sister's possessions. The observer wrote:

> Lilli goes to collect a book from the table and brings it to mother. Then she sits on her lap and turns the pages. It is a grown-up's book, and then she wants the observer to have a look at it. . . . She then wants a book which belongs to her sister. Mother allows her to look at it but she soon loses interest and points to a box which also belongs to her sister. Mother tells her that the game inside is too difficult for her, but Lilli insists on trying and mother lets her play with and find out for herself. She soon gets frustrated with it and eventually gets her own toy postman's van. She opens the door of the van and takes all the shapes out of it and wants to put them back in again through the hole. Mother helps with the first two and then Lilli is able to carry on by herself. She is thrilled with excitement and pleasure. She claps her hands and wants mother and the observer to do the same each time she succeeds. She does it over and over again; they praise her and she claps her hands.

It is important to know that both parents and sister spent most of their time reading, so that reading appeared to Lilli to be an enviable activity. She had to come to terms with the fact that she could not yet read; mother was helpful in letting her find that out for herself. At 22 months:

> Lilli points to a wall where lots of her sister Ella's drawings are hanging. Mother shows me the one done by Lilli at 20 months and comments that it is impressive. While she is talking about her children's artistic gifts, Lilli climbs on a chair and begins to make

unspecified noises. Mother asks if she wants to do a poo, Lilli nods, and mother gets the potty and removes her nappy while she is standing in the middle of the room. Lilli then goes to her potty looking very solemn. It is a serious business. She performs and immediately afterwards gets up with a little smile. Mother wipes her and as soon as she is let free she begins to run around the room and to march up and down still half-naked. She then runs in and out of the kitchen with a satisfied smile on her face.

From this description it can be seen that the painting and performing on the potty were linked in Lilli's mind. They were both tremendous personal achievements of which she was proud and which made her feel good about herself.

Lilli's mother was tolerant; she supported her child's struggle and patiently encouraged her to gain confidence and bear frustration. Such a parental attitude is, in my view, the one that helps a child to build a benevolent and helpful super-ego authority, to cope with failures and inadequacies without too much shame, and to integrate the unwanted side, the shadow within the ego structure.

Ricky had a different experience from Lilli's. He was five when he was referred to me for therapy at the clinic; initially I saw him twice weekly. The symptoms reported by his parents were lying, soiling, heavy swearing, destructive attacks on toys and furniture in the home, desperate clinging to his father and difficulty in concentrating at school. He also exhibited some speech problems and at times his words were incomprehensible. His parents had divorced when he was three. His mother had left the home, leaving him and his two brothers of five and nine with their father, a very caring man but unable to look after the children. A year later the father married a young divorcee with a seven-year-old son.

Ricky's symptoms worsened from the time the step-mother appeared on the scene. Anxiety about him, both at home and at school, had escalated to such a degree that the family and the child psychiatrist had come to consider hospitalization for Ricky.

In the first interview Ricky appeared very lively, warm and responsive, but looked persecuted, tense, muddled and confused. He entered the room accompanied by his step-mother and the social worker. He was a tiny fellow with a large head set on a disproportionately thin and small body. His face was pale and wrinkled like that of an old man. This old man appearance was reinforced by his holding himself upright and pacing stiffly up and down the room, carrying a book under his little arm like a man with his daily newspaper. Despite this act he looked very frightened, tense and uneasy, crouched on the floor by his step-mother as if in search of protection, well away from me and turning his back on me.

At one point, while his step-mother told of an improvement in school, he turned around and looked into my eyes, giving me a thorough look. He seemed reassured and accepted the paper and pencil I was offering and moved closer to me to display his writing abilities. Then as soon as his step-mother moved on to talk about the problems with him at home he began to draw a house. At first it was a small house where he, his father and his two brothers lived. He portrayed his middle brother just like himself with a very large head and big ears, and scornfully called him the "big-headed and big-eared." There was no mother in the house. The two brothers were at the windows while he drew himself and his father holding hands going through the front door. The house looked crowded; I commented that it looked a bit small for all those people. He then drew a bigger house next to it where the people had more space, but again with no female figure in it. His step-mother, who had been watching him drawing, commented on the absence of the mother, and evidently taking it as an attack against herself, added, "He is exclusively attached to his daddy and pushes me away." I suggested that therapy would be able to help with that problem and went on to make arrangements for treatment. By now Ricky had settled in the room and was exploring the toys. He had moved away from me and was playing with the dollhouse, arranging furniture in the various rooms, very concentrated and quiet.

At the end of the session his omnipotence manifested itself. He collected the drawings he had made and told me he was going to take them home to show his dad. I suggested he leave them here but he baffled me by marching out of the room with the drawings under his arm, looking like an executive with his work projects. I realized that he was provoking me to a battle. At that stage, I could not interpret his behavior and I let him have his way. He had reached the exit and I had re-entered my room when, suddenly, he ran back into the room, kissed me goodbye and rushed out through the door again. Note that his approach to me occurred after his step-mother spoke of his writings. When she mentioned his shortcomings and inadequacies he drew the house excluding her, and displaying his wish that the father get rid of her. At the end of the session he did the same with me. Taking no notice of what I said, he seemed concerned only with his father and wanting to please him.

The following session he sounded very confused about me and thus puzzled and anxious. He seemed to be projecting his anxious and confused feelings about his own identity and everybody else's. I commented about them to him and a flood of muddled-up and confused questions to himself burst out, leaving no time for any answers on my part. How many mothers did he have? He told himself he had an "old mum" and a "new mum." He seemed to ask me which was his real mum. "How many brothers do you have?" I asked. This confused him too. Then he said that his old mum had a brother living with her; was he his new dad? Who were all these people? Who was he? Who was I? All these questions seemed to pile up in Ricky's mind and he could not get any answers. He was helplessly mixed up and insecure.

I began to feel that confusion and mental mess muddling up everyone and everything, was his defensive maneuver against helplessness and unbearable anxieties about not knowing, about being a dependent baby. It was at this stage that his language also became muddled up and incomprehensible. However, he would swiftly come out of this confusion, shifting to a precarious identification with the big-man-father, looking like a man going to work, or using reading and writing as a way of proving to me and to himself his abilities, in an attempt to deny and ward off the chaotic feelings of the baby inside himself. Thus I found myself during the whole of his treatment having to work with a pair of opposites, big and small. Big, I later discovered, meant to him a state of idealized order, power, knowledge and invulnerability, whereas small was equated with mess, helplessness and vulnerability.

This is, of course, quite a usual feature of the way little children think, due both to their experience of reality and to the interplay of archetypal projection—their own and that of the parents—which becomes quickly constellated in the transference. However, in Ricky's case the polarization between big and small had reached a high degree of autonomy that obscured all other pairs of opposites and blocked the natural developmental processes that Fordham (1957) calls deintegration and reintegration; Ricky could not allow a full deintegration to take place for fear of remaining a helpless, messy baby. The consequence was his defensive shifts from baby to old man, both in the treatment and in the outside world. His parents, too, had great fears of showing their vulnerability and helplessness and expressed self-denial, strength and ability. They identified with the wise old man/woman, while both the mother who had left and Ricky had to carry their projections of incompetence, weakness and uselessness. At the same time Ricky's behavior was intolerable for them and prompted them to do anything possible to help.

In the early phases of the treatment, I felt that there was a great deal of his big-boy act that I had to permit and I restrained my interpretations about his other side, the messy baby, in order not to shame him and add to his persecutory guilt. I made occasional comments about his wish to show me how good and competent he was at doing his school work, in order not to make him feel attacked and persecuted by interpretations aimed to draw out his baby side. I felt I should wait for him to introduce his inner baby when he was ready, thus allowing him to feel in charge and myself to be the helpless child in the session. Indeed, many sessions were spent in his reading one school book after the other, and making me feel totally useless, controlled and shut off like the baby inside himself to which, as yet, we did not have access.

When I felt that this stage had lasted long enough I asked him one day during a pause in his reading, in which he had appeared particularly threatened by the silence, what was he afraid would happen to him if he stopped reading; did he think he had come to the clinic like a school? Why was he coming to see me? For a while he did not answer; but soon after, dropping his book, he began, in a very hyperactive manner to go around the room touching everything, opening drawers and dashing about at such a speed that it paralyzed me. Meanwhile he was flooding me with all sorts of questions. These, too, shot out at such a speed that it was obvious to me that they did not require an answer. "Do you live here? Do you sleep on that bed?" Then, touching something on my desk, "Can I take it home? What is this?

Can I have it?" His behavior was escalating into a frenzy of activities, questions and excitement that suddenly filled the whole room, and I felt their aim was to render me impotent; there was no room for me to say anything at all, except to take up and exert a controlling stance like a super-ego authority, which I did not want to do.

I thought that now that the big-man mask had been dropped I was beginning to see the chaotic baby and his terrifying confusion, resulting from his persecutory shame and guilt. The interesting feature of the shift was its automatic swing from one position to its opposite without any in-between stage or transition time. He took me by surprise and I began to understand what the difficulties must have been like at home. It also gave me an idea of how much he had felt that things happened to him and suddenly changed, finding him totally baffled and unprepared; I had found myself confusing him in this way. This led me to speculate on his weaning, and how his mother's departure must have occurred very suddenly without any explanation being given to him, and without giving him any time to adjust to it.

The session which followed was one in which what I term the big mess took place. He rushed into the therapy room, again carrying a book in his hand and, without a word, checked that everything was in order. Then he began to read. I said that he was starting to read again to avoid getting out of control, as had happened on the previous occasion, and he feared that I might tell him off. His face looked much more relaxed than in previous interviews. He dropped the book and moved to the table where pencil, paint and paper were displayed and said, "I want to do a proper painting." He sat down at the little table in front of a large sheet of paper and, as I was pouring out some water from the tap into a pot for his brush, he started painting a square with large strokes of dark, blackish paint. While mixing the paint with the brush in the pot he became excited. "I am drawing a house," he explained; "It is a black and white house." As he was struck by the contrast of the black and white lines he said, "No, it is gray," smearing the colors one into the other and adding more colors while naming them.

While asking his questions he had begun to show his manic hyperactive behavior of the previous day by pouring out all the paint from each individual pot on the paper. He looked at me defiantly and said, "I need more water and more paint," and this continued until a thick, slimy mess had covered the paper and was beginning to flow from the paper on to the table and down to the floor. He was looking increasingly anxious. He went to the tap and busied himself with filling the pots and pouring out the water from one into the other, mixing into it all the remaining paint. Then taking the brushes and sprinkling water all over the place, he said, half defiantly and half fearfully, "They are having a wee." He then filled up the pots and poured water directly on to the painting until the water became a puddle on the floor. Then very anxiously he ran to the table, spread both arms around it, and tried to prevent the water from overflowing on to the floor. In a very peremptory way he ordered me: "Stop that tap." "You are asking me to help you to stop the uncontrollable mess you feel is pouring from inside you, which is making you feel very anxious and frightened," I said.

This interpretation shifted his behavior defensively. Here he was the big man again. Very competently he asked me for a wiping cloth, said the painting was too soggy and threw it away. Then he wiped his hands clean and rushed to where the toys were placed and began to play with some little cars, taking a sedan car and attaching a small trailer to it. All the time he had been very curious about the contents of my big cupboard, giving it inquisitive glances. Then suddenly he reached the cupboard in which were kept the toy boxes of my other patients, opened it wide, climbed into it and tried to get hold of one of the toy boxes. I said he wanted to have everything inside the room and inside the cupboard.

Realizing that he could not have it his own way he said, reaching for the door handle, "I am going to my daddy," and waited to see my reaction. "You want to go back to your good daddy," I said, "because I have now become a bad person by not letting you have what you want." He smacked my hand and stepped back from the door he had opened. I closed it and as I was saying that he had smacked my hand because he had got very angry with me, he sat back very stiff on his chair and started reading his school book aloud to himself. The story was about Janet and John helping mother to make cakes. He changed the words of the story and read out loud angrily: "You make horrible cakes," "You feel I am a horrible mummy," I said, "and you want to go back to your good daddy because I deserve to be left by you for being so horrible." He took some small pieces of paper from his desk, wrote on them, and hid them under the telephone on my desk, ordering me, "I want to find them still there when I come back next time, but I will not write my telephone number on them because you are horrible and should not ring me up!" Having said that, he made a little drawing on another piece of paper which, he said, was a nice present for me, and then offered to fix up my drawer which, he said, was broken.

I commented that he had attacked me and smacked me when he felt I was being horrible to him, but now he also wanted to please me and repair the damage he had done as he felt he had made me into a "broken-up mummy." This reference to a broken-up mummy unleashed his persecutory guilt and anger, and once again he attacked me and turned the room upside down in a sort of manic frenzy, running about with much disorganized activity. He was in the grip of persecutory anxieties of the sort stirred up by archetypal fantasies of the bad mother-breast, resulting from his aggressive impulses and destructive wishes against me as the frustrating mother re-experienced in the transference.

In the first interview, the father and the step-mother had projected heavily all the badness onto the mother who had left, confusing their own personal infantile unresolved problems with Ricky's situation. There was a lot of hatred and resentfulness on the part of the father toward his ex-wife that he also directed at Ricky. In fact, I found out from the boy that he thought he was bad, and that it was his bad messiness that had made his good inner and outer mother abandon him because, in his view, she had left in order to punish him. It was his misery and guilt that induced his "bad," regressive behavior, as he could not forgive himself and did not want anybody else to forgive him either. His super-ego was quite merciless.

It was only through the work we did together, and his becoming aware of his own infantile fantasies as something distinct, no matter how similar to real events they appeared to be, that he was able to feel "good" again. For this to take place the influence of the destructive collective shadow projection within the family had to be put into the right perspective; thus both his own archetypal fantasies and those of his parents had to be sorted out so that the relationship with his mother, both internally and externally, and his love for her could once again come to the fore and be re-established. Only this could make reparation possible, and allow forgiveness of her and of himself to take place. But for this to happen he needed the analytic space, and me in it making a space inside myself to let him be and feel each time as he truly felt, protected from collective archetypal shadow projections. It was my awareness of his need for such space and my analytic sensitivity that held me back from making, in the beginning, some obvious, stock interpretations, waiting until I felt in touch and in tune with what he was to bring me in the sessions. In this way I avoided humiliating him and reduced his consequent shameful feelings because I did not compete by knowing better.

During sessions he became persecuted easily by comments pointing to his baby side, if I omitted to stress first his able and competent side. Any hint about his messy side shamed him, tended to make him become—rather than feel—totally helpless, incompetent, and incontinent. Becoming helpless immediately produced a defensive, all-knowing, omnipotent, false reaction. When he experienced excessive persecution and guilt in the sessions his ego tended to splinter, and at these points he would usually become very excited and physically hyperactive. In such moments interpretive work become totally impossible and I experienced him as a very disturbed and difficult patient.

On the other hand, when he exhibited his grown-up adult-like behavior, his own control of the baby within was so strict that again I felt he was unreachable. In addition, he could not come frequently enough for intensive analysis. Consequently, I had to be very aware and sensitive of his level of tolerance of frustration and distress during sessions and between them, in order that the treatment should not break down. Thus I had to devise a method of responding and almost anticipating his sudden shifts between the opposites in order to keep him in the center area, that of the ego, where the therapeutic alliance could take place, and to phrase the interpretations in such a way as always to bring together the "good" and the "bad" sides, in his case the big and the small. I adjusted my responses to avoid inciting manic flights and unbearable persecutions in him, both on the part of the archetypal images of the super-idealized man (senex), or of the devalued messy baby (puer). In mentioning senex and puer I am referring to cultural patterns of his environment where only adults are valued; little children are devalued.

I also had to avoid restraining his behavior by active intervention, as he would experience it as a controlling hand on my part. I would become the controlling parent, and he would then defy me to exert more control with the aim of repeating in the sessions the battles over toilet training that he was fighting with his stepmother at home, and the battles he had fought over going to sleep with daddy, when both parents had either been defeated or had had to resort to physical violence in order to make him comply.

He had a great passion for painting which—as it later emerged—he had inherited from his mother, who had been an art student. He used pots of paint both to express himself and to make diabolical messes, which he always cleared up in a very agitated and compulsive way. The messes always began, as in the first interview, by colors being mixed together and water added to them, which made the mixture unmanageable. The mixing of colors and the brushes and paint pots contained primal scene fantasies that had to be analyzed throughout his therapy.

What emerged in his treatment was his need to develop a containing boundary around the baby and his mess in which he could feel safe to express himself, that is to say, to assimilate to his baby shadow. He worked hard at it by himself, making the best he could of my comments, interpretations and presence. It was clear, however, that he was building his own inner containing frame within the sessions, which he experienced as holding the whole of him together. This process was manifested in the way he asked questions for which he did not want answers but wanted me there in the game he played to build frames. He was a very determined, intelligent and humorous child, and I felt at later stages that his sense of humor helped me to put his behavior into perspective for him; he could then have a good joke about himself and his siblings and the way they would gang up and drive daddy and mummy mad, or joke and pull my leg in the session and enjoy being a funny clown and having fun about himself, making a mess, being unable to do something, or talking baby talk. He could allow himself to be muddled, foolish, not-knowing and little, and not worry too much as he came to accept both sides. He could feel more often like a baby, loved and appreciated by mummy, both his inner one and his real mother outside, rather than an abandoned, messy, unwanted baby who had to delude himself, to be grown up, in order to feel loved. In brief, his shame had decreased because he had been able to start integrating his shadow.

REFERENCE

Fordham, M. (1957). *New developments in Analytical Psychology*. London: Routledge & Kegan Paul.

Discussion: Marcello Pignatelli (Rome)

From Melanie Klein to D. W. Winnicott to Michael Fordham, studies have re-evaluated the child with regard to pathology and to individual development. The alternation of deintegration and reintegration represents in miniature the parameters of the adult's experience. These processes include the discovery, rejection, and projection of bad objects; hallucinatory fantasies of good objects; aggressivity as response to frustration; and attempts at control of instincts. Investigating such mechanisms in childhood, when details are enormously magnified, makes it possible to perceive them before they are deformed or obscured by larger patterns.

I do not think it is possible to identify the moment of the birth of the ego. It seems certain, however, that at that moment conscience too is born, peculiarly human and endowed with ethical capabilities.

From the beginning, the medley of instinctual and psychoid elements leads the child to a confrontation with two fundamental experiences: abandonment and guilt. Although these experiences are both integral to the trauma of birth, the abandonment is more evident than the guilt. The persistence of guilt, however, suggests the Christian idea of "original sin."

Sidoli's paper describes and synthesizes the concepts of guilt and shame and presents two brilliant clinical cases. The feeling of insufficiency and impotence that engenders guilt is present from birth because the newborn perceives immediately the possibility of living without being dependent. The omnipotence projected on the person who takes care of and nourishes the infant is conceivable only if an image of such omnipotence pre-exists, an image that corresponds to the *imago dei*, an archetypal image.

The search for the origin of such an archetype leads to a transcendental being or to the representation of the parental couple. This couple may be perceived as one sphere constituted by two complementary parts, male and female.

Thus the classical formulations, which attribute to the mother the primary psychodynamic influence on the child's development, need to be integrated with the archetypal determination of the ideal ego. It becomes absorbed into the imperatives of the super-ego which are present from the very beginning. If they were not present, we would not be able to comprehend what the guilt feelings and attempts at reparation (described by Klein) are due to.

Aggressivity in the child engenders more or less conscious reactions of punishment or rejection in the mother. One cannot assume, however, that child behaviors are shaped by experience only, without the introduction of a preconstituted disposition, the super-ego. We all agree that the id—the unconscious—is innate. The super-ego, however, is connected to the ideal ego and may precede the ego.

Sidoli has described the activity of the super-ego in the case of a girl less than two years old and of a five-year-old boy. She points to the negative influences when, in response to aggressive tendencies, the super-ego exerts a disproportionate repression and induces a hastened adjustment to adult collective patterns. In contrast, when the super-ego acts in a positive manner, it benevolently adopts the authority principle and, coming to terms with weakness, allows a gradual delimitation of the power of the child's narcissism.

The authority principle is connected to the paternal figure, the determiner of order and chaos. Thus, the father archetype is active early in the child's life, unless the father does not connect concretely with the child. In the development of the personality, especially in the first phases of life, the idea of alternation between the maternal and paternal interventions is merely theoretical, because it does not take into account the timelessness of the unconscious. This statement is even more true if, instead of saying mother and father, we talk of feminine and masculine.

The education of children is one of the unrenounceable prerogatives of parents and society; it seems to have escaped the extreme permissiveness of the recent past. This time period has been confused and fundamentally revolutionary. Poorly understood psychoanalytic theory has contributed to placing all the blame on parents and society and removing responsibility from children.

At present we believe that we have a better knowledge of what education means: to allow and facilitate development in obedience to the child's physical and psychological nature and to the moral code. The code provides the norms of the historical-cultural context whose reality the person must acknowledge in order to establish a dynamic balance.

Therefore, in addition to the environmental influences, we must take into consideration the organic structure of the individual. As a physician I wonder, for instance, to what degree Ricky's psychological disorder was determined by his physical condition: his big head on a thin and emaciated body, his face wrinkled like that of an old man.

At the same time, we must not overlook the importance of frustration, imposed by the limitation of space and time, by illness, and by awareness of death. The super-ego expresses itself through these limitations. Some people maintain that Psychoanalysis is merely a kind of pedagogy. It is well known that Freud attributed a decisive therapeutic role to tolerance of frustration. I hope that the image of the gratifying Jungian is on its way to extinction, without devaluing either the therapeutic alliance—the one with the "grown child" within us—or the prospective dimension of the work.

In order for the alliance to work, the therapist must acquire a quality that is desirable for everyone but indispensable to therapists: humility. Beneath the technical competence, it is the analyst's human depth that counts, including teleological virtues that have always been explicit in religion and ethics. The analyst cannot take the role of the old sage who confines the other person to ignorance and shame; one must present oneself as a simple person who salvages, with difficulty, the lightness and irony of childhood.

To achieve these qualities, one must mediate between small and big. The small cannot be omitted without serious loss; it has an equal claim to existence. In the 1970s people used to say "small is beautiful" to show the correspondence between infinitely big and infinitely small, between the whole and its parts, between work and play. The big meaning is an attempt at an all-encompassing answer, but it is the sum of individual meanings. In order to obtain access to such goals one must confront the initial chaos that has both phylogenetic and ontogenetic roots and that can burst again, dramatically, into one's life at any moment. I am suspicious of those who think that they can single out ways and reasons why confusion and folly steal in suddenly; a strange language is not necessarily the fragmentary one of the child, but may be the unknowable one of the divine.

We must establish a dialectical relationship to the opposites. Ricky was not able to do that. Struck by the black-and-white contrast, he believed that he could transcend it by means of the gray or a chaotic mixture of colors. Such a mixture may imply archetypal fantasies of the primal scene; the coniunctio is felt by the one who has no access to it but to whom it is fascinating and terrifying.

The emphasis on the first phases of life and on the vertical relationship with the parents does not exclude the importance of other crucial moments, such as puberty. At that time the desire for and fear of becoming an adult trigger conflicts exacerbated by the power of the sexual urges.

Alfred Adler has told us of the psychological value of the horizontal relationship between siblings, of the social factors of the will to power. To understand these factors, it is necessary for us to keep them all in mind without adopting an ideology of privilege.

Recent years have shown us once more the devastating power of aggressivity, as Sidoli indicates. The optimism of the will must reckon with the pessimism of reason. War seems to be inescapable as if it belonged to a natural law that is impermeable to culture.

Freud wondered appropriately whether neuroses were the recapitulation of primordial fears. An unpublished manuscript from 1915 was found among Ferenczi's papers. It has been published in Italian with the title "Synthesis of Transference Neuroses." In it Freud showed that he was a good biologist of the psyche; he was attentive to Darwinian and Lamarckian formulations, with a preference for the latter. He formulated a phylogenetic fantasy, hypothesizing a parallel between the child's life and the childhood of humankind: The anguished hysteria of the first phases of life is the echo of the most remote past; the conversion hysteria that arises at around the age of four sends us back to the traumas of the glacial era; the obsessive neurosis that appears during puberty represents the end of the big chill and the uneasiness of civilization. Nevertheless, we continue to hope, invent, and act in order to feel alive. But we must also accept loss, which reintroduces the shadow that must be integrated.

Thus, I return to guilt. It exists only if there is a determined intention to damage oneself or another, whose freedom and will would be compromised, without any possibility for good to result. This intention is one of action and does not include the activity of the imagination.

It seems impossible to pursue the purposes of the ego, even the most sublime, without error or damage. Thus, evil belongs to life; it is included in the realm of shadow, is archetypal, and thus is a necessary entity. In this way, abandonment and guilt acquire a tolerable dimension, leaving us more aware and light-hearted in the face of life's questions.

Translated from Italian by
Guilia Colaizzi
and Jennette Jones

Black Shadow—
White Shadow

Martine Drahon Gallard (Paris)

I am sitting on the grass under the starry sky. The weather is very beautiful and I am letting myself be penetrated by the sweetness of the evening, by its scents and by the song of the cicadas. I am biting into an apple and I am watching my parents' bedroom window. I know that they are in bed and I am listening to any noise that could reach me. I am five years old.

The dreamer remembers the feelings that she had at that time of her life: the perception of being in harmony with the whole earth, the sensation of being dissolved into the smells, the colors. The adult world fascinated her and, as in the dream, she was alert to any sign that would make it possible for her to understand anything sensual or erotic in her parents' life.

Here we are in the presence of a primal scene phantasm which introduces us into the realm of desire, of human sexuality and of one's personal origin. The child's eyes are fixed on the parents' bedroom, expecting revelations and, of course, answers to the questions: "Where did I come from? Who did I come out of?"

This young Eve bites greedily into an apple as if she knew precociously that, in the likeness of her mythical mother, she was stealing some forbidden knowledge full of promise that she would find pleasure and the knowledge of Good and Evil. For it is by the discovery of our sexual identity and by setting up in ourselves the dynamics of the other sex through the interplay of anima/animus that each of us gains access to human knowledge and that we exercise our intelligence.

This dream shows the two fundamental components of the unconscious:

—Belonging to a family, being the third party in a couple's desire, a situation that shapes the most individual and the most primordial part of one's personality.
—Belonging to a cosmic world with all its elements: the mineral, the vegetable, and the animal world.

Between the two, the intermediary layers correspond to the different groups we belong to and, what I want to emphasize here more specifically, are the traces left in the unconscious by historical events.

The Shadow

The formation of the shadow starts from a root point in our individual history, as shown in the previous dream. This point allows the encounter between the two components of the archetype: the activation of the drive and its capacity for representations (imaging). These components use all the potential of the collective unconscious as matrix to representation. Bringing into play such a system allows the development of consciousness and its shadow, of personal experience and representation.

At the beginning of analysis we know that bringing the shadow into consciousness is not an easy matter; it requires the divestment of infantile objects and taking back whatever projections have been made onto others. The paranoid is the typical example of an individual who is unable to part from these projections and, therefore, is unable to build a shadow that would enable entry into subjectivity. The paranoid is dangerous because of this inability.

Only when one has become aware of inner duality, of the existence of an inner figure with whom it is possible to dialogue, can one begin to speak of one's own shadow. The shadow is what gives us our substance and human depth. One who is conscious of one's shadow is incarnate and, because of this, often feels crucified and diminished. Consequently, one must act, not only in relation to the conscious personality, but in relation to the content of the shadow which is often in contradiction with consciousness.

The integration of the shadow requires inventiveness and daring; it is a mercurian game in which what is desirable does not always come out as good and where evil is unavoidable. The relation between the ego and the shadow modifies both of them. This relation never ends, for it is a matter of structure; the shadow by definition will always remain dark.

This typically Jungian method of dealing with the unconscious gives to the treatment of the Freudian repressed and of primary object relations a very particular approach, using images in a dynamic way. In dreams these shadow figures, of the same sex as the subject, bring two kinds of information to us Jungians.

—Shadow figures give us information on infantile repression caused by implicit and explicit parental interdictions and by the censorial role of the subject's super-ego.

—The content and shape of the shadow figures refer to a world different from that of the patient. It uses ancestral, cultural, and collective imagination with all its creative and vital content. This way of looking at the unconscious opens to a new vision of the psyche which can now be seen in perspective; we can then have a dialogue with personifications of the shadow.

Thus, the ego acquires a greater flexibility and ceases to strangle the Self which, in my opinion, always comes out of the shadow. Paradoxically, the aim of individuation is not to make the shadow non-existent, but to come to know the shadow we cast and to know the effects it has on the ego and on other people. Familiarity with our shadow is an indication of our true subjectivity, of the place that we occupy in the world. The more conscious we are, the more aware we are of the weight and breadth of our shadow and of its effect on others.

A major point of Jung's theory of energy is that the psyche functions thanks to the tensions between two opposite poles. It is impossible to extend the field of consciousness without extending the field of the shadow. Each group and cultural circle we belong to has its norms, its values, its ideals and consequently its own shadow. This is what I call the BLACK SHADOW.

There is another shadow, however, a WHITE SHADOW that we cannot encompass. We encounter this shadow when a silence, a secret, something which cannot be named by one or both of the parents creates a blank, a hole in the psyche. This is in contrast to the repressed experience which would create a black stain, a shadow with a shape.

A patient with such a shadow requires analysis, specific work dealing with the unconscious of the parents and the grandparents. A French analyst, Dumas (1985), following the work of Nicholas and Maria Torok, calls this the "genealogical unconscious"; it appears to be situated between the personal unconscious and the collective unconscious of Jung. In the work on the genealogical unconscious we try to discover the affective event that was buried in the parents' unconscious, an experience that they were unable to communicate to their children even though it is quite important for them. This experience may have been too shameful or inhuman and the parents may have been unable to integrate it; it may even have remained unconscious.

What characterizes this moment of the analysis, what makes it possible to lift the repression, is the discovery of something foreign in the parent. It is a discovery in the other that gives access to an aspect of oneself. Like the missing part of the puzzle, it gives meaning to the whole. The subject comes to understand the parent and gains self-understanding. In "Analytical Psychology and Education" (CW17) Jung was very firm on the subject. He stated that, in case of neurotic symptoms in a child, the first thing to do is to deal with the parents' unconscious:

> Nothing influences children more than [the] silent facts in the background. . . . The children are infected indirectly through the attitude they instinctively adopt towards their parents' state of mind: they fight against it with unspoken protest (though occasionally the protest is vociferous) or else they succumb to a paralysing and compulsive imitation. In both cases they are obliged to do, to feel and to live not as *they* want but as their parents want. The more "impressive" the parents are, and the less they accept their own problems (mostly on the excuse of "sparing the children"), the longer the children will have to suffer from the unlived life of their parents and the more they will be forced into fulfilling all the things the parents have repressed and kept unconscious. . . . The repressed problems

and the suffering thus fraudulently avoided secrete an insidious poison. (pars. 153–54).

What appears right and quite normal to us now is astonishing compared to the Freudian approach of that time, which attributed to the child the origins of neurotic phantasms and was not concerned with the unconscious state of the parents. For Freud, it all happened in the actual memories and the chance libidinal fixations; this view was sustained by the thought that such a development is supported by a structure culminating in the Oedipus complex. Jung's statement, which was written in 1924 and revised in 1945, shows the child's extreme susceptibility to the parents' unconscious. In the cases that I will discuss, the parents' silence created a blank; I will attempt to show how the missing link in the genealogical chain was restored.

Mark was seven years old. He had not learned to read and write or even to recognize colors, in spite of a normal intelligence. His mother brought him to the sessions; she showed a great deal of aggressiveness. She talked about Mark's laziness and ill will. Eventually she said that Mark was not the son of her present husband, with whom she had two other children. Mark had his mother's birth name and the other children had the father's name, but Mark was not expected to notice this anomaly. His mother never explained this to him because she was afraid that he would reject the man he thought of as his father. Consciously, she wanted Mark to have access to knowledge, but she did not want him to know the story of his origins.

Faced with the difficulty of this couple and the pressing need of the child for therapeutic help, I started therapy without demanding that the secret be revealed immediately, but I asked the parents to tell the boy when they were ready.

Therapy started very quickly with explicit drawings. They depicted a woman who had killed or chased away a man. Mark described this image in numerous ways and always with a lot of emotion. I only intervened to bring out associations, but without stating that he was telling me his own story. I thought that it was up to the parents to make this revelation. At the same time that he was able to give shape to his story, to tell it to his therapist, he began to learn in school, to understand what his teacher was saying. Until then his teacher had thought that he was mentally defective. Expressing his unconscious knowledge in a metaphor and experiencing it in the transference had allowed him to gain access to learning. Once he had done his inner work and his inhibitions in school had diminished, his parents were able to talk to him about his origins.

There are more complicated cases where the missing link is related to collective events. Some people cannot tell us their story because it has been stolen from them. Nobody in particular and at the same time everybody has done this. It is History with a capital H. Historical events have distorted the personal history of a person who was implanted in a particular place, with a precise environment, a specific family, a particular body. The link that attached the individual to the line of generations has been broken, disconnected by the violence of human collective actions — actions belonging to nobody and also to everybody. "Someone" stole their history. This way of putting it describes well the feeling of dispossession and the anguish attached to it: There is something somewhere that belongs to you, that is part of you, but you don't know where to look for the key to the enigma of your suffering.

What has been imprinted and then lost pursues us like a ghost. Such deprived beings feel exposed to all winds. They are not able to set boundaries, with an inside and an outside. What I am describing may apply to all neurotic persons in certain respects, but in the neurotic person this state is caused by repression; the knowledge one seeks is within oneself. The neurotic lived through an experience which engraved traces and left memories that can be restored through analysis. This is the part of the unconscious explored by Freud, for which he gave us a powerful tool of understanding. Such is not the case of the persons I am talking about.

Marie had difficulty in establishing an inner world. She was 30 years old and recently divorced. She had started a new profession and had an ovary removed. She was in a severe state of uncertainty and anguish. From the beginning, her attitude of mistrust toward me as her analyst was so extreme that I wondered if she (we) would be able to overcome it.

Her initial dream already bears the mark of the forbidden: *My father tells me to close the door, to beware. I notice that the room where we both are has a closed gate, then another door, and finally an open door*. It was only after the analysis had begun that I understood how heavy was the paternal interdiction and that opening the doors of Marie's unconscious meant to unveil a secret about her father.

It was not a total secret, since she had some knowledge of it through her mother. Her paternal grandfather had committed suicide when his son was only nine years old. But this fact remained surrounded by mysteries and with many questions unanswered. She had not heard the fact from her father and she felt that he had cut off his access to his suffering and to the psychic consequences it had for him. Something was broken inside him and he had been unable to rebuild the link to his father to find healing. He was still in mourning; his daughter had inherited a series of closed doors that functioned like a hole in her psyche, inside of which lived a ghost. She could be said to be partly excluded from her own psyche.

Marie's story was rendered more complicated by the war situation in which she had lived. Born in Algeria, she had witnessed several acts of terrorism, she had heard gunshots, and most of all, she had suffered from the anguish of her parents in this situation. She explained her present state by the traumas she had lived through, and her fear of men by the fear of Arabs which she had been taught as a young girl. It is in this context that I speak of a stolen personal history. In Marie's case, she needed a great deal of time to let go of the crutch of explanation by trauma and to reach the part of her animus that was kept in prison by her father's neurosis. She was invaded by a white shadow produced by collective events that were beyond herself. She was also invaded by her father's secret which deprived her of a part of herself. These were communicated to her from unconscious to unconscious. As long as she was a captive of the white shadow, she was unable to look inside herself and to gain access to her own intra-psychic productions.

Our Destiny, Our Desires Are Shaped by History

Michael, 23 years old, asked for psychotherapy for various kinds of somatizations, sleep disturbances and anxiety. His parents were quite representative of the political and social trends

of our times. His mother was from Paris, Jewish, Marxist; his father from Algeria, a member of the Algerian National Liberation
militia during the Algerian war. Their meeting ground was their
common ideal of the liberation of humanity. Their love did not
survive the end of the war and the liberation of Algeria. Living
in the new independent country, they wanted to take part in its
organization, but now the collective was unable to help them
avoid the clash of their antagonistic cultural backgrounds. They
separated. The young man before me was the product of this an-
tagonism. On the collective level he was the link between two
communities that excluded each other and that were hereditary
enemies. This case of a cross-bred individual enabled me to get
a better understanding of the intricacies of personal and collective identifications in the mental structure of the individual.

This degree of complexity is difficult to live with. Michael lived
in Paris with his mother; he excluded his father from his immediate field of consciousness. Michael explained how he had lived,
torn by an anguish bordering on physical sickness, when, for example, he had to respond to acts of terrorism between Israel and
Palestine. He said that he was unable to take the part of one side
against the other without coming close to fainting. As a young
boy becoming conscious of the split world in which he lived, he
could only choose one and exclude the other, while waiting for
something better. He chose his Jewish identity, rejecting his
Arab name. In this way he recovered some kind of unity.

He came for consultation at a time when, having started to
study history, he did not know how to consider his own future.
He could not go on living without building a bridge over the split
which he had created in himself between the defects of his primal
scene and the representations which derived from it. Listening
to this young man, I was thinking about his parents. They met
because of their common political commitment, because they
had desired to promote unity and fraternity among peoples.
What they projected into their action expressed a split within
themselves, a lack of something, a great suffering, the urge to repair something in the outside world corresponding to their inner
wounds. Their son represented their attempt at union, but they
had only provided very few meeting points for him and he had
to build his own bridges or face inner dissociation.

The archetypal structures responsible for our development

must be filled by human contents. The fundamental mother and father archetypes must come into contact with differentiated human beings. If the real persons embodying these archetypes have not been satisfactory, the child must call upon collective representations. Social and political commitment may fill this need.

I am especially interested in the influence on the psyche of history and collective experience. Because I am French, born during the Second World War, and my father died in a concentration camp, I have been confronted directly with the phenomenon of cultural and parental silence concerning what happened during that war. I know how difficult it is to constitute a shadow for one's self.

Independently from our personal histories, we are all victims of this century's history. We have to understand what happened and deal with its "inheritance." In this search for understanding, I was very impressed by Alice Miller's (1985) book *For Your Own Good*. She painted a frightening picture of the methods of education of past centuries. She showed how each of us tends to repeat the kind of life we were required to live.

The child who has been too strictly trained, and has not been able to rely on personal feelings and sensations will do anything as an adult rather than experience them. In order to avoid them the person will be ready to obey any order that comes from someone in a paternal position; avoidance of thinking and obedience will be an absolute principle. Such a person will go as far as persecuting others, without realizing it, because in this mental system feelings must be cut off. This psychological attitude endures only because it preserves a certain idealization of the parents. As children, it was of the utmost importance not to notice that we were mistreated and despised by our parents. The hate that might result could bring about the other person's destruction and the collapse of oneself.

On this subject, Jung says: "The libido that is withdrawn so unwillingly from the 'mother' turns into a threatening serpent, symbolizing the fear of death—for the relation to the mother must cease, *must die* and this is almost the same as dying oneself" (CW5, par. 473).

The stakes are so high that it is difficult to take such a risk. We prefer to know nothing and to project on to others the evil of the world. This relentless repetiton is enough to make us shudder, but because of its logic, we can find a way to dismantle it.

Miller (1985) showed in a detailed way that all of the great leaders of the Third Reich were submitted to such an education. "Honesty and courage, etc. are not mental categories or virtues; they are the consequence of a destiny more or less favorable. An individual who is alive is able to be only himself. He does not want to lose himself" (p. 105).

People whose childhood has been destroyed cannot help but pursue in others their own weakness and their lost child. Thus, although it is difficult to accept, atrocities, cruelty and persecutions are human actions, not really foreign to the ordinary person. We are shocked by these atrocities, as if they were inconceivable. But I rather agree with Woody Allen when he imagines the following dialogue in his 1986 movie "Hannah and Her Sisters": "How could there be so much evil in the world?" asked some one. Another person answered: "Knowing humanity I wonder why there is not more of it."

The question therefore is: How do these collective atrocities concern me and what can I do with them? Their intensity and enormity leaves us speechless and unable to act. They seem to be of a different essence; we cannot imagine that we or any one close to us would be able to commit such acts—could even consider it—and derive pleasure from it. The kind of fascination created by such acts defies reasoning.

It seems to me that we could undo this fear-fascination, which leaves the problem untouched, only by entering into communication with the destructive violence and the splitting of the schizo-paranoid position within ourselves. If we are able to let rise in ourselves the violence that grabbed us in confronting the frustration and the desire we felt to tear up the mother's breast, these atrocities will become a little less strange to us. We will be able to feel the humiliation and the pain.

There is, however, a world between wanting to kill someone and doing it. Human beings try with all their might to forget that they have had the desire to kill. It is not acceptable morally and it happened in the archaic past, when they felt in great danger of disintegrating. They do not like to remember the despair they felt or how dependent they were on their mothers, especially if they blamed her for something. But these feelings do exist inside us. The most common way to try to master them is to project them onto someone else and create a scapegoat. This enables us to feel unified, without contradictions, identical with our conscience, and with a well-delineated inner space. The ones that are like me are good. The others, who are different, are dangerous and should be destroyed. They are the shadow, as opposed to light; from the shadow, from the night come the monsters.

Something that I have noticed in my practice seems to confirm what I have said above on the schizo-paranoid position. People who suffered as children because of unsatisfactory relationships with their parents use in their phantasms, in their representations, images borrowed from the concentration camps: tortures, ghettos, sealed wagons, gas chambers. These seem to be the aptest collective images to account for what a child might have suffered from the conscious or unconscious persecution of the parents. That someone physically and psychically thousands of miles from war and concentration camps dreams of entering a gas chamber perplexes me. When the same person wakes up and realizes that the dream is an adequate picture of existential anguish and that it connects to the feeling of insecurity and affective threat experienced in childhood I think that, in spite of our denials, these states are not far from us.

Sometimes I have been able to feel, even in homeopathic doses, that the Nazi atrocities might have the same origins as a display of disproportionate rage caused by suffering. Then I have felt depressed, without recourse. Is there nowhere a bit of good that is inalienable? I have been invaded by fear and I have become conscious that this fear made me more sensitive to murderous madness. I become more vulnerable but also more able to recognize this madness and defend myself from it.

Concerning the genocide of the Jews, a question keeps coming back and Bettelheim (1979) asked it very clearly in his book *Survival*: How is it that this whole community did not organize itself to resist? How could they believe in the pacifying words that were said to them? I am not going to answer this question. The fact that it is asked, however, means that there are other possible choices and that our thinking is not paralyzed by the weight of obedience to ancestral stereotypes such as "We have to believe our parents. They want what is good for us. The leaders have to be believed and obeyed." Thus we become accomplices to the destructive actions that others exert against us.

"There is, in my opinion, no ground for the assumption that Eros is genuine and the will to power is bogus" wrote Jung (CW7, par. 42). But it is very difficult for us to accept it.

Tales and myths, however, tell us all the time about monsters, dragons, powers of evil that we have to defeat, that we have to face and change into a different shape. The other one, the stranger, the evil one, the enemy has been our traveling companion since the beginning of humankind. Only very rarely has humanity found a livable arrangement in the confrontation with enemies. But we do not read enough fairy tales. We are too serious and too convinced of our intellectual superiority. It is this absence of mythical reference that makes us prey to the white shadow. In the Judaeo-Christian world we despise evil and try to eliminate it from the human heart. The study of myths of another culture is a precious antidote and enables us to realize better the content of our own collective shadow.

I have been surprised to find that the Hindus in the Nahabarata are able to stage the destructive sides of life. Life is conceived of as a battle, a game where powers come into play in a positive or negative way, depending on the way in which they are used. The Hindus do not possess a sense of individual narcissistic identity, where one believes oneself to be the center of the universe. Rather they understand themselves as the place where the components of humanity are incarnated. They are bearers of something they must transmit. Their life is an element in the cycle of repeated transformations. The forces of destruction are as important as the forces of life; the Hindus have gods to represent both.

This inverted mirror is very interesting to us. This Archimedean point of view enables us to look at ourselves from the outside in a more objective way. Each civilization produces a specific zone of repression different from any other. The complexes arrange themselves in different ways, even if we can recognize the same nuclear structures of the psyche.

Earlier I quoted Jung: "Repressed problems and the suffering . . . fraudulently avoided secrete an insidious poison" (CW17, par. 154). I hope that I have shown how experience — traumatic reality — which is not suffered and not made conscious creates a history in the line of descent; it reaches the children in

the guise of a white shadow. By this I mean the unconscious contents, the complexes are the affective support of the subject. By
their noxious quality, these contents hinder the formation of the
subject's shadow. This process creates a feeling of the unreality
of existence, a dull anguish, an atrophy of feelings and sensations and a compensatory hyperdevelopment of the intellectual
function.

In some cases, there is identification with the hidden part of the
parent's story. Thus a daughter, through her anorexia, will come
to weigh as little as her mother weighed at the same age—in a
concentration camp. This white shadow can create serious
somatizations, such as some types of cysts in the body similiar
to cancer growths. In analysis, I have noticed that it is difficult for
these persons to approach this particular question. After mentioning their origins they do not bring up the subject again, as if
there were nothing more to say about it. They can talk about their
little personal stories all they want; this does not change in depth
their life problem. It is up to the analyst to suggest that it might
be beneficial to look into the dramas that occurred earlier instead
of disposing of them so quickly. Then sometimes we have rivers
of tears. The analysand did not know that this was so important.

In conclusion, I would like to discuss something which I believe is important, which I think is partly a consequence of the
white shadow of our century and which influences our choice of
values and the direction of our thoughts. I have found in the texts
of the German analysts A. and M. Mitscherlich, in the book *The
Impossible Mourning* (1972) an analysis related to my own reflections. "There is a cause and effect link between political and social ultra-conservatism or the backwardness that reigns now in
West Germany, on one side—and on the other side the stubborn
negation of certain memories, specifically the barrier against an
affective participation in facts of the past that have actually been
totally negated" (p. 9). These authors also see Germany's frantic
race toward material success as a result of its being unable to lean
on tradition.

Western people have in the shadow, regardless of history, an
executioner who watches and persecutes. We use all our intelligence to repress this dangerous enemy. To this end, we develop
in a grotesque way our knowledge and our know-how to exploit
our planet. We have expended our fantasy in the outer world, to

conquer space. We have robbed the people of the Third World and we are pushing ahead everywhere as conquerors. We are unable to understand the evil which our shadow carries and we are surprised to see aggressivity rising everywhere. In other words, we are afraid of our potential for evil, of death and of old age; we prefer the illusion of eternal youth.

This collective shadow is evident in the education system that we choose for our children. Television feeds them with aggressive stories; war and murder are their everyday images. But as parents, we take great care to respect their development and not to inflict any restraint on them, but we also repress severely the expression of their personal and collective aggressivity, not by blows, but by a very subtle moral constraint.

We want to protect our dear children from evil, from insecurity, from suffering, but we push them toward culture. They must be scholars; they must have degrees. Thus, they need the best schools possible, the best informed teachers, possessions, money. All you have to do is to listen to parents during analytic sessions and you hear the stereotype that our consumer society fosters. None of us can escape, because this model is stronger than we think. Movements of return to nature, on the one hand, and increasing numbers of acts of terrorism, on the other, seem to be attempted answers to the constraints we are subjected to.

Our civilized world is dominated by the supremacy of the ego. Adaptation has become an obsession with us. We are standardized, unidimensional. Our mind works fast and is used to all kinds of calisthenics. It works horizontally, allowing all combinations from the significant to the meaningless. But the vertical dimension, that which relies on history and takes its significance from the past, makes our mind feel much less clever. But access to the collective dimension of the unconscious and the activation of the polarity between the ego and the Self is a much more difficult balance.

I said that our children are condemned to culture. I should have said to "knowledge"; culture implies exactly this dimension of history, of taking root in the evolution of our thought with its complexities and its reversals, and it implies that a shadow is taking shape.

Here is an obvious split in our modern world: There are the people who have enough to eat and those who do not. This division fits into my color metaphor: The whites are masters of technique; they eat more than necessary to appease their hunger and spend energy and money to lose weight. The other races barely make ends meet. But that does not stop them from laughing and from transcending this unsteady life in a way which does not seem reasonable to us at all. But does our reason help us to understand the world better and to organize it better? We need a little more humility in regard to what we judge incoherent behavior.

We spend our days with beings who suffer and come to us asking to be delivered from their sufferings, from the moral anguish that they experience. I sometimes think that they simply ask me to be delivered from living. Fortunately, when the weight of their neurosis becomes lighter, they no longer wonder if they suffer. I am happy when an analysand is delivered from a self-imposed burden and acquires balance that makes possible a view of the world, a pleasure in understanding it and finding an active role in it.

Is not one of the values of Jung's Analytical Psychology that it provides us with tools to understand the collective dimensions of our lives?

Translated from French by
Paula Kondrick

REFERENCES

Bettelheim, B. (1979). *Survival*. Paris: Laffont.

Dumas, D. (1985). *L'ange et le fantôme*. Paris: Edition de Minuit.

Miller, A. (1985). *C'est pour ton bien: Racines de la violence dans l'éducation de l'enfant*. Paris: Aubier.

Mitscherlich, A. et M. (1972). *Le deuil impossible: Les fondements du comportement collectif*. Paris: Payot.

Discussion: Verena Kast (Zürich)

The concept of the black shadow that Drahon submitted is a familiar one: The shadow contains the repressed, the infantile or what was presented to us as infantile; it contains that which our parents have forbidden us explicitly or implicitly and also whatever does not correspond to our own ideal ego. Therefore, it has to be repressed. In addition, we always belong to groups, cultural circles, social strata, and historical time. Each of these categories has norms, values, and ideals that they represent and that therefore exclude other norms and values — their shadows. The white shadow presents more difficulties to the understanding, when we take seriously the statement that one cannot encircle the white shadow. It is important to some therapeutic experiences but difficult to grasp. In trying to understand the white shadow, I felt powerless and furious. Perhaps these feelings represent a form of countertransference with this "white shadow"; if that is so, perhaps it also characterizes the emotions of other people who have to deal with this shadow.

As I understand Drahon's idea of the white shadow that cannot be encircled, it is created when parents have secrets, when certain things must not be talked about. This creates a "hole" in the psychic functioning. The hole is the mark of the white shadow in contrast to the black shadow, which is formed. Something that causes shame to the parents cannot be conveyed to the children, even though they are affected. The parents' emotions may be unconscious to them also. By analyzing the unconscious of parents and grandparents — the genealogical unknown — this repression is removed. The discovery of the alien element in the lives of the parents then leads to the discovery of a part of oneself. Without these discoveries, the children live their parents' lives instead of their own. This white shadow, visualized as a phantom or a ghost, prevents the formation of the personal shadow. The result is a feeling of the unreality of existence, combined with deep fear, avoidance of feelings and an overstressing of the intellect. Thus, Drahon has described some essential aspects of the psychodynamics of people who suffered a disturbance in their early parent-child relationship.

Now my reflections. It is of great importance to our analytic work that we consider the effect of the secrets that are handed down from one generation to another. These secrets can nurture many fantasies and be a source of constant insecurity. Drahon's cases demonstrate their effects. Yet not all secrets have the same impact and secrets will function in different ways according to the quality of parent-child relationships. Further, either the secret itself or the approach to the secret has to be special in order to produce a white shadow. Not every secret has such consequences in the next generation.

Drahon speaks of the defense mechanism of mild denial, and connects it with splitting and with projection. The parents would then have avoided a lifelong problem, by inflicting a "hole" on themselves. Subsequently, however, Drahon says that, if one analyzes the unconscious of the parents and grandparents—here I would like to know how she would go about this—the "repression" is removed. The repression, however, was mentioned previously in connection with the formation of the black, formed shadow.

Evidently, this white shadow is so packed up or stowed away that the person cannot form a personal shadow. This supposition is supported by the statement that these children live the lives of their parents instead of their own.

Two questions force themselves upon me: Is it true that these children cannot develop their own shadows? Or is it rather that they cannot separate themselves and their ego-complex from the parent-complexes at the appropriate age, so that they continue to identify with these complexes? The consequence would be that they cannot form a personal shadow and they would obey unquestioningly. Formed shadows presuppose a structured ego. During puberty and adolescence the person lives the shadow complexes of the parents and of society. Eventually, these complexes become integrated into the ego complex. Then a separation from the parents takes place, which allows a re-connection later on. If the ego-complex is not sufficiently coherent, if it is tangled up with the intangible shadow of the parents, then such a development cannot take place and no individual shadow can be formed.

I suggest that we call in Asper's (1986) concept of the shadow in narcissistic disturbances, in relation to Drahon's description of the white shadow. Asper mentioned that narcissistic people do not have shadows, but are within the shadow, feeling unloved and guilty. Correlated to these feelings are hatred, fury, jealousy, fear, and lack of a safe basis in life. These people have no clear-cut shadow figures to connect with the Self, as a compensation for the conscious standpoint. When making this connection, Drahon postulates that family secrets contribute to this narcissistic form of psychic development. Or conversely: In the case of narcissistic people, family secrets have inhibited the personal development even more.

Drahon carries her argument one step further: There are people who cannot talk about their own history because it has been taken away from them by the history of the world. This lost knowledge now persecutes them like a phantom or a ghost and leads to a state where they cannot sufficiently separate the outer world from the inner life. She gives the example of Marie who experienced the incidents of war in a traumatic way and therefore could not approach a secret of her father's. In this case, war incidents covered up inner experience with similar base themes—death, violence, despair, fear.

What is to be understood here by the white shadow? Access to the personal history and the family shadow cannot be found because the collective shadow has had such an important impact upon experience. I think, however, that the two traumas experienced by Marie cannot be separated from each other because they relate to the same complex.

In the concept of the white shadow, denial is not so much in the foreground, but rather repression, displacement and fixation onto a collective happening. Individual responsibility—the personal possibilities for change and awareness—cannot be perceived. This example indicates that collective historical events can cause the personal history to fade into the background, yet that the emotional significance of personal experiences can be magnified enormously by world history. As a consequence, an approach to these personal problems, especially to shadows, is no longer possible. Further, these collective cruelties cannot be understood as solely the shadow of an individual person, even though that person participates in them.

And yet the task presents itself to contact this destructive force within oneself. What needs to be denied so steadily, according to Drahon, is the destructive force that we have developed in early childhood in the face of a threat to our life. She makes a connection between the cruelties that were committed in the Nazi period, for example, and the homicidal impulses of the infant who wants to tear the mother's breast out of fury due to frustration. In this context I point out a paper by Hans Dieckmann (1986) about the enemy figure. In reflecting which archetypal structure underlies the enemy figure and in view of the feelings that we connect with this, he postulated that there is more at the root of it than the fury of the infant about the absent breast. The images triggering the destructive aggression are the negative side of the Great Mother. She is experienced as devouring, dismembering, enslaving, cannibalistic. This image, Dieckmann wrote, is projected on our enemies and then wakens in us the destructive impulses to protect our own life, to delimit our own territory. This demonic element of the mother archetype that originates in the imagination is brought into interaction with the concrete mother during the course of development and can also turn positive abruptly and then form the basis for the friend figure.

Basically, this destructive force is a matter of a reaction to a fundamental threat. I refer to the theses of both Drahon and Dieckmann. Genetically speaking, this form of experiencing is to be placed at the time when splitting is the predominant defense mechanism, where the child still spits out the evil object. With the individual, an empathic response to fear and a building up of the sheltered aspects may help to deal with this destructive feature, but not to master it. It is a matter of experiencing the good-bad mother as imaginary and as concrete also (See Mara Sidoli's paper in this volume). Thus, we do not identify with the attacker within us nor act out our destructiveness. It is a matter of empathic handling of fear, of our life possibilities, and of our destructiveness.

In conclusion, Drahon reflects on the effect of the white shadow in our century. Here again, she mentions the splitting of the bad, the attacker that we all have in our psyche, and the formation of compensation in the domain of our intelligence and of our myth of unlimited powers. She also links this splitting to the inability to mourn. In view of these ideas I propose some theses regarding the effects of historical events on individual shadow-formation.

1. Thesis: History in the largest sense is part of our lives. It includes political history, social history, the history of ideas and of ideologies. These influence one another and also create an atmosphere into which we have been born. This is an aspect of our destiny.

2. Thesis: Every form of this history creates an ideal; thus the shadow is already present. This "shadow" is the basis of what we call development or change. For example, in art history, naturalism is followed by abstract art, the latter by photo-realism; an especially subtle, dreamy phase is followed perhaps by the neo-primitives.

3. Thesis: All possible forms of historical development, and the confrontation with them, stamp the philosophy of life of the parents. By arguing with our parents, we are also coming to terms with yesterday's history; we tackle collective values and a collective shadow. Personal and collective shadows are closely linked, almost inseparable. Certain aspects of the shadow are in the foreground. The shadow of the parents may be processed, repressed, split by them—some of each is perhaps always the case—and thus the shadow-like becomes a task for the next generation, so that a new dynamic equilibrium between the ideal and the shadow is reached.

4. Thesis: A shadow-theme that is currently very stirring is the world-wide force of destruction. Yet it is not the only current shadow-theme, and a person has the possibility of surpassing these brutal forms of encounter. War history is really the history of the destructive shadow. People whose lives are prescribed by warlike situations and their accompanying cruelties are shadowed in their historical identities, not necessarily because of secrets, but because of features that are too shameful, too mortifying, possibly also because the individual has a hard time gaining distance from the effects of being human; one can never answer for that as a whole. As expressed in the discussion on the white shadow, I feel that here also the ego is taken in by a shadow without outline, and that this situation is so agonizing that a resort to the time before the shadowing—and for the Germans that would be the time before Hitler—is not possible. To this shadowing in historical identity, by the way, often corresponds a demand for a very high morality in one's personal life, which of course again creates new shadows. It is probably

often the next generation that can take a look at this shadow and can deal with it more empathically. Furthermore, I think that the analysis of this shadow becomes the task of all people—and thus also spreads to the non-participating peoples—as a human eventuality that has turned into reality and frightens everyone. This involves unpleasant feelings that in turn have to be warded off. As the defense mechanisms of splitting, projection, and delegation are used collectively and employed politically, the individual cannot withdraw from this shadow-anxiety by long-practiced defense mechanisms of splitting. Thus, we return to the starting point.

Translated from German by
Yvonne Cherne

REFERENCES

Asper, K. (1986). Narzissmus und Schatten problematik. *Zeitschrift für Analytische Psychologie, 17–1,* 1–24.
Dieckmann, H. (1986). *Gedanken über den Begriff des "Feindbildes." Zeitschrift für Analytische Psychologie, 17–1,* 25–38.

Archetypal Foundations of Projective Identification

Nathan Schwartz-Salant (New York)

In 1946 Melanie Klein (1975) coined the term *projective identification*. In the same year Jung published the "Psychology of the Transference" (CW16). Klein's paper employed the mother/infant object-relation and a conception of "parts" of one person put into and identified with another person, the process of projective identification. Jung's study employed the arcane symbolism of alchemy to grasp the same phenomenology. Klein's paper, as Meltzer (1973) has noted, had an "electrifying impact [upon] the analysts who were closely working with her" (p. 20). Jung's hardly had such an impact. For most Jungians, let alone analysts of other schools of thought, his alchemical model often seems too abstracted for here-and-now clinical practice. Yet in Jung's study of the transference, I believe that we can find an approach to the phenomenology of projective identification which richly elaborates the findings of Klein and other psychoanalysts for whom the concept is central.

Projective identification is a psychic mechanism whereby the self experiences the unconscious fantasy of translocating itself, or aspects of itself, into an object for exploratory or defensive purposes. Projective identification can lead to a state of confusion, to a weakening of consciousness that allows for emotional flooding by unconscious processes. In extreme instances a relationship dominated by projective identification can trigger psychotic episodes. Through projective identification one has the unconscious fantasy of being invisible. This can become extreme, leading to a sense of a "loss of soul" and a terror that the self can never be found.

Negative aspects of projective identification, such as confusion, identity loss or panic often appear dominant. However, projective identification also has the power, as Gordon (1965) has explained, to break down inner psychic boundaries as well as between a person and the object world. This breakdown of structures is essential to any qualitative personality change.

Gordon noted that Jung's *participation mystique*, unconscious identity, psychic infection and induction are synonyms for projective identification. She also pointed out the process Jung called *feeling-into* as representing positive aspects of projective identification, here underlying esthetic awareness (CW6, par. 486), and empathy. I believe that his work on alchemical proesses can significantly expand our understanding of this key clinical phenomenon.

Jung often stressed negative features of what Klein called projective identification. His goal in therapy, as stated in his commentary to the *Secret of the Golden Flower*, is the dissolution of participation mystique (CW13, pars. 65–66). But this goal appears questionable; Jung explained that, once the Self becomes the center of personality, participation mystique is done away with and "results in a personality that only suffers in the lower storeys, as it were, but in its upper storey is singularly detached from painful as well as from joyful happenings" (CW13, par. 67). It would appear from this statement that accepting a degree of mind-body splitting is the price one must pay for doing away with processes of projective identification.

In these remarks Jung was centering upon what he called the "compulsion and impossible responsibility" (CW13, par. 78) that can accompany interactions dominated by participation mystique. Then again, in his study of the *Visions of Zosimos*, Jung struck a different tone and regarded participation mystique as underlying alchemical projections which "are a special instance of the mode of thinking typified by the idea of the microcosm" (CW13, par. 123). Generally, Jung was aware of the potentially creative and destructive aspects of participation mystique, and thus of the phenomenology of projective identification. He was influenced by both possibilities to a strong degree in his analysis of the alchemical imagery from the *Rosarium Philosophorum*, his

Ariadne thread through the complexities of the transference (CW16, par. 401). The dominant image there is of a hermaphrodite, which often represents the soul or *vinculum*, the linking aspect between male and female opposites, and between mind and body. The hermaphrodite can represent negative fusion states, but also sublime states of union, both of which can include projective identification.

"Psychology of the Transference" (CW16), Jung's main statement on the transference, is centrally concerned with the phenomenology of projective identification. There he addressed unconscious processes that "have an inductive effect on the unconscious of . . . the doctor" (CW16, par. 363). This theme repeats itself in variations throughout his study (e.g. pars. 364, 365, 367).

Jung described the phenomenology of projective identification as activating the unconscious and the archetypal transference. "The doctor becomes affected, and has as much difficulty in distinguishing between the patient and what has taken possession of him as has the patient himself. . . . The activated unconscious appears as a flurry of unleashed opposites (such as hate and love) and calls forth an attempt to reconcile them, so that, in the words of the alchemists, the great panacea, the *medicinia catholica*, may be born" (CW16, par. 375). Thus, the Self may be born out of the process initiated by projective identification as it uncovers the prized states of the *nigredo* and *massa confusa* (CW16, pars. 376, 383, 387).

Since this paper employs Jung's approach to the *Rosarium*, I want to emphasize that he used this alchemical set of woodcuts and associated commentaries in a most extraordinary way. The alchemical tradition only rarely employed two people working together; there was certainly little expressed concern for mutual processes. This tradition, like Tantricism with which the imagery of the *Rosarium* has important similarities, was primarily interested in the union of opposites within the individual; interpersonal interactions would have been, at best, a tool along this path. Yet Jung took the *Rosarium* as a series of images representing the unconscious process between two people. I think that represented a great stroke of genius. But we are led to follow up the implications of his model. In this regard we must recognize that alchemical speculations addressed processes in what they

termed the subtle body. Jung's analogy was to the linking between anima and animus, not the conscious personalities of two
people. Yet, the problematic issue that we must focus upon is
that of where such processes occur. They do not take place inside
or outside individuals. As Deri (1978) has emphasized in her critique of D. W. Winnicott's idea of transitional phenomena, transitional phenomena cannot be located either inside, outside or
even in between people. These phenomena refer to another
dimension of existence that can only be perceived with the eye
of imagination. In fact, notions of location are inadequate to begin with.

Generally speaking, the alchemist's approach addressed
processes in a *third area*. They called this area Mercurius; he also
was the process occurring there and his transformation was a
goal of the opus. My main point in this paper is that projective
identification has the goal of transforming the third area. We may
often refer to it as "in between" two people, or as a transitional
area, for it can sometimes be experienced in this way. But the
more deeply it is entered, the more such spatial considerations
vanish. We are dealing here with an imaginal world, a *mundus
imaginalis* that has its own processes and can also evolve. Individuals can partake of its processes. Indeed, as Jung said,
when two parties get involved in the transformation of the third,
Mercurius, they themselves are transformed in the process
(CW16, par. 399). Mercurius or the subtle body is usually a hidden area through which projections pass, as Jung (1939) explained. Alchemical speculations addressed its reality and its
transformation, for which projective identification was a vital
force.

Projective identification, wrote Grotstein (1982), may be employed for exploratory or defensive purposes. "Employed defensively, projective identification rids the contents of one's mind
or, when the experience is severe, the mind itself. An object,
hitherto separate, becomes either the container for the negated
contents, or confused with it through identification" (p. 124).

Such workings of projective identification can be painful to the
object who is to be the "container" for contents projected into it
by the subject. Here is an example.

A man began a conversation with me, midway through which
he paused. This pause appeared suddenly; in the context of our

conversation it would have been more natural for him to have continued with a remark or some question. He behaved as if nothing was wrong. It soon seemed that each of us wanted the other to say something. As he looked at me I began to feel awkward. The pause rapidly became more painful. I felt called upon somehow to bridge what was becoming intolerable.

During the painful pause, projective identification was occurring. He was putting his blank mind into me, attempting to use me as a container for his absence or mental blankness that overtook him midway in our conversation. He was putting this absence, encased as it was in a paranoid shell, into me, and then watching me while hoping I would somehow give him his (functioning) mind back. Consequently, when I said something to disengage and end the encounter, he was angry. I was left with the guilty feeling that I had failed a test; I then felt coerced to return to emotional contact with him and somehow repair the break between us. He did not get his mind back during the pause. But his anger jarred him out of his schizoid state and into more affective contact. Thus, the event just passed by, unintegrated in its meaning and certain to occur again.

As important as it is for communication, projective identification has a larger role: It is goal oriented. It can both create and break down imaginal structures between two people, structures that are as real as the phenomenon itself. These structures, like dreams, are normally unseen in waking or consensual consciousness.

For example, in the previous vignette of aspects of a person's mind being projected into me, one could imagine an unconscious structure defining our interactional field: an image of a hermaphrodite with one body and two heads, familiar from the alchemical woodcuts from the *Rosarium* (McLean, 1980). The conjoined body could be an image of the fusion desires between us which I felt in the form of a need somehow to maintain contact with the man, while the two heads could represent the contrary tendency toward splitting, evidenced in my desire to lose contact with him in order to avoid the pain of mental blankness.

Projective identification can initiate the process of gaining access to and transforming interactive fields of linking or relation. These fields are imaged, for example, by the couples in the *Rosarium*. The alchemical process is devoted to overcoming the dangers of fusion states, of the tendency to concretize process in the third area into something belonging to the ego. The entire process may be seen as a continual refinement of the hermaphrodite's shadow side, which is a regressive fusion with the ego personality. Jung was extremely critical of this aspect of the hermaphrodite in "Psychology of the Transference" (CW16).

The existence of what we know as projective identification was crucial for the initiation of the alchemical opus. Apprehending it was synonymous with the *fixing* of Mercurius, and could result in finding the *prima materia* or the *massa confusa*, or of arriving at the *nigredo*. In clinical practice, whatever the artful ways of the practitioner, identifying projective identification is dependent upon being somehow distanced from extremely strong feelings which, a moment ago, seemed perfectly justified. Bion (1961) described this distance as a "temporary loss of insight" (p. 149) without which the analyst would continue to play out a part in the patient's fantasy, and would fail to recognize being manipulated to play that part. Just how the analyst gains emotional distance and reflection varies greatly, over a spectrum ranging from one's own splitting to the moral act of imagining the effect on the patient should the analyst actually speak or behave in the ways the patient feels are so totally justified. Such imaginal acts will often jar the analyst out of arrogant complacency, and into the awareness that a very complex and dangerous process has been at work.

For example, during a session with a patient I began to feel that her existence, even her right to breathe and have any thoughts at all, had to be preceded by flowing through me. I was a dictatorial container. I felt as if it were right that she be contained in me, that all her autonomy and thoughts existed only if these were contained by me. I felt them to be for her own good. This dictum was seething through me. Until I jarred myself out of this state, it felt perfectly right. In the previous vignette of the pause, which was a non-analytical example, I was able to recognize only later that I was being manipulated to recover someone's lost mind. During the pause I had a strong belief that my reactions were totally justified. The following case demonstrates the kind of imagery that can evolve out of imaginally reflecting projective identification dynamics.

A woman began her session by looking at me in a very

penetrating way and saying: "When I see that bored look on your face, that is, when I believe I see it, I just want to go away. I get anxious and I withdraw."

I felt stung by her criticism. Was I bored with her? I had been in the past. I did not feel that way today, and certainly not when she had spoken to me. Why did I feel jarred by what she said? Where was she seeing clearly? I realized that if I retained contact with her while also being connected to myself, she became very anxious and withdrew. I told her this.

She acknowledged it, and after some reflection she looked at me. I then found myself looking away, just for a second; but ever so slightly I did avoid her. I acknowledged this to her, but she had also seen it. As she reflected on her experience of my looking away from her, she became very upset. This occurred, she realized, not only with me, but with all her experiences with men, for as she expressed it: "They don't want to contact me, they run away. Why did you run away?"

I had no answer. In fact I felt surprised by her question. In revealing that I had ever so slightly tended to withdraw, I felt I was offering something that could make her grateful. Instead, she was now angry with me. I had clearly opened up more than I had bargained for. I thought about it; why did I run away? Did I want any emotional contact with her? I realized that the slight looking away I did was actually chronic in our interactions.

I then began to have very angry feelings and thought that she wouldn't let me have any of my own process. I felt I couldn't be in myself at all, but always had to be linked to her and focused on her and our interaction. After a moment my anger passed and I came to my senses. I told her of the thought and process I had just gone through. I did not totally ascribe my state to an induced process, but it did have the sense of foreignness common to projective identification. I wasn't sure where it came from – me, her, or the interaction – and in telling her about it I had hoped to bring these destructive contents to consciousness. I was open to the fantasy's being not only a product of her psyche or my own, but also a spontaneous product of our interactive field, a *mundus imaginalis* that cannot be reduced to individual psyches.

Communicating these feelings, noting both their foreignness and that they were part of my own reactions, led her to a flood of memories of how she had so often been treated exactly as I had described, as a greedy and controlling person who allowed no other person's autonomy. Her careful and genuine response then caused me to wonder if the reason that I slightly turned away from her, and often had in the past, was simply a projective identification dynamic, in the Kleinian sense of her putting into me this withdrawing, sadistic expectancy. Would any reflections on third areas and imaginal couples only be a way of distancing from a more direct encounter?

Seeing the projective identification as something of hers being acted out by me was useful, but it soon felt unsatisfying to both of us. After all, why did I act it out? What did this say about me and my feelings about her? Thinking these thoughts gave me an urge to protest that I actually did a good job of not acting out, that I only barely succumbed relative to the experience she had had of other people. But small or slight withdrawals can be more sinister than outright accusations that someone is boring, for these withdrawals cloak themselves in the lie of only being a slight failing in a state of otherwise real contact. If I were going to be truthful, something else was needed.

So I returned, with her, to examining our interaction. It seemed clear that we were acting as a couple who did not want union. In this dynamic, when she contacted me I withdrew, and when I contacted her, she filled with anxiety and withdrew. We seemed to be ruled by an interactive couple whose roles we alternately played out. In approaching our interaction in this way we submitted to a third element having its way with us. Like the alchemical Mercurius described by Jung it was "the elusive, deceptive, ever-changing content that possessed the patient like a demon [who] flits about from patient to doctor and, as the third party in our alliance, continues its game, sometimes impish and teasing, sometimes really diabolical" (CW16, par. 384). Most crucially, such a presence could be sensed through an imaginal act, a metaphorical grasp of our interaction, a way of speaking about it as if we were constructing a dream that might be going on, a dream that was filling in for our missing consciousness. Our interaction could best be grasped by thinking that two couples were present: the patient and I, and an unconscious one.

In this way we established the presence of an imaginal couple that seemed to thrive on sadomasochistic dynamics. For example, I could follow its rhythms and withdraw from her ever so slightly, causing her pain with surgical precision. She, in turn, could flee from me and have a similar effect, a painful non-mirroring of my eros. The act of imaginatively seeing this couple freed us from its power, much like the technique in active imagination of objectifying an affect. The result was that a new field of felt union began to manifest. That was the crucial item: Active imagination, imaginal sight had a transformative result on the nature of the couple. We could feel ourselves then, working together in an interactive field that seemed to have its own creativity; images and feelings appeared that had a new-found spontaneity that we had rarely known together.

I now found myself in the midst of an awful fantasy: I began to see, in my mind's eye, and fleetingly in the space between us, a wild red-haired man, much like old pictures of Ares, the wild man. He and I tended to merge, and he-I was very angry with her. The anger, indeed rage had the following voice: "Anything that goes wrong here is your fault. If you dare to split from me or in any way mess up now you're in for it."

I was very surprised by the power of this fantasy, and when I told it to her she recognized it as her greatest fear. She became upset and told me that she had always been held accountable for anything that went wrong in states of union.

Now what about the wild man? In a sense he is the sadistic urge that I had partaken of in small amounts in withdrawal. It was now revealed in its more devastating, persecutory form. But the act of imagining this together, with reference to the couple—both creative and soulless—that seemed to be structuring our interaction, now led again to something else. For she recognized the "wild man" to be her energy, her libido or yang power that she had always felt men hated and withdrew from. When she dared to feel this power, men accused her of being unrelated. At least in that moment she had the experience of her phallic power not being destructive, not ruining union.

As long as I was dealing with the parts put into me by the patient, or parts I put into her in counter-projective identification that, in rage, she would then attempt to put back into me, I was approaching our interaction through a Kleinian metaphor. I was dealing with projected parts, and attempting to understand them through a kind of Cartesian-Newtonian spatial grid of insides and outsides. But when we perceived the interactive couple in mutable and interchanging states of fusion, union, or radical non-union, felt as states of deadness or complete absence of linking, all of which could change into each other, we began to enter a different kind of space, one not of parts projected, but of couples and their relations.

This space of relations is, I believe, a transitional area between the space-time world where processes may be characterized as an interaction of objects, and the collective unconscious, or what Jung also called the *pleroma* (CW12, par. 629). The physicist David Bohm (1982) has called this the *implicate* order. Healing, for Jung, depends upon linking to the pleromatic level.

Images have the capacity to lead us into the mystery of the pleroma or implicate order. Marilyn Ferguson has described this beautifully, writing that T. S. Eliot's poems are full of such images: "The still point of the turning world," she noted, "is neither flesh nor fleshless, neither arrest nor movement. Eliot said: 'And do not call it fixity, where past and future are gathered. Except for the point, the still point/ There would be no dance, and there is only the dance.'" (1982, pp. 24–25). Ferguson also recorded a Buddhist Sutra as the most extraordinary ancient description of this level in which oneness, not separable events, is the guiding thread and experience:

> In the heaven of Indra there is said to be a network of pearls so arranged that if you look at one you see the others reflected in it. In the same way, each object in the world is not merely itself but involves every other object, and in fact *is* every other object. (1982, pp. 24–25.)

One further item: The physician and scientist, Alex Comfort (1984), has recently suggested that Bohm's idea of an implicate order is the same as a space in which relations, not things related but relations per se, are the central feature. While images have the power to link to the implicate order, the particular images that mediate to relations may have a special role here. By discovering an unconscious couple through its fragments known from projective identification, we move into a third area that can link to the pleromatic fullness of the implicate order. We thus follow the fragments known in projective identification back to their pleromatic roots; the couple itself then becomes an image with the power to engage us in the oneness of the implicate order. There, as Jung taught, healing resides, consonant with the ancient and Hermetic tradition.

The space in which we can grasp the imagery of a couple, whose everchanging dance is the only reality, is a third area that links to the unitary world of the implicate order. Becoming conscious of this area is a new level of awareness. It is best not to identify the third area with either implicate or space-time orders, but to allow it to be a linking domain that cannot be cast in spatial categories. The third area is neither inside, outside, nor in between persons. This area is also neither material nor psychic, "neither flesh nor fleshless," but rather a subtle body, a realm of ethers, of concepts long since discarded but in need of our reconsideration.

How did the alchemist apprehend what we call projective identification processes and turn them into creative, structure-creating and transforming modes? How did he approach those processes in which, as Jung says, the alchemist "no longer knew whether he was melting the mysterious amalgam in the crucible or whether he was the salamander glowing in the fire." This process of "psychological induction," Jung went on to say, "inevitably causes the two parties to get involved in the transformation of the third and to be themselves transformed in the process" (CW16, par. 399). The key to the transformation, Jung said, lies in the containing power of the archetypes. The primordial image that best suits this task is the coniunctio, the union of opposites.

Discovering an unconscious couple and recognizing that it is the creative source of an interaction beyond the powers of the conscious personality, is often a discovery accompanied by awe. This can be a numinous moment; it is a here and now experience of the archetypal transference. The discovery of the couple, through being affected by the inductive processes of the third area, can lead to its introjection as an internal center (Meltzer, 1973, p. 85).

Jung's alchemical approach to the transference allows us to situate projective identification in a proper container for its Mercurial-like ambiguities. Through the woodcuts from the *Rosarium* we may recognize the workings of projective identification as it is coupled with the larger process of the evolution of the third area of relations. This evolution includes transformation such that compulsion and the tendency toward concretization is gradually refined away. Projective identification plays a key role in creating the illusions and arrogance that would identify the ego with such processes, but it also leads to the capacity to discover the unconscious couples which are the central images of the third area.

Picture one of the *Rosarium*, *The Mercurial Fountain* is "an attempt to depict the mysterious basis of the *opus*" (CW16, par. 402). At the top of the picture is the divided (or two-headed) serpent. It "spews out the poisonous fumes of the *prima materia* which contain the seven planets or metals in evil mixture and disorder" (Fabricius 1976, p. 18). Jung said: "These are the two vapours whose condensation initiates the process which leads to a multiple distillation for the purpose of purifying away the . . . clinging darkness of the beginning" (CW16, par. 403).

We have in this picture a combination of several ideas. On the one hand, there is the imagery of the massa confusa or prima materia, the hostile elements which appear through projective identification. On the other hand, the soul is represented in a split "upper" and "lower" form (McLean, 1980, p. 120). Splitting and projective identification are thus portrayed. But, most crucially: The upper and lower are connected through the fumes.

These vapors, which as Jung has said initiate the process, form a perfect analogy to projective identification. Through working with them, the alchemist sublimated or distilled away the states of unconscious identity filled with split and hostile opposites. They link above and below, the mind-body, or spirit-instinct split inherited in our western tradition since Plato and before. The awareness that projective identification can link above and below, instinctual and mental processes, is thus a clear part of the alchemical image in the Mercurial Fountain. This role of projective identification has been clarified by Grotstein (1982) who, following Bion, portrayed it as a "conduit for the id into the ego, and from both into the superego" (p. 161).

In the Mercurial Fountain these vapors are shown in their ambivalent form. They link above and below; yet, as commentaries (CW16, par. 403 & n.10) on these fumes show, they also block the sun and the moon. Projective identification, which obscures the light of consciousness and the imagination appears here—like the alchemical sulphur—as a captor of the imagination, rendering it dull and lifeless in states of the nigredo. Yet through imaginally working with the fumes, their sulphuric quality can be transformed (CW16, par. 403). The alchemical process had to transform the state of projective identification into a positive one, without undervaluing its dark and negative form. The art, apparently, was to value the obstruction of the sun and moon by the two vapors. We have to value the darkness and unpleasantness of despair and the tormenting, soulless state of mindlessness, lessons we have to learn in psychotherapy over and over again.

The alchemical model in the *Rosarium* works with the imagery of a couple that must be transformed through states of dangerous fusion and confusion. For example, projective identification dominates picture two, the left hand contact. (The following survey, as in Jung's study, only considers the first ten pictures of the *Rosarium*. The entire series of twenty has been printed by Fabricius, 1976, and also by McClean, 1980). The "perverse fascination" of incest (CW16, par. 419), wrote Jung, "like tentacles of an octopus twine themselves . . . round doctor and patient" (CW16, par. 371). But there is a goal, for the hidden meaning of the incest is revealed to be a repulsive symbol for the *unio mystica* (CW16, par. 419). Furthermore, the incest energies, which here are thoroughly identified with projective identification, link and identify spiritual processes with the cthonic depths of sexuality (CW16, pars. 418, 455). This inclusion of the bodily-erotic element, through projective identification, is essential to the alchemical work. Through it, further transformation of the interactive field can take place, but not without a careful attention to the duplicity and dangers of projective identification.

Picture three addresses this for, in the commentary to "Naked Truth" (CW16, par. 450), we have what amounts to a litany against narcissism, especially against the pride and arrogance that would lose sight of the greater-than-ego powers at work. In picture four the process again returns to the erotic energies exposed through projective identification, the energies which are now a mysterious bath for the transformation of the unconscious couple. This leads to picture five, the "coniunctio." Here alternating states of fusion and distance, the opposites whose painful conflict is usually denied and falsified by the deceptions of projective identification, is transcended in a rhythmical harmony.

Following the coniunctio, we see the emergence of new, hermaphroditic structures now defining the nature of the third or transitional area. This appears in picture six, the "nigredo," a state of death traced to the incestuous intertwining of projective identification. This both causes the death of the coniunctio and leads to its further transformation.

Picture seven, the stage in the *Rosarium* known as the "extraction of the soul," is likened by Jung to a schizophrenic dissociation (CW16, par. 477). Up to this point in his analysis he had largely employed the model of union or the coniunctio based upon the image of the hieros gamos — a state that can reflect the unconscious relationship between two people. In analyzing picture seven Jung moved more toward another root of the coniunctio, namely the unio mystica, the solitary ascent of the soul to God. This is significant: While two people engaging in the state depicted by picture seven may experience extreme disorientation, more is happening than meets the eye. Analyst and analysand may experience a severely soulless condition, an absence of linking.

This condition is common in dealing with borderline patients. Metaphors such as being in parallel or alternate universes come to mind. The experience is often frightening and, for the analyst, can be humbling unless one's narcissistic defenses are too strong. For the state of being in no true contact is difficult to accept for anyone who feels adept at connecting to people and to psyche. At this juncture, many projective identification interpretations are possible, but these will only falsify the painful state of a complete absence of linking. For example, states of psychic deadness and impotence, which the analyst may feel, can readily be interpreted as an inductive effect. But this is off the mark, and takes into the interpersonal relationship archetypal aspects which are truly beyond it. As Jung says, "The psychological interpretation of this process leads into regions of inner psychic experience which defy our powers of scientific description" (CW16, par. 482).

The state imaged by this picture is notably also called the "impregnatio." The hint here is that, while the interpersonal relationship feels soulless, and while the individuals themselves may each feel no inner connection to the unconscious, a mystery is being enacted. The soul is ascending toward God in the unio mystica. It is a time when projective identification ceases to have interpretive value, and in fact has only the value of humbling us within its clumsy attempt at true understanding. It is a time shrouded in mystery and a sense of analytical failure. What happens here is often unknown, even to the eye of the imagination. The mystics knew this level. This is beautifully portrayed in the following tale from Rumi, the Islamic mystic of the 13th century:

> A seeker knocked at the door of the beloved – God – and a voice from inside asked: "Who is it?" The seeker answered: "It is I"; and the voice said: "In this house there is no I and You." The door remained locked. Then the seeker went into solitude, fasted and prayed. A year later he returned and knocked at the door. Again the voice asked: "Who is it?" Now the believer answered: "It is You." Then the door opened.

The eighth picture, the "mundificatio," depicts the process of washing away the inflations that attend engaging the third area, and further refines the fusion and splitting tendencies that reside there. In other words, its evolution is furthered; this process goes on through the entire series of 20 pictures. Jung only attended to the first ten; I also limit myself to them in this paper. In picture nine the soul returns, reviving the structure that has been forming in death, and becomes the Rebis of picture ten.

Now we meet a major level of achievement in the *Rosarium*, the creation of a structure that can be understood as a shared self between two people. It is the "third body" of which the poet Robert Bly wrote: "They obey a third body that they share in common./ They have made a promise to love that body." This is subtle body or structure that yields wisdom, knowledge and most crucially, kinship. It has its own autonomy within the third area. To some degree, but never fully, it can become a self within an individual, a self with male and female polarities. Such shared experiences and structures seem to me to be the goal of projective identification. Jung's study of the transference thus allows us to grasp the Mercurial nature of projective identification, and recognize it as both a trickster and wily god of revelation, forging structures in the third area.

REFERENCES

Bion, W. (1961). *Experiences in groups*. London: Tavistock.

Bohm, D. (1982). *Wholeness and the implicate order*. London: Routledge & Kegan Paul.

Comfort, A. (1984). *Reality and empathy*. Albany: State University of New York Press.

Deri, S. (1978). Transitional phenomena: Vicissitudes of symbolization and creativity. In *Between reality and fantasy*. S. Grolnik & L. Barkin (Eds.). New York: Jason Aronson.

Fabricius, J. (1976). *Alchemy*. Copenhagen: Rosenkilde & Bager.

Ferguson, M. (1982). In K. Wilbur (Ed.), *The holographic paradigm*. Boulder, CO: Shambala Press.

Gordon, R. (1965). The concept of projective identification. *Journal of Analytical Psychology, 10–2*, 127–51.

Grotstein, J. (1982). *Splitting and projective identification*. New York: Jason Aronson.

Jung, C. G. (1939). Psychological analysis of Nietzsche's Zarathustra. (Parts 1–10, 1934–39). M. Foote (Ed.). Private publication.

Klein, M. (1975). Notes on some schizoid mechanisms. In M. Klein (Ed.), *Envy and gratitude*. London: Hogarth.

McLean, A. (1550/1980). Commentary on *The rosary of the philosophers*. Edinburgh: Magnum Opus Sourceworks.

Meltzer, D. (1973). *Sexual states of mind*. Perthshire, England: Clunie.

Discussion: Mario Jacoby (Zurich)

Schwartz' paper is challenging, and, like his other publications, reflects his concern for furthering, expanding, and
differentiating the clinical potential of Jungian psychology. This
paper helps me to grasp that intriguing concept, "projective
identification." Although this Kleinian term alludes to familiar
experiences of the psyche, its meaning has tended to escape me.
I am relieved to know from Schwartz' presentation that projective identification is linked to the spirit Mercurius in alchemy.
Just as Mercurius never lets himself be pinned down, this term
is fluid, many faceted and "tricksterish." Thus, I found that my
difficulty in grasping the concept and hold it is not just my blocking but part of its phenomenology.

My understanding is that, for projective identification to occur,
there must be either a regressive loss of boundaries or a state
where boundaries have not yet been established. To a minor degree this happens to all of us in our relationships. Rosemary Gordon's work on projective identification explained that what Jung
called *participation mystique* or unconscious identity and psychic
infection or induction are synonyms for projective identification.
Why, then, is it necessary to introduce this multisyllabic Kleinian
term? It must convey something more specific than what Jung
meant by his terminology. I also wonder in what way the
phenomenon of projective identification is different from Heinz
Kohut's concept of fusion with the self-object: that the other cannot be experienced as a separate, autonomous being, but is seen
as part of oneself. I wonder, finally, why Schwartz chose to use
the concept of projective identification above all others for the title of his lecture. Though he says that it expresses key clinical
phenomena as described by Jung, at first I had difficulty when
reading phrases such as "Generally Jung is aware of the potentially creative and destructive aspects of projective identification," or, "The alchemical process had to transform the state of
projective identification into a positive one." Schwartz is more
careful, saying for example, "Jung's main statement on the transference is centrally concerned with the phenomenology of
projective identification." But again, if the phenomenology

amounts to the same, why introduce such a mechanistic sounding term?

The second part of Schwartz' paper however, reveals what he is aiming at. By very impressive case-examples he can demonstrate how a patient unconsciously induces a content in the analyst, who then must function as a container. This process may produce a feeling of being controlled in the analyst, who then becomes aware of what Michael Fordham called the "syntonic countertransference-reaction."

Indeed projective identification seems to be the basis of this important therapeutic instrument, the instrument of syntonic countertransference. Maybe, I thought, by using this term one lays the accent more on the activity of unconscious interplay than when we talk about "unconscious identity." I also felt that the concept of projective identification may be useful in sharpening one's awareness of some subtle emotional transactions. For me it proved to be so, at least in several instances, once I focused on it.

But apart from the terminology which Schwartz uses to describe clinical phenomena, I like this second part of his exposition best and find it extremely important. Its importance lies in the fact that he can show us the alchemical king and queen couple "in action," so to speak. King and queen virtually make their appearance in a surprising way during the analytic session. I had always felt that Jung's concern, in his rich dialogue with the *Rosarium*, had much to do with the great questions of humanity and with the individuation process in terms of the coniunctio — the interplay and final meeting of the opposites. At no place, however, is there in "Psychology of the Transference" (CW16) a detailed account of its impact on the interactions of two persons in the here and now of the analytic situation. In this area Schwartz fills a gap. He is able to fill it because of his extraordinary sensitivity and his intuitive gift to become aware of the most subtle implications which are part and parcel of the analytic dialogue.

Of course, one might say, every Jungian analyst knows about participation mystique, knows about the fact that the analytic process involves both patient and analyst, and knows that both will be transformed by the constellated archetypes. It was Jung's genius that had discovered this, long before the therapeutic value of the countertransference or the ideas of modern systems theory had been elaborated. Yet because of the preponderant interest of Jungians in what is called the "symbolic material" from the unconscious, the sensitive awareness of how the unconscious affects the here and now of the analytic encounter has remained largely in the undifferentiated shadow. (I know of course, that there are many important exceptions to this general statement.)

Thus, I want to accentuate the merit of Schwartz' attempt to become aware of the archetypal impact of the personal interactions in the transference/countertransference. From this point of view I can understand even better why he has chosen the term projective identification as the starting point of his investigation. From the realm of the dynamic personal interchange, he can feel "parts put into [him] by the patient," but also parts put into the patients by the analyst in what he calls "counterprojective identification." But Schwartz wants to go to a deeper level. He shows us step by step how, during the interactions with his patient, he came to realize the effect of what he calls "the third area" which is neither inside nor outside, nor in between persons. In this imaginary area we cannot talk any more of interactions of objects. I hope that I do not over-simplify his ideas if I put it this way: It is not just I who unconsciously affects you, nor the other way around. But there are archetypal forces in the unconscious which affect both of us; they affect and even structure the interactions we are having.

This is classical Jungian knowledge, but in Schwartz' paper it becomes a here-and-now experience. He can visualize spontaneously what the unconscious pair of opposites, as described by alchemy, is doing to him and to his patient. To me the effect of the third area in the analytic situation feels crucial, but it affects me more in the form of distinct feelings of an atmosphere in the room, a tension, a rhythm, a melody, sometimes an intuition.

I am pleased that Schwartz does not seem to be always in awe of all this numinosity, but also sees its seductive danger and the importance of emotional distancing. I like very much the pertinent example of how he stepped out of an identification with a grandiose countertransference response. Also, his idea that it is essential for an analyst to imagine in advance what effect a certain response may have on the patient is very much to be supported. He is speaking here about empathy.

In the last section of his paper Schwartz interprets several pictures of the *Rosarium* in quite the same style as Jung's except that Schwartz focuses on the theme of the symbolic alchemical couple's effect on projective identification in analysis. My scepticism tells me that, when an analyst begins to interpret such a set of symbolic pictures, they stimulate the imagination. Consciously, the analyst intends to talk about interactions in the transference with the patient. But the patient, as well as the transferential situation, may become imaginary because the analyst is carried away by an inner need to make a coherent and pertinent interpretation of the picture series. The danger is that what happens with the patient has to fit into the picture interpretation and not the other way around. I am also curious to know in what way the alchemical couple affects the third area when analysis takes place between persons of the same sex.

Schwartz' paper is stimulating and important, especially in that he begins with the here and now in the analytic situation and leads us step by step, experientially, to the archetypal foundations as symbolized by the *Rosarium*.

Jung's Shadow Problem with Sabina Spielrein

Aldo Carotenuto (Rome)

Letters written by Jung to Sabina Spielrein, along with her diary (1909–1912), reveal an aspect of Jung's personality that might never have surfaced had he not found himself involved in a singular experience with his patient. The relationship succeeded in dislodging a dimension which apparently surprised even Jung, as evidenced by one of his letters to her. He wrote that, "At times it is necessary to be contemptible in order to survive" (Carotenuto, 1986, p. 223). That phrase expresses his discomfort at finding himself confronted by a struggle between two commitments: first, the professional one to a person objectively weaker than himself psychologically; and second to himself, a man in love. What to do in such a predicament?

The tendency is to compromise. But compromise is never adequate when we are dealing with our own salvation. Jung was thinking more of his own psychic dimension that that of his patient. I believe that it was in that process that he perceived the real meaning of the psychological shadow. Our image remains clean as long as we are not confronted with situations that put us to the test. In such situations elements emerge which have been kept at a distance because they are reprehensible. These moments are necessary because they allow us to "exteriorize our demons," a term that Jung used often in his letters to Spielrein. During this period in which Jung was constrained to defend himself from attacks — absolutely justifiable — by a patient in love, he began a pattern of behavior that could be described, according to the tenets of common morality, as reprehensible.

It seems that Jung, pressured by Spielrein's demands, wrote a letter (Carotenuto, 1982, p. 94) to the young woman's mother.

> I moved from being her doctor to being her friend when I ceased to push my own feelings into the background. I could drop my role as doctor the more easily because I did not feel professionally obligated, for I never charged a fee. This latter clearly establishes the limits imposed upon a doctor. You do understand, of course, that a man and a girl cannot possibly continue indefinitely to have friendly dealings with one another without the likelihood that something more may enter the relationship. For what would restrain the two from drawing the consequences of their love? A *doctor* and his *patient*, on the other hand, can talk of the most intimate matters for as long as they like, and the patient may expect her doctor to give her all the love and concern she requires. But the doctor knows his limits and will never cross them, for he is *paid* for his trouble. That imposes the necessary restraints on him.
>
> Therefore I would suggest that if you wish me to adhere strictly to my role as doctor, you should pay me a fee as suitable recompense for my trouble. In that way you may be *absolutely* certain that I will respect my duty as a doctor *under all circumstances*.
>
> As a friend of your daughter, on the other hand, one would have to leave matters to Fate. For no one can prevent two friends from doing as they wish. I hope, my dear and esteemed Madame, that you understand me and realize that these remarks conceal no baseness but only experience and self-knowledge. My fee is 10 francs per consultation.
>
> I advise you to choose the prosaic solution, since that is the more prudent one and creates no obligations for the future.
>
>   With friendly good wishes, etc.

Our task here is to comprehend without passing judgment; moral evaluations teach us nothing. It is not my intention here, nor has it ever been, to take up Jung's defense. What is important is the effort to understand psychologically what happened.

The simple fact of bringing money into play could be interpreted as an attempt to introduce a new element into the relationship or of providing a pretext. Money, as a third element in the relation, became a possible insurance that Jung could relate to Spielrein within the limits of professional correctness. That point of view is not exactly a mistaken one because the analytic relationship is particular insofar as it is based on sentiments that are otherwise not revealed. The exposing of extremely delicate and private sentiments can present dangerous implications, as there is no situation in which an individual is so vulnerable as in analysis. The exchange of money can restrain the analyst from letting oneself go in a seductive situation. It defines a contract, the intent to provide therapy and not gratification. Money is a reminder: "Remember, psychotherapist, you are providing a professional service. The patient who pays your fee has the right to the conviction you will not lose your head, even if the patient in the meantime does everything possible to make you do just that." Thus, the patient expects the impossible from the analyst.

It should also be clear that the contract imposes an imperative for finding a solution to this paradox. We cannot negate both requests. We must let ourselves become involved, getting into it up to our necks, but without drowning. On the other hand, using the swimming metaphor, I can think of colleagues who insist on swimming with their heads high out of the water in order not to dampen their hair, and end up swimming badly.

Freud also drew a few lessons from the Jung/Spielrein situation. Through it Freud came to an understanding of the problems of transference and countertransference; he began discussing countertransference precisely on the basis of Jung's experience. As Cremerius (1986) wrote:

> It would seem that the doctor/patient relation referred to by Carotenuto opened Freud's eyes. If one follows the sequence of the Spielrein tragedy, it becomes obvious that the dates on which Freud learned more about that episode coincide with the dates of his discoveries of new aspects of the dynamics of transference and counter-transference. If up to that point he had sustained that only transference occurred in patient/analyst relations, he discovered in Jung's letter of March 7, 1909 (in which Jung refers to a patient— obviously Sabina—who was threatening to unleash a scandal because he did not want a child with her) and Jung's letter of March 9, that analysts as well can be scalded by the sort of love with which we must deal. These are the risks of our profession. (pp. 9–10)

(Cremerius refers to FJ, pp. 207, 210, and 228–29.)

After Jung informed him on June 4, 1909, of the relation,

Freud's reply three days later demonstrated how deeply the problem affected his reflections on his theory:

> Such experiences, though painful, are necessary and hard to avoid. Without them we cannot really know life and what we are dealing with. I myself have never been taken in quite so badly, but I have come very close to it a number of times and had *a narrow escape* [English in original]. I believe that only grim necessities weighing on my work, and the fact that I was ten years older than yourself when I came to [Psychoanalysis], have saved me from similar experiences. But no lasting harm is done. They help us to develop the thick skin we need and to dominate "counter-transference," which is after all a permanent problem for us; they teach us to displace our own affects to best advantage. They are a *"blessing in disguise"* [English in original]. (FJ, pp. 230–31).

This is the first appearance in psychoanalytic literature of the expression, "countertransference," which subsequently became an accepted scientific term. Freud recognized immediately the importance of the phenomenon. In March of the following year, in a lecture entitled, "Future Prospects of Psychoanalytic Therapy," he stated:

> Other innovations in technique relate to the physician himself. We have become aware of the "counter-transference," which arises in him as a result of the patient's influence on his unconscious feelings, and we are almost inclined to insist that he shall recognize this counter-transference in himself and overcome it. Now that a considerable number of people are practicing psycho-analysis and exchanging their observations with one another, we have noticed that no psycho-analyst goes further than his own complexes and internal resistances permit. (SEVI, pp. 200–201)

At that point, Freud made a proposal in which we recognize the intensity of his preoccupation with reducing this danger: "We consequently require that he shall begin his activity with a self-analysis and continually carry it deeper while he is making his observations on his patients. Anyone who fails to produce results in a self-analysis of this kind may at once give up any idea of being able to treat patients by analysis" (SEXI, pp. 144–45). Freud stated further that the doctor must be alert to the sentiments which arise within the relation in his role as "male," because everything experienced must be interpreted in the specific psychological situation. One must guard against believing that certain dimensions originate in the personal reality of the analyst instead of the patient's projected image. The analyst is perceived as a protective god, but must in no way identify with that perception. To avoid doing so requires a fine self-knowledge, as that projection acts forcibly, rife as it is with such powerful and seductive contents.

Jung was very young and had not been in analysis, at least not as we know the analytic process. Thus, it was not difficult for a patient with serious disturbances to unleash psychological elements in Jung which had been hidden up to that time.

Under Spielrein's influence Jung discovered his "polygamous" nature, in that he came to know how necessary it was for him to keep his emotional world active by means of plural interests. A single experience was not sufficient to appease that emotional hunger to relate to another soul. It became clear to him that monogamy had been a cover, maintained by repressive elements.

When Jung, already married, met Spielrein, he realized that his sentiments had been affected. "Such a thing could only happen to me, and I curse the day that I met you" (Carotenuto, 1986, p. 189) he wrote to her. A new psychological aspect was brought into focus in which his belief in fidelity was destroyed. He discovered a side of life which was exhausting and fraught with problems. He desired a love from Spielrein which was "different" — free, liberated from the bonds of bourgeois respectability. However, as Jung had no intention of giving up that respectability (which was represented by his marriage), he accepted in himself what I call his polygamous dimension. In order to rid himself, at least partially, of his sense of guilt at having embraced so censurable an éthic, he resorted to an accusation of complicity. "In this situation I have given too much consideration to the ideas of Otto Gross," he wrote to Freud on June 4, 1909: "Gross and Spielrein are bitter experiences. To none of my patients have I extended so much friendship and from none have I reaped so much sorrow" (FJ, p. 229).

In a previous letter to Freud, Jung had explained the ideas of Otto Gross:

Doctor Gross tells me that he puts a quick stop to the transference by turning people into sexual immoralists. He says the transference to the analyst and its persistent fixation are mere monogamy symbols and as such symptomatic of repression. The truly healthy state for the neurotic is sexual immorality. . . . It seems to me, however, that sexual repression is a very important and indispensable civilizing factor, even if pathogenic for many inferior people. . . . I feel Gross is going along too far with the vogue for the sexual short-circuit, which is neither intelligent, nor in good taste, but merely convenient, and therefore anything but a civilizing factor." (FJ, p. 90)

In the same letter Jung confessed to Freud that he envied Eitingon (FJ, p. 90). Jung turned to Freud, as an older and more expert colleague, the moment the Spielrein case had become his own case as well. The motivation for the correspondence may have been Jung's desire to discuss that experience with Freud; by the second letter Jung had already mentioned the case even if, at the time, he did not provide the patient's name. However, he mentioned it in such an elliptical and enigmatic way—probably due to his sense of guilt—that Freud had great difficulty in putting the problem into perspective..

Another theme emerges, typical of Jungian psychology: the formulation of a psychic aspect of the Other, a counter to the conscious sexual identity. When a man feels attracted to a woman, Analytical Psychology affirms that the attraction is mediated by the internal feminine dimension, the anima. (The male dimension of a woman is the animus.) The possibility of dialogue with the opposite sex, theorizes Jung, is not so much connected to the actual person we are dealing with, as to the inner translation of the female or male image. We could hypothesize that such a proclamation was a direct result of Jung's meeting Spielrein. He would write in his memoirs (MDR) that, in a hallucinatory state, he spoke with female voices. Thus, he became aware of the existence of a psychic contrasexual part, and discovered that the external aspects which interested him were in reality the projections of his own desires. To him the glance which entices and captures has no connection with the objective reality of the other person, but is a reflection of subjective psychic reality.

On the scholarly side, as regards Jung's development of the

anima/animus concepts, we know that he had a strong aversion to the Freudian concept of a sexual interpretation of human behavior. However, this refusal to concede a determining importance in human life to the sexual dimension, finds a singular counterpoint on the practical, biographical and even anecdotal plane.

Jung was never at ease in relations in which sex appeared on the scene. It is easy to suspect that his theoretical no to Freud's pansexualism was a retreat before a burning issue. We can deduce with reasonable certainty that the female figure was perceived by Jung as a disturbing element, attracting him and frightening him at the same time.

However, if we are to put Jung's inner anima figure into better focus, we must ascertain what the existing female image was in the historical epoch and in the society in which he was educated, so as not to mistake as individual what was a commonplace for an entire culture.

The presence of Sabina Spielrein in Jung's life and in Freud's allowed both of them to discover new and unexpected elements inherent in the analytic relation, including countertransference. It also permits us some historical perspective on their understanding of women. When Spielrein became estranged from Jung, she grew closer to Freud and told him the story of the intense love and emotional involvement which bound her to her doctor, her friend—a person who, while still her doctor, became her lover. At the beginning, all the attention was focused on Spielrein, whom Freud deemed to be solely responsible for what had occurred. The moments of intense emotional involvement between patient and analyst were considered to have had nothing to do with reality, but were merely part of the feminine emotional dimension.

This is not surprising if we remember that in Freud's time the contemporary idea of woman was the voracious, destructive female, or at the very least seductress. The same Jewish-Christian-Islamic culture which, in the Middle Ages, had created an eponymic hero, Don Juan, reversed the roles and institutionalized the great seductress. It only follows that when, during analysis, the element of seduction appeared, the cry was "watch out for the woman!" At the time, the woman was always the patient and never the analyst. Thanks to Victorian morality which, although

named for a woman, was custom-tailored to the measure of man,
the consulting rooms of psychotherapists were frequented almost exclusively by women, single and married.

Consistent with the patient-as-seducer view of the problem, at
the beginning Freud defended Jung and, when questioned by
Spielrein, furnished her with an exclusively endopsychic interpretation of the episode. The external situation and the real
figure of the analyst had no relevance whatsoever. Later, perhaps because in the meantime his relation with Jung had deterio-
rated, Freud had much less difficulty in admitting that a share of
the responsibility rested with the therapist. It was possible, even
probable, that the emotional storm engulfing Spielrein was not
exclusively the result of the interior requirements of the woman,
but also directly connected to external impulses which originated
with her analyst. The countertransference or "transference of the
analyst" was only later considered to be equally responsible for
what occurred in the analytic setting.

It is interesting to note that Freud's point of view altered after
1910. He came to speak of countertransference unwillingly and
rarely; the last mention of it in his theoretical work was in 1914.
Focusing on countertransference, calling into question the
responsibility of the analyst, signified a burden rendering the
work even more difficult.

Freud's discovery of transference and countertransference was
offered to him on a silver platter, so to speak, as he was involved
only as observer in Jung's experience with Spielrein. Freud was
in Spielrein's debt, also, for a theory drawn later from a study of
hers—the theory of the death wish opposed to the life instinct.
This theory, which became the foundation and the mythology of
Freudian psychology, was proposed by Freud in 1920 in *Beyond
the Pleasure Principle* (SE18); Spielrein formulated the theory 10
years earlier in her study, "Destruction as the Cause of Coming
to Be." In that study an important message takes shape: Humans, in their rapport with death, confront and conquer not only
destruction but also rebirth. This work, a central one in Spielrein's thought, was dedicated to her analyst Jung and she considered it a spiritual child, a product of their love. In her diary she
intuited that, if her work were accepted and subsequently published, her love relationship could be concluded. The possibility
of their being dead for each other was always on the horizon,

because from that dying a birth would result. Birth or becoming, from Spielrein's sentimental point of view, assumed the aspect of a work on the death wish.

Freud was struck from the very beginning by Spielrein's extraordinary concept: life consisting of two contrasting drives, life and death. However, he was not persuaded and 25 years later he wrote, apropos of that refusal: "I remember my own defensive attitude when the idea of an instinct of destruction first emerged in psychoanalytic literature, how long it took before I became receptive to it" (SE21, p. 120). Here, Sabina Spielrein was not referred to by name, nor was she in Freud's study, *Beyond the Pleasure Principle* (SE18), in 1920.

We know that certain theoretical formulations are drawn directly from our experience. Spielrein had perhaps understood that her relation with Jung could not continue. It had to die and, in order to overcome the dimension of mourning, it was necessary for her to create a theory which would permit that death to generate something else.

In keeping with that world-view, Spielrein desired the rapprochement of Freud and Jung. In her letters to each of them, she always spoke well of the other. In 1914, when the theoretical dissension between Freud and Jung had reached the proportions of a religious war, she was forced to make a painful choice of camps; she made it in favor of the Freud Society. When, on that occasion, Freud wrote to her, "There will be a warm welcome for you if you stay here, but then you will have to recognize the enemy over there," she answered, "I like [Jung] and would like to lead him back into our fold. You, Professor Freud, and he have not the faintest idea that you belong together far more than anyone might suspect. This pious hope is certainly no treachery to our Society! Everyone knows that I declare myself an adherent to the Freudian Society, and [Jung] cannot forgive me for this" (Carotenuto, 1982, p. 112). According to Spielrein, the disasters that had occurred originated not from rational disagreement, but from emotional incomprehension.

We come now to the intrinsic significance of the Jung/Spielrein relationship. In some of her letters, Spielrein lamented the fact that Jung could have "conducted experiments" on her. She was unable to comprehend that Jung, as any analyst, had to experiment in the beginning because each analytic situation was

unique. No matter how prepared one is theoretically or culturally, that preparation becomes secondary when dealing with individual circumstances. In 1909, Spielrein wrote: "For over three
months I have analyzed everything, I withdrew into nature to try
to save myself and my idea; finally I spoke with a colleague of
mine, or, rather, showed her all the letters, with the result that
I felt much lonelier than before, for my beloved could not be
saved, and the thought that he might be a complete no-good,
that he was using me for his first experiment, etc., etc., drove me
absolutely wild" (Carotenuto, 1982, p. 92).

For analysts, strength of character as regards our sentiments is
not a quality we come by naturally, but must be developed and
earned throughout our careers. We must learn to understand the
inner modulation of our requirements and our sentimental expectations. At the beginning, this requirement approaches impossibility, especially if we have a wounded personality which
no analysis has been able to cure. Thus, it should be clear that
there is danger of deep involvement. Psychological, neurotic and
psychotic disturbances are not something qualitatively different
from sanity, but simply a difference in degree. We can consider
that Sabina Spielrein was psychotic, in the sense that her disturbance was a very deep one and had undermined her ego structure. Such people have the particular capacity to "enter into"
other people, unhinging them, opening them up to understand
their psychological workings. That capacity is possessed to a
lesser degree by the neurotic and does not exist in the normal individual. Working with a psychotic is difficult because we are totally unprotected from that capacity to understand and perceive
us.

For a suffering soul, (i.e., Jung, who was about 30 and in a marriage that did not satisfy him), the experience of being understood by a young woman little more than 20 years
old—intelligent, passionate, in love and able to read into the very
depths of his soul—disarmed him completely. According to
Spielrein's diary, Jung was so disarmed that he, the analyst, proposed to the patient that she read his personal diary. To arrive
at such a point suggests unconditional surrender. However,
Jung did have a part of himself—the less admirable part
perhaps—which entered into a conflict of commitments. On the
one hand, he understood that he was bound to maintain his atti-

tude of doctor, and on the other the love dimension had captured him and destroyed him. In the earlier letters this ambivalence is apparent. He used terms of admiration and at the same time made movements to escape.

This attitude of giving and withdrawing oneself, being present and not present, must have been very painful for Spielrein. At that time she was going through a psychotic crisis, in which condition an individual loses the sense of reality. The ambivalence of the doctor would increase the patient's confusion and the confusion in the relationship.

Jung's ambivalent attitude was the basis of his love relationship with Spielrein, and was thus also destructive. He wrote in one of his letters: "How happy I should be to discover that you are a strong spirit, not side-tracked by sentimentalism, whose true intimate condition of life is liberty and independence" (Carotenuto, 1986, p. 190).

Jung could give himself to her in direct proportion to her degree of independence, which protected him from her ever needing him. But to the person who is loved and who loves us we cannot say, "Be independent." We can say that only when we are already sure that the other cannot do without us.

Jung also talked about himself, and so doing, judged himself a good person. However, he was unaware that he was abusing the power he wielded. In an analytic setting, the patient — and Spielrein was a patient, even if she was in love — cannot risk losing the analyst. That is, when one enters into an analytic situation, a condition of "analyst-dependence" results which is similar to drug addiction. Thus, requests like Jung's, "I want you to be independent," are unconsciously in bad faith.

The problem of the abuse of power is one that marks the life of every analyst. There exists no other situation in which power can be exploited in so insidious and deceitful a manner. Such power is never explicit, but functions by means of secret maneuvers of which we are usually unaware. In the analytic environment that power is deceiving, as the analyst appears simply as a smiling and compliant person, someone who usually says exactly what the patient wants to hear. But in reality, that person emanates considerable power because of the type of profession the analyst practices.

The problem of power and its abuse was a recurrent theme in

Jung's life. In his correspondence with Freud, examples of the subject often came up and referred to actual experiences. For example, as a child Jung went through a dramatic experience, when he was violated sexually by a person who was a father substitute, a man he trusted. That experience, which is mentioned in the correspondence with Freud, was a fundamental one for Jung; it undermined his sense of confidence in others. With Freud he had that problem; he accused Freud of treating his students in the same way that an analyst would treat patients. Here again we have the problem of power.

In Jung's letters to Spielrein (e.g., Carotenuto, 1986, pp. 195–96) we discover something unbelievable. He attempted to instruct the young woman as to the manner in which she should love him. He did not allow the sentiment to grow and mature in her but expected that love to follow a defined pattern. It is as if he were saying: "I do not love you for what you are, but for what I wish you to be." This is a trap into which we are all capable of falling.

I refer here to the most important letter sent to Spielrein. It is dated 1908, and it is, I believe, the one which led Jung's heirs to refuse permission for publication. It was written at the moment that Jung had understood that he had fallen into a trap. He was heartbroken, and he admitted to being ill, asking her openly to help him in his hour of suffering, as he had helped her when she was in need, devoting to her all his energies and his professional skills. We are dealing here with moral blackmail. However, when confronted with suffering, it is not easy to refrain from such behavior.

This letter was the last which Jung would write to Spielrein in this vein before another sort of correspondence took over in which it appears that the crisis had been resolved. I believe that that stormy moment had been overcome because Jung had begun another sentimental experience in which he could give form to his emotions. It is an age-old method of saving oneself from painful love complications. Jung had become friends with a student/patient whom he described as sensitive, intelligent, a scholar of philosophy and history of religion. She would in fact become his companion and remain thus for 40 years. We could hypothesize that Jung had always needed such a relationship with a female figure in which his presence as analyst was a constant, and in which the woman's dependence was stimulated and maintained by the analytic experience.

These are the circumstances that revealed Jung's psychological shadow. However, the greatness of a man, the intensity of his light, exist in direct proportion to the measure and intensity of his shadow.

Translated from Italian by
Joan Tambureno

REFERENCES

Carotenuto, A. (1982). *A secret symmetry: Sabina Spielrein between Jung and Freud*. New York: Pantheon.

Carotenuto, A. (1986). *Tagebuch einer heimlichen Symmetrie*. Freiburg: Traute Hensch.

Cremerius, J. (1986). Prefazione a A. Carotenuto, *Tagebuch einer heimlichen Symmetrie*. Freiburg: Traute Hensch.

Discussion: Peter Mudd (Chicago)

We all, I am sure, have speculated privately on the content and intensity of the shadow of Jung, but to reveal publicly what were privately-held analytic insights regarding a collectively-revered ego ideal is disconcerting. In analyzing Jung, we analyze and reveal a deeply cherished element of our own psyches as well. Even as I share some of my observations about Jung's character structure, I say without hesitation that respect is my first and most consistent reaction to this paper and to Carotenuto's body of work that seeks to shed light on Jung's shadow. Carotenuto has proved himself a possessor of analytic courage as well as careful scholarship.

My comments in this paper are divided into three sections:

1. A general response to the nature of and approach to the paper's content.
2. A section dealing with the "polygamous component" of Jung's personality.
3. A section dealing with the aspect of power in Jung's intrapsychic and interpersonal life.

My general reaction to the nature and approach of Carotenuto's paper is a sense of frustration stemming from two separate but related sources. The first is not having access to Jung's letters to Spielrein and so not having the opportunity to see where Carotenuto's points originate. The second is a lack of linkage between Jung's personal history and the dynamics of his shadow in relation to Sabina Spielrein.

The first source is a matter of Carotenuto's respect for the wishes of Jung's heirs not to publish his part of the correspondence. The second is an apparent difference in analytic style of approach. Carotenuto has concerned himself with the history of Psychoanalysis and Analytical Psychology rather than with the personal history of Jung. Thus, the voyeur was constellated in me and I was left both frustrated and fascinated.

Jung's theory of unconscious compensation in the service of individuation was perhaps his most important contribution. Through many readings of the *Two Essays on Analytical Psychology*, I have been impressed by one statement:

> A collapse of the conscious attitude is no small matter. It always feels like the end of the world; as though everything had tumbled back into original chaos. One feels delivered up, disoriented, like a rudderless ship that is abandoned to the moods of the elements. . . . In reality, however, one has fallen back on the collective unconscious which now takes over the leadership. (CW7, par. 254)

This utterance could have been a description of Jung's experience in his encounter with Spielrein. It also describes the seemingly demonic, dark side of the Self which ruthlessly enforces the law of compensation. It is an ironic synchronicity that Speilrein's (1912) major theoretical contribution, whose creation paralleled her relationship to Jung, was entitled "Destruction as a Cause of Coming to Be." My private opinion is that a major incongruity of the Jung/Spielrein relationship was that Spielrein had already learned through her psychosis what it is to die, while Jung's sense of death remained entirely on the symbolic level. Thus, she had something of a psychological edge.

In keeping with Jung's statement about the collapse of a conscious attitude, an inquiry into the construction of that attitude — sometimes called personal history, psychohistory, case fiction or simply projection — would be a useful complement to Carotenuto's approach. Related to this attitude are the shadow elements of polygamy and power.

Carotenuto has proposed with convincing evidence that Jung's encounter with Spielrein was his initiation into the experience of the anima and was the source of that theoretical concept. The supplementary questions that occur to me are: Who was Jung's anima? What was she like? Where did she come from? The paper outlines beautifully the cultural sources of the content of the anima; I need not focus there. Rather, I bring your attention to the evidence present in Jung's memoirs (MDR); this work enables us to identify personal elements that contributed to the development of what Jung called his "polygamous components." I suggest that Jung's polygamous dimension was an attempt to heal a deep and troubling split in the anima, a split that began in his relationship to his mother.

By Jung's own report we know that his mother was hospitalized when he was about three years old. He wrote: "I was deeply troubled by my mother's being away. From then on I always felt mistrustful when the word 'love' was spoken. The feeling I associated with 'woman' was for a long time that of innate unreliability" (MDR, p. 8).

We also know that he was cared for by an unmarried aunt and a young maid servant who reportedly saved his life when he nearly fell from a bridge, an event which he said pointed to "an unconscious suicidal urge" (MDR, p. 9). Jung said that this maid was the prototype of one of his anima components: "The feeling of strangeness which she conveyed and yet of having known her always" (MDR, p. 9). Further, we know that Jung divided his mother's personality into personalities number one and number two: a normal, typical, everyday mother and an uncanny, frightening embodiment of the "natural mind" who was the subject of anxiety dreams and the voice in the famous man-eater dream.

These experiences with women seem to embody several polarized components of Jung's anima. Jung's self-confessed separation trauma, rescue from death by the maid, and subsequent relationship to an unstable, changeable mother leave us with the impression that his level of anima development at the time he met Spielrein was minimal and problematic. In an attempt to cure the "innate unreliability" (MDR, p. 8) associated with such a figure, and protect his ego from being overwhelmed by the anxiety associated with the negative pole of this complex, it appears that Jung chose to relate primarily and defensively to the number one aspect of his mother and anima, while repressing the frightening number two personality who could shake the foundation of ego identity and challenge the reality of everyday experience.

Like all of us, Jung developed a persona in accordance with the needs of the ego to remain intact and in control. His wife Emma, who has been viewed as a sensation type, must have offered safe refuge in her solid embodiment of the mother's number one aspect. Her practicality and attention to the everydayness of living would have reinforced the defenses which Jung had developed in the process of ego consolidation. This element of containment eventually proved to be only a temporary bulwark against the dark Self whose intention was to insure a destiny quite different from the one Jung himself must have had in mind.

The earliest public manifestations of the compensatory movement which sought to balance Jung's preference for a number one lifestyle can be located in his interest in the occult and his staunch defense of the spiritual element, in his Zofingia lectures (CW supplementary Vol. A). Even so, his doctoral dissertation, in its attempt to analyze his cousin Helly Preiswerk's mediumistic experiences in a rational, quasi-Freudian manner, could be viewed as a defense against the powerful forces of the collective unconscious. Helly was among the first projective carriers of the compensatory anima who would insure Jung's fateful plunge into the archetypal depths. As we know from his memoirs, Jung cited his female patients as those who precipitated his most fruitful discoveries. Babette, whom Freud found so ugly (MDR, p. 128), fascinated and enchanted Jung with her symbolic inner life and language and is another manifestation of this anima element.

The need for conscious reintegration of the split-apart elements of the mother imago and the anima occupied a major portion of Jung's energies for the greater part of his life. I believe he came to a profound and much clearer understanding of this problem through his near-death experience in 1944. Impending death convinces us that we are separate units of being, no matter what attachments we have contrived. The essay on the transference (CW16), published in 1946, and its rosarium pictures can be understood as Jung's recognition and delineation of his own separate status. Coinciding with the increasing estrangement from Toni Wolff the pictures seem to evidence an intense transformation.

As Jung stated in his essay on marriage: "A dissociation is not healed by being split off, but by more complete disintegration. All the powers that strive for unity, all healthy desire for selfhood, will resist the disintegration, and in this way [the containing partner] will become conscious of an inner integration, which before he had always sought outside himself. He will then find his reward in an undivided self" (CW17, par. 334). Jung knew this in 1925 but he lived it in 1944 when his heart attack provided an experience of profound disintegration even more powerful than his confrontation with the unconscious.

Thus, Jung's shadow problem of his polygamous dimension was the result of his splitting and projecting the mother and anima dimensions and their subsequent appearances in Emma

Jung, on the one side; his maid in the middle; and Helly Preiswerk, Babette, Sabina Spielrein, and Toni Wolff on the other. These paradoxical and problematic elements were reunited through Jung's fascination with the feminine in her multiplicity. At that time the elements were imagined by Jung as a concrete polygamous dimension rather than a psychological polygamy.

With regard to the aspect of power in Jung's shadow, I believe that Jung's attraction to Spielrein was a compensatory movement by the Self, an attempt at healing a damaged wholeness and restoring a sense of the protective immortality of the prenatal state. Jung said of relationship born of unconsciousness: "Even more is it a return to the mother's womb, into the teeming depths of an as yet unconscious creativity. It is, in truth, a genuine and incontestable experience of the Divine, whose transcendent force obliterates and consumes everything individual; a real communion with life and the impersonal power of fate" (CW17, par. 330).

This passage eloquently describes that aspect of relationship which Carotenuto has characterized unerringly as the trap into which Jung fell. Despite all his extraordinary powers of perception and deep wisdom, Jung succumbed to his human longing for completion.

Motivated by an intense drive to heal his own inner division Jung, like Pygmalion, created a woman and fell in love with her. The projection was utterly addictive. Carotenuto spoke of Spielrein's addiction to Jung, and he was correct. Jung's addiction to her was qualitatively different but quantitatively equal. Carotenuto cited the deep division Jung must have experienced between his professional commitment to his patient and his commitment to the vicissitudes of love.

If we consider this kind of love, as Jung did in his marriage essay – an essay surely informed by this experience – we can see how easily the abuse of power in the service of an intrapsychic need becomes inevitable. "You always hurt the one you love," the song goes, describing the intense desire to annex the beloved as the projected part that promises eternal bliss. Jung's attempt to instruct Spielrein in how to love him, blatantly selfish as it was, indicates a dim awareness on his part of what he needed. Tragically for him and for her, the awareness succumbed to

Jung's inability to see it symbolically. When he failed to control Spielrein, to compel her to play the intrapsychic part that he needed, the spell broke. Spielrein and Jung were propelled into a more fully interpersonal realm and an ever widening gulf opened between them. Jung's still unresolved need for completion had already begun to create an even deeper coniunctio with another female patient who would accompany him during his confrontation with the unconscious and beyond.

One last point about the power aspect concerns the sexual assault which Jung suffered as a boy. This event had perhaps an even more powerfully shaping effect than Jung's problematic relationship with his mother. This trauma must have shaken to the point of near non-existence, Jung's ability to project the Self or appropriately idealize men. Only the figure of Freud seems to have held the possibility of cure, but the issue of authority, or rather of Freud's refusal as Jung's analyst to submit to Jung's dominance, closed the matter once and for all.

Jung's ability to trust and confide in men must have been inhibited by the fear of repetition of the intense pain created by his fallen father figures. This fear would have shifted the weight of trust completely onto women; one recalls the touching attempts which both Emma Jung and Sabina Spielrein made on Jung's behalf to halt the demise of his relationship with Freud. In this dimension of his personal life Jung became a tragic figure, isolated and wounded, enraged and desperate, but most of all hungry for an empathic, loving mirror who would see him as he needed to be seen. Jung also became, through this experience and others, a full human being; I welcome him as a model of faith in the Self and the human ability to endure life's alchemy.

Carotenuto's paper is to be commended for its unwavering analytic insight and impeccable scholarship and for its ability to teach in images that reveal deeper levels of perception with each reading. These abilities become even more impressive because his compassion and respect for Jung as an "analysand" are so clearly present.

REFERENCE

Spielrein, S. (1912). Die Destruktion als Ursache des Werdens. *Jahrbuch für psychoanalytische und psychopathologische forschungen, 4,* 465–503.

The Shadow Archetype in Anorexia Nervosa and Depression

Part I: Grassi de Marsanich (Rome)

Part II: Patrizia Baldieri (Rome)

Part III: Daniela Iorio (Rome)

Part I

In recent years the anorexia nervosa syndrome has captured the interest of numerous Jungian writers and analysts, especially women. The abundance of medical literature on the subject indicates how much interest anorexia has generated since the turn of the century, although its impact on western society at large was minimal until the Second World War. My reflections on the subject seem appropriate in relation to the shadow archetype in our divided world.

The anorexic young woman is truly a shadow figure of female adolescence. She is "a skeleton covered in skin" (Morton, 1694), "a corpse among the living" (Binswanger, 1958). She is a modern *memento mori* (reminder of death) in our affluent and materialistic society.

Once relatively rare, anorexia nervosa has reached epidemic proportions, especially in the upper social classes; 77 per cent of all anorexics come from the wealthier classes (Bruch, 1978).

Perusal of medical and psychoanalytic literature indicates that the origins of this disorder are diverse, as are the treatments and therapies applied. Frustration and perplexity are common denominators uniting those who have dealt with these young women. Freud devoted only a few lines to the problem of anorexia, defining the illness as "a state of melancholy relative to an underdeveloped sexuality" and suggesting that anorexics should not be treated analytically.

The difficulty in capturing the essence of the anorexic is reflected in the growing Jungian literature on the subject. A frequent approach is to try to understand the anorexic through parallels with mythological figures, particularly Greek. However, as noted by Spignesi (1983, pp. 114–15), the most striking feature is, again, the multiplicity and variability of these identifications.

Joanne Stroud (1980) related the anorexic to Puer, Persephone and Artemis; Shorter (1980) to Athena; Woodman (1980) to Athena, Demeter and Dionysius; Joyce Stroud (1980) to Puer and Dionysius-Eros. Spignesi (1983) highlighted the problem using figures such as Gaia, Hecate, Demeter, and Persephone, and substances such as alchemical sulphur. Woodman explained psychic multiplicity as a way for the anorexic to bring out disparate hidden and inferior aspects of other people, and stigmatized the anorexic's destiny with the statement: "She may . . . be the harbinger of the shadow in almost all situations in which she finds herself" (1980, p. 80).

These authors have assisted me in my analytic work and have offered valuable material for my own thinking. Their works are based on brilliant intuition and reflect the profound and multiform experiences with anorexic patients. They have helped me to hypothesize another image which encompasses all of these experiences: the mirror. Anorexia is a mirror for all of us—of our dark side; and of the illness, the divisions and repressions inherent in our modern society. To understand the pathology of the anorexic, we must identify our collective consciousness and contrast it with the negative aspects of this moment in our history. This process can help us to understand the significance of the anorexic's suffering. Let us listen to the messages she sends us through her illness.

During the time of passage from adolescence to adulthood, the anorexic young woman's growth is blocked. Her relationship to food becomes increasingly illusory. On one hand, food is seen as poisonous and therefore its consumption must be reduced to absurd levels. On the other hand, eating becomes most desirable. To it she dedicates the major part of her energies, inventing increasingly bizarre, compulsive rituals.

Her goal is total emaciation, and she concentrates all her energies to reach this goal. The roundness of the female figure horrifies her. "The desire to remain *thin* remains a constant in my thoughts. . . . This compulsion (regarding food) has become the damnation of my existence, it pursues me when awake and asleep; it hovers about me like an evil spirit, and I feel that I can never escape it." So Ellen West confided to Binswanger (1958) during her treatment. A patient of mine, a philosophy student, described it thus: "I try to study as soon as I wake up; I force myself to sit at a desk, and I try to make all the words in the book enter into my body, so that they fill me totally, so that I have no space to think of eating, but this thought is inexorably present and does not give me a moment's peace."

At the time of passage into the adult sexual role, the anorexic, who has identified with the pre-pubescent male, falls "into a narcissistic existence without sex" (Thoma, 1967); she cannot achieve a female identity at the genital level and "she removes herself from a conventional sexual gender" (Spignesi, 1983).

Psychoanalysis first identified the pregnancy fantasies of the anorexic female. Waller, Kaufman and Deutsch (1940) held that: "The desire to become pregnant through the mouth sometimes gives rise to compulsive eating and, at other times, to a guilt complex with subsequent refusal of food; constipation symbolizes the child in the abdomen, and amenorrhea is a direct psychological repercussion of pregnancy fantasies. This amenorrhea may also be part of a direct negation of genital sexuality."

This interpretation led to a new definition of the syndrome, locating its causes in the period of ego formation. An ego which lacks primary support regresses and is deformed. The impact of the changes at puberty, frequently sudden and violent, can overwhelm such a weak ego, thereby influencing adolescent identity and role formation. Indeed Meng (1944) spoke of anorexia as the "deformation of the ego."

A dream reported by one of my patients presents this psychic situation: *I'm in a large university class. I have my father's bearded face. Two of my classmates in an ironic, almost mocking manner make me understand that I cannot keep that face. I take it off, but what am I to do? Who am I? I have a condom in my hand. I open it with my mouth. There is a milky white solution inside. It is like glue. It spreads onto my teeth and glues them together. I open my mouth to get rid of it, but I'm not able to close it. I remain with my mouth open.*

The body is progressively perceived as a prison which holds the anorexic in the material world, the world of biological and physical needs. Meanwhile, she tends more and more toward being "outside, beyond the world" (Binswanger, 1958).

There is no suicidal intention in this stubborn mortification of the body; there is no death wish. Rather, there is a desire to control a body which does not allow her to be totally spirit. "They (the anorexics) seem to be indifferent to their physical deterioration; this may be traced back to the delirious idea that they are capable of living by nourishing themselves with their own substance, in a sort of autarchy" (Thoma, 1967).

At the same time, this quest to be a spirit, to exist outside of this world, brings her to refuse human feeling, to live in antiseptic isolation. Spignesi (1983) saw this antiseptic isolation as an attempt to enter the world of Hades. Thus, the anorexic attempts to go beyond space and time, beyond the good and evil of the terrestrial world.

If we attempt to put together all these fragments in an effort to form a complete picture of the anorexic and her world, we are reminded of an earlier world view: gnosticism. While orthodox Christianity insists on the sinful nature of people and on the division of God and humanity, gnosticism insists that the division is not between humanity and God, but between humans and the world, between the soul and the body. In opposition to the Christian view that the world and the body are somewhat imperfect reflections of God, the gnostic argues that the world and matter are sources of all evils and all sufferings, created by an inferior, malevolent figure—the demiurge—or created by the sufferings of a female aspect of the divinity, Sophia, mother of all beings.

One of the great gnostic myths is the tale of the fall of Sophia. She was the youngest daughter of the primordial couple, the Abyss and the Silence. She was overcome by a passion, which she interpreted as love, to know her father. This passion led toward self-destruction. She was stopped by a power which freed her from her passion and returned her to her original place. This passion, separated from herself, became the lesser Sophia, from whose sufferings matter was born.

The pneumatic, spiritual part of humankind finds itself in this world like a foreigner, "the alien whose origin is elsewhere, who does not belong to the here" (Jonas, 1963, p. 49). Thus the world is a trap, a prison, a devalued and denigrated body.

In the Gospel of Thomas, Jesus says "if the spirit has truly come to exist due to the body, it is a wonder of wonders. In truth, I am amazed at how this great wealth (the spirit) has made its abóde in this poverty (the body)."

And, finally, a fragment of a Mandean lament exclaims "How much pain, how much anguish must I suffer in this body-envelope, into which they have taken me and thrown me. How many times must I remove it, and how many times must I replace it. Time after time I must die and never see life in the Sh'kina" (Jonas, p. 56).

In the separation of matter and spirit, femininity is experienced ambiguously. On the one hand the female principle, Sophia, creates matter, which has within itself a spiritual aspect. With the discovery of the gnostic library at Nag Hammadi, many texts were found containing references to God, not a monotheistic and masculine god, but a god that exists in a pair (dyad), having masculine and feminine elements. Some female figures are re-evaluated, among them Mary Magdalene, who was known as a close friend of Jesus.

On the other hand, gnostic thought finds femininity exclusively in material nature and scorns it. Thomas the Protester's book contains this phrase: "Woe to you who love intimacy with women and have contaminating relations with them" (Pagels, 1979, p. 66). Another Nag Hammadi text, the "Periphrases of Shem," describes the horror of a nature "which turns her obscene vagina and expels the power of fire which has been in her since the beginning, through the knowledge of darkness" (p. 66).

Furthermore, in the Gospel of Thomas, Jesus says that Mary must become a man to be "a living spirit resembling men, because every woman who transforms herself into a man will enter the Kingdom of Heaven" (p. 67). Thus a woman is a mere human being, while a male is divine.

Therefore, according to the gnostics, anything material, including femininity as a synonym for nature, is solely negative, a cage which one must escape through asceticism and through the denial of everything that is linked to the material world: sexuality, procreation, material possessions, food, sociability. This concept has continued despite its repudiation by orthodox Christianity.

Some gnostic ideas have remained as undercurrents in the dominant culture and have surfaced from time to time in various heretical movements. The devaluation of femininity as nature and body without the exaltation of its spiritual aspects reappeared, for example, in the dualistic movements of the Middle Ages, namely Catharism. Jonas (1963) saw in twentieth-century existentialism the gnostic idea of a scorned nature and described it as the "devaluation of the concept of nature which obviously reflects the spiritual impoverishment perpetrated by Science."

The parallel between the symbolic message which the anorexic sends us and the gnostic concept seems to be valid. The search for autonomy, the rebellion against adults, the freedom to exist as a separate individual, the administration of one's own power in interpersonal relationships are typical for the period of adolescence. In anorexics, these values cannot be expressed and therefore die. They succumb to the external environment, often represented by an "aggressively hyperprotective and impervious mother,. . . unable to conceive of her daughter as a person with her own rights" (Selvini, 1984, p. III). This power, which might have been exercised appropriately in interpersonal relationships, is transformed by our young person into an intra-psychic relationship, and her body becomes the scapegoat for her impotence and her inability to exist.

Many people agree that the anorexic's mother has a determining role. In my therapy practice I have encountered mothers who were mortified, self-sacrificing, and anguished; some of them hide this under a confident attitude. But is it their own fault that they are that way? Chernin (1985) examined the problems of today's women, as new immigrants through the borders of the business world—the world of being male, to which the female body has not been invited. In view of these new rites of passage, the daughter must reject the values of the traditional maternal world almost completely. In choosing to be different, the daughter is commenting on her mother's life and living out explosive conflicts. The anorexic, confronted with her mother's failure to realize herself, renounces her own growth and development.

The current access women have to male prerogatives produces a profound sense of guilt which brings the young woman to sacrifice herself in order to revitalize her mother and, through self-destructiveness, express both her own anger and her mother's hidden and denied anger.

Crucial in a woman's life today is her shame of displaying her body and of expressing her sentiments naturally. Society requires women to be well-groomed, thin, odorless and capable. It reinforces this message through advertisements, television commercials and magazines.

Our young woman accepts these requirements totally, without criticism. The bitterness that all this provokes within ourselves was well expressed by Chernin (1985): "Dressed in her shorts, her androgynous body covers pages of magazines, a sad reminder of how easy it was to rob us of our most profound existential battle; it is returned to us, reworked into empty images that mock our inability to reach the substantial conquests evoked by those same images."

It is true, I believe, that we women, both as mothers and as daughters, must recognize that we force ourselves to sacrifice our "otherness" to the patriarchal society. It is at least equally true, however, that the western culture in which we live rests on a basic misogyny of the Christian religion. The Virgin Mary is exalted, but as the "bride of God and Queen of Heaven [she] enjoys the place of the Old Testament Sophia" (CW11, par. 625). She does not share the original sin of humanity. Jung continued:

> This arrangement, though it had the effect of exalting Mary's personality in the masculine sense by bringing it closer to the perfection of Christ, was at the same time injurious to the feminine principle of imperfection or completeness, since this was reduced by the perfectionizing tendency to the little bit of imperfection that still distinguishes Mary from Christ. . . . Thus the more the feminine ideal is bent in the direction of the masculine, the more the woman loses her power to compensate the masculine striving for perfection, and a typically masculine, ideal state arises which, as we

shall see, is threatened with an emotional enantiodromia. (CW11, par. 627)

The threat of this "race in reverse" is desperately represented by the anorexic who is warning us, with her grotesque emaciation, that perhaps a new and previously unknown famine is about to occur: the famine of philanthropy.

Translated from Italian by
Mary Rubin

Part II

So long as a woman lives the life of the past she can never come into conflict with history. But no sooner does she begin to deviate, however slightly, from a cultural trend that has dominated the past than she encounters the full weight of historical inertia and this unexpected shock may injure her, perhaps fatally. Her hesitation and her doubts are understandable enough for . . . she finds that she is not only in a highly disagreeable and dubious situation, where every kind of lewdness and depravity abounds, but actually caught between two universal forces – historical inertia and the divine urge to create. (CW10, par. 267)

In this 1927 passage Jung indicated some of the historic difficulties in the development of the female personality, difficulties which are pertinent and timely even today. Indeed, a woman's transformation is still played out between historical inertia and the divine urge to create. The aim is an individual and not a collective existence.

A complicated interaction of intra-psychic and cultural factors increases the incidence of depressive pathologies in women. These pathologies occur when the possibility of conceiving an individual project of self-realization has been lost or where ego integration has not occurred. My reflections here have developed through my clinical experience and are based on the premise that depression, seen as a feeling of loss of meaning, is a weakening of the symbolic function. We must ask ourselves why this weakening occurs so often.

I am referring here to a situation that occurs repeatedly in clinical observation. It happens within the context of a negative mother complex, from which the difficulty in activating the symbolizing process springs. The formation of the symbol is, for Jung, the transformation of energy. The very concept of energy presupposes the existence of an opposition. The symbol then unites the opposites, giving rise to a new movement and to a new synthesis. This conceptualization will be very important as I try to formulate a hypothesis regarding a difficulty that exists in relation to the symbol. This difficulty in the maternal realm carries the deepest meaning of many depressions of women.

It is important to remember, within the context of this presentation that, whereas for the male the relationship with the mother presents itself with its characteristic of otherness, a thou experienced as distinct and differentiated from the ego, for the female the mother is both the first object of love and the privileged model for ego identification. The effect is that the resulting long-term identity brings with it in its regressive aspects and in the presence of a hypertrophic mother figure, the risk of being completely absorbed, of being unable to differentiate oneself, a hardening of the evolutive possibilities of consciousness. These intra-psychic levels of the relation between mother and daughter help us understand the blockage of the symbolic activity which expresses itself through the feeling of loss of meaning. This blockage is the inability to set in motion a transformative work through passage from the simply perceptive world to the symbolic world of images.

The feeling of loss of meaning occurs in a regressive situation where, even in adulthood, narcissistic elements strive to maintain a symbiotic relationship with the maternal iamge. What is undifferentiated in the mother-daughter relationship is fusion-confusion metaphor. The captivating power of this mirroring results in the abandoning of oneself to narcissistic identification and the failure of the symbolization process. What is lacking is an experience of otherness. Development of the symbol requires dialectical tension, contrast, bipolarity, encounter with what is different.

Many cases illustrate that the relationship with the mother, through the confusion of identity, the lack of differences and the exclusion of the masculine polarity, can become an obstacle for the female psyche's moving into the symbolic dimension. The possibility of interiorizing a positive masculine may be lacking because of a particular family constellation. The mother herself may not have a good relationship with the masculine, which is cut off or too unconscious to activate a dialectic between the opposites. For either reason or both, the woman remains closed in the trap of narcissistic identification with the mother. Losing sight of the Other in oneself closes off the symbolic dimension, halting one's development.

The relationship with the mother becomes then, for the daughter, the archetypal arena where a type of collusion is played out between narcissism and depression. Within this context the feeling of depression seems to express a suffering linked to the failure of the transformative aspect of the feminine. By narcissism, in connection with the feeling of loss of meaning, we mean its specifically feminine dimensions, represented in the Narcissus myth by characters such as Liriope and Echo and materials such as water and atmosphere.

The feeling of loss of meaning is connected with the feminine parts of the myth, and these feminine parts are characterized by elements such as passivity, incompleteness of development, inability to make decisions, and inability to find meaning unless it comes through the reflection of the Other. We make a distinction between the concept of the dyadic or narcissistic structure — sometimes indiscriminately used — and the imaginal world which connotes the symbolic feminine dimension. This dimension can be seen in many myths, including that of Narcissus.

My point can be emphasized and illustrated by a specific mythological element which can be used as an imaginal point of reference; this element contains within itself a correlative of the shadow. I do not turn to those myths that tell of the failure of the transformative aspect of the feminine through a regressive conversion into elementary forms of life that are lacking in individual consciousness. Nor do I turn to those that connect this failure with a loss of contact with the masculine or the inability to bring about a coniunctio. I turn instead to the myth that illustrates how an opening to the symbolic overcomes the undifferentiated mother-daughter reality in which many depressive pathologies originate. This myth shows that the overcoming occurs through the intervention of a masculine which introduces the experience of Otherness. This experience makes possible an approach to the symbolic dimension.

I refer to the myth of Demeter and Kore. In it the masculine attacks the idealizing symbiosis of the mother-daughter relationship and draws the outline of the archetypal shadow in the background. In a case of mother-daughter symbiotic relationship, an animus is contaminated by the shadow and completely cut off from consciousness because its aggressive contents attack the fusional quality of the relationship. The Demeter-Kore myth presents both the prospect of totality—a Self which is born from the dialectic between the maternal feminine and the masculine— and the complex obstacle, the breaking away from the mother. The myth illustrates how the painful integration of this shadow can give birth to a widening of existential horizons for a woman. An internal aggressive masculine, not subject to the dominion of the Great Mother, supplies the push and the energy necessary to bring about a separation.

If we want to understand better how this type of mother-daughter relationship can be charged with hidden depression that often emerges as full-blown pathology, it is enough to think of the unconscious ambivalence and repressed aggressiveness— which are the roots of depression—that are present in every symbiotic idealizing relationship. An encounter with the divine masculine, a mixture of the animus and the shadow, makes Kore the lady of the underworld, a participant in the mystery of immortality and transcendence. This new condition marks the passage, even though it is a painful passage, from the elementary character of the feminine to the transformative character, from historical inertia to the divine urge to create. The passage includes attainment of a symbolic perspective; within this perspective the tension of the opposites characterizes a psychic model that goes beyond the borders of one-sidedness.

I conclude this brief presentation by referring to our cultural context. In the psychic constellation described here, the dominance of the maternal image and the absence of a positive masculine makes the process of symbolization impossible and gives rise to depression. This constellation is characteristic not only of a patriarchal western culture where traditional roles make it hard for the woman to break with the maternal world and develop an autonomous animus. Many depressive pathologies of this type have been observed over the last ten years in women whose involvement with feminism has contributed to an accentuation of the pre-existing individual problems. These women may regress to the archaic maternal which is matriarchal. Because it is full of negative projections, the masculine is also cut off. Many such women may experience a hardening of the symbolic function due to their inability to set up a masculine-feminine dialectic.

The result may be the appearance of severe depressive states. It is difficult to treat such a state in these people who, because of their extreme ideological positions, and because of an excess of defensive rationalizations, have a tendency to deny the need to reconcile the opposites. Thus they refuse the symbolic message of the depression itself.

Translated from Italian by
Beatrice Rebecchi Cecconi

Part III

Some women, affected by severe long-term depression, have become aware through analysis that depression can arise from the lack of living femininity as a dimension of their lives or a mode of their experience. In the cases that will be described here, the analytic work has touched—at the root of depression—the feeling of a threat to psychic identity or to their feminine existence. This feeling has caused a stalemate in the ego-Self axis. The ego gives voice to the suffering which comes from this threat, in unceasing oscillation between the poles of despair and guilt. Even more, in these cases the ego tries to impose itself as a voice which is superior, indomitable and accusatory. At the beginning, there is an entanglement of accusations. Later their target is revealed in the mother as the carrier of the projection of the Great Mother who has abandoned, rejected and betrayed.

This position of the ego, similar to Jung's image of Job against Yahweh, is an achievement of the analytic work through its efforts to reach the meaning or to offer a clarification of the initial contradictory accusations. Here we are dealing with a number of women whose psychological development, despite individual differences, has been precociously dominated by the paternal figure or the paternal world around them. This domination has created a systematic devaluation, if not an outright attack, on femininity itself. Emotionality, sexuality and cognitive development have all been the objects of indiscriminate control and influence, through the anticipation of meanings and the pressure for values of consciousness such as intellectuality, reasoning and will, as privileged goods in themselves. The result is a state of enslavement continuously acted out by a blind and rigid ego which adheres compulsively to a model, to the exclusion of anything else. A daughter of this type completes her studies and goes to work—while in the clutches of a corrosive sense of waste.

Though feeble on the surface, the relationship with the mother is charged, at a deeper level, with denigration and anxiety. The more this relationship is kept at a distance, the more it proves to be petrifying or menacing when it comes concretely close. Such a mother figure carries in herself an archaic and senseless shadow, full of poisonous emotion, because the paternal world and its predominating ability have absorbed consciousness. The narcissistic greed of an artistic father competes, in one case, with the maternal figure; the urge for social revenge of a patriarchal farm clan annuls, in another case, the maternal figure. In both cases, the mother withdraws, gives up and, inevitably, colludes with the invasive father. This mixture of giving up and collusion affects the daughter massively and deeply: on the one hand, the inability of the mother to give herself to the daughter and to protect her; on the other hand, her ability to be absent or present through insurmountable silences. The daughter's perception, increasingly and unbearingly, is of a mother who is rigid and mortified, suffering or disappointed, nevertheless haughty and distant.

This situation produces a psychic event that conditions the daughter's personality toward depression. This event can be described mythically as the Goddess, the ancient and the eternal one, who sinks down into the depths or, fairy-tale like, as the dark women who isolates herself in the woods. The fundamental sense of Self as unity and potentiality is offended, frightened and even hardened. Like a pearl inside a shell it moves downward until it rests on the very bottom. Survival is attained, but depression ensues. The Self, as the function of totality, is blocked at the maternal level and acts as paralyzing identification with the

mother as offender and offended. The ego, disarmed and suffo-
cated, reacts bitterly by collaborating with the paternal influence
though preserving, hidden in the maternal function, that threat
to psychic identity that stimulated the sinking down of the Self.

The Self is in a frozen state of ambivalence. Adolescence is the
time when failure explodes outward and conflicts implode in-
ward. In my analysands, of ages varying from 27 to 40 years, the
depressive blockage has marked their personality ever since: devoid of rhythm, lacking in images because lacking in mystery,
the personality seems to be continuously grasping for something
else, or for "new spaces which then always fade away" (as Ute
Dieckmann, 1974, p. 110, underlined in a similar case) in the anguish of maternal lack, defeat and rejection.

The depressive combination of impotence and self-accusation,
of a despairing inability to live and the stubborn use, at the same
time, of the weapons supplied by the "enemy" (the father) and
turned constantly against the maternal, which also carries the
image of Self, is better understood as a paradox. The depressive
tyranny is produced by the sinking down of the Self, but the Self
treats the ego more as an incomplete sense or as an interrupted
image, rather than as an overwhelmingly negative function, as
Wilke (1978) and Cornes (1985) have stated, referring to clearly
psychotic depressions. Neither is the sinking down of the Self a
purely passive and reactive event resulting in the denial of Self,
which occurs in the narcissistic character disorder described by
Schwarz-Salant (1982).

The threat to psychic identity takes us back to the ego-building
function of the Self. By blocking the ego in that feeling of threat,
the Self is preserving itself. The identification with the mother as
offender and offended is the prison of the "divine figure" of the
Self, the aspect of its unexpressed potency. The personal and the
archetypal aspect of such an identification is a negative symbol;
the ego feels that it is the carrier of the negative symbol as well
as the victim. An abortive or defeated maternal Self tends to
leave its mark on every love relationship of the ego, on every
push toward planning or accomplishing anything. The ego is
blocked in a self-image as an unproductive and bad mother, from
which it must flee. The more she flees elsewhere, the more such
a depressed woman finds herself in a pseudo-symbolic land of a
thousand and one masks. She denies her identity and loses even

more. There are no children except for aborted ones in the histories of these analysands, nor are there lasting love relationships. Loss spreads out as loss of forms, connections and strength. It is as if life itself becomes invisible: The ego, indeed, does disappear but not the compulsive motion to do something or to devote to something. It is a sort of secular creativism, non-naturalistic and not compensatory, as if one were trying to solve the riddle of life through a piece of work without having the grace of art, or by cloistering oneself into a particular commitment without having a vocation for the convent.

These depressed women need what they fear most and what nails them down obsessively to their inability to transform. They need to face the maternal in themselves and redeem it from the condemnation as a negative symbol. The shadow which links the mother and the daughter is within the Self; the freeing of the Self comes about through the redemption of the shadow – which the mother has not been able to accomplish. In one case, the accusation of refusing the child's love, of abandoning and betraying, was translated into the offended and rejected maternity of the daughter. Her melancholy traced its origins back to the unconscious refusal of maternity itself on the part of the mother: maternity as duty and the child as the only fruit of the Self. In another case, the shadow tied itself to both mother and daughter as carriers of death: the mother, because she responded to a humiliating conjugal situation by keeping maternity for herself as her only good, both too big and too little to be shared; the daughter, because she identified the mother with death to cover her fear and envy of her. By performing fatherly commands in life, she was indeed a false Bacchante who, unknowingly, kills her child.

As von Franz wrote: "The mother goddess wants to incarnate in a human daughter, but the impulse remains abortive. It has nowhere been carried through and become a religious event" (1972, pp. 21–22). But a daughter can humanize the chaotic impulse of her mother by following its intent, or she can break the "total reaction" of the unmirrored divinity by fulfilling the task of the abortive shadow. To do this she must transgress against forced maternity in favor of tolerance and acceptance of herself; or she must expiate destructive maternity and, through acceptance of her mother, gain a hold on her own life.

Regression and paradox are in contention in the psyche. The

greater the possibility of symbolizing the maternal, the greater the redemption from psychic invalidism. The underlying eros melts the bond to the Self as crystallized divine figure and brings forth new images of I and Thou. The other way around, the bond to the Self gives such depressed women a touch of extreme modernity. Indeed, sense and feeling, reason and emotion, eros and logos need and seek each other in them as well as in those men who, today, do not live the fall of physical and metaphysical masculine supremacy as a psychic crash.

A weak minority, perhaps—such women and such men—in front of the schizoid scientistic society of the year 2000: the one which, on one side, manipulates values in favor of the return to family life and, on the other side, wants to section the female and male bodies in order to make of male pregnancy a sort of talisman, perhaps, against the nuclear threat.

Translated from Italian by
Beatrice Rebecchi Cecconi

REFERENCES

Binswanger, L. (1958). *The case of Ellen West*. New York: Simon & Schuster.

Bruch, H. (1978). *The golden cage*. Cambridge, MA: Harvard University Press.

Chernin, K. (1985). *The hungry self, daughters and mothers: Eating identity*. New York: Times Books.

Cornes, T. (1985). Symbol and ritual in melancholia: The archetype of the divine victim. *Chiron*, 203–22.

Dieckmann, U. (1974). Ein archetypischer Aspekt in der auslösenden Situation von Depressiven. *Analytische Psychologie*, 5, 97–112.

Jonas, H. (1963). *The gnostic religions*. Boston: Beacon Press.

Meng, H. (1944). *Psyche und Hormon*. Bern: Huber.

Morton, R. (1694). *The phthiosologia or a treatise of consumptions*. London: Smith & Walford.

Pagels, E. (1979). *The gnostic gospels*. New York: Random House.

Schwarz-Salant, N. (1982). *Narcissism and character transformation*. Toronto: Inner City Books.

Selvini-Palazzoli, M. (1984). *L'anoressia mentale*. Feltrinelli.

Shorter, B. (1980). The concealed body language of anorexia nervosa. In J. Beebe (Ed.), *Money, food, drink, and fashion and analytic training*. Fellbach: Bonz.

Spignesi, A. (1983). *Starving women*. Dallas: Spring Publications.

Stroud, Joanne. (1980). Flesh gone in inquiring of the bone. *Dragonflies*, 2–1.

Stroud, Joyce. (1980). Anorexia nervosa and the puer archetype. *Lapis 6*.

Thoma, H. (1967). *Anorexia nervosa*. New York: International Universities Press.

von Franz, M. -L. (1972). *The feminine in fairy tales*. Dallas: Spring Publications.

Waller, J.; Kaufman, M.; Deutsch, F. (1940). Anorexia nervosa, a psychosomatic entity. *Psychosomatic Medicine, 2*, 3–16.

Wilke, H.-J. (1978). On depressive delusion. *Spring*, 105–114.

Woodman, M. (1980). *The owl was a baker's daughter*. Toronto: Inner City Books.

Discussion: Ian Baker (Zurich)

The three papers I am discussing bring a most valuable contribution to the practical problems raised by the archetype of the
shadow in anorexia nervosa and depression. The papers thrust
us again into the dilemma of what to do when we are faced with
these problems in the split world which our practices mirror. The
topic is so wide that it merits down-to-earth confrontation with
what it implies for our practical analytic work. My short paper
highlights the excellent points made by my Italian colleagues and
also proposes some ideas which may provoke discussion or even
controversy.

Baldieri sees an important phenomenon in her presentation:
the weakening and loss of the symbol-forming function in the
psyche. If a person is unable to move into a symbolic dimension,
there can be no possibility of reaching the creative space between
polarities. For men, the relationship to the unconscious feminine
is always colored by its very otherness; for women that maternal
unconscious is always linked to ego identity and cannot allow objective distancing. The mother-daughter relationship, unless dissolved, contains the risk of complete mutual absorption and
blocks the opportunity for the daughter to differentiate herself.
What then occurs is a collusion between narcissism and depression, since there is no space for the creation of individual symbolic space. Fusion with the maternal is complete and confusion
of identity follows.

This situation is confounded if the mother does not have a
good relationship to the interior masculine, or for that matter to
the exterior. On a mythological level, this reminds us of the
Demeter-Persephone constellation where the masculine (Hades)
forces the break, albeit incomplete, within the symbiotic collusion of mother and daughter.

At the same time, because of the common collusion between
mother and daughter and the lack of space for growth which this
implies, we are forced to face the vexing problem of the mother's
animus and the faulty shadow development which this constellates. We are asked to look at the dynamics of a shadow contaminated by the animus, where neither shadow nor animus can be
properly differentiated and experienced. This situation is con-

founded by the inability to relate on any level to the father-lover and by the consequent alienation from the archetypal masculine in general. We have to admit that we have not yet faced what this animus/shadow contamination means on a practical level.

Baldieri points out that the encounter with the divine masculine opens the woman to the dilemma of the contamination between shadow and animus which, on the one hand, blocks her earthly life and, on the other, leads her into a new relationship to mystery and transcendence. But in cases of anorexia and depression, the access to this higher feminine consciousness is blocked.

This problematic situation leads us to ask the question: Is it correct to link anorexia with depression? The anorexic, according to my observation, does have a form of depression, but it is compensated by the curious phrenetic activity and buoyancy which seems to be a byproduct of fasting. This phenomenon leads us to examine the remarkable lack of anxiety of anorexics and, indeed, the strange lack of fear in the face of death from starvation. It leads us also to the examination of the strange split between body and soul; the patient seems comfortable with being in a realm between spirit and flesh and at the same time seems unable to realize that body is soul and soul is body. The exquisite maintenance of an existence which thrives on a delicate balance between life and death absorbs all the energy and brings the feeling of exaltation and triumph which is so difficult to comprehend. As far as I can see, depression comes only when insight into the danger of the game becomes conscious. It is thus a depression linked with the sense of loss of youth and the inability to make good what has been thwarted in development—the sorrow of futility.

In addition to the question of the mother-daughter relationship is the problem of the missing father. Much of the literature on anorexia deals with the disturbed relations between mother and daughter. In the work I have done with anorexics, however—11 cases to date—I have found a far deeper disturbance in the father-daughter relationship than is usually recognized. A consequence is that, with anorexia, the analyst must break the analytic vessel insofar as one must deal with the client's family. This is a situation for which most of us are untrained. In the 11 cases I have mentioned, I managed to see both the mothers and the fathers. The three papers have correctly assessed the disturbed relationship of mother and daughter, but in the fathers I found certain characteristics which were too marked to be ignored.

First they were all in what might be called second positions. They wanted to be doctors but were dentists; they should have been bank managers but were assistants; they wanted to be in the army but were minor city officials instead. Second, they came reluctantly to see me and were strangely indifferent about their daughters' fates except in the sense that they were having to pay for therapy. They were markedly cold and indifferent to their daughters' suffering. Third, they all evinced a subliminal cruel, sadistic streak when they described the physical danger in which their daughters found themselves, as if they experienced some perverse, distant enjoyment. Fourth, they expressed a sexual desire for their daughters when puberty started, either overt desire or veiled in sentimentality. All had made some "off-color," usually denigrating remark about their daughters' developing bodies. Fifth, each had ceased sexual relationships with his wife when the daughter's anorexia started. For this cessation they put the blame on the wife.

When talking to these men, it struck me that these facts were too prevalent to be ignored. It also made me think how often Analytical Psychology dwells upon the negative mother and made me wonder about what one might call the St. Joseph archetype.

Much of our imaging of the family is based, in western culture, on the ideal family for which we, perhaps unwittingly, use the Holy Family as archetype. But the Holy Family is a faulty archetype, in that Joseph is not the genitor but merely the figure-head. He is two-dimensional, bland, benign, and teaches his son his trade. More than that, we have no knowledge about him. It strikes me that this missing father image and its base upon a distorted archetype may be more important that we have admitted. This has been brought to light oddly by the feminist movement, where suddenly women are aware, not only of the damage done by masculine-dominated culture, but of the fragile role the father has played in our cultural development. It is relatively easy to write off the Great Mother in a psychological way, but we leave the Great Father to the theologians.

One of the aspects of our split world lies in just this problem — the missing father or, worse, the father figure-head who is present but at the same time absent and lost in the collective. The death of the old king makes little sense if he is, as a man, already non-existent.

It strikes me that, using Analytical Psychology and its terminology, we could gain new insight into the dynamics of anorexia. For it touches upon our other psychological split—between body and psyche, between nature and spirit. Moreover, the syndrome of anorexia is increasing among males.

Iorio defines the relationship of daughter and mother in a new way. She sees that, though the relationship to mother is feeble, this is only a surface manifestation; underneath lies a confining closeness which has strains of denigration and anxiety. This petrifies development in the daughter and reveals the mother as caught in her own archaic but senseless shadow. At the same time, the paternal world, though promising certainty and light, in fact denies consciousness by absorbing ego energy. There can be no protection from the maternal and only abduction from the paternal. This leads to a state of frozen ambivalence and also a fictional sense of being and time. There is no space to reach for something else and, even when such space opens up, that new space recedes into a sense of lack, defeat and refusal. This situation eventually leads to a depressed sense of shame and guilt which can only be relieved by attacking the enemy, the body, the maternal, but the paternal at the same time traps the woman in a spiritual yet motherly way.

Iorio builds her argument upon a statement of von Franz who suggests that the mother goddess wants to incarnate in a human daughter, but the impulse to do this remains abortive. Nowhere has it been carried through to become a recognizable religious event. The daughter of the great goddess remains non-incarnate. Moreover, the daughter, at least in western culture, can never reach the Dionysiac, because there is no feminine counterpart to that great god.

Grassi de Marsanich views the anorexia epidemic as a milestone in the history of the development of medical and psychological trends, and as a manifestation of the shadow of our affluent and materialistic society. It is just one of the manifestations of the shadow in this split world of ours. Not only is the anorexic a victim of her own shadow; she is the harbinger of the shadow wherever she finds herself, in that she is the mirror of the divisions and repressions of modern society.

But we might see the anorexic as suffering, not via the mirror of Narcissus, but more in the one-way mirror of Echo. The body of the anorexic does not allow her to be spirit. She must then live in a repetitive stubbornness, repeating the pattern of half-life, reiterating the search for a perpetuum mobile between life and death, always searching for antiseptic isolation.

In Grassi de Marsanich's paper we are asked to consider a new approach to anorexia, that is, in terms of the world view of the gnostics, with their devaluation of femininity as nature and body and denial in the feminine of the exaltation of spirit. This, in combination with many aspects from these three unique papers, must stimulate discussion on the wider implications of the feminine psyche, sick and healthy, in our present social and cultural climate. For we are asked once again to view the problem of scorned nature in both a clinical and a symbolic format, and as yet seem not so blessed with the seal of success.

Masochism: The Shadow Side of the Archetypal Need to Venerate and Worship

Rosemary Gordon (London)

Richard had been in analysis with me for 18 months. A year before he came to me he had terminated a long analysis with a colleague because an uncomfortably close professional relationship had developed between them. He was in his early fifties, a lecturer in a theological college, and married with three grown children, two sons and a daughter. He was of average height, had some middle-aged spread, and always wore dark and very conventional suits. He looked his age. He complained of finding it very difficult to be alone in his home and felt easily abandoned by his wife even if she went out for only a short time to do the shopping.

The main theme in many sessions was his preoccupation with death. Closely related was his anxious concern about the existence of God. Indeed, he felt angry and resentful that God did not prove His existence to him. In spite of a life ruled by his belief in God, Richard was a man of the scientific age of concrete proof, dependent on belief because he was unable to give himself over to faith. In time his belief became threadbare, and the existence of God seemed to him increasingly unconvincing. Then fantasies of being beaten began to possess him, fantasies that excited him sexually. As they intensified he found himself driven to act them out with women he picked up. He felt intensely disturbed, guilty and very angry with analysis, with me, and with God, much in the way that Sartre cried out through one of his characters: "He does not exist, the Bastard."

Working with Richard impelled me to speculate on the connection between masochism and the belief in, and worship of, a deity. I remembered a number of patients who had told me of masturbation fantasies in which religious rituals had taken on a markedly masochistic quality. One woman had described lying on an altar and being solemnly whipped. Another woman saw herself on an altar in a convent being held fast, hands and feet, by four nuns while the mother superior whipped her in full view of all the sisters. Another woman patient dreamed of being beaten; she woke to find that she was having an orgasm.

Patrick, a schoolmaster, whom I described in an earlier work (1978), told me soon after he started analysis with me that he was much involved with the Greek goddess Artemis; the worship of Artemis had included an annual sacrifice to her in which the most perfect youth was beaten to death. The masochistic experience of this rite governed his masturbation fantasies; in fantasy he experienced himself as this perfect youth-victim. The sadistic role of the sacrificer tended to be enacted in his relationship with one of his male students to whom he was attracted, and whose qualities he admired and idealized.

These experiences and reflections led me to the hypothesis, expressed in the title of this paper, that masochism is closely related to a human need, probably archetypal, to venerate and to worship some transcendent object or being. Masochism, that impulse to expose oneself to pain and suffering, is the shadow side of this need. Though not often seen in these very stark and extreme forms, masochism is a frequent and pervasive factor in clinical work. I think it worth exploring here.

Masochism seems to figure very little in Jung's writings; there is not a single reference to it in the Index (CW20) to his *Collected Works*. However, Neumann (1954) related masochism to his concept of uroboric incest in which a weak ego dissolves in the Self, and this "unconscious identity with the stronger solvent, the uroboric mother, brings pleasure, which must be called masochistic in the later perverted form" (p. 277). Another valuable contribution has been made by Williams (1958, 1962). She wrote:

I will now make the assumption that there are two main ways of avoiding the fear of death. In the sadistic method the individual forms a counter-phobic identification with death as the destroyer. The victim is then the mortal who must die in fear and pain while the destroyer experiences the ecstasy of immortality. . . . The masochistic method derives from the sadistic method and must be understood in terms of the latter, for masochism is a counter-phobic reaction to unconscious sadism. The sadist identifies with the invulnerable destroyer and projects his mortality on to his victim. The masochist identifies with the mortal victim and projects the invulnerable destroyer; thus the destroyer is sought as the saviour who will rescue him from his mortality. (1958, p. 16)

Like Neumann, Williams talked of the ultimate aim being "death in ecstasy."

Freud distinguished primary masochism from secondary masochism. While he regarded secondary masochism as a turning upon oneself of the sadistic impulses and feelings experienced toward another, primary masochism was to him the direct expression of Thanatos, the death drive. Its object is still one's own self; it is not the consequence of aggression that, as a defense of oneself, has been directed outward.

In Klein's theories, however, the death drive has taken on a primary and crucial role. She saw its manifestation in the ego's struggle to preserve itself. She wrote: "The threat of annihilation by the death instinct within is, in my view – which differs from Freud's on this point – the primordial anxiety and it is the ego which, in the service of the life instinct, possibly even called into operation by the life instinct, deflects to some extent that threat outwards" (1957, p. 31).

There is some convergence of the ideas of the foremost pioneers, Freud, Jung and Klein, concerning the roots of masochism, for all three are led back to an original death drive or death wish. But Freud and Klein did not seem to pay attention to such concepts as the transformation of impulses, death and rebirth, the symbolic meaning of death, or to humanity's basic need to search for something transcendent. I believe, however, that if we are to understand masochism, we must consider those ideas too. After all, masochism is evinced not only in the pursuit of physical pain, but also in such psychological states as longing for surrender, for dependence on others, for helplessness, for self-abnegation or for immersion and unity in and with another person. While some regard masochism as a means of symbolic self-annihilation, others understand it as a way of resisting ego annihilation and asserting instead an identity and proof of ego-consciousness. It is then seen as a sort of "pinching oneself to know one is awake" (Joseph, 1982, p. 634).

To me the most meaningful contribution by a psychoanalyst to an understanding of masochism has been made by Khan (1979). He argued that the individual needs psychic pain to be witnessed silently and unobtrusively by the other, and that it is this need which has "led to the creation of the omnipresence of God in human lives" (p. 211). With the increasing disappearance of God as the witnessing Other, "the experience of psychic pain has changed from tolerated and accepted suffering to its pathological substitute, and the need has rapidly increased for psychotherapeutic interventions to alleviate these pathological masochistic states" (p. 211).

Khan's thesis meets quite naturally my reflections about masochism in religious rites and rituals and in ascetic and mystical practices. The presence in religions of frustration and denial of physical and emotional needs, and indeed the actual infliction of pain on oneself or on others is almost ubiquitous and universal. Circumcision, sub-incision, flagellation, fasting, abstinence — sexual, social, appetitive — and sacrifice are well known. Physical postures also express and communicate humility, surrender and abandonment: folding arms, clasping or joining hands, bowing, kneeling and prostration.

There is indeed a very thin line between the sincere desire to surrender to something or somebody beyond oneself and a perverted masochism, where the experience of pain has become an end in itself. Such perversion parallels in some ways Arnold Hauser's description of the mannered style in art, which he has defined as the perversion of a given style through concentration on inessential details, raising them to the central feature. Thus when pain, suffering, and self-abasement have become the primary objective rather than only a preparation for an experience of surrender to the holy, the eternal, the transcendent, then we are indeed dealing with a perversion, with pathological masochism. The realization of this distinction led the Buddha in his search for enlightenment to abandon rigorous asceticism for the middle way—that is, the reining in but not the total rejection and destruction of one's personal needs.

I return to the theme of sacrifice, which is so prominent in religions. Here I find Humbert's (1980) paper to be quite seminal. He pointed out what is actually obvious, yet rarely noted or remembered, that etymologically "to sacrifice" denotes "to make sacred" (p. 32). He discussed and analyzed the human willingness to forego satisfaction of needs and impulses such as hunger in order to find or create the symbolic, and so give meaning to life, personal and social. A powerful example of this impulse to escape from a sense of comfortable meaninglessness by a quest for the unknown is described in a short story by D. H. Lawrence entitled "The Woman who Rode Away." Married to a rich self-made American silver mine owner living in Mexico, the woman used a few days' absence of her husband to leave home, drawn by a "vulgar excitement" to encounter somewhere, somehow, signs of the Indian people she had heard described as "ancient, wild and mysterious savages." She met men who, without using force, constrained her to follow them up to their mountain village. She lost all self-will and self-direction. There was no struggle in her against this, though she was also given potions to ensure further her loss of sense of self. She was treated like a precious object: fed, housed, massaged and clothed in blue—"the color of the dead" she was told—but she was kept in isolation, except for the daily visits of a priest and of the only interpreter. "They were gentle with her and very considerate. . . . They watched over her and cared for her like women." But she was left in no doubt about her fate. Indeed, at the very moment of the winter solstice, after a day of much ritual dance and ceremony, when "she felt little sensation, though she knew all that was happening," the oldest man, the priest, "struck home, accomplished the sacrifice and achieved the power."

In this short story Lawrence portrayed the almost orgiastic abnegation of consciousness and the willing, near-ecstatic acceptance of self-sacrifice.

How can we understand this drive to sacrifice? I believe that such abnegations and self-denials have as their aim the suppression of what is felt to be but a temporary, transitory part of ourselves. This part aims to liberate us from the domination of body over mind or psyche. We know that the body returns to dust quite shortly after death; we have all observed the unreliability of this body when it begins to let us down in the course of the aging process. Is asceticism a rehearsal of death, an attempt to experience death in this life, so as to rob it of its capacity to surprise us or to find us unprepared? In Buddhist tradition it was wisdom, or rational foresight, that made the king Kapilavastu, of Suddhodana, try to prevent his son, Gautama, from ever seeing illness, old age, and death. He knew that knowledge of this would draw his son away from his palace and into the forest in search of enlightenment.

In our analytic work, masochism is frequently the expression, albeit often perverted, of the need to worship, venerate and to search for the transcendental. Its goal is usually more earthbound and less lofty, but it is often in the service of securing love and admission to the admirable, the idealized. As Joseph (1982) suggested, the masochist, building on childhood experience or misunderstanding of how to gain or to maintain the parents' love, believes that the price to be paid for this love is the surrender of personal separateness and individuality.

It is worthwhile to remember that Freud recognized three forms of masochism: erotic, moral, and feminine. The patients I mentioned at the beginning of this paper showed primarily the erotic form of masochism. The patients I will describe next show the interaction of complex and differing psychological mechanisms.

Bob had been in analysis for many years. He was a designer, eager to use his creative resources. His longing to become a good, inventive designer had been one of the main reasons for coming into analysis.

He was the elder of two boys. His father, an engineer, a quiet and somewhat withdrawn man, had been away fighting in the Second World War when Bob was between eight and 12 years old, the very years when he most needed the presence, encouragement and inspired companionship of a man.

His mother had been a professional ballet dancer who, after the birth of her two sons, and then the absence of her husband, became a teacher of dance and drama. She was, from Bob's description of her, a very lively person, somewhat self-centered, devoted to her work and profession, with easy access to her feelings and her creativity, but not really interested in, or talented for, homemaking or giving attention to her children. She had a close woman friend with whom she collaborated in her professional work.

Bob was a tall, quiet, shy, timid, diffident, insecure and passive person, who looked ten to 15 years younger than his age. He had great difficulty in asserting himself personally or professionally. He seemed cut off from his affects and impulses; his feelings in the transference were subdued. Only when he could tell me of some new failure or mishap, some new loss of prestige, achievement or argument did a flash of masochistic triumph enliven his facial and verbal expression.

The analysis jogged along quietly, yet he had many interesting dreams and some of them were filled with strong emotions. There were several about a birth-giving; either he or some domestic animal, such as a cat, was bearing a baby. But even this potentially forward-looking theme tended to be vitiated in some way or other: There was not enough food for the new baby; or instead of milk the baby was offered shit; or he, the birth-giver, was rejected and socially excluded and shunned; or the baby was damaged or disposed of as rubbish. There was, in these dreams, much hurt and pain, but he would tell them in his quiet, gentle and bland manner, as if they had been dreamed by someone else.

Strangely enough, my own feelings for him in my countertransference remained consistently patient, affectionate and maternally caring. Why, I often wondered, did I not at least sometimes react with impatience, anger and/or irritation, as, indeed, his father had expressed to him when he returned from war service. As Bob remembered, his father did not seem pleased with the way his elder son had developed. His father may have experienced Bob as part of his own shadow, as a caricature of himself, representing his own lack of a positive and secure confidence in his masculinity.

I began to suspect that there was no lively and potentially creative center to be found in Bob. When both of us came close to a loss of hope—and yet there were the dreams—he decided to try some art therapy. The results were truly surprising. His paintings were a revelation: They were remarkably lively, colorful and full of imaginative forms—of persons, of animals, of objects—expressing joy and fun as well as fear, anger, violence and even horror. They showed a previously unseen capacity to be playful.

I use the word "playful" here in Winnicott's sense when he described it as the "child manipulating external phenomena in the service of the dream." But at first, as with his dreams, Bob displayed and discussed his paintings without much affect, enthusiasm or even involvement.

Now my own reactions to him changed: I became more fierce and challenging. I felt anger, as if on behalf of these pictures, his pictures, at what seemed to me to be his dismissal of them, and at his churlish and almost sadistic refusal to acknowledge as his own the paintings before us. As I began to express some of these reactions it seemed as if a father, a more potent and potentially enabling father than he had experienced in his own personal history, had become activated inside each of us and between us. At first Bob reacted with sullen, sulky and hurt withdrawal into more silence. But then, slowly, he rose to my challenge: He became overtly more resentful, sometimes abusive and finally openly and honestly hostile and aggressive. This seemed slowly to enable him to protect and defend his creative work and to acknowledge it as his. He was then able to protect that part of himself from which his pictures had drawn their existence and their aliveness.

Now he seemed to begin to extricate himself from envy and impotence in relation to his lively and artistic mother; to emerge also from the belief that all creativity belongs to the woman, the mother, who castrates males and leaves them eunuch-like with only a slavish, flirty, and admiring way of associating with the forces of creation.

However, before Bob achieved this extrication, and while he was in the midst of this mother-father-transference work, he had an auto accident. It was not altogether his fault, but had he been more alert and attentive, he said he might have been able to avoid it.

It took many months, in the relative safety of the consulting room, to understand the meanings of this accident and to work through its emotional aspects. What emerged was that, psychologically, the accident was indeed a murderous attack on the much admired and much envied mother. It was also a murderous attack on the father, whom Bob thought of either as absent and unavailable or, if present, as inadequate and impotent because he had not succeeded in taming and containing the

mother. He had also been unable to guide Bob into true and enjoyable manhood. But, inasmuch as Bob identified sometimes
with the enviable mother, sometimes with the inadequate father,
the accident was also a suicide, a killing of him who had been
swamped and taken over by one or both parents. This suicide
was then an expression of his despairing of ever being able to
shed the incorporated and introjected Other; becoming himself.

As we worked through the emotional experience and the symbolic meaning of the accident, it took on the quality of murder
and suicide, but also of parturition, birth and sacrifice. Sacrifice
is, of course, the essential and always present constituent of rites
of passage.

Bob's case illustrates idealization, projection and incorporation
of the person carrying an idealized part of oneself. In Bob's case,
the mother had been experienced as a somewhat alien presence
inside him, and hence as an obstacle to discovering his true Self
and his own creative powers. The fact that his creative, idealized
mother had remained like a foreign body inside him provoked
murderous envy. The sadistic attack on the internalized mother
ended in the masochistic attack on his own body. This was a dramatic example of a sado-masochistic acting-out. It also shows the
power of envy and how the search for one's true Self, in cases
where there has been much internalization, can produce the
simultaneous enactment of both sadism and masochism.

I want to give one other, less dramatic example of masochism.
Leslie, a man in his late thirties, had several desirable ex
periences which had raised his hopes that he might eventually
have more time to do what most fulfilled him: painting and writing poetry. However, two nights later he dreamed an "absolutely
horrible dream" which left him in a bleak mood. He told me the
dream in the next session:

> I have to go somewhere, to my office I think. I am at a bus stop. But I have
> to wait a terribly long time. I turn round for a moment; and just then the
> bus I have been waiting for rushes by—without me. And then I see that
> though I wear a shirt I have no trousers on, which is most embarrassing.
> Then I am back in my flat; I am now properly dressed. And now I realise
> that where I want to go is actually nearby; I do not need to take a bus at
> all to get there.

As we talked about the dream I became aware that the happy

ending did not make him happy at all. The grim mood persisted; he seemed to cling to the first, the negative, unhappy part in what I felt to be a masochistic way, a tendency in him with which he and I were quite familiar. This bleak mood continued through the next session. I ended the session asking, "What do you need all this pain for?" I kept to myself the possible answer, "To attack you" (the analyst) and "to attack myself" (the patient). When he came to the following session he felt and looked much more cheerful. He had remembered suddenly that his mother used to dampen any joy at achievement. And he remembered the day when he had won the first prize as the best actor in his school and indeed in the county. But he remembered that his mother, instead of congratulating him, warned him, "You know such a talent might suddenly disappear." "She always spoiled a good experience," he added. "Am I now doing this to myself? After all, only my father was allowed to be great." Fortunately for this patient, the unconscious identifications were more accessible to consciousness than had been the case with Bob. In Leslie's case the self-attack seemed to emanate from an internalized mother; he probably colluded with her in an attempt to placate, obey, and please her in guaranteeing that father alone was the great and powerful one. But he did resent it, and felt angry about it.

Masochism inevitably has clinical consequences. It is often one of the root causes of the negative therapeutic reaction, for it tempts the patient to cling to hurt, suffering and unhappiness and to memories of sad events and circumstances of the past. Interpretation touching on painful areas does not easily evoke compensatory drives, memories and attitudes that could then challenge the sufferer to do battle with causes underlying the pain. Rather, he or she is likely to grasp the pain, hold fast to it and relax into its pleasurable effects. Also, unless an interpretation is painful, it feels like none at all.

Naturally the analyst's countertransference is very difficult. I find that either I am drawn into the masochistic mood, in which case I may start to share the patient's despair, or get bored and perhaps even sleepy. On the other hand I may be irritated and feel arising in me a sadistic reaction to the patient. Then I am likely to experience anxiety and guilt, though I usually try to protect the patient from my reaction. Sometimes, however, such sadistic reactions may have a function. I felt just such irritation with Leslie, and I admit it was out of that irritable and sadistic reaction that I had asked him why he needed his pain. In his case my reaction bore fruit, for he then dredged up the memory of his mother who "always spoiled a good experience."

It must be clear from my comments and descriptions that masochism usually has multiple causations; it is rarely a single event, or even a single trauma that can explain or be held responsible.

However, in all these patients there was a desire to reach through love, surrender and submission something or somebody beyond themselves, idealized probably, but nevertheless experienced as beyond and superior to themselves. It is true, in the cases of Patrick, Bob and Leslie, that the apparent cause was the relationship to the real and earthy persons of the mother and/or father. In Patrick's and Bob's cases the father was absent but he was overwhelmingly present in Leslie's case. In the case of Patrick his mother—seductive and mysterious—appeared to him as a goddess. Bob longed to reach that fascinating creative spring, that muse to which only women, it seemed to him, could have any access. Leslie's masochism appeared to be rooted in the fact that his mother and so many others rendered willing and selfless homage and devotion to his famous father; refusal to join them, or to compete with him was experienced by Leslie as rebellion, if not blasphemy.

Summary and Conclusion

If my hypothesis is valid, if behind the masochistic phenomenon lies an archetypal need to worship something transcendent and sublime, what effect could this knowledge have on our clinical work and on our reflections about the wider world?

I believe that the recognition of a link between masochism and the shadow side of the need to worship and venerate could affect countertransference feelings toward masochistic patients. It may stir us to ask, for instance, what the patient is seeking as a valid object of veneration. How can we help the patient to assimilate projected idealizations for conscious use? It may be our task to assist the transfer of worshipfulness away from persons and to-. ward the admired qualities and talents, or at least toward a personage, such as God, who may represent these qualities more suitably.

Furthermore, if we recognize that this need to worship and venerate is archetypal and intrinsic, then we must remain alert lest the object of this archetypal need be harmful or evil. Such an object incarnates the heroic but also the diabolic in us, a poisonous mixture of our envy, rage, murderousness, and disenchantment with the unattainability of the good. The gang leader, the terrorist, the self-styled freedom-fighter, the demagogue, all exploit the human need to surrender, follow and worship.

I doubt that such an archetypal need can be eradicated. But we analysts may be able to affect the choice of the object to be worshiped, and inform and alert those outside our consulting room of the glimpses that we have gained in our work with our patients.

I close with a sentence from Jung's paper on "The Psychology of the Trickster Figure" which I think touches prophetically, in a personalized form, on what I have suggested here: that there is a link between masochism and the search for meaning, for spirit.

> The unpredictable behaviour of Trickster, his senseless orgies of destruction and his self-appointed sufferings, together with the gradual development into a saviour and his simultaneous humanisation. It is just this transformation of the meaningless into the meaningful that reveals the trickster's compensatory relation to the "saint." (CW9-I, par. 458)

REFERENCES

Gordon, R. (1978). *Dying and creating*. Library of Analytical Psychology, Vol. 4. London: Academic Press.

Humbert, E. (1980). Le prix du symbole. *Cahiers de Psychologie Jungienne*, 25–2.

Joseph, E. (1982). Addiction to near-death. *International Journal of Psycho-analysis*, 63–4.

Khan, M. (1979). *Alienation in perversion*. London: Hogarth Press.

Klein, M. (1957). *Envy and gratitude*. London: Tavistock Publications.

Neumann, E. (1954). *Origins and history of consciousness.* London: Routledge & Kegan Paul.

Williams, M. (1958). The fear of death (Part 1). *Journal of Analytical Psychology, 3–2.*

Williams, M. (1962). The fear of death (Part 2). *Journal of Analytical Psychology, 7–1.*

Discussion: Rudolf Blomeyer (Berlin)

My approach to discussing Gordon's paper is to present a series of statements which I will examine as a whole without referring to each of her points.

A statement that I have always felt to be one of the main principles of Analytical Psychology is: A patient who comes with a religious problem has a sexual one; one who comes with a sexual
problem has a religious one.

Another important statement comes from a paper by Guggenbühl (1982) about anarchistic sexuality:

> All the bizarre sexual fantasies, all that wild and chaotic acting out
> of sexuality can be understood as symbols of individuation. Maso-
> chism, for example, would be confrontation with the suffering ex-
> perienced through the medium of sexuality. . . . But Jungian
> psychology, too, is not able to grasp sexuality in all its aspects. . . .
> Certain compulsive, monotonous, repeated, "perverted" sexual
> fantasies or activities, for example, can hardly be understood any
> longer as parables or symbols for individuation. (p. 66)

The terms masochism and sadism were introduced by Krafft-
Ebing (1892). Freud remarked on the naming: "Other authors
prefer the more restricted term of algolagnia which stresses the
pleasure gained from pain, . . . while the names which were
chosen by Krafft-Ebing put in the foreground the pleasure gained
from any kind of humiliation and submission" (GWV, p. 56).

Very early Freud connected neurotic and religious contents or
exercises with each other and remarked that "the little accom-
paniments to the religious ceremonial make sense and are to be
understood symbolically, while those of the neurotic ceremonial
appear silly and pointless. Compulsive neurosis furnishes a half-
comical, half-sad caricature of a private religion." The difference
would soon be made clear by analysis. "One learns that the compulsive acts make sense. . . in all. . . their details, that they
serve important interests of the personality,. . . that they have
to be interpreted historically or symbolically" (GWVII, p.
131–32). Example: In the story of the "wolfman" (GWXII) the
masochistic attitude toward the father appears to be sublimated
in an identification with Christ.

Freud distinguished between erotogenic, feminine, and moral masochism; the first form underlies the other two (GWXIII, p. 373). Here Freud used the term of erotogenic as he had introduced it in the "Three Essays on the Theory of Sexuality," where the term refers to particular zones of the body; in these zones sexual arousal can develop. "The zone behaves in every respect like a part of the genitals. . . . In the sexual instinct's component of pain and cruelty it is the skin which takes on [that] role" (GWV, pp. 68–69).

Wilhelm Reich thought that the masochistic fantasy essentially contained the fantasy of bursting in the sense of a wish for and a fear of orgiastic relaxation. He noted: "Religious ecstasy is completely set up on the model of the masochistic mechanism." Thus, God is expected to give loosening of and deliverance from the inner (sexual) tension. "The masochistic orgies of the Middle Ages, Inquisition, the mortifications and torments" had to be understood in this sense (1927/1976, pp. 112–13).

Gordon mentions Masud Khan (1979). He thought that humans need to have psychic pain tacitly confirmed by another. This need led to the creation of the idea of God's omnipresence. The more God as the perceiving and testifying Other has disappeared from our imagination, the more psychic pain has turned from a borne and accepted suffering into a pathological substitute, that is, masochism. For Gordon, Khan's reasoning was the most important contribution of a psychoanalyst to the understanding of masochism. For me, too, the reasoning sounds appealing and convincing, but "the more . . . the more" makes me skeptical. It sounds as if masochism had not existed in the good old days, but that it had come into being only since God has more and more "disappeared." In my opinion only the name is new, but the phenomenon is very old.

Humans as suffering or enduring beings are described by Frankl (1950) and Weizsäcker (1956). It is important to distinguish between masochism and suffering—bearing it, accepting it, mastering it. A disciple of Frankl, Polak (1959) agreed with Gordon that, for the masochist, suffering becomes an end in itself.

Among the forms of masochism named by Freud, feminine masochism is especially interesting for our discussion. Freud did not mean a form of masochism which can be found especially in women; he meant a feminine-masochistic attitude in men. He described this attitude: "Being gagged, bound, beaten in a painful manner, whipped, somehow maltreated, forced to unconditional obedience, soiled, humiliated, . . . treated like a little helpless and dependent child. . . . [When] the masochistic fantasies have undergone an especially rich elaboration, one can easily discover that they put the person in a situation which is typical for femininity, i.e. being castrated, copulated, or giving birth" (GWXIII, p. 374).

All the men described by Gordon belong to this field: Richard, who lets himself be beaten by women picked up off the street; Patrick (with a narcissistic accentuation), the chosen victim of Artemis; Bob, the pregnant man, the one who gives birth, with the castrating mother; and finally Leslie, whose mother undermines all progress.

I return to the comment on religion and sexuality. Jung commented on the pictures of the *Rosarium Philosophorum*, and especially on the picture of the coniunctio:

> As to the frank eroticism of the pictures, I must remind the reader that they were drawn for medieval eyes and that consequently they have a symbolical rather than a pornographic meaning. . . . Union on the biological level is a symbol of the unio oppositorum at its highest. . . . The opus becomes an analogy of the natural process by means of which instinctive energy is transformed, at least in part, into symbolical activity. . . . Many alchemists compute the duration of the opus to be that of a pregnancy, and they liken the entire procedure to such a period of gestation. (CW16, pars. 460–61)

The statement on analogy and symbolism, of course, is valid not only for the beautiful image of the coniunctio, but also for the repulsive images of and fantasies about the torments of the alchemistic procedure. In order to extract the pure substance, body and soul are subject to medieval torture: killing, murder, decaying, burning (CW16, par. 467) and "cutting up the limbs, dividing them into smaller and smaller pieces, mortifying the parts, and changing them into the nature which is in [the stone]" (CW16, par. 478).

Jung commented on "the motif of torture," on "torture" and "torment" in the "Philosophical Tree": "Take the old black spirit and destroy and torture with it the bodies, until they are changed: . . . [the] plucking of a live cock, the drying of a man over a heated stone, the cutting off of hands and feet, etc." (CW13, pars. 439, 441). Other passages, for example the section about "the sacrificial act" in the comment on "The Visions of Zosimos," mention the self-sacrificer, dismemberment, and a "bowl-shaped altar . . . in which a multitude of people were boiled and burned" (CW13, par. 91). Jung scarcely ever used the term "masochism." But in connection with transformation he wrote a lot about fantasies and symbolic acts which in our patients we would not hesitate to describe as sado-masochistic.

At the end of her paper Gordon quotes Jung's work "On the Psychology of the Trickster-Figure." We learn among other things that the trickster "can turn himself into a woman and bear children" (CW9-I, par. 472). Jung reported on several parallel figures: Mercurius, poltergeists, shamans. They all have an inclination to partly amusing, partly vicious, even sadistic tricks. At the same time they are subject to tortures of all kinds. If one considers also an approximation to the savior, that the sufferer takes away suffering, pronounced sado-masochistic elements are associated with the figure of the savior. Jung wrote:

> These . . . features extend even to the highest regions of man's spiritual development. If we consider, for example, the daemonic features exhibited by Yahweh in the Old Testament, we shall find in them not a few reminders of the unpredictable behaviour of the trickster, of his senseless orgies of destruction and his self-imposed sufferings, together with the same gradual development into a saviour and his simultaneous humanization. It is just this transformation of the meaningless into the meaningful that reveals the trickster's compensatory relation to the "saint." (CW9-I, par. 458)

Trickster elements in the individual, according to Jung, are a "sort of second personality, of a puerile and inferior character," that is a typical shadow figure with "the personal shadow [being] in part descended from a numinous collective figure" (CW9-I, par. 469). The ego consciousness finds it unpleasant and amusing, perhaps also vicious or even a source of masochistic suffering.

Gordon's view is that masochism is the shadow side of the tendency to venerate and worship. We generally assume that the shadow is opposed to the conscious. But Gordon's hypothesis actually is not about an opposition but about something which on different levels is principally similar: the need to give oneself, to subject oneself with humility, to venerate and worship. Satisfaction is sought either on the sexual level or, linked with highly developed mental products, on the level of religion. But the original tendency remains contaminated with the more sublime one; the sexual element remains part of the religious one. And in spite of a continuous and careful torment, in analysis not all tricksters become saints.

Translated from German by
Dagmar Henle-Dieckmann
and Sabine Osvatič

REFERENCES

Frankl, V. (1950). *Homo patiens*. Wien: Franz Deuticke.

Guggenbühl-Craig, A. (1982). Anarchistische Sexualität. *Gorgo*, 8–4, 63–73.

Khan, M. (1979). From masochism to psychic pain. In *Alienation in Perversion*. London: Hogarth Press.

Krafft-Ebing, R. (1892). Bemerkungen über "geschlechtliche Hörigkeit" und Masochismus. *Jahrbücher für Psychiatrie, 10*, 199–211.

Polak, P. (1959). Zum Problem der noögenen Neurose. In: Frankl, Gebsattel, Schultz (Hg), Handbuch d. *Neurosenlehre u. Psychotherapie*, Vol.II, 664–91. München/Berlin: Urban & Schwarzenberg.

Reich, W. (1927/1976). Die Funktion des Orgasmus. In: *Ausgewählte Schriften*. Köln: Kiepenheuer & Witsch.

Weizsäcker, V. (1956). *Pathosophie*. Göttingen: Vandenhoeck & Ruprecht.

The Pathological Shadow of the Western Cultural Self

Carlos Byington (Sao Paulo)

In developing my ideas about the pathological shadow, I have synthesized the thinking of my predecessors and have added my own concepts (1986) to those of Jung, Michael Fordham, J. J. Bachofen, and Erich Neumann. Jung (CW9–I) formulated the concept of a collective shadow. His description of the individuation process in the second half of life was enhanced by Fordham's (1969) theory of ego formation through the process of deintegration of the Self and by Neumann's (1954, 1973) conception, following Bachofen (1861/1973) of collective and individual archetypal development of consciousness through successive matriarchal and patriarchal phases.

I have substituted a concept of structural evolutionism for Bachofen's and Neumann's "linear" development or "staircase" evolutionism. In my (1983) model the matriarchal and patriarchal phases are cycles which initially succeed one another but, once implemented, function concurrently throughout life. In each such archetypal cycle, as consciousness is being structured by an archetype, we distinguish a more active or passive attitude of the personality. The passive predominates in the first part of these cycles and the active in the second.

In addition, I have added two more archetypal cycles to the matriarchal and patriarchal: the otherness cycle, patterned by the anima, animus and coniunctio archetypes; and the cosmic cycle, patterned directly by the central archetype (diagram 1). The postulating of four archetypal cycles recognizes that some archetypes, once they are constellated, function side by side throughout life and give importance to the fact that these cycles may be antagonistic to each other during individual as well as cultural development. This four-cycle model is central to my understanding of shadow formation, mainly regarding those symbols of the shadow which become dissociated because of defensive structures and thus form the pathological shadow.

The concept of these four archetypal cycles describes four different patterns for symbolic elaboration and the operation of consciousness. This use of the concept of the archetype as a pattern of relationship was described by Jung (CW10, 12, 13, 14) in reference to the anima as mediator between conscious and unconscious. It is found also in Neumann's (1973) presentation of matriarchal and patriarchal dynamisms. Klein's (1952) schizo-paranoid and depressive positions can be regarded also as archetypal patterns of relationship.

In order to by-pass methodologically such polarities as inner-outer, psyche-nature, mind-body, and individual-society, I have formulated inclusive concepts of psychic energy and symbol to express all existential dimensions, subdivided for practical purposes into a quaternio: social, physical, ecological, and ideological-emotional (diagram 2). This concept of symbol encompasses all psychic dimensions, representations, and functions, including defenses; it means that every symbol has a historical-personal and an archetypal aspect.

If we admit that consciousness and the ego have different patterns of operation in each archetypal cycle, and thus are restructured and archetypally transformed throughout life, we must reformulate many psychological concepts. We need new skins for this new wine. To try to fit life-long patterns into concepts formulated by Jung to express archetypal activity exclusively in the second half of life is a strait-jacket attitude. This formulation is one explanation of Jung's reductive and non-archetypal treatment of many psychological concepts. He tended to equate archetypal psychology with the ego's being transcended in the second half of life, and the psychoanalytic model with ego formation in the first half. Thus many concepts of Analytical Psychology dealing with ego formation have been contaminated by psychoanalytic, non-archetypal reductionism.

Jung's fixing of ego development in the first half of life and archetypal activity predominantly in the second half may explain also his reduction of unconscious functioning primarily to compensation rather than to the creative aspect of the whole personality, the Self. To consider compensation of consciousness as the essence of unconscious functioning overlooks the primary creative function of the Self, which includes compensation but goes beyond it in the potential creative capacity of the central archetype.

From the perspective of lifelong development, the Self and the central archetype cannot be used as synonyms, a fact which Perry (1957) also remarked on when studying the shattered ego of schizophrenics. The Self as the sum total of conscious and unconscious processes is not the same as the archetypal matrix of psychic development.

In considering the second half of life, in which the ego supposedly is transcended, the archetypal aspect of ego and persona as well as the psychodynamics of shadow symbols are easily overlooked. But when lifelong archetypal development of consciousness is postulated; persona, ego, and shadow become the actualizing structure of the central archetype. Thus conceived, the persona ceases to be reduced to the secondary or defensive aspect hiding the shadow, and becomes instead a set of social roles worked out through the creativity of culture to further collective and individual symbolic elaboration. The pathological defensive persona hides symbols; the normally creative persona enhances symbolic development. The masks of Greek actors indicated their role and were constructed to intensify their voices. ("Persona" combines "per," meaning through, with "sonare," to sound.) This modification of the concept of the persona is essential for understanding the creative transformation of collective consciousness, along with individual consciousness.

From this developmental perspective, consciousness and the ego also cease to be reduced to their defensive usage — as in the ego's permanent resistance to the repressed unconscious in the psychoanalytic model — and become instead the creative product of archetypal activity. Similarly, shadow symbols are seen only secondarily as that part of the personality which consciousness has difficulty in accepting. Primarily, they are insufficiently elaborated symbols, and so are inadequately expressed in personality, institutions, and cultures.

The conscious/unconscious axis—Neumann's ego-Self axis—constitutes the functional expression of the Self and, in this perspective becomes the symbolic axis. If we acknowledge the common individual and collective archetypal development of consciousness, we can conceive a collective as well as an individual self. The Self functions through the symbolic axis to express the four existential dimensions patterned by various archetypes and coordinated by the central archetype. Diagram 2 expresses the structure of the individual Self, and diagram 3 that of the institutional or cultural self. Their similarity is elaborated to show the analogy of individual and collective consciousness formation.

Individual and Collective Symbolic Psychopathology

My concept of the pathological shadow is based on a theory of symbolic psychopathology which differentiates normal structuring functions from defensive structures operating along the symbolic axis. I have presented this theory in an earlier work (1986).

The indiscriminate use of fundamental psychic polarities (such as creative/defensive projection, delimitation/repression, centroversion/regression, creative/compulsive repetition, and creative/defensive transference) has established a conceptual confusion in psychopathology which hinders its being understood as a variant of normal symbolic-archetypal development. This confusion of creative and defensive structures may be interpreted as a defensive projection and rationalization of the cultural self onto psychological theory.

Creative structuring functions such as imitation (predominant in matriarchal dynamism) and delimitation (predominant in patriarchal dynamism) are archetypal structures which operate along the symbolic axis to enhance symbolic elaboration and consciousness structuring. (Jung's "transcendent function" is active in the elaboration of all symbols.) Defensive structures are variants of creative functions. They also express symbols along the symbolic axis but compulsively prevent these symbols from entering consciousness for ultimate discrimination. Such symbols form the pathological shadow.

Projecting a symbol in order to identify with it (projective identification or creative projection) is quite different from projecting a symbol in order compulsively to resist identification with it (defensive projection). In this manner, the concept of the creative structuring functions, elaborating every symbol in consciousness and in the normal shadow, is the basis of normal symbolic development, whereas the concept of defensive structures, expressing symbols in the pathological shadow, is the essence of symbolic psychopathology both in the individual and in the cultural self.

Institutional Analysis

Once we recognize the common archetypal development of individual and collective consciousness, we can undertake a symbolic/archetypal analysis of institutions and cultures. This analysis presupposes a model for the structure of the group or cultural self (diagram 3), and a model for the inter-relationship of the four developmental archetypal patterns of individual and collective consciousness (diagram 1): the matriarchal, patriarchal, otherness, and cosmic patterns.

A symbolic/archetypal analysis of the institutional self must be centered around five main issues. First, anamnesis—the historic and present interrelation of the four dimensions of the institutional self. Second, identification of the main symbols constellated at a particular moment in order to discover the developmental process underway. Third, differential diagnosis of symbols that operate freely from those in the normal and pathological shadow and thus encumbered by defensive structures. Fourth, further differentiation of symbolic parts caught up by defensive structures through elaboration in the live interaction of therapist and members of the institution under analysis, with the constellated archetypal field of the therapeutic self; this part, when productively undertaken, coincides with the beginning of treatment. Fifth, prognosis and treatment. This issue must be considered dynamically during therapy, so that the course for working through the polarity defenses and symbolic elaboration can be altered strategically whenever necessary.

The Institutional Distortion of the Christ Symbol

As I have pointed out elsewhere (1980), the Christ symbol continued the development of Messianic thought from its roots in Jewish mysticism. It was constellated, synchronistically, on the eve of a genocidal confrontation, in 70 A.D., between Rome and the Jewish people—two cultures distinguished by an extraordinary development of the patriarchal pattern.

That pattern structures consciousness in an asymmetrical I-Other polarity; autocratic behavior leads to a delimitation of the field of consciousness and resultant shadow formation. Collectively, the patriarchal pattern tends to an organization of society characterized by hereditary class privileges that include private property. The tension built up by the power drive in such a cultural self is alleviated through scapegoating and cultural power expansion. In the patriarchal pattern, opposing pairs are not treated as equal; any confrontations between such pairs meet with intense delimitation and even repression, so that asymmetry is maintained. The extreme consequence of this attitude is one pole's being oppressed or eliminated by the other. When it occurs collectively, this situation can lead to war and, in ultimate cases, to genocide. It is not difficult to conclude that, under this patriarchal pattern and present technological development, any serious international crisis may lead to the destruction of our species.

In the post-patriarchal otherness pattern of development, consciousness includes the capacity to function with the I-Other polarity in an egalitarian, creative, and dialectical inter-relation. The I becomes able to expose its shadow symbols in the same way that it can detect the shadow of the Other. The otherness pattern of consciousness is therefore quaternary; it expresses the actualization of the quaternio structure of the central archetype. I have associated this consciousness pattern with the structuring capacity of the anima, animus, and coniunctio archetypes. In individual development the pattern corresponds in part to the phenomenology described by Jung in the individuation process. Collectively, the otherness pattern of consciousness expresses the search for the social democratic state, and its great ideal of freedom, equality and full human development.

The Christ symbol in the Jewish-Christian tradition is the main expression of the otherness pattern of consciousness in western culture; this pattern is expressed also in the Kabbala and in alchemy. After the Renaissance, the otherness pattern appeared in the natural sciences and, from the end of the nineteenth century onward, also in the search for the social democratic state. It may seem far-fetched to link the Christ symbol with such extensive occurrences as the development of the natural sciences and the search for the democratic state. This link becomes more intelligible and acceptable, however, if we consider the historical transformation of the cultural self as inseparable from archetypal patterns and symbols. The Christ symbol was not the historical cause of the Renaissance, the natural sciences, and the search for the democratic state, but these events are meaningfully (synchronistically) linked to the symbol through the otherness pattern, as constellated in the cultural self.

In order to understand symbolic elaboration through the otherness pattern of consciousness, it is important to realize that this pattern functions through the synchronicity principle. In the same way that magical causality may be detected in the functioning of matriarchal consciousness and demonstrative causality in the patriarchal pattern of consciousness, synchronicity is the main principle in the functioning of the otherness pattern of consciousness.

From a symbolic/archetypal developmental perspective, it is comprehensible that such a powerfully charged symbol as that of Christ should suffer many historical distortions during its institutionalization. It is also to be expected, and even predicted, that these distortions should come from great resistances of the patriarchal pattern to the otherness pattern; resistances lead to the formation of shadow symbols. When these are dissociated by defensive structures, pathological shadow symbols appear. Because of the prospective characteristic of the psyche, these future events are likely to be present in this symbolism from the start. All these variations of the Christ symbol can be found in Christianity under various guises.

It is a meaningful coincidence that the apostle Peter, whose name means rock, betrayed Jesus three times before sunrise but was chosen to institutionalize Christianity. In this betrayal we can see symbolically that the institutionalization of the message, even before it could be expressed in the new pattern of collective consciousness (sunrise), would suffer a severe distortion (three denials). It is also significant that John, who first mentioned the Antichrist (I John 2:18), received visions of the apocalypse in a cave on the island of Patmos and that Patmos was destined to be the center of one of the four Greek Orthodox churches that originated in the first great schism of Christianity.

My approach to the history of Christianity differs from many others in distinguishing between institutional Christianity and its archetypal symbolism. Documents such as those of the Nag Hammadi library show how much the institutionalization of Christianity distorted this original message, censoring a good part of its Dionysian element.

Perhaps the most important symbol that was repressed even more than distorted in Christianity was that of Mary Magdalene, the woman apostle and announcer of the savior's resurrection. The defensive patriarchal minimization of her symbolism crippled the hero's adult masculinity and reduced his meaning to the son child in the Trinity. Even Jung (CW11), complemented the masculine triad almost exclusively by the femininity of the hero's virgin mother. Through this dissociation, the prostituted patriarchal femininity is not saved as the messiah's anima and remains exiled in Christianity, sharing the devilish qualities of Adam's Lilith.

The Antichrist and Devil Symbolism

Historically, western culture and the church have projected the Antichrist and the devil—a collective Christian shadow. The formation and intensification of Antichrist and devil symbolism was structured in a patriarchal manner, through the suppression of the matriarchal-Dionysian aspects of the Christian symbol. When the four gospels were canonized, as we see clearly in the Nag Hammadi library, the new religion already was mutilated greatly. The institutionalization proper, marked by the conversion of Constantine and the Roman Empire, allowed two of the greatest patriarchal cultures of all times to unite for the first time. The legendary sign of Constantine's conversion joined the cross and the sword.

The matriarchal dimension was suppressed along with gnosticism: for example, a representation of Christ as a serpent around the cross. Increasing patriarchal dominance was expressed by the Council of Nicaea (325 A.D.), because it suppressed Arius' differentiation of the nature of the Father and Son in the Trinity and because this suppression was based on the explicit agreement (required by Emperor Constantine himself) to have only one version of the nature of Christ.

This patriarchal domination is the main psychological reason for the schisms of Christianity; it took over the Church, and later became the inspiring guide of the Holy Office during the Inquisition. Psychodynamically, this domination became the main defensive structure which prevented an adequate elaboration of the Christ symbol and led to expression of the shadow. Herein lies the basis of the Antichrist symbol, defensively projected as evil on any creative manifestation that differed from orthodoxy. These defenses may be classified as psychotic. How else can we classify torture and homicide in the name of love?

One of the central themes of this paper is to propose that Christian heresies are archetypal ways to elaborate and assimilate the Christ symbol. Heresy (from the Latin *hairesis*) means a school of thought. How could such a powerful symbol be elaborated except by many different schools of thought? The repression of this plurality was accompanied by the repression of Dionysian-matriarchal polytheism, which reappeared in alchemical imagery.

Latin American Colonialist Identity

After the symbolism of death in the Middle Ages, Christianity was resurrected in the Renaissance through the natural sciences. Then the term Antichrist was thrown against natural science by the Inquisition. The aftermath of this encounter was the separation of science from religion and, in the eighteenth century, the rise of so-called objectivity.

During this religious struggle the rich New World was discovered. The black and Native American offer of the Dionysian *joie de vivre*, perhaps the greatest of these riches, was answered with catechizing, genocide, and slavery by Inquisition-dominated Europeans.

An immense difference marked the German-English Protestant colonization of North America, compared to that of Catholic Portugal and Spain. Northern immigrants, mainly family-oriented, founded a new country with social democratic idealism which had had been cherished in their home countries.

In South America there was never the idealism of founding a new country. On the contrary, the great difficulty was finding colonists. The majority who came plundered and returned to Europe. Not only riches, but the very land was divided among noblemen who seldom visited and, once in the new country, longed to go home. This practice led to the formation of a colonialist identity in Latin America which, even after independence, remained essentially European-centered.

The economic models offered their colonies by Catholic Portugal and Spain and by Protestant Great Britain and Holland were fundamentally different. Most of the Portuguese and Spanish nobility were economically unproductive. They used the riches obtained from their colonies to repay immense sums borrowed from England to finance their armies and luxurious court life. England in turn used these riches to finance its industrial revolution. Thus, Portugal and Spain remained culturally in the Renaissance and only recently, together with Latin America, began the differentiation of their identity as modern industrialized nations.

Miscegenation was the second great difference between northern and southern colonialist identities. On both continents there was genocide of the indigenous peoples and black slavery; in South America miscegenation occurred on a much larger scale. Through inter-breeding the great indigenous empires in Mexico and Peru had a large influence in the colonial era.

Under such circumstances the Antichrist symbolism and heresy persecution, extended by the Inquisition to the colonies, influenced massively the formation of Latin American identity. In North America black slaves were converted and Native Americans isolated; in South America they intermarried with Europeans while being exploited and religiously persecuted. A whole interbred population was formed, lacking identity because the white immigrants themselves had no New World identity but maintained a cultural and economic orientation toward Europe and later the United States.

Latin American Post-Colonialist Identity

For all these reasons, the post-colonialist identity of Latin American countries was long delayed. Its formation is only now underway, guided by large social themes such as agrarian and social reform, labor unionization and political representation. The present transformation of Portugal and Spain, and their cultural, political and economic participation in Europe, play an important part in this effort.

The present quest for identity in Latin American societies may be termed post-colonialist because it involves, for the first time, the differentiation of these societies from their European roots. However, collective identity in a multicultural, inter-racial society can be furthered only through the otherness pattern of consciousness. This archetypal pattern, which underlies both the individuation process described by Jung and the social-democratic form of government, encounters many difficulties in becoming institutionalized, including the reactionary drive of the class-privileged elite. The difficulties of the progressive forces are not seen easily because they are largely projected on the privileged elite, whose power then becomes exaggerated. These difficulties spring from the matriarchal as well as the patriarchal dimensions of colonialist identity. A transformation in both dimensions is needed to build post-colonialist identity.

Latin American black and Indian cultures contain an important component of matriarchal dynamism which permeates and enormously enriches popular culture, but which was severely wounded during the period of slavery and genocide. The European immigrants' repression also hinders creative elaboration. This dysfunction of matriarchal dynamism is at the root of many cultural problems such as disorganization and corruption. The *caudillo*, the most common political prototype in these countries, is an archaic paternalistic figure, a matriarchal image of magical leadership. The defensive patriarchal pattern, imported from Europe with its class-struggle ideology, historically has been the great trigger of military repression.

The need for the otherness pattern to build the post-colonial identity has constellated the Christ symbol. The Church plays a central role in this quest. It is divided into a traditional and a progressive sector; the latter sides largely with a revolutionary cause based on Marxism and the theology of liberation.

This new historical constellation of the Christ symbol may enhance the otherness pattern, which is indispensable for the formation of post-colonial identity, or it may be transformed again into its shadow, the Antichrist, to favor fratricide, terrorism and cultural stagnation.

A dynamic examination of Church history could lead to an understanding of the present patriarchal quality of Marxist dialectics and of the current reduction of the search for class interaction to a mere class struggle. The transformation of the socialist democratic message into the totalitarian state shares the same archetypal structure as the patriarchal spirit of Christianity expressed in the Inquisition. In both situations, the otherness pattern is reactionary and defensively patriarchal.

A contribution to the search for Latin American post-colonialist identity can be made by an archetypal understanding of the nature of the collective otherness pattern, showing how this identity may be further mutiliated by Christianity through the defensive use of the Christ symbol.

The Developmental Symbolic Cycles of the Individual and Cultural Self

Predominance of
Active Position of the ego in
the ego-other polarity

Predominance of
Passive Position of the ego in
the ego-other polarity

SECOND HALF OF LIFE   *FIRST HALF OF LIFE*

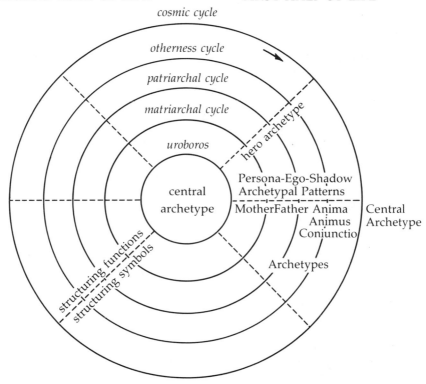

Each archetypal cycle has a typical person-(ego-other)-shadow pattern of relationship. Cycles begin in stadial succession, but function side by side throughout life. Their psychological dominance also occurs in stadial succession which does not prevent each dynamism from becoming again dominant whenever necessary.

Diagram 1.

The Symbolic Structure of the Individual Self

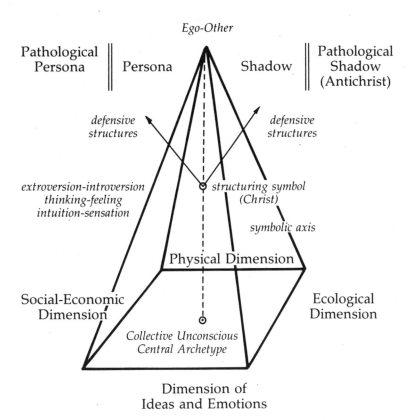

BEHAVIOR

unconscious-subconscious   subconscious-unconscious

CONSCIOUS

Ego-Other

Pathological ‖ Persona   Shadow ‖ Pathological
   Persona ‖   ‖   Shadow
                                     (Antichrist)

defensive   defensive
structures   structures

extroversion-introversion   structuring symbol
   thinking-feeling   (Christ)
  intuition-sensation

                              symbolic axis

Physical Dimension

Social-Economic   Ecological
   Dimension   Dimension

Collective Unconscious
Central Archetype

Dimension of
Ideas and Emotions

Diagram 2.

The Symbolic Structure of the Cultural Self

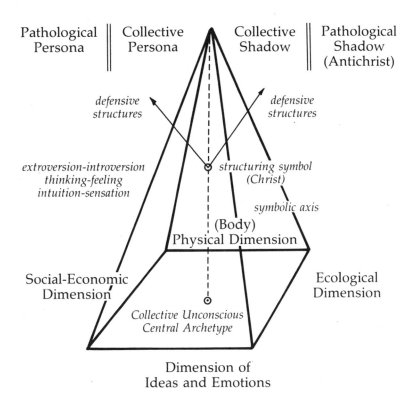

BEHAVIOR

unconscious-subconscious   subconscious-unconscious

*COLLECTIVE
CONSCIOUSNESS*

Pathological ‖ Collective   Collective ‖ Pathological
Persona   ‖ Persona   Shadow   ‖ Shadow
                                             ‖ (Antichrist)

defensive   *defensive*
structures   *structures*

extroversion-introversion   *structuring symbol*
thinking-feeling   *(Christ)*
intuition-sensation
                                   symbolic axis

                                   (Body)
                                   Physical Dimension

Social-Economic   Ecological
Dimension   Dimension

                Collective Unconscious
                Central Archetype

Dimension of
Ideas and Emotions

Diagram 3.

REFERENCES

Bachofen, J. (1861/1973). *Myth, religion, and mother right*. Princeton, NJ: Princeton University Press.

Byington, C. (1980). Symbolic psychotherapy, a post-patriarchal pattern in psychotherapy. In J. Beebe (Ed.), *Money, food, drink, and fashion and analytic training* (pp. 441–72). Fellbach, West Germany: Bonz.

Byington, C. (1983). O desenvolvimento simbólico da personalidade, *Junguiana, Journal of the Sociedade Brasileira Psicologia Analitica, 1*, 8–63.

Byington, C. (1986). The concept of the pathological shadow and its relationship to the concept of defense mechanisms within a theory of symbolic psychopathology. In L. Zoja & R. Hinshaw (Eds.), *The differing uses of symbolic and clinical approaches in practice and theory*. Zurich: Daimon.

Fordham, M. (1969). *Children as individuals*. London: Hodder & Stoughton.

Klein, M. (1952). Some theoretical conclusions regarding the emotional life of the infant. In M. Klein (Ed.), *Developments in psycho-analysis*. London: Hogarth.

Neumann, E. (1954). *The origins and history of consciousness*. New York: Pantheon.

Neumann, E. (1973). *The child*. New York: Putnam's.

Perry, J. (1957). Acute catatonic schizophrenia. *Journal of Analytical Psychology, 2-2*, 137–52.

Destructiveness in the Tension Between Myth and History (A Discussion Among Three Analysts)

Arvid Erlenmeyer (Berlin)

Anne Springer (Berlin)

Klaus Winkelmann (Berlin)

We live and work as analysts in the western part of Berlin, a city whose division is the result of World War II. The Iron Curtain which, as Jung said, represents the split in the human psyche, goes right through the middle of the city. Berlin, as representative also of the global split, influences profoundly our practical and theoretical analytical work. Moreover, Berlin is of special significance for Psychoanalysis. In the course of Freud's and Jung's separation the focus of the analytic movement shifted from Zurich to Berlin under the leadership of Karl Abraham. Our training institute (The Institute for Psychotherapy) gathers under the same roof Jungians and neo-Freudians (mainly followers of Harald Schultz-Hencke) who work together, with some difficulty at times. The neo-Freudians consider themselves to be successors of the Berlin Psychoanalytic Institute which was founded in 1910; the "orthodox" Freudians, however, have their own institute which is named after Abraham. Our training institute is seen as successor of the Reichsinstitut under Matthias Göring which, after the seizure of power by the Nazis, united the different depth psychological schools with the aim of establishing a "German psychotherapy" purified of orthodox Freudian thinking.

In recent years, colleagues from the German Psychoanalytic Association, the professional association of Freudians, dealt intensively with the history of Psychoanalysis in Nazi Germany. Initial steps have been taken toward a historical clarification of the role Jung and Jungians played in the Third Reich and especially in the Reichsinstitut. Among Jungians Jaffé (1985) dealt with Jung's role in the Third Reich and Blomeyer (1982) took up the story of Freud's and Jung's separation. Wilke, as the editor of our journal as well as author of a paper (1985) about this subject, initiated a discussion assessing Jung's statements on National Socialism.

Our own work has roots in Ute and Hans Dieckmann's seminar "On the Inner and External Nature of Man" which began in 1979. In connection with the ecological and nuclear threat it has been dealing more and more with questions of contemporary history (see Dieckmann, 1984). Since 1982 this part of the seminar's work has been carried on by a subgroup which has examined the reflection of events in contemporary history in the transference-countertransference relationship. (See Erlenmeyer, 1984 and Springer, 1984.) It seems to be not by chance that, after separation processes within this subgroup, we remained apart from other colleagues as a triangular configuration—a return of the repressed. The oedipal dynamics of this configuration had a productive effect on our work. If it is true that the Oedipus concept guarantees historical relevance in biography, we had to pose its questions to ourselves and to our personal and analytic parents.

How did Jung deal with the historical reality of his time, which was full of collective destructive eruptions, including mass extermination of human beings and destruction of whole cultures and their spiritual and intellectual property? Does Jung's theory and his way of dealing with his personal and political history allow us suitable identifications with regard to our personal and intellectual background? Does Jung offer us a mythologizing of history—a defense against the torturing reality of contemporary history? Do Jung's theory and language seduce us into an ideological view of reality and too easy explanations? Do we thus

avoid the suffering from reality and a socio-political transformation of reality instead of learning to deal with it by mourning?

Throughout our three-way talks, which were sprinkled with
affects of anger, fear, and shame, the dominant theme time and
again was the necessity to clarify our own identity against the
background of our personal and professional history. When we
told each other the stories of our lives it turned out that depth
psychology had a different value for each of us, even though it
had led us all to the same professional identity.

After reporting some typical items from our life histories we
found that our choosing this particular analytic school was not
because we considered it the most excellent blossom of the tree
of depth psychology. The choice was determined by our
histories – by motives which only now have become accessible to
us. The relevant events occurred before we met our training
analysts and the onset of transference.

But these motives rarely seem to be scrutinized in a training
analysis; they threaten too much the formation of a professional
identity. Such an identity is enhanced by the simultaneity of
analysis and training. When training has been completed and
one has come to a relatively stable identity as analyst, however,
we are able to analyze, emotionally and intellectually, the process of forming professional identity.

Erlenmeyer:

Of the three of us I was the one who was most identified with
Jung and his theory when I started my analytic training. At 21, I became acquainted with some of Jung's main works and I decided to
change my study program from Arts to Medicine, in order to become a Jungian analyst. I had discovered that Jung dealt with questions which, in my adolescence, had nearly driven me to despair.
He offered those who were not given the "charisma of faith" an empirically founded theory – if not of God, at least of God's image in
the psyche. I was fascinated by Jung's axiom of a collective unconscious and archetypes. His theory made me hope that, when applying it to myself, I would experience God after all.

In adolescence I was disappointed by my father whose embittered
withdrawal from the family I had observed, earlier, quite empathetically. After the war my father, a Nazi and member of the Nazi party, had returned from a denazification camp. I remember him
gaunt, confused, wrecked, and ashamed. In my unconscious I

probably mixed up the two kinds of camps – the allied prisoner camps and the Nazi concentration camps. While I remember having had an affectionate relationship with him in pre-puberty, I experienced him later as full of contempt for himself and for humankind. Apparently he could accept himself and accept me only by constantly demanding from himself and others, in an almost maniacal manner, efficiency and fulfilment of one's duty. Thus, he could ward off shame and sorrow about the recent past. Behind an offended silence he hid his shameful story.

Today I feel that the silent God of my adolescence reflected my silent father. Freud's "Outline of Psychoanalysis" (SE23) which, fortunately, I came across at that time, offered a first solution. Freud gave expression to the son's inquiring about the father and about the history they share.

In retrospect I feel that my later reading of Jung was a temporary seduction into a grandiose denial of the personal father problems and of the history which is hidden in the father imago. I was fascinated by Jung's one-sided emphasis of the Great Mother, of myth, meaning, and introspection. My over-identification was not shaken fundamentally even by the fact that he had polemicized against Freud – whom I still admired very much – and against Psychoanalysis.

Springer:

My biography up to now has been characterized by being in-between. My father's and mother's families were characterized by marriages which joined German, Jewish, and Russian identities; and Protestant, Catholic and Mosaic faiths. My childhood and adolescence, my choice of profession, and my political and intellectual preferences were strongly influenced by my mother's Jewish origin. It also underlay my early and continuing love for Freud and for the tradition of Enlightenment which contributed to my political thinking. My mother disliked Jung for his earlier sympathizing with the Nazis, but she appreciated his post-war statements on the Germans' collective guilt. While idealizing my father I experienced non-Jewish German elements in a highly ambivalent manner.

My family background, especially the mixed marriage of my parents, constellated the beginning of my training analysis; in the first interview I felt that I was accepted with the background problems which affected the transference situation. The difficult and necessary de-idealization of my parents (as victim and heroic "exceptional German") could proceed only after a long phase of denying the Jungian character of my analysis and by maintaining the fantasy of undergoing a Freudian training analysis. This de-idealization could succeed only because my training analyst, an "Aryan" Jungian, presented himself as a historically determined person. His countertransference was determined by showing his commitment to his experience of history. The familiar element, of being in-between, probably will remain a constitutive element of my identity as analyst.

Winkelmann:

Our work led me back, like the other two, to my adolescence, of which I have unpleasant memories. The liberal moral concepts and ideologies of my father weighed heavily on me as an unbearable pressure which I could not get rid of at that time. It became clear to me only recently that I had been subject to my father's assignment to live the image of an Aryan-German youth, personifying the illusion of an unbroken German identity. My childhood in Argentina intensified the racial stereotype because of my Aryan physiognomy. I still experience this image as alien; it is completely inconsistent with the conscious statements of my father, a historian, on what happened in the Third Reich. A strong identification with the Prussian claim to power and elitism helped him to deny the extent of the Nazi regime's destructiveness. Although fully capable of viewing the events without prejudice, his education to Prussian hardness forbade him to admit to himself the emotional parts of his participation in Germany's history.

The introjected tension between my father's assignment and his inability to mourn the Nazi regime's destructiveness make understandable my tendency to self-contempt and self-depreciation. My active participation in the leftist students' movement and my interest in Freud and the Freudian Marxists were first attempts to resolve this tension.

Why did I become a Jungian, nevertheless? Jung's temporary affinity to National Socialism was known to me. I idealized Freud, but with a Jungian training the assignment from my father has found a place where it can become conscious, as this paper shows. When we worked on Jung's ideas about "Aryan" and "Jewish" psychology, affects of shame and anger became clearer to me. Previously, with all due respect for Jung, these had been hidden behind a kind of ironic contempt.

It is not easy for us to present ourselves in this way. All three of us are learning or practicing group analysis. We know that individual elements become part of the matrix and the inner process of the group. Thus, the paradigm of individuation applies not only to the individual members, but also to the whole group. Are our life histories representative of the local, national and perhaps also of the international professional association? Individuation in the group and individuation through the group happens by the telling of histories. Confrontation with the critical views of the others calls into question the mythologizing of one's own history; the others help me to detach from my fantasies about myself. Does this separation process not involve mourning? And does not a historical image of myself arise out of this disillusionment?

Our three-way talks time and again touched on the same times in the history of Analytical Psychology and of Psychoanalysis: Jung's and Freud's separation shortly before World War I, and the revival of the old conflict between Jung and Psychoanalysis in the beginning of the Nazi regime. With Freud's and Jung's separation, the group process of the young psychoanalytic movement came to a temporary end. The conflict between Freud and Jung is not comprehensible without the dynamics of the group process, including a lot of homo- and hetero-sexual triads and triangles. These dynamics also influenced the formation of the theories.

It is one-sided to blame the splitting of the psychoanalytic movement solely on Freud and Jung. As we know from group dynamics, all members of a group contribute to such process; remember Alfred Adler who had already split off. The triangular configurations were substructures of the group, with their oedipal love and hate affects, their alternating formations of pairs which exclude the third, and their death wishes, rivalry and competition. Of central importance is the envy which comes to the fore in this situation.

Such splits continue to affect the group process. To think that we have rid ourselves of an unpleasant part through splitting it off indicates a denial of our own incompatible and destructive parts. It is not our task here to describe what role Jung played (and plays) for the Freudians after the separation. But the role Freud played for Jung became clear shortly after the separation; Freud and his theory of sexuality became for Jung the object of his projection of evil. We learn from a letter to his friend H. Schmid-Guisan which he wrote in 1915, shortly after he had

separated from Freud, how these destructive parts become effective: "The symbol wants to guard against Freudian interpretations, which are indeed such pseudo-truths that they never lack
for effect. With our patients, 'analytical' understanding has a
wholesomely destructive effect, like a corrosive or thermocautery,
but is banefully destructive on sound tissue. It is a technique we
have learnt from the devil, always destructive, but useful where
destruction is necessary"(Let-1, p. 31). Important for us here are
not Jung's attempts at criticizing the contents of Psychoanalysis,
but the images he used to characterize its alleged destructive
effects, especially the one of the devil. This idea and the affect
which goes with it were developed more distinctly about 1933.

The split with regard to the theory became visible in Jung's central work of 1911–12, *Transformations and Symbols of the Libido*
(now CW5, *Symbols of Transformation*), as well as in the lectures
given in September 1912 at Fordham University, New York
(CW4, pars. 203–522). In these works he qualified the meaning
of the central complex of the neurosis, the Oedipus complex.
This was a newly-developed concept, to which all analysts felt
themselves to be under obligation. Jung extended the Freudian
concept of the libido to cover the schizophrenic diseases.

Beyond the relatively well-known territory of the oedipal configuration an unknown territory opened whose preliminary map
Jung drew. The regressive libido of Miss Miller (described in
CW5) encountered a symbol-forming mythopoeic layer in which
Jung was to immerse himself during his "journey to Hades" on
the occasion of the separation from Freud. At that time, still striving for enlightenment, Jung considered myth as a denial of infantile memory; later he considered it as the foundation of the
individual and the collective and even as producer of history. In
the revised version of this work (CW5), published in 1952, he
took into account the concept of the collective unconscious and
of the archetypes, a concept which had matured in the
meantime.

The idea of the myth as fundamental to the individual and the
collective affected the second period of Jungian history with
which we dealt intensively. By 1933 Jung had found and formulated his own point of view. He presented himself already as one
who would be known later by a world public. In retrospect it
seems as if he no longer needed the paradigms of Freudian Psy-

choanalysis, not even those he had modified during the phase of separation. For Jung, the biographical background of the individual's development lost much of its importance in favor of the theory of the collective unconscious and of the archetypes. Even though he continued to concede their due to Freud's reductive psychoanalytic methods, after the split Jung dealt no more in an essential way with the development of Psychoanalysis. And since then the Freudians have largely passed him over in silence.

Jung had won world-wide recognition. He was known to the German-speaking psychotherapists as representative of Kretschmer, the well-known psychiatrist and president of the German Society for Psychotherapy. Jung took the presidency when Kretschmer resigned in protest after the seizure of power by the Nazis. According to Jaffé (1985), Jung internationalized the Society in June 1933, a few weeks after his assumption of office, in order to ensure German Jewish psychotherapists admission to an international professional association. The process of decision and the consequences of assuming such an office as a non-German are documented in letters of the time and in other publications. As we can gather from these documents, this decision provoked violent affects and accusations against Jung, in his correspondents and his adversaries. The situation was aggravated as Jung became more deeply involved in events which had become largely determined by the Nazi regime.

Jung considered the rise of National Socialism as the expression of a change which affected all of Europe. He identified the youthful élan of fascism with the Germanic gods, humiliated by Christianization and now emerging from collective repression, and he interpreted National Socialism as the expression of a puer-senex psychology. Keeping a distance although clearly fascinated, he said in a 1932 lecture, "The huzzahs of the Italian nation go forth to the personality of the Duce, and the dirges of other nations lament the absence of strong leaders" (CW17, par. 284). In this work he also compared the leader with Christ or Buddha: the one who is able to lead the confused political masses out of their distress. He applied his psychology of individuation (the process of differentiating the ego from the collective psyche) to the concept of the leader's personality. At the same time, the socio-political changes in Germany led him to intolerable defaming polemics against his analytic father and later adversary, Freud, and against his theory. These polemics became especially visible in "The State of Psychotherapy Today" (CW10, pars. 333–70), published in 1934. Occasional earlier statements on the necessity of a distinction between a "Jewish" and a "German" psychology culminate in this work and in other statements of that period.

Jung made statements in that period in which historical-cultural differentiations were obliterated in favor of a biological concept of race. There can be no doubt that, at that time, his views included a biologically defended anti-Semitism.

We have discussed among ourselves and with others a text (Jung & Weizsäcker, 1933) which is largely unknown, that of a radio dialogue recorded on the Berlin Radio Hour on May 26, 1933. The dialogue was published in the volume, *Berlin Seminar*, which was meant exclusively for participants in the seminar. A remark in a letter to James Kirsch the following year gives the impression that Jung did not remember the broadcast: "Neither have I addressed Hitler over the radio or in any other manner, nor have I made any political statements" (Let-1, p. 161). In a simplified form, this remark to one of his disciples reflects the position Jung held at that time.

In his broadcast address, Weizsäcker carried out what had been announced: to set Jung's "constructive psychology" against the "undermining psychoanalysis of Sigmund Freud." He characterized Psychoanalysis as "nothing-but analysis" which, with good reason, had become suspect. It would distinguish itself by constant "enquiring and undermining in an intellectual manner" (Jung & Weizsäcker, p. 166). The German public must have known that, on May 10, 1933, Freud's and his disciples' works had been publicly burned.

For Weizsäcker it was crucial that Jungian psychology "not offend, . . . not tear to pieces, . . . not undermine or corrode the element of immediacy in our psyche, the creative element which, especially in our German history of ideas time and again has played the decisive part" (Jung & Weizsäcker, pp. 166–67). Before coming back to the contrast between Jung's psychology and Freud's, Weizsäcker discussed the "Seelenlage des reichs-deutschen Menschen" (psychic condition of the citizens of the German Reich), that is, of the National Socialist movement.

In the conflict between the generations which had broken out through that movement, the 58-year-old Jung sided with the Nazis, whom he seemed to experience as youthful with a "natural and necessary impulsiveness" (Jung & Weizsäcker, p. 168). In accordance with his theory of archetypes, which had been conceptualized in the meantime, he considered the "general confusion of today's Europe to be compensated by 'instinctive,' that is to say, natural powers. . . . The need instinctively arises for a comprehensive Weltanschauung [world-view] . . . which would allow us to embrace . . . an over-all view and therefore to see the inner meaning of the whole movement" (Jung & Weizsäcker, p. 170). According to his conception, which was formulated later, that the archetypal image or idea underlies the instinct, he attributed an underlying archetypal meaning to the National Socialist world-view.

As Weizsäcker understood Jung, his psychology is best for grasping this world-view. He left to Jung the characterization of the practical part his psychology plays for the whole of life and the whole of the people. Jung emphasized the role of the individuation process which he called here "self-development of the individual" (p. 170). As he had pointed out before, he considered individuation to be the only possibility for escape from the threatening danger of mass suggestion. He said, "Only the self-development of the individual—which I consider to be the first aim of all psychological efforts—produces a responsible upholder and leader of the collective movement. As Hitler said recently, the leader must be able to be lonely and have the courage to go forward alone" (Jung & Weizsäcker, pp. 170–71).

Without doubt Hitler—after Christ and Buddha—had become the representative of a personality which is led by the inner voice; he had become the Fuhrer. When Weizsäcker referred again to the opposition between Jung and Freud, he stressed more clearly the opposition between a "Jewish" and an "Aryan-Germanic" psychology, even if this attribution did not appear expressly. Jung's reply appears especially shocking in view of the National Socialist anti-Semitism and of the persecution of the Jews which had already begun. An important aspect of his answer is that he characterized Freudian—and Adlerian—psychology with the regressive and destructive metaphors which characterized the National Socialist movement. Thus, the

Jewish psychoanalysts, representatives of the Jewish minority which was already being persecuted and singled out, were made out to be culprits although in reality they were victims.

These statements, which reversed the actual situation, do not reconcile with Jung's efforts to help his Jewish colleagues in Germany by the internationalization of the Medical Society for Psychotherapy, which efforts were under way. While in Germany the Jews were being singled out and "Jewish science," that is, Psychoanalysis was also being defamed, Jung in this broadcast claimed to have an eye to the "whole of the creation," ("Ganze der Schöpfung") that is, to the "whole of the people" ("Volksganze") – the whole which did not exist any more. Jung's actual words were:

> It is one of the most beautiful privileges of the German spirit to take in without any conditions the whole of the creation in its inexhaustible variety. But in Freud as well as in Adler one single individual aspect, as for example sexuality or the striving for dominance and power, is contrasted critically with the whole. Through this a part is singled out and broken into smaller and smaller pieces, till the sense which is carried only by the whole is distorted to the point of nonsense, the beauty inherent only in the whole to the point of absurdity. I could never become reconciled to this hostile attitude to life (Jung & Weizsäcker, p. 171).

For this answer Weizsäcker was "especially grateful" to Jung, and he said that "for many a person it will have the effect of a release." We must ask ourselves, a release from what and for what? On the one hand it is certainly about the release from the evil, from the destructiveness which is projected here onto the Jewish psychoanalysts as representatives of the Jews themselves. On the other hand it means the justification for releasing forces which encourage the segregation of the Jewish element described as "hostile to life." Jung, whom Weizsäcker called in his introduction "the most advanced researcher in modern psychology," soothed the possible feelings of guilt his listeners might have had for their active participation in the events of the time. Did Jung – seduced by the specific historical situation and the situation of the dialogue – take revenge for the fact that Freud did not want to understand him and his "transformations" any more and had called Jung an anti-Semite? Jung's next statement that "each movement organically culminates in the leader," was applied to Jung himself by Weizsäcker in his closing remarks: "Today we live in a phase of our renewal where it is crucial that what we have gained and conquered is inwardly consolidated and extended, far into the soul of the individual. For this undertaking we need leaders like you are who really know something about the soul, about the German soul and whose psychology is no intellectual chatter but a vivid knowledge of Man" (Jung & Weizsäcker, pp. 172–73).

The group in Berlin discussed this text and tried to clarify the differences in the positions we tend to take, according to our different personal backgrounds. The discussion showed again how much we as Jungians must experience such a text as full of conflict. In their content and emotions the contributions shifted between two poles which are known to us from our group's work: spontaneous displeasure and feelings of relief because one's own thoughts and affects had been confirmed.

When we chose the topic of Jung as political man, our interest was to confront ourselves with our own shadow, that is something which we as Jungian analysts, especially, should be able to come to terms with. The working through of old identifications — which, in fact, also determines our daily work with our patients — cannot and may not stop short of the formation of our own identity and ego ideal. It is our unavoidable task as analysts to ferret out false mythologizing and to be aware of the fact that we, too, contribute to producing new myths.

With the example of the Freud-Jung relationship we tried to show what a dangerous shadow quality old identifications can carry when one deals with conflicts but omits the process of mourning the split-off adversary. Thus, the one who has not been mourned turns into an enemy. The history of the subject degenerates into mythologizing. Omitting the mourning process leads to the demonization of the adversary; thus, Freud became a Jungian demon.

Such enemy images, as we can learn from the example of Jung's being seduced, make us susceptible to being seduced and used politically. We can experience this threat in ourselves and in our patients in the outer world as well as in the transference-countertransference situation. We must be aware of Jung's being seduced and of our own constant susceptibility to political seduction which roots in defense against anxiety and in wishes for idealizing an omnipotent object, which might become true, after all. Unconsidered finding of the meaning and a rash search for the myth might hinder us and our patients from painfully realizing and actively perceiving culprit-victim constellations, which continue to exist intra-psychically. There is a constant temptation to avoid the work of mourning, but a high probability of reproducing situations which threaten to be destructive to us.

Translated from German by
Dagmar Henle-Dieckmann
and Sabine Osvatič

REFERENCES

Blomeyer, R. (1982). *Die Spiele der Analytiker: Freud, Jung, und die Analyse.* Olten, West Germany: Walter.
Dieckmann, H. (1984). Psychologische Gedanken zum Problem der atomaren Bedrohung. *Analytische Psychologie, 15–1,* 19–36.
Erlenmeyer, A. (1984). Die Wirkung geschichtlicher Ereignisse auf die Psyche: Die Wirklichkeit des Bildes—das Bild der Wirklichkeit. *Analytische Psychologie. 15–4,* 273–84.
Jaffé, A. (1985). C. G. Jung und der Nationalsozialismus. *Analytische Psychologie, 16–1,* 66–77.
Jung, C. G.; Weizsäcker, A. (1933). Stenogramm des Zwiegesprächs von C. G. Jung und A. Weizsäcker in der Funkstunde Berlin, 26. Juni. In *Bericht über das Berliner Seminar,* 166–73.
Springer, A. (1984). Kassandra: Eine Seherin der Destruktivität. *Analytische Psychologie, 15–4,* 285–93.
Wilke, H.-J. (1985). Nationalzocialismus Vergangenheit: Ein Aktualkonflikt. *Analytische Psychologie, 16–1,* 9–32.

Acedia:
Collective Depression in a Jungian Psychiatric Clinic

C. T. Frey-Wehrlin (Zurich)

When *André's* parents first inquired about treatment for their son, he was 25 years old. A few weeks elapsed until he arrived in Zurich; his condition had not allowed him to travel directly from France to Switzerland. The report from the French clinic painted a somber picture of paranoid schizophrenia. André had been in the habit of smearing the walls of his room with feces and therefore he had been treated with electroshock. The marks on his temples were still visible when he arrived. He reported that he had recently had a crisis; he had heard voices and smashed objects. When his mother came and told him to send the voices away, he had done that.

He also told us that he was able to see on other people's faces what he was supposed to do. At the age of 22, he had seen Christ hanging on the cross in a church. The voice of God had told him that not Christ's legs had been broken on the cross but those of the two sinners on either side. He, the patient, was the son of God and in the next two years he would see even greater signs. "He adores me," said the patient, adding that he felt God's love for him growing by the day.

During the days that followed, the patient appeared to adapt well to his new surroundings. He made friends with a young schizophrenic woman patient; we had to watch them, as they tended to disappear into a bedroom together. Once, he smashed a tray of dishes on the floor, but on the whole, our first impression of an amiable young man seemed to be confirmed. The dosage of neuroleptica he received was of average strength.

On the eighth day of his stay in our clinic "without any warning whatsoever," according to the medical report, the patient jumped from the second story window onto the pavement in front of the entrance to the clinic. The injury to the cranium was severe, and he died from it two days later.

We were unanimous in concluding that this was not a case of suicide; it was likely that the patient suffered from a delusion of being able to fly.

At the time—September 25, 1978—we were in no position to realize that it was only the prologue to a series of nefarious events.

Birgit was 31 when she first sought refuge in our clinic from her overwhelming depressions and death wishes. She was a teacher, had attended a training school for teaching the handicapped and had taught mentally disturbed children. She felt that she had never had a genuine relationship with her parents. The medical history is evidence of our therapeutic helplessness at all levels. The medication ranged from anti-depressants to neuroleptica and back; the psychotherapist complained of Birgit's almost total passivity and unproductivity. The patient's attempts to find part-time jobs and living accommodations were legion. Her rare dreams depicted burning houses, fire falling from heaven, her sister suffering from hemorrhage of the brain while giving birth to a child, and the dreamer herself being exposed to sadistic tortures.

In the subsequent three years her state of mind fluctuated a great deal. Off and on she worked as an auxiliary nurse over relatively long periods of time. She was very sensitive and circumspect in her work but emotionally she was flat and not flowing. A strong undercurrent of feelings became noticeable when she complained about her worthlessness, the lack of meaning in her life and, most particularly, when she indulged in death fantasies with imagery of cemeteries and being buried. Even at the very beginning of her stay at the clinic she had one very specific suicide fantasy: She wanted to take some pills, add some alcohol, and then drown herself in the sea.

Despite all this it became possible to "discharge" the patient after 3½ years. This meant moving to a one room flat near the clinic and working for us as an auxiliary nurse. But after just 1½ years she had had to be interned again in a state of acute depression. A Szondi test showed up her strong feelings of worthlessness, self-hatred, and dissatisfaction. The depression turned out to be a defense against her fear of sliding into schizophrenic psychosis.

After a month she was discharged once again, but only for three-quarters of a year. During her third spell in the clinic, tension developed between her and the psychotherapist. In February 1979, the patient applied to the staff conference for another therapist. After close examination and intensive discussions, the conference rejected the idea of a change. As a result, the patient applied to the medical director, who was absent at the time for reasons of illness. He explained his objections in a detailed letter to her. Subsequently he assessed his position as having been "appropriate but wrong."

Two days later the patient disappeared from the clinic. Later in the evening of February 4, 1979, she called to inform us that, this being the tenth anniversary of her father's death, she would drown herself in the lake of Zug. The police, who were alerted instantly, arrived too late.

Corinne was 20 and had just passed her university entrance exams when she was referred to us by a university psychiatric hospital, with the diagnosis of a "very serious borderline neurosis, possibly simple schizophrenia." Her parents brought her to the clinic. Before departing, the father, a tall and bearded internist, had given the admitting physician a written statement relieving the clinic of any responsibility in case his daughter committed suicide during her hospitalization.

Corinne's stay at the clinic was hard on everyone. Because she was extremely suicidal, we had to keep her in the closed ward almost continuously, where she spent most of her time in bed indulging in her suicide fantasies. Aside from a brief initial "honeymoon" period, the therapy dwelt almost exclusively on her hopelessness and yearning for death. In compensatory fashion the dreams highlighted a close and exclusive tie with the father. In one, she was sitting with him, separated from the other members of the family, on a float which tilted and threw both of them overboard into the water.

Time and again the parents, especially the father as a medical doctor, interfered, compelling us to grant occasional home-leaves against our better judgment. At the end of January 1979, after Corinne had been at the clinic for seven months, we requested the parents to sign a formal declaration cancelling our obligations. Consequently, they took the patient home against our advice. Shortly thereafter the parents went on vacation, leaving their daughter alone. On the morning of February 8, 1979, she was found dead in the garden. She had taken an overdose of sleeping tablets.

David was 27 when he was transferred to our clinic, in February 1978. Five years earlier he had had a psychotic breakdown, after which he had never become his former self again – quiet, sporty, intelligent, according to his mother. Gradually he had become more of a loner and had changed his course of studies repeatedly. He was living alone in his student quarters surrounded by many law and psychology books. It never became quite clear whether he had understood these books, or had even read them.

The patient's hospitalization resulted from a weekend visit at home, during which he had assaulted his father and beaten him until he had drawn blood. Neither in the first mental hospital nor in our clinic did the patient show any insight into his pathology. He contended that he knew nothing of the events that led to his hospitalization and resisted any attempt at verbal interaction with staff members.

It was perfectly consistent for David to request discharge at the end of February 1979, to resume his university studies. He was neither prepared nor able to recognize that, given his passivity and inability to concentrate, he was in no position to meet the demands of study and that he was bound to slide into isolation and physical neglect yet again.

We discussed the situation and the assessment of it with him, and it seemed as though he had taken with a certain amount of detachment the news that we had rejected his request for discharge. On March 1, 1979, he managed to leave the clinic and jump to his death from a high bridge over a motorway near Zurich.

You can imagine what a tremendous impact such an accumulation of deaths in a 35-bed clinic is bound to have on survivors, patients and staff. The knowledge that, even with these four cases, the statistically expected suicide rate for the time span involved had not been reached, is of little consolation and misses the mark when you think of the actual experience of such a disaster. The resultant feelings and emotions ranged from grief, guilt, fear and dejection, to resignation. The reactions were particularly marked in the closed ward where the nursing staff refused to take any further risks. Patients' leave time was curtailed and the physician responsible for the ward increased the doses of medication for patients at risk to the extent that they were immobilized. In some cases he gave orders for patients to be strapped to their beds. No one was prepared to remonstrate with him, to point out that along with the risks, he was also blocking the possibilities for positive development. Fear had gripped us all.

After some time, four of us mustered the energy to discuss the situation with an analyst colleague who was not working at the clinic. What remained with me from this discussion was his comment that, in most cases, the intent of suicide included an attack on the surviving, an attempt to leave them with the guilt for their failure by committing a last-ditch act of desperation. To enable us to overcome our helplessness and to resume work with the patients at the clinic, in a more or less meaningful manner, it was no doubt necessary for us to be told something of the kind at that time. To avoid total resignation, we first had to get rid of this dark shadow — no matter how — and defer until later the job of going into it in depth and digesting it. I hope that this paper will make some contribution to this process.

As it happened, we were not left in peace for long.

Ernst was in his late thirties when he joined our medical staff in 1978. He proved himself to be a sensitive doctor and a pleasant colleague. He was admitted to the Zurich University Hospital in August 1982; the news of his death shortly thereafter came as a complete surprise.

Fabian joined our outpatient service as a young psychiatrist at the beginning of 1982 to complete his training. Toward the end of the year he noticed a recrudescence of a malignancy for which he had been operated on years earlier. Apparently he was not prepared to undergo another round of treatment, with all the uncertainties it involved; shortly before Christmas 1982, he killed himself.

And now the time has come to tell about the death of our medical director and friend of many years, *Dr. H. K. Fierz*. The clinic had been directed by him since its inception. In his generation, he deserves primary credit for having carried on, deepened and enriched the clinical tradition of Jungian psychology. He died in January 1984, after a long and painful illness.

Gertrud came to the clinic as a patient in the autumn of 1972, at the age of 32. For much of the time she worked as a nurses' assistant, which she continued to do even after she was discharged. In March 1983, she had surgery for breast cancer. A year later metastases were diagnosed and she died in October 1984.

Between 1979 and 1983 a number of the medical, therapeutic and nursing staff suffered health problems, though none of them were fatal:

Hilde, a relative newcomer on our staff, was taken home by car by a colleague after a social evening in the clinic. The driver failed to see a stop sign at a very dangerous crossing, and his car was rammed by a much heavier vehicle coming from the right. Hilde suffered severe injury to her spine and became quadriplegic. It took her several years of intensive rehabilitation work to regain her private and professional independence. She has since returned to work in the clinic.

Ivo went through a difficult personal crisis at the beginning of 1982. It was associated with very unpleasant vegetative disturbances.

For nearly a year, *Katya* had to cope with somatic complaints of an unidentified nature which seriously impaired her entire life-style off and on. Ultimately these complaints proved to be of a rheumatic nature, accompanied by fairly serious colitis. Her condition improved considerably during the second half of 1983.

Shortly thereafter, *Lena* also began to suffer from rheumatism, which kept her away from work for several weeks.

Max, who had joined the staff shortly after the clinic opened, underwent surgery for a malignant growth in 1983. He was incapacitated for the major part of a year.

At this point I can no longer avoid talking about myself. In the spring of 1979, I had a gall bladder operation from which I recovered physically but my psychic recovery was slow. For several years my leisure time was taken up by reading authors like Christa Wolf, or listening to romantic or impressionistic music — usually in a minor key. To begin with I attributed my depressiveness to the after-effects of the anesthesia, a blood count which failed to come back to normal, and even nicotine withdrawal symptoms, for I had stopped smoking.

Ultimately I had to acknowledge that the low had set in long before the operation. The connection between my condition and that of the clinic became manifest. I had to recognize that the symptoms of "decline" had begun to appear as early as 1976. At that time, we had begun to prepare a paper on our clinical experiences for an international meeting in 1977. In the course of these preparations we came across a colleague's announcement that he planned to report on his cures of schizophrenic patients and the statistics of his unheard-of success. We decided not to take up the challenge and to report instead on our failures, that is, our experience in the treatment of incurable, chronic patients (Frey-Wehrlin et al., 1978). Those of us who participated in the venture became clearly sub-depressive during the period of researching into our observations and writing them up. Subsequently, Florian Langegger, our present senior registrar, wrote a book (1983) entitled *Doctor, Death and the Devil*.

Two other occurrences deserve mention in this context. In 1982–83 the foundation that supports the clinic came into difficult financial straits; the situation cast doubt on the clinic's continued existence. The profit and loss account for the two years showed a deficit of nearly SFr. 250,000. In addition, for the first time in the clinic's nearly 20 years, serious differences of opinion surfaced among the members of the board of trustees.

The events I describe could be represented on a curve, which begins to decline in 1976, drops sharply in 1978–79, and stays at that level until 1984. Since then it seems to have climbed again slowly, though I hardly dare say this out loud. [*See author's end-note.]

I do not think that it is only the parallel movement in my own curve that induces me to think in terms of a collective depression in the Clinic on the Zurichberg. When an institution set up to promote health and life is afflicted by a concentration of so many analogous cases of death and illness in a relatively short time and gets into a financial as well as a leadership crisis in addition, it is bound to be affected in a most vital manner. For those involved it becomes unavoidable that they reflect on this state of affairs in order to understand the chain of negative events and to get some inkling of their possible meaning. The similarity and snowballing

of these events indicated that we were faced with a case of synchronicity, in other words, the intervention of the unconscious.
As we know from experience, synchronicity tends to be compensatory, that is, it offsets a one-sided attitude. Put in different
terms, we would say that the shadow is activated to counteract
a split situation and a process of this kind is inevitably accompanied by emotion, pain and resistance.

When it was at its worst, our frame of mind and emotional state
could be described as a time of deep dejection. The world was
dark and gray; everything seemed devoid of color. There was a
feeling of resignation about our therapeutic possibilities, of being
at the mercy of spontaneous and nefarious processes and events,
and of guilt. The causal chain of events, which led to several of
the disastrous developments I described, suggested that they
may have been induced by us as individuals, a team, or an organization. Decisive mistakes were made which later seemed
perfectly avoidable. Moreover, the general feeling of failure
seemed to carry the hallmark of some unfortunate finality.

You probably have noticed that the diagnosis unmistakably
points to a depression. As it was due to the specific events that
I mentioned, you might assume that it was of the reactive type.
Yet, it seemed to display clearly endogenous features. Whatever
the case, I thought that I was on the right track when I attached
the label of "collective depression" to our condition.

At that point a colleague, Alfred Ziegler, drew my attention to
the phenomenon of "acedia," which used to strike the residents
of monasteries, especially in the early and late Middle Ages. A
uniform description of this condition or epidemic seems to be
lacking, but I will give you an impression of what is meant.

Acedia is derived from the Greek *akedia*, or *akedeia*, whose root
is *kedos*, for care, anxiety and grief. The first meaning of a-cedia
would therefore be "care-lessness." One meaning of the Greek
kedos was grief, which in turn was derived from Avestan, *sādra*
for sorrow. In the Germanic languages the Indogermanic root
was modified to *haz*, which was Old High German for hate. In
Old Norse it was *hatre*. In Gothic *hatris* (wrath). The association
of acedia with hatred in modern English (and German *Hass*)
seems to link it to the realm of passion. The kind of "careless-
ness" implied here relates to sloth and indolence and it even extends to the Greek expression *akedeutos* for an unburied corpse

(Jehl, 1984, p. 7). Another obvious term that comes to mind in this context is the Latin *pigritia*, which means sloth and laziness in English. I may be indulging in lay etymology, but via *acidia*, or *accidia*, the association with *tristitia* may not be so far out. Before turning to the nature of the relationship between melancholia and depression and acedia, I want to offer you the description of a concrete manifestation of acedia as reported by Cassian.

> When this spirit . . . takes hold of a weak mind, it generates restlessness and drives the monk out of his cell; he experiences scorn and contempt for his brothers, irrespective of whether they live in close community or loose association with him, as though they were neglectful and not sufficiently concerned with spiritual matters. The spirit makes him feel lazy and slothful about any activity in his cell. It will not allow him to dwell there, nor to devote proper attention to his reading and the monk thus afflicted sighs that he is not making any spiritual progress despite the fact that he is trying to spend more time on it; . . . he moans and regrets that he is not getting anywhere with his spiritual quest, that he is feeling empty . . . inasmuch as he is not edifying anyone . . . and has not enriched people by his teachings, or doctrine. The demon praises far-off monasteries and describes these places as being far more useful for accomplishment and more suitable for spiritual and physical well-being. (Cassian, 1965, pp. 365–67)

In the permanent malcontent of the monk who is tired of his duties, tempted to leave his cell and to go out into the world — where he would no doubt be faced with the same restlessness and discontent — we easily recognize an agitated form of depression. Acedia also appears to be a forerunner of the "spleen" and "ennui" we find in French Romanticism (e.g., Baudelaire) and of the twentieth-century boredom described in Thomas Mann's *Magic Mountain*, in Sartre's *Nausea* or in Walser's *Gallist's Disease*. This enumeration is by no means exhaustive.

The fact that Bonaventura (thirteenth century scholar and mystic) distinguished clearly between depression and acedia is of decisive importance for our present considerations. Depression, or melancholia, he asserted, is a disease caused by a disturbance in the balance of the body juices. Acedia, on the other hand, is a sin or rather a vice. Essentially it is therefore a mental and moral problem. Jehl (1984) says that "every time a sin is committed and so also in the case of acedia we are dealing with a person, who turns away intentionally from . . . the sublime, the highest good and true bliss, which is the ultimate goal of his nature and through which he would achieve perfection" (p. 307). We shall have occasion to return to this intentionality later.

If we translate this dogmatic statement into the language of Analytical Psychology, we can say that acedia is capable of overcoming any striving for perfection and compels us to turn away from otherworldly ideas in favor of the reality in the here and now. Inasmuch as this reality includes our instincts and passions, it also implies a withdrawal from pure logos in favor of eros. Instead of perfection and dissociation the goal becomes completeness and wholeness.

Could it be that *perfectio* (desire for perfection) was involved in the optimistic intentions with which an enthusiastic team opened a Jungian private clinic on the Zurichberg in Zurich's best residential area, where growth and progress are concretized in the form of luxury homes? Was our claim that, thanks to Analytical Psychology, we possessed the appropriate tool for understanding and therefore for curing neuroses and psychoses? Could it be that, quite imperceptibly, we were subverted by the spirit of positivistic psychiatry, which believes that ultimately it would be able to overcome suffering, disease and death by means of scientific progress? That is, were we subverted by an excess of paternal logos, which knows with its arrogant pretense at feasibility, that it is in line with the "Zeitgeist" and therefore the collective?

If this is so, what does it mean that this clinic came to suffer an attack of acedia, a vice which was considered at various times to be one of the mortal sins? What does the word sin mean in this context?

There are things I do knowingly that I also know "one" does not do. These are two kinds of knowing which seem to exist side by side in me and, at times, they may even have an inkling of each other's existence. Both are conscious and unconscious and cannot be distinguished from each other in a clear-cut fashion. Sometimes they merge and intermingle but then again they light up brilliantly (*scintillae*). I would like to term the blurred line of demarcation between them the penumbra. As long as I am "one," or collective, I am all right. But when I do things, which "one" does not do, I am not collective, but an individual who is. And the etymologies of "is" and "sin" appear to be interrelated. To be someone in one's own right, different and individual, seems to be closely associated with sin.

It is informative to read how the pious resisted the temptation of acedia. According to Palladius, a nun of Saint Melania answered a question on the subject as follows: "From morning until the ninth hour (3 p.m.) I pray by the hour while spinning flax. During the remaining hours, I mentally recite the names of the patriarchs, prophets, apostles and martyrs. And after having eaten my bread I await the other hours persevering faithfully and prepared to accept the end with expectant delight."

This means that coping with acedia is associated with repression and with the help of "the fathers," that is, the patriarchal principle, whenever the negative cannot be avoided any longer. For example, in the thoughts of the end or death, the pious ego is only a suffering victim; it never takes any action. It is active and engaged more than anything in adhering to a prescribed paternal order so as to keep out disorder and chaos.

Yet we are told "Do not resist evil!" That is, illness, incurability, even death must not just be fought but also accepted. This may mean that we should understand illness as expressing something that is not in harmony, as an attempt to right something that has gone wrong; or, to put it into our language, as an attempt at compensation, which failed in the first instance. "The symptom is always right," we say in line with Jungian thinking.

In one of our earlier reactions to acedia we noted that even chronic illness must be accepted. (Frey-Wehrlin, et al. 1978). At that time we concluded that, in cases like these, trying to change things was not the point, but that chronic patients needed us to accompany them, to be present with them. There seemed to be a hint at a possible erotic motif, which would strive for relatedness and toleration rather than the strict implementation of rules, regulations and order. What comes to mind in this context is the "fatherless society," a concept which was no doubt prompted by a utopian principle but might also humanize a one-sided, disciplined order. Furthermore, we should not overlook the fact that acedia used to manifest itself primarily in western monasteries, those with strict rules, such as the Benedictines. In the East things were probably always more anarchical; there was less fear of chaos. The questions which therefore arise are: How much order and how much disorder is wholesome in a psychiatric clinic? Is chaos as essential as order in accompanying the sick soul? For, as we pointed out earlier, individuality and therefore individuation are unthinkable without a person who is (someone in his or her own right), nor are they possible without sin.

In this context it is worth mentioning that often, though not always, depression may be accompanied by an odd feeling of pleasure. Perhaps it presupposes that we have given ourselves leave to be depressive and refused to meet the demands of the outer world. I cannot help but think that these pleasurable feelings are the very result of this refusal, of our "no" to the demands of what is outside and alien, thus at the same time a "yes" to the individual self. What is particularly palpable is the feeling of well-being that is experienced in staying with oneself, in feeling oneself. It seems that this feeling of well-being is possible only because it corresponds to an inner urge—perhaps a drive.

It seems clear that refusal of outer demands meets the instinctual needs of the Self rather than the strivings of the ego. It would not be much of an exaggeration to say that depression may be as seductive as a femme fatale. The feelings of pleasure experienced in depression are like a bonus awarded by the Self for one's refusal, while the negativity associated with the condition would be the penalty for a recalcitrant ego that continues to identify with the demands of the outer and resists the Self's refusal.

It is hardly surprising that the collective morality cannot brook this kind of withdrawal. For this very reason tristitia has always been considered to be a sin, even a mortal sin. The unquestioned, glad acceptance and approval of creation is a human duty, for humans are the crowning of that very creation. If the Self turns out to be a source of evil, something must be wrong with creation, at least from a Jungian point of view. A compensation of a one-sided affirmation of life by means of negating depression is only conceivable when this positive attitude toward life turns hostile or even threatening. For the Self is always in the service of life—a life, however, which also encompasses its opposite, the end and its ultimate goal.

Any unconditional affirmation of life, however, denies the shadow and therefore also reality. This is to be taken quite literally; a photograph, especially in black and white, taken with the sun in the back, gives no depth of field. A picture derives its depth, power and beauty from the slanting shadows, which come with the late afternoon or autumn light. This is the time of day, or year, which announces the end. The shadowless noon hour on the other hand sets loose the demon of midday, the dread disease which Hillman (1972) associated with the terrors of panic; and the church fathers, with acedia.

We should not fail to note that other schools of psychology are also concerned with the timely topic of the lost shadow. Thus a splinter group of Zurich psychoanalysts expressed their concern under the heading of "The Malaise of Psychoanalysis" (Lohmann, 1983). They emphasized the repression of the death instinct in Psychoanalysis, which therefore tended to degenerate into a "harmless kind of common-sense psychology," or into "psychoanalytical short-term therapy, which is being applied to deal with the equally harmless symptoms displayed by the members of a middle class looking for some meaning in life" (p. 50). The repression of the death instinct, it was said, turned Psychoanalysis into a unipotent science, whose inherent unconscious destructive tendencies have become so terrifying to us. This trend was attributed to the growth of medico-centrism, a predominantly medical approach to therapy, as well as the socialization of psychoanalytic therapy to bring it in line with the requirements of health insurance schemes.

To counter this trend, contributors said it was essential that we learn increasingly to live with the naked truth about ourselves, especially the inhuman behavior "which threatens us under the cover of so-called civilizing efforts (p. 7). At this juncture it would appear that the medico-therapeutic and the socio-critical trends in Psychoanalysis are at odds with each other; one branch can thrive only at the expense of the other. It reminds me of how horrified I was when Michael Fordham told me 30 years ago that analysis was meant to be a scientific and not a therapeutic tool; it just might produce a cure as a by-product.

Since then my attitude has changed. Theoretical considerations were of minor importance in bringing about this change. Jung's ideas on the self-healing tendencies of the soul were well known to me even 30 years ago but they did not impress me very much at the time. On the contrary, I am acutely conscious of the suggestive and manipulative measures I resorted to in order to give some impetus to these self-healing tendencies. As time went on and I gained experience, I became painfully aware that manipulation achieved next to nothing. But more than anything, the change in me was brought about by the kind of growing detachment that comes with age, by faith in the process rather than confidence in some superior knowledge, an attitude that is not without a religious component. I do not know how else to describe an attitude that expects a patient to improve or even to heal just on the basis of "disinterested" concern for the patient's state of mind. Those involved must be prepared to expose themselves to trouble and even suffering. This is the premise of the long-term therapeutic approach of our clinic. It is worth noting that the religious element has also found expression in the above-mentioned writings of "leftist Freudians." Lohmann, editor of *Psyche*, wrote about "the members of an invisible church" — those who recognize the existence of the death instinct — and branded "the fixed idea that science has all the answers" as "the superstition of the century" (1983, p. 54).

There is another reason, however, why the scientific attitude needs to be compensated by a religious element. Because its methodology operates exclusively according to general laws and on the basis of statistics, the scientific attitude cannot do justice to the individual. Myth, on the other hand, focuses on the individual case — which is set aside by science as a mere coincidence — and makes sure that an individual assessment is made. The millstone crushing the title character in the Grimm's fairy tale "Herr Korbes" is God's punishment and therefore proof of his wickedness. Similarly, we do not confine ourselves to administering specific quantities of medication, statistically certified through double blind tests, in the treatment of our patients, but respond to them individually by offering psychotherapy as well. By doing so we move from the scientific-causal to the mythically meaningful determination, which manifestly belongs to the realm of religion.

Insofar as our analytic work is based on a religious attitude, we discern a characteristic which we share with the monk in the monastic community. In the way we work and live we rely on a faith which, as such, is pre-scientific but provides the necessary context for scientific facts. Acedia can develop only where the very foundations of faith have been shaken. Faith that is intact keeps acedia away; a pious person will not be deterred from striving for perfection.

But what is the role of faith in psychotherapy, or even more so in psychiatry, both of them scientific disciplines? Even if their scientific method does not measure up to the strictness and exactness of some of the natural sciences and even if we are prepared to look at our work as an art, most of us would tend to insist that the basic facts of our profession require knowledge. At the same time, we must acknowledge that the chief principle of Analytical Psychology, synchronicity, is based on the notion of meaning, which escapes any kind of scientific generalization and reveals itself only in individual, subjective experience. This is a realm where we are not primarily concerned with logos and knowledge but with myth and faith.

The supremacy of knowledge is open to question from another point of view as well. I shall first illustrate what I mean, by way of an anecdote. When I was investigating the effectiveness of psychotherapy a few years ago, I asked a professor to give me a bibliography of the most recent publications in this field. I undertook a careful study of the relevant literature and came to the conclusion that our successful work boiled down to very little and just barely exceeded the number of spontaneous remissions (Frey-Wehrlin, 1983). During the discussion that followed my lecture on the subject, the professor in question expressed the view that Mr. Frey would not have arrived at these obviously erroneous conclusions had he used the most recent literature on the subject!

Here we get into an area where "things that must not be cannot be" and, where basic vital interests are at stake, faith is always stronger than knowledge. But the disturbing relationship between faith and knowledge is not confined to this anecdote. Any naive realist whose eyes have been opened by the Kantian critique of reason inevitably will be caught up in anything from the "philosophy of the as-if" (Vaihinger, 1911), to the "invented reality" of constructivism (von Foerster, 1976). And the Jungian theory of the archetypes is an important station on this road. The archetypes enable us to know things on the basis of inborn forms of cognition. And we survive because these inborn forms or categories correspond to a reality, which will never be entirely within our reach.

An existing faith, we have said, is shaken when acedia strikes. It involves more than a loss of faith in adhering to the rules of the order. Doubt is cast on the goals of the entire undertaking; life's highest values are questioned. The greatest good of happiness in the beyond is replaced by a temporal good in the here and now. This means that the believer gives up striving for perfection. In a monk such a turn-about is equivalent to a breakdown. Now I want to draw some practical conclusions from these findings for our Jungian psychiatric clinic.

The events I described at the beginning of my lecture led to a breakdown in our clinical community. From the "beyond" of our utopia, our pretentious expectations at healing, we were forced into the here and now of modestly accompanying our patients analytically. On the one hand our medical treatment continues to obey the statistically well-founded rules of modern psychiatry. On the other we leave room for a conscious open-mindedness in respect for deviations and even for inconsistencies, depending on the individual process. We are prepared to sin against science.

Paradoxically this also leaves us to speculate about our original therapeutic enthusiasm, which may have been the sin we needed to acknowledge and for which we had to assume responsibility. In a higher sense this may include the responsibility we bear for the destiny of the patients and colleagues I mentioned. I hope that I am making myself very clear: There is no causal relationship involved here; to postulate one would be presumptuous yet again.

Acceptance of the shadow into the inevitably split world of everyday psychiatric work is one of the major responsibilities of a Jungian clinic. The suffering of tensions, insecurity, chaos and guilt provides the essential counterpoise to the structure and order of medico-scientific activity. Our awareness of this counterbalance must not be lost again, even if it shows up little or not at all in the persona which our clinic presents to the outside world.

Translated from German by
Ruth Horine

*Author's Note: Unfortunately, this trend did not continue. In the spring of 1987, I was obliged to resign from my post at the clinic and it is by no means certain that the Jungian spirit will survive under the new administration.

REFERENCES

Cassian (1965). De institutions cénobitiques 10, 2; J. C. Guy (Ed.), *Patrologia Latina* 49. Translated from Latin by Martin Odermatt.

Frey-Wehrlin, C. T. (1976). Reflections on C. G. Jung's concept of synchronicity. *Journal of Analytical Psychology*, *21*–1, 132–38.

Frey-Wehrlin, C. T. (1983). "Wie war zu Köln es doch vordem. . . . " Fortschritte in der klinischen Psychotherapie? *Analytische Psychologie*, *14*, 186–203.

Frey-Wehrlin, C. T.; Bosnak, R.; Langegger, F.; Robinson, C. (1978). The treatment of chronic psychoses. *Journal of Analytical Psychology*, *23*–3, 253–57.

Hillman, J. (1972). An essay on Pan. In *Pan and the nightmare*. Dallas: Spring Publications.

Jehl, R. (1984). *Melancholia und Acedia: Ein Beitrag zu Anthropologie und Ethik Bonaventuras*. Paderborn: Schöningh.

Langegger, F. (1983). *Doktor, Tod und Teufel: Vom Wahnsinn und von der Psychiatrie in einer vernünftigen Welt*. Frankfurt/M: Suhrkamp.

Lohmann, H.-M. (Ed.). (1983). *Das Unbehagen in der Psychoanalyse: Eine Streitschrift*. Frankfurt/M: Suhrkamp.

Vaihinger, H. (1911). *Die Philosophie des Als-Ob*. Berlin.

von Foerster, H. (1973). On constructing a reality. In W. Preiser (Ed.), *Environmental design research*, Vol. 2, (pp. 35–46). Stroudsburg.

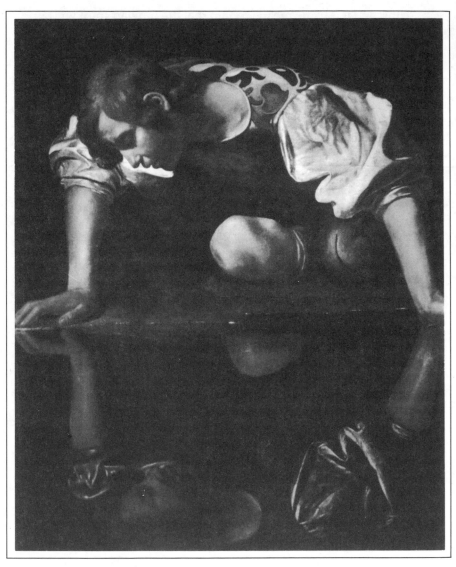

Figure 18-1.

Ovid's Narcissus and Caravaggio's Narcissus

Christian Gaillard (Paris)

Why invoke a painter, and a painter of the sixteenth and seventeenth centuries at that? Because his work, at least the work that we will consider here, is mute. It is so manifestly mute that it surprises us, arrests us and, in turn, silences us.

The silence imposed on us by this painting is all the more surprising and useful because it concerns a figure, a story, a myth that had already provoked much discussion in the painter's lifetime, and that provokes still more discussion in our day: the figure and the myth of Narcissus. More precisely, this representation of Narcissus explicitly concerns the themes of the shadow and separation.

What can this painting tell us about these themes? And how does our knowledge as clinicians help us to understand this work that is, by its muteness, so surprisingly demanding?

This work always surprises the first-time viewer. It remains surprising, however, when one becomes familiar with it. The least that one can do is to pause and open oneself to the first phase of interpretation. Thus we make room for what comes up before facing it directly.

The first surprise is due to the fact that this painting is quite removed from Ovid's Narcissus. The familiar Narcissus myth, in Caravaggio's day as in our own, is primarily Ovid's version.

Ovid (43 B.C.–18 A.D.) was the first in our cultural tradition to have truly given shape to the myth of Narcissus, before Pausanias. He based his poem on the versions known in his day, which were Beotian. Ovid was a poet. A subtle and mobile poet, he reworked the old story of Narcissus in his own period, that of Augustus (63 B.C.–14 A.D.), and told it with characteristic elegance in 172 lines. He told of the birth of Narcissus, son of the river god Cephissus and the nymph Liriope; and of the words of the soothsayer Tiresias, who foretold that Narcissus "would live a better life if he did not look at himself." Ovid told also of the passion that young men and women had for Narcissus; his insensitivity and arrogance; his impossible dialogue with the nymph Echo; his discovery of his own image by the edge of a brook; his desperate love for this image, his vain attempts to embrace it, his death, his passion for this very image, even to the edge of the Styx; and, finally, the flower–the narcissus–that blooms in place of his body.

Here, in this painting, there is no narrative. This work does not tell a story. It imposes itself on the viewer with the impact of a photographic snapshot.

Painting in Caravaggio's day knew how to be narrative, however. It knew how to tell the stories of the gods and those of humans that were related in myths and in Christian tradition, or that were related in worldly and civic life and in domestic life. The task of painting in those days was to bring its subjects closer to the daily life of the world, to bring the sky down to earth. Caravaggio in particular sought these objectives, with such predilection for ordinary life that he ended up shocking rulers in the Church and in the city and, even more, the bourgeoisie.

But here there is no story, not even a title; the painting is a snapshot that, nonetheless, undeniably refers to the myth of Narcissus. What then is going on here that comments on the ancient myth?

There is no flower in the painting either. One looks in vain for the expected narcissus; it appears neither as an emblematic reminder nor as a discrete part of the landscape. In fact, no element of scenery is represented here, with the exception of the water line, to which I will return later; nothing offers itself to rest the gaze. The background is black and closed.

Ovid, in contrast, had left out neither the springtime nor the flower. In unfolding his story step by step, from one line to the next, the poet had not missed the opportunity to charm his reader by evoking the sylvan pleasures of the hunt, the beautiful bodies basking in the sun, and the freshness of the brook. He had taken special pleasure in describing the gracefulness of the young man, leading his reader nearer, through sympathy and identification, to the charm that was seemingly timeless, almost eternal, yet also ambiguous.

At the same time, Ovid needed to note the distance that exists between a reader and such a singular tale. To do so, while still maintaining his taste for well-balanced drama, he had chosen to reprimand his Narcissus, as he fell in love with his image in the water:

> Why try to catch an always fleeing image,
> Poor credulous youngster? What you seek is nowhere,
> And if you turn away, you will take with you
> The boy you love. The vision is only shadow,
> Only reflection, lacking any substance.

The admonition is clear. Yet even through these lines shimmers Narcissus' image—an ideal figure. The poem plays on the fascination that this figure evokes. And under the cover of the lesson that he pretends to teach the young man, the poet plays sufficiently on the fascination to set his reader dreaming. In the end, the reader understands that the poem, like the daydream it inspires, closes on the image of the flower. We grieve, we weep over the unhappy fate of the young man, but we remain filled with the ideal bliss that this story, which comes full circle, leads us to comprehend.

This painting, on the other hand, is devoid of flower and story. They are beside the point, outside its pictoral scope. What tension, what suspense!

The ambiguity of the poem and the poet's subtle ambivalence are no longer with us. The lesson of the myth, as it was heard and understood before the time of Caravaggio, is suspended, perhaps in order to lead directly to the heart of the myth.

What tension? What suspense? Shall we say that in this painting, as in Ovid's text, Narcissus dives into the bewildering embrace of the perfect image that fascinates him? On the contrary, this young man is leaning on both arms, peering over the vision that is rising up and frightening him.

Ovid talked about shadows, but in the meaning used by philosophers, the meaning adopted by the Renaissance neo-platonic philosophers after Plotinus: the vain reflection, which does not exclude pleasure, even to the edge of the Styx. Here, shadow reigns manifestly over the bottom of the painting, where it takes the shape of a body: the fearsome body and visage of that other Narcissus, in whom he will soon recognize himself. From there, the shadow tends to overcome the whole picture. It rises and threatens the figure of the young man in the light; this figure, in turn, is altered by it. The shadow gnaws at the beautiful and alters it.

This canvas denies the flight and motion expected since Ovid. It reverses them. It reveals a threat. And this threat is not only the threat of the young man's wavering before the disquieting strangeness of the double, his own double borne on the mirror of the waters. It is the threat of an encounter, an inevitable one which is also a discovery, a disclosure.

This threat emanates from this other, distorted visage of himself, which Narcissus discovers with fright. This discovery overtakes the image the young man had and gave of himself until then, his representation in full light of day. The threat dismantles him, dismembers him, and almost buries him, in pieces. This discovery is precisely our problem of the shadow. We must call upon more than the question of the narcissistic double as it is developed in Freudian discourse, in order to account fully for this Narcissus.

For these reasons this canvas, which carries no more signature than it does a title, is generally attributed to Caravaggio. Not a painter of conventional beauty and ideals, Caravaggio was a profane painter who was called a profaner. And he was precisely a painter of shadow. Caravaggio's painting caused a scandal in his own day because of his taste for standing ancient and biblical themes on their heads, because of the movement he gave to classical shapes, and because of his predilection for the shadow, which makes him go against the grain of the light.

His painting passionately explores the real, more than it plays the expected and flattering game of conventional representation. With Caravaggio, painting moves into a new environment and new scenery. It moves from the domain of established projections and representations into that of the world and its encounters.

And here the world opens up on that which is hidden. The

encounter comes from below, from the waters, and not those waters that call for bathing, or that create a calm mirror, but somber waters that are both troubled and troubling. One would look in vain for such waters in painting before Caravaggio.

This is an event in painting, a transforming event. Not only does it challenge painting's blissful games with light, but the event also destabilizes painting, overthrowing its center of gravity. With this painting, we see and we live a loss of equilibrium against which, like Narcissus himself, we have good reasons to defend ourselves.

It is not a coincidence that this event took place in the same era in which Copernicus, and then Galileo, inflicted upon humanity a wound that Freud later called narcissistic, a wound that pushed humanity out of its supposedly central position in the universe, out of its cosmological comfort.

With Copernicus and Galileo, the decentering was upward. With Caravaggio, its direction is downward. Painting is transformed by this decentering and, taken in reverse, is thrown off balance. Moreover, our own relationship with painting and our position before it are collapsed and are transformed.

This canvas is a snapshot, not the narration of a story. A close-up snapshot, with no scenic or architectural frame to reassure the gaze. Where does one look when facing this canvas? Not only did this work want nothing to do with Ovid's poem, with its ambiguity between pleasurable fascination and warning, but it also has no use for that magisterial invention of the Renaissance— perspective.

Perspective is the certainty of a point of view. It is a scenic invention, in the end, which assigns to the world a theatricality that is all the more convincing and compelling because it is said to be natural. Perspective controls our understanding of people and things. The artist takes a position outside the canvas by taking a removed stance that assures mastery over the whole.

The pleasure of the Renaissance was one of mastery, a mastery which was presumed to be cosmological. This was a new cosmology, in comparison to the cosmology of earlier days. But this particular work, which departs from the comfort of scenic and architectural frames, leaves to others the mastery of perspective.

In refusing to use his easel as a window open onto the sky or onto the theater of the world, Caravaggio refused to examine space itself and to order it according to established laws. He made it manifestly flat, so that it imposes itself frontally, at eye-level. We do not enter into this painting as into the perspective spaces opened up by the Renaissance. This painting speaks out to us and takes us to task.

By virtue of its directness, and because it looks at us more than it offers itself to our gaze, this work prohibits the certainty of any established point of view. Ovid, who pleasantly cultivated both the flower and the lesson of the myth of Narcissus, did not antici-pate this prohibition. Perhaps Caravaggio did not either, and his contemporaries even less. At the same time that they honored his work, they questioned it so much that the painter had to en-dure rejection. This repudiation of the painting became more em-phatic over the seventeenth and eighteenth centuries, giving Caravaggio's work notoriety instead of oblivion.

Thus it is said that Poussin (French painter, 1594–1665) who, in matters of painting, had his own ideas and prejudices, could not tolerate Caravaggio. Poussin said that Caravaggio was put on this earth to destroy painting. The expression is violent, but it is fair. Caravaggio's work is about destruction – not wavering, like the affectations of painters of his day (1570?–1610) and before – of earlier or recently enshrined modes of representation and of our position in relation to paintings. This was Caravaggio's genius concerning Narcissus: his desire to come as close as possible to partaking of true happiness on this earth and to the ideal image that we make of ourselves and encounter in the eyes of others.

What we have here is not the problem of the mirror and of the double, as we might have thought after too quick an observation of the work. These problems, including all surprises and hesita-tions, are imprinted as unchanging memories. They are projec-ted in a form that is supposedly eternal and at times posthumous – like Ovid's flower, or in an esthetic of need and impossibility.

This painting is about an encounter with the shadow, a ques-tioning of one's primary identity, the encounter of the unity of Narcissus with the world, and of the ideal unity of his image of himself. The painting is also about the unity that we expect – or expected – from painting, and that we dream of for ourselves.

Where then shall we look when we face this canvas? In fact, the answer is right there: When looking at this work, the gaze itself is divided, just as the canvas is divided, cut in half, almost at the middle, by the line separating the earth from the water. The painting is a close-up of this separation which occurs in all of us.

The encounter with the shadow does not occur without loss or destruction of primary and ideal unity. Without such a separation within the subject and loss of his dream of oneness, Narcissus can regain it only in an impossible embrace. This embrace is all the more impossible because he turns defensive, standing firm against the fear of an all too human face that rises toward him.

It is a mark of Caravaggio's modernity that he showed that fear and imposed it upon whoever permits oneself to be examined by this work. This rising of the shadow, with the division that it induces, is the rise toward our modernity.

Yet is it only in this mood, that is quite diabolic, and only by its impact, that this work stands up and commands our attention? To conclude this would be to see quite poorly. There is certainly a downward decentering here, a return from the cave, and thus a separation and a threat of disfigurement and dismemberment. And this threatening invasion of the shadow almost buries the dismembered subject. The young man in the painting thus has very good reasons for defending himself against the shadow, just as we, like Poussin, have very good reasons for refusing to countenance such a painting.

But how can we see this scene without the desperate wrenching of Ovid's hero, without the grieving cries of the people around him, and without the posthumous consolation afforded by the metamorphosis into a flower? This work is obedient neither to Narcissus' point of view on his own fate, nor to that of his close relations, nor to that of the master painters of the Renaissance. Yet we can understand it on its own terms because it has its own unity. We can see this better today than yesterday.

The arc formed by the young man's arms as he leans over the line of the water is in opposition to, but also answers, the arc that rises from the water. The arc thus structurally forms a whole which is addressed to us, the viewers.

We can see it better today than yesterday, precisely because we have learned not to read paintings as the representation of an already known, an already seen, an already lived. We have learned not to engage ourselves as with a controlled space, inhabitable

before us. We have learned to receive the pictorial effect in the
terms that order it and support it, often subliminally, through the
shock and defeat that engender this effect and that it provokes.
We have learned this notably through the diffuse vision of Monet
(1840–1926) the frontal approach of Manet (1832–83) the acceptance of the ruptures of cubism, and the unexpectedly frequent
pleasures of that art we call abstract.

Yet it is precisely on this point, the recognition of the structural
meaning of the work, that psychoanalytic interpretations di-
verge. What I have said about the rising of the shadow does not
all appear in the analyses of this work by our Freudian colleagues. However, with the support of clinical evidence, it is possible that we could come to some agreement. There is a radical
divergence between the interpretation that I am proposing here
and earlier ones. I am thinking of the works of Damisch (1976)
and Wajeman (1984, 1985), to whom I owe a great deal, as I do
even more to the works of Marin (1977). This divergence concerns the unity implied by this painting. The unity is structural;
we are enjoined to see it through this scene and in the very particular shape of Narcissus.

Damisch and Wageman draw directly on the neo-Freudian
teachings of Jacques Lacan, which focus narrowly on the theory
of the mirror and repeatedly denounce imaginary phenomena.
In reference to the structural unity of this painting, they talk of
an illusory achievement of the unity of the subject, of an imaginary circle or totality, and even of a unity of the ego, that they
immediately dismiss as imaginary.

On the other hand, I prefer to talk about the play of the Self – in
the meaning that Jung gives to this term – at the very moment of
the rising of and encounter with the shadow, at the very moment
of the clear separation, and at the very moment of the most frac-
turing tensions.

I must be more precise, however. It is important to underline
the fact that Narcissus himself knows nothing of this. He is all
caught up in this moment of his story. He is this image of himself
at the edge of his own loss. That is why he hangs on.

Not only is he hanging on to the image he had of himself until
then. He is hanging on to his world. And he is defending his
world as much as he is defending himself. He wants to stay in

his world and maintain it. He would have liked to embrace it totally. We can understand this as the attachment to the ego that
Jung talked about.

Narcissus knows nothing of the general movement in which
this moment is caught up. He knows nothing of the possible
meaning of his story, of this moment of his story. But the meaning here is given to us to see in the specific framework in which
this moment of the story of Narcissus is played out. The meaning
is laid out for us when we look at this scene just as when, in our
clinical work, we hear our patients and their one thousand and
one tales that appear to make no sense.

I must emphasize also that if there is a meaning to this story,
to this moment in the story of Narcissus, to this segment of his
story, which is a segment of the myth, this meaning is not forthcoming. Why? Because we are dealing with a painting. We see
the scene as outsiders to it, when we face this work that speaks
out to us. Consequently, we see the whole story. It is we who
reconstruct the dynamic that occasions this frightened separation.

We can now understand why Caravaggio, unlike Ovid, did not
reproduce the entire story of Narcissus, but chose to represent
this moment of suspense in his story. It is clear why, in constructing this work, he did not choose to place himself as master of the
point of view, in the manner of the master painters of the Renaissance. We understand this canvas better when we look at it in the
same way that we listen in our clinical work, than when we look
at it through Ovid's text.

In fact, Caravaggio is a modern, partly because of his pictorial
understanding of the shadow and of the encounter he portrays
with the shadow and its effects. But he is a modern especially because of the composition of this canvas, in which is inscribed the
critical decentering of Narcissus, and because of this structural
composition that organizes it and brings us to talk of the Self.

If the Self is really the organizing element of this canvas, that
does not mean that it is perfect in its current state, or that it
promises perfection. The totality that is presented here is not one
of perfection, or of completeness, but it is one of connection. It
includes the separation and makes it possible. That is what the
work means to us.

And that is the reason, the only reason, why the work is tolerable, I might even say restful. Not for Narcissus himself, who finds no support, no perspective. Rather, it is restful for us.

This restfulness comes for us through the pictorial evidence that the crisis, the decentering, the separation take place within a dynamic whole that is meaningful and can give meaning to this moment. The painting coldly objectifies this critical moment of decentering but in a visual mode so that, without promising Narcissus anything, without making a flower for him, we can know – and if need be, he can know – that the whole story is not absurd. What Jung referred to, since 1916, as the transcendent function is signified here in the very composition of the work.

There is a crucial divergence on this point of the meaning of the work, between ourselves and our Freudian colleagues. Is it irremediable? Does it not send us into a region of psychoanalysis where we are alone, no longer in contact with them?

This divergence is not so certain if we engage in discussion with them on another aspect of this painting which I have not yet addressed: At the center, almost, of the work, is this light spot, Narcissus' sunlit knee. From its place above the line of the water, it thus strangely attempts to balance the whole scene. This light spot strives to be the pivot of the composition, the hub of the wheel that it forms. It does not succeed, however, because it is not precisely centered.

I hesitate before saying any more about this. For this is where there appears to be the widest gap between the pictorial evidence and the vocabulary that we need in order to interpret it. Here we must speak of phallus. This statement would certainly have astonished the painter.

On the other hand, what appears in the picture dispels my hesitation. I conferred with some who allow themselves to look at a painting through its immediate literality, who look at it through a floating gaze that draws the attention to what a painting shows or leads one to perceive without saying or representing it explicity. The obvious imagery in the composition of this piece is truly that of a phallus.

It is quite possible, in fact, that my hesitation is due to one very simple and banal fact: Our conceptual vocabulary evades that which informs it. The imagery of the phallus is primarily that of

power and mastery: that omnipotence in which impulse identifies itself in such a way with the narcissistic that such power is
more of the order of being than of the order of having. The ob-
verse appears in ordinary clinical practice: the threat of castra-
tion, which is always at least underlying or held at bay but
which, here, is at the heart of the picture.

Thus received and considered, this painting sheds light on the
myth of Narcissus. It helps us to understand the sexual distance
maintained by Narcissus from all object relations, in particular
with Echo. His phobic distance is that of a "touch me not," destined to keep himself safe and sound, far from all threat.

This painting also helps us to understand better the complete
excitement that Narcissus experiences through his presence in
the world, as well as the threat of annihilation, the enormous risk
of disintegration that is the opposite of this complete excitement
and that is manifest in the carving up of the composition of the
painting.

We could respond to certain of our Freudian colleagues at this
point, especially the British, in their new vocabulary, and speak
with them of "the ideal self." We can be even more direct, I believe: Narcissus is the phallus, or rather, he was the phallus. This
painting specifically shows and proves this, by showing how this
character is untenable, if only because he is centered on an ideal
representation and he is without a split.

My conclusion is that this painting is no more restful than it is
frightening. The tension and equilibrium within it are not immediately and literally perceivable, but are structural. It leads us
to see, or rather to receive, the tension and equilibrium between
the Self—which sustains this moment in which Narcissus is
finally divided within himself and decentered to the point of being threatened with perdition—and the phallus, the ideal self.
There he remains; there he would like to remain.

In fact, this painting represents a surgical cut through the knot
of myth, while Ovid, instead of becoming a surgeon, preferred
to compensate his poet's fascination by playing on therapists'
common sense and feelings of grief.

Returning to the question that was already present in our first
surprise: From what knowledge does such a work proceed?
From what mute knowledge, absent from all other language, be

it earlier or contemporary, that today we have so much difficulty in recognizing and expressing as correctly as this painting does?

Translated from French by
Colette Hyman

REFERENCES

Berne-Joffroy (1959). *Le dossier Caravage*. Paris: Minuit.

Damisch, H. (1976). D'un Narcisse l'autre. *Nouvelle Revue de Psychanalyse, 13*.

Wajeman, G. (1984). Narcisse ou le fantasme de la peinture. In *Art et Fantasme*. Seyssel: Champ-Vallan.

Wajeman, G. (1985, Automne). Narcisse spectateur et peinture. *Cahiers de psychologie de l'art et de la culture, 11*.

Marin, L. (1977). *Détruire la peinture*. Paris: Galilée.

The Split Shadow and the Father-Son Relationship

Donald Sandner (San Francisco)

My main purpose in this paper is to expand Jung's concept of the shadow, and to demonstrate its bipolar nature. To illustrate this bipolarity, I focus on the father-son relationship. The first section gives a brief developmental background, based on Eriksonian psychology, tracing the split shadow from infancy to adolescence. The second section uses a Navaho myth to elucidate the archetypal foundation of the split shadow in adolescence. The third section gives a detailed account of the split shadow in psychological terms; in the fourth section this account is illustrated by a clinical example of a weak father-son relationship. In the fifth section an account of a Vietnam war veteran's experiences is used to show the split shadow in a strong father-son situation, and the archetypal structure of the father-son initiation process is explored in the myth of a Navaho war ceremony. The last section sums up the concept of bipolarity on a collective basis and relates it to the current world dilemma.

The Initiatory Stage

In the first part of a boy's life the mother — or her substitute — plays by far the most important role. She is the archetypal center, and the home is her symbolic womb. When the father shares in early care, plays his part in the oedipal romance, and labors in the outside world, he supports this pattern.

The boy's initiatory stage reaches its peak in adolescence, following the stages of ego development posited by Erikson (1950, 1980). The first three stages are based primarily on the maternal archetype as expressed through the personal mother. The first stage involves the balance of *trust vs. mistrust*, the basis of comfort in the world. It does not depend on actual quantities of food or demonstrations of love, but mainly, as Erikson said, "on the quality of the maternal relationship" (1950, p. 221). Here are the roots of existential being in the world, the ability to live with good and bad objects (and objects that are sometimes one and sometimes the other), with the inner assurance that basic needs will be met. Here also is the basis of meaning. Erikson wrote: "[The parents] must be able to represent to the child a deep, and almost somatic conviction, that there is meaning to what they are doing" (1950, p. 221).

In the next stage, *autonomy vs. shame*, the boy encounters authority. Society demands that he regulate his bodily functions. This is his first encounter with the outside father-world of law and order, though the experience is still actively mediated and ameliorated by the mother. There is special somatic concern for the backsides of the body, the buttocks and the anus. As Erikson cogently puts it:

> This reverse area of the body with its aggressive and libidinal focus in the sphincters and in the buttocks, cannot be seen by the child, and yet it can be dominated by the will of others. The "behind" is thus the individual's dark continent, an area of the body which can be magically dominated and effectively invaded by those who would attack one's power of autonomy and who would designate as evil those products of the bowels which were felt to be all right when they were being passed. . . . This finds its adult expression in paranoid fears concerning hidden persecutors and secret persecutions threatening from behind and from within the behind (1950, p. 224).

In these first forceful impositions of authority lie the seeds of the sadomasochistic aspect of the boy's relationship with the father. We will return to that topic.

In the third phase, *initiative vs. guilt* (the phallic phase), the hegemony of the maternal archetype is challenged. Having accepted the first great imposition of authority, mainly through the mother's animus, in the preceding stage of autonomy vs. shame, the boy can now identify with it and begin his struggle for individual assertion. The incest taboo is activated and the masculine ego begins its long climb to autonomy. Archetypally, this is the inception of the hero's journey.

Ego development steadily continues through the next stage, characterized as *industry vs. inferiority*. Through enhanced mastery, the ego assimilates its heritage. The boy receives, somewhat passively, the learning and culture accumulated by his society. This encourages a certain freedom from the matriarchate, and the beginning of a decade-long confrontation with the father-world as conveyed by the personal father and other representatives. If the boy fails here he will bear the onus of inferiority which will handicap him in the ensuing masculine initiation.

Now the boy enters adolescence. His sexuality emerges and he enters into the struggle with what appears to be ungovernable instinct on one hand and unyielding authority on the other. In the struggle the boy will be molded by the initiatory archetype into the kind of man his culture determines him to be.

This is not a clean and well-defined effort. There is a split in the psyche, an unavoidable wound which has been there from the beginning. Erikson characterizes his stages as essentially either-or: trust vs. mistrust, autonomy vs. shame, initiative vs. guilt, industry vs. inferiority, but they may be viewed, alternatively, as pairs of opposites to be negotiated in childhood, and as not essentially different from those encountered later in adulthood. In the early stages, if the experience is "good enough," then the trust and autonomy predominate but mistrust (suspicion) and shame maintain their underground existence in the form of split-off feeling-toned complexes. Erikson said of the stage of initiative vs. guilt: "Here the most fateful split and transformation in the emotional powerhouse occurs, a split between the potential human glory and potential total destruction. For here the child becomes forever divided in himself" (1950, p. 225).

Viewed from another standpoint, the boy has been divided against himself from the beginning. The psyche is fundamentally split, and the seeds of what we know as the shadow are laid down in earliest infancy. First there is a split between the essentially good and unsuitably bad breasts (to speak in somatic symbolism), then there is a turning against parts of the body and its products as nasty and repulsive, and finally the incest wound in which the part of the psyche that wants to stay protected, gratified, inflated, rebellious, and unconscious is at war with the part that wants to be independent, assertive, productive, admired, and conscious. The stage is set for the emergence in adolescence of the archetypal opposition of the trickster versus the hero (characterized by Erikson as *identity vs. role diffusion*), and its resolution in an encounter with the father, the laws of society and the tribal gods.

A Navaho Myth

The hero-trickster myth from the Navaho healing ceremony Big Star Way provides a parallel to the development of the young male. I will give a shortened version of the myth of this rite as related to me by Natani Tso, a medicine man, at his ceremonial hogan on the Navaho reservation in northeastern Arizona. (A version of this myth appears in McAllester, 1956.) In the myth, Badger is the cultural hero and Coyote the Trickster.

> Badger was the one who started this chant (Big Star Way). Coyote came to Badger and said: "Come on, let's go to the top of these cliffs. There are some young eagles up there." Coyote was interested in Badger's wife and hoped to play a trick on him. Coyote persuaded him to climb up the cliff while Coyote stayed down below. When Badger got to the top he was disappointed because he saw no eagles, only grasshoppers.

Coyote plays on Badger's greed to get him to make this strenuous and dangerous climb which results in an almost fatal inflation.

> While Badger was on the top, Coyote blew on the butte from each of the four directions and it started rising up in the air until it almost reached the sky. Badger had no way to get down, so he had to stay up there for four nights. There was nothing to eat or drink, so I don't how he got by.

Coyote traps Badger in his own inflation, in order to get him out of the way so that Coyote may seduce his wife. But there is a spiritual dimension with which Coyote has not reckoned.

Four racer snakes saw Badger from the sky. These racer snakes were divine beings. They were like sentries in the upper world. The Holy people told the racer snakes to get Badger and bring him up the cliffs to the upper world.

When he got into the upper world Badger saw that the divine beings there were living together in a community. They gave him deer meat and he told them all about himself. The Star People, for that is who they were, then gave him secret knowledge concerning dead people. Badger stayed up there for four years learning different branches of the Big Star Way until he knew everything perfectly. Then he was told to return, taking his healing knowledge back to his people.

A large part of the myth is omitted here, in which Badger undergoes various ordeals in the sky world. He becomes stronger after each ordeal until finally he is able to help the Star People against their enemies.

Finally the racer snakes crisscrossed again and took Badger down to his earthly home. Then they disappeared into the sky. It was four years since he left, and his home was abandoned. He found out from the poker that Coyote had kept his family here for a year and then moved on to the east. This happened four times.

When Badger came to the fourth hut, he found his wife and children in a pitiable condition. His wife was thin and sick, and his children were dressed in rags. They didn't even recognize him because he'd been away so long. He gave them all deer meat from the Holy People, and this made them stronger.

Then he heard Coyote howling outside. He was returning with an old flea bag full of rabbits. Coyote called Badger's children beggars and commanded them to come out and welcome him home as they were supposed to do. As he came in he was startled to see that they were with their father, Badger.

Once more Badger and Coyote meet; this time Badger is much stronger and less easily tricked. He is a spiritual person, and Coyote is at the disadvantage.

When Coyote came in he immediately saw the deer meat which Badger brought from the upper world. It was much better than the skinny rabbits he caught. He said: "Cousin, give me a piece of that deer meat for taking care of your family while you were gone." Badger gave him a piece of meat, but wrapped in it was a piece of star from the upper world. Coyote ate it all down ravenously. All of a sudden Coyote gave a loud yelp and took off around the house. You could hear his footsteps as they ran; all of a sudden they just stopped. Badger went out and saw that Coyote was dead. The star had burned his throat. Then Badger saw that his wife was sick because of her long stay with Coyote, so he determined to perform his new ceremony over her and the children.

Here the spiritual principle triumphs, but only for the moment. The Holy People decide that Coyote is indispensable and must be brought back to life again.

A little inch worm came and dragged the dead Coyote to the North, the place of evil. There he was revived again. Meanwhile Badger went out to the woods to find some special berries for his wife's ceremony. As he was looking all around, Coyote's skin came over him. It covered his whole body and his eyes so he couldn't see. It was Coyote back again as full of lust for the woman as before.

Where lust is concerned Coyote never stops, but the sudden covering of the hero with Coyote's skin reveals their hidden identity. Badger, the hero, is also Coyote and even though as the hero he has attained his spiritual quest, the trickster in him is never dead.

In a further part of this account Natani Tso told how Badger, covered with Coyote's skin, spent four nights blindly crawling around the forest. Finally he asked Big Fly, who was a spiritual messenger, to call the Holy People. They came and held a Big Star ceremony in which Badger crawled through five special wooden hoops. As he passed through each one, the skin came off him a little further until at the last one he was free.

Here the archetypal split in the Navaho psyche is clearly revealed. Coyote is the forbidden instinctual side, closely connected with what is repulsive and repressed in the Navaho culture. As an archetypal trickster, he bears a close relationship to the Freudian id and the Jungian shadow. Reading the Coyote stories we can recognize, all too easily, our shadowy likeness.

Opposing him, and yet in a certain complementary relationship with him, is the hero, Badger, who is idealistic, sensitive, spiritual and able to learn divine secrets of healing. But the hero is also easily inflated, cut off from his natural base in the earth, forgetful of his humanity, and too much concerned with his own spiritual welfare to care about his wife and children. While he is on his transpersonal quest he leaves his family with Coyote, thus expressing a pointed critique of spirituality.

The archetypal dimension of the split psyche is outlined in the development of the Navaho culture hero, but the split must be resolved in some way by every young man as an initiatory stage leading to maturity and marriage. Let me bring this into clinical focus and put the split psyche with its hero and its trickster into a psychological perspective.

The Split Shadow

The concept of the split psyche suggests an extension of the Jungian idea of the shadow, especially regarding its clinical manifestation. The shadow can be seen as a bipolar or split complex, characterized in the myth as trickster versus hero, which expresses itself on the personal, cultural and archetypal levels. This view of the bipolar nature of the shadow was presented in an early form by Perry (1970) and expanded by Sandner and Beebe (1982). In a specific culture one side is always bad or undesirable, something to be hidden or repressed, but still contains vital instinctual energy. The other side is good or ideal, something to be encouraged and developed. The masculine ego, in the developmental process, integrates as much of each side into itself as it can, leaving parts of both unintegrated, unexpressed and unconscious. These unintegrated parts become the adult split bipolar shadow complex.

On the personal level, the negative pole of the complex contains culturally undesirable qualities that have been repressed. These are usually primitive, lustful, aggressive, hateful, envious and anti-social qualities – the familiar shadow material. In other cultures almost any qualities, including those we idealize, can be considered undesirable and repressed and vice versa. In dreams and other unconscious fantasies these repressed qualities are usually represented by such sinister figures as toughs, murderers, aggressive animals, menacing intruders. Though always seen negatively by the particular culture, this pole contains great instinctual vitality.

The opposite pole, the relatively positive side, carries idealized qualities represented by superior, noble, heroic, spiritual or religious figures. These qualities tend to inflate the ego, though they also carry genuine spiritual values.

In adulthood both poles of this complex are still available to the ego for further efforts at integration, most notably in analytic work. Both poles are rightful extensions of the ego's domain and may be designated as ego-aligned. This designation does not mean that these complexes cannot be projected. Of course they frequently are; it only indicates their natural connection to the ego.

This concept of the bipolar shadow differs from the Freudian concept of id and superego (which derives from the same clinical data) in seeing these components not as separate institutions but as a dynamic, polarized entity (the complex) containing energy and specific qualities, complementary to each other as well as in opposition, and rooted in both biological and spiritual archetypes.

The bipolar shadow complex and the ego complex together contain the full range of masculine qualities in any cultural pattern. Any quality not expressed by the ego is held in potentia by the complex. Thus, no matter what the overall pattern, there is a resulting conservation of overall qualities.

I have illustrated one cultural pattern in the Navaho hero-trickster myth. In Balinese culture (Indonesia), for another example, the qualities of close group cooperation, detailed orderliness, and highly developed spiritual refinement are idealized while any gross, animal-like, disorderly or idiosyncratic behavior is discouraged, sometimes violently. This differs sharply from the American cultural ideal of rugged individualism; thus what is idealized in the United States is shadowy in Bali. Every culture has its own pattern which extends to the formation of masculine identity in its own unique way.

A crucial governing factor in determining how much of the masculine shadow will be expressed and how much will remain unconscious is the quality of the father-son relationship. I will describe two examples, one a weak father-son relationship involving a boyish (puer) son, and the other a strong father-son relationship involving an aggressive (warrior) son to show how they differ functionally.

The Weak Father-Son Relationship

My first example is a young man in therapy: He was single, in his early thirties, and a teacher. He was born and raised in the Southwest, and retained a deep love for the deserts and mesas of Arizona and New Mexico.

He was bisexual in his instinctual orientation. In his early twenties he had been both emotionally and sexually in love with a young woman, but he also was strongly attracted to men. Especially interesting to us is one of his sexual fantasies, containing a great deal of energy, which was tied to his father.

The predominant conscious feeling of this young man for his father was one of disgust and disappointment. He thought the old man stupid, vulgar and mean. Far from appreciating the comfortable life style his father's labors had procured for him, he saw it all as money-grubbing pretentiousness. All through his adolescence the patient was aloof and inflated. His father treated him superficially with some tolerance and consideration but an overall indifference masked his deeper feelings of jealousy and anger. There was bitter rivalry for the mother/wife, but this was never made conscious and father and son never confronted each other. Thus the negative father archetype was never fully invoked and mediated by the personal father, and the son was never initiated into manhood. He remained on the brink of it, unable to proceed further without help. There is an old saying that what the father has spoiled, only the father can repair. His father never forcibly claimed the son as his own, never risked a display of intense love or anger that would have gripped the son and pulled him into the process. Now the initiatory father for this young man can be found only in the symbolic transference-father of analysis, and that is where he came for help.

But the initiatory process had not been entirely absent. There was an unconscious fantasy which was an important part of his erotic life. He fantasized that his father, in a surge of anger, would take him out to the woods alone, bend him over, and beat him until he promised to be respectful and obedient. This had never happened to him, but by means of the fantasy he preserved his connection to the chthonic, instinctual masculinity that can only be transmitted by the father. He was obsessively fixated on an essentially initiatory ritual. But it is a solitary fantasy, not sanctioned by the society of men (the outer collective). It is an unconscious product of the trickster, and the trick is on him (as it was on Badger in the Navaho myth). He is erotically bound inwardly to the very act of submission to the father which he outwardly abhors. As long as the meaning of the fantasy remained unconscious he was doomed like Tantalus to be initiated again and again without resolution.

For the initial elucidation of a fantasy of this type we must first turn to Freud who wrote a paper in 1919 entitled "A Child is Being Beaten" (SE17). Freud commented that to the young male, being beaten stands for being loved. The boy's beating fantasy is passive and is derived from a feminine, incestuous attachment to the father which has remained unconscious. This is on the mark, but what Freud omitted was that this incestuous fantasy is also a part of the archetypal initiatory process. It is the necessary submission to the father, the necessary endurance of pain as an act of masculine love, and the acceptance of symbolic death of the mother's child (unconscious identification with the mother) as a prelude to rebirth into manhood.

In an early dream the patient reported: *I was walking down a dark, deserted street with three black guys. They were intent on destruction. Then I was on a motorcycle being pursued by three tough characters. One was an older man. I threw the emergency switch and was able to speed away up a hill.*

Here as in other dreams he is in close contact with the aggressive aspect of his (ego-aligned) shadow complex, but there is danger from the tough characters, and he can escape only by using his emergency energy (motorcycle). The older man may be an early appearance of the therapist in his dreams.

In a second dream the patient *is in the Palace of Fine Arts* (his inflated side), *being attacked on all sides by blacks who are intent on killing every white in the building.*

The shadow complex is full of murderous rage. Only an appeal to the inner father who is also tough can lead him out of this mortal danger. At this time in therapy the patient was suicidal; all his efforts to change were failing. In one dream: *I was trying to cross the Golden Gate Bridge, but it collapsed. I was underneath. It started sagging down. Water started to come in. Finally it was like a tunnel, and I just got out to the other side before the water flooded in. Lots of people were killed.*

In spite of such repeated attacks the ego was still able to identify with the inflated heroic pole of his bipolar shadow: *I was in
a big opera house singing an important aria. The stage began slanting
down like the leaning tower. I was quite high up. I had to sit down and
block myself from sliding, but I was still slipping. Someone, maybe the
stage manager, on the left was bracing me. Thousands and thousands
of people were waiting for me to sing the Etruria* (combination of erotic and Etruscan). *I did get through and it was very well received.*

In a dream he tried to get help from his father: *I went on vacation
and left my parakeet in a cage. I asked my father to take care of it but
when I got back he hadn't taken care of it at all.*

Then the patient dreamed that *he saw his father dressed in leather
pants and boots, and having an affair with a 19-year-old boy. The father
was whipping the boy with a leather belt.* The feeling of the dream
was of mixed disgust and jealousy of the boy.

The dreams in this case show the typical pattern of the weak
father-son relationship. The dream ego, as well as the actual ego,
identifies itself with inflated heroism, ready to sing for "thousands and thousands of people." But it is under attack by the instinctual shadow complexes symbolized by the blacks and the
toughs. There were many other, similar dreams. In the last two
dreams cited the father complex is activated again. Though at
first there is the expected betrayal, in the sadomasochistic dream
the father becomes an ambivalent figure that fascinates the son;
my patient thought the boy might be a younger version of
himself.

Of over-riding inflation, prominent in the opera dream and in
the patient's life, Henderson (1967), in his important work on the
initiation archetype, said: "Every educated person comes out of
childhood with the impossible expectation of achieving some
kind of godlikeness. I have already called attention to the immense social danger of this illusion unless it is corrected. What
we can excuse in a boy and even admire, because of the enthusiasm with which he may enliven his elders with his divine
discontent becomes both a private and public danger in a grown
man" (pp. 130–31).

Here the transference comes into play, as Henderson (1967)
said once more: "The patient's acceptance of his therapist as both
trustworthy and humane suggests that in his transference of feeling from mother to father, he accepts the role of the doctor as a

transitional figure, a master of initiation, who is both mother and father, firm and skillful in the use of his instruments, but also compassionate" (p. 97).

The therapeutic initiation process means lowering and grounding the god-like expectation. To do that requires activating symbolically an inner archetypal structure that consists of submission, fusion (in the transference/countertransference), and re-emergence as a man. This structure is the basis for every initiatory therapy. Thus, in the case of a young man, an older man is often the most appropriate therapist. In such therapy the inflation of meaning over substance, and the hegemony of the spirit, is sacrificed for substance, grounding and energy for life itself.

If, however, the above process is obstructed, as in our clinical example, then the symbolic substratum might surface as a sexualized compulsion for male-male sadomasochistic acts. Many of these acts—submission to the father-master, the posture of humiliation, being bound or immobilized, the infliction of physical pain, and even penetration by the stronger masculine phallus—originally represent necessary stages in the flow of initiatory symbolism. All of them can be found as parts of initiation rituals in tribal cultures. Symbolically, every part or product of the father's body becomes an avenue for longed-for fusion by means of which the transfer of genuine masculine power takes place. But if there is an obstruction in the process and the libido is caught in the repetition-compulsion of a specific sadomasochistic act, then it will remain in that form until the libido is once more restored to the underlying, initiatory process.

Here caution is necessary on the part of the therapist. No therapist can know the true relative strength of the contending complexes, nor can one in any particular case know how far the initiatory process can and should go. Every part of the initiatory archetypal way is sacred in its own right and contains a secret symbolism of its own which binds the devotee to a way of life, both sexually and emotionally, which has its own divine patronage and fatefulness. Individuation does not demand perfection. In all these secret scenarios, if they are genuinely experienced, the sacrifice of godlikeness, hubris and youthful inflation is performed, and that is the all-important step. Then—and only then—the sacrifice of the spirit can be made which leads of its own accord to moderation of the flesh.

The Strong Father-Son Relationship

In the strong father-son relationship the son readily accepts psychological fusion with the father, the deflation of his childhood divinity, and his own identity as an ordinary instinctual man. Then he becomes the father's son, the culturally approved man; often this also means becoming the patriotic warrior. He has undergone the initiatory process, and has accepted the currently official form of manhood for his society. But this does not mean that his problems are over. Far from it. If he is aware he will become conscious that not only his own masculine identity, but also the culture that shaped it, is seriously flawed. Then he, too, must bear the burden of individuation. This situation is well described in an essay by Broyles (1984), founding editor of Texas Monthly and past editor of Newsweek. The essay, "Why Men Love War," is unflinchingly honest and describes Broyles' own wakening to consciousness. He seemed to refer to fathers' sons when he wrote:

> It is no mystery why men hate war. War is ugly, horrible, evil and it is reasonable for men to hate all that. But I believe that most men who have been to war would have to admit, if they are honest, that somewhere inside themselves they loved it, too, loved it as much as anything that has happened to them before or since. And how do you explain that to your wife, your children, your parents, or your friends? (p. 55)

Of course, men never explained because, as he said:

> We were mute, I suspect, out of shame. Nothing in the way we were raised admits the possibility of loving war. It is at best a necessary evil, a patriotic duty to be discharged and then put behind us. To love war is to mock the very values we supposedly fight for. It is to be insensitive, reactionary, a brute. (p. 56)

Here he described the split that is the main theme of this paper. On the one side is the idealism which is publicly approved by the outer culture, and to which we must all appear to conform; on the other side is the nakedly aggressive shadow rooted firmly in the dark primitive side of the masculine (father) archetype.

Broyles went on to describe the dynamics of that archetype: "Part of love of war stems from its being an experience of great intensity; its lure is the fundamental human passion to witness, to see things, what the Bible calls lust of the eye, and the Marines in Vietnam called eye-fucking. War stops time, intensifies experience to the point of terrible ecstasy" (1984, p. 56).

Finally, with relentless self-analysis he concluded: "The love of war stems from the union, deep in the core of our being, between sex and destruction, beauty and horror, love and death. War may be the only way in which most men touch the mystic domains of our soul. It is for men, at some terrible level, the closest thing to what childbirth is for women: the initiation into the power of life and death" (p. 61).

In many tribal cultures, the love of war is openly and unashamedly displayed. War is part of life and must be lived with the same vital enthusiasm. But it is often ritually regulated. The Navaho again offer a prime example in the War Ceremony collected and presented by Oakes (1943). This was a ceremony given for young men going to or coming home from war. It provided a path for the return of the warrior to peaceful life. It also laid out the archetypal path of initiation in the clearest possible way.

This is the story of the Navaho warrior twins, Monster Slayer and Child Born of Water, and their journey to find their father. They are born of the great Navaho fertility goddess, Changing Woman. She carefully protects them from the monsters, but when they are 12 years old they can no longer be prevented from setting off to find their father, who is the Sun, giver of all warmth and life.

The basic split I have described is echoed in its Navaho form even in the twinship of the heroes. Monster Slayer is bolder and more aggressive, while Child Born of Water is softer and more gentle, the favored of the mother. He is the one for whom she weeps when both twins leave. Their journey is fraught with terrible dangers, which are described in great detail in the myth. Before they go far they come upon the house of Spider Woman. She is the Navaho version of the wise old woman, always shrewd and sometimes helpful. She has a very small house, but they find they can enter it nonetheless. One of the things she gives to each of them is a sacred feather which she has obtained secretly from Father Sun himself. These feathers represent the secret, spiritual connection with the father, and in spite of the many terrible ordeals the twins must undergo, the feathers keep them safe. Finally they come to the trackless ocean (what better symbol for the boundless collective unconscious) and with the help of the feather find their way to Sun's house.

Sun's daughter tries to hide them in the cloud coverings, but when the Sun comes home he is very angry, because he has seen from the sky strange men approaching his house. He hunts until he finds them, and then, appearing to disbelieve their claims to be his sons, puts them through a series of ruthless tests.

The first is a sweathouse heated to an unendurable temperature until the rocks inside are so hot they explode. This would have killed the twins except that Sun's daughter helps them. She digs deep pits inside the sweathouse and in these the twins hide themselves to escape the heat and flying rocks. Sun is surprised to find them still alive, but he devises another test. He offers them poisoned mush. Only half of it has the poison. Little Wind, their spiritual advisor, tells them which part to eat. There are several other ordeals, but finally Sun takes them to a high platform placed over sharp, out-thrusting knives, and pushes them off. They are sure to be killed, but the feather guides them safely down past the blades. Then Sun relents and recognizes them as his sons. He changes completely, becomes very generous, and offers them all the bounties of his earthly domain. But all they want are his terrible arrow weapons to kill the monsters who are ravaging the earth. Sun is sorry to hear this because the monsters are also his sons, but he does give them the arrows. One by one they slay all their enemies, but when the task is accomplished, and the earth is free from the oppression of the monsters, they cannot stop. They want to go on killing and must be restrained. Sun takes back his powerful arrows because the twins can no longer handle them. War chant ceremonies are held to cleanse them of the blood they have shed.

In this part of the Navaho myth the core of the initiation archetype relating to the father is laid out. The hero(es) must leave the land of the mother. This leaving itself means going outside time and space, against strong obstacles. They must finally penetrate into the objective (collective) psyche (the trackless ocean) and there they find the father's house. At first he is the terrible father; he meets them with suspicion and hostility. He subjects them to tests they could never survive if they did not have secret connections to his other, spiritual side. These are the feathers from Spider Woman (the feathers represent a spiritual connection between the earth and the upper world), Little Wind – another such spiritual connection – and Sun's daughter who, like Brunhilde, knows the father's tender heart. When they pass his tests he knows they are his sons and all the bounty of the earth and heaven is open to them. They choose weapons. Their lust is to kill and nothing else interests them. Even after the monsters threatening civilized progress are dead, the heroes cannot give up the lust to kill. Finally the first performance of the War Ceremonial is given on earth to cleanse them of the killing, to renew contact with the peaceful, spiritual father who dwells in the upper reaches of the psyche, and to return to the ways of peace. It is that ceremony for which the whole world now, it would seem, stands in need.

Conclusion

We are in a crucial world situation. The split between instinct and ideal is strained to the uttermost. In a world threatened by total nuclear destruction on the one hand and relentless overpopulation on the other, the core instinctual experiences of life and death in both men and women will have to be changed if we are to survive. For a genuine transformation to take place, a sacrifice is necessary on both sides of the bipolar shadow. If humans are to sacrifice the intensity of their animal nature they must also sacrifice their divine pretensions. Their sacrifice will not be, as in the past, for the perfection of Christian virtue or eastern enlightenment, but rather to become complete human beings beset by unattainable idealizations and by instinctual temptations. The path is a narrow one between the opposites, but it is our nature to be at home with (to paraphrase John Gower) "this warring peace, this sweet wound and this enjoyable evil" (quoted in CW16, par. 353).

REFERENCES

Broyles, W., Jr. (1984, November). Why men love war. *Esquire*, p. 55.

Erikson, E. (1950). *Childhood and society*. New York: Norton.

Erikson, E. (1980). *Identity and the life cycle*. New York: Norton.

Henderson, J. (1967). *Thresholds of initiation*. Middletown, CT: Wesleyan University Press.

McAllester, D. (Ed.). (1956). *The myth and prayers of the great star chant*. Navajo Religion Series, Vol. 4. Santa Fe: Museum of Navajo Ceremonial Art.

Oakes, M. (1943). *Where the two came to their father, a Navajo war ceremonial*. Princeton, NJ: Princeton University Press.

Perry, J. (1970). Emotions and object relations. *Journal of Analytical Psychology, 15*–1, 1–12.

Sandner, D. and Beebe, J. (1982). Psychopathology and analysis. In M. Stein (Ed.), *Jungian analysis*. LaSalle, IL: Open Court.

The Shadow Archetype and the Hemispheric Disconnection Syndrome

Romano Fiumara (Rome)

In the introduction to Neumann's work *The Origins and History of Consciousness* (1970) Jung stated, "The author has placed the concepts of analytic psychology—which for many people are so bewildering—on a firm evolutionary basis, and erected upon this a comprehensive structure in which the empirical forms of thought find their rightful place" (p. xiv). The present paper is biologically-based and therefore follows an evolutionary perspective. On these premises I propose some ideas in support of the topic designated in my title.

1. *The unconscious is the seat of forgotten memory, and the mechanisms of progressive forgetting can be used for the purpose of evolution.*

To support this statement we may let Jung himself speak. In "Analytical Psychology and Weltanschauung" (CW8), originally a lecture delivered in 1927, Jung pointed out that, from a Freudian point of view, "unconscious psychic activity . . . appears chiefly as a receptacle of all those contents that are antipathetic to consciousness, as well as of all forgotten impressions" (par. 702). But some paragraphs later Jung said something more:

> The collective unconscious is in no sense an obscure corner of the mind, but the mighty deposit of ancestral experience accumulated over millions of years, the echo of prehistoric happenings, to which each century adds an infinitesimally small amount of variation and differentiation. Because the collective unconscious is, in the last analysis, a deposit of world-processes embedded in the structure of

the brain and the sympathetic nervous system, it constitutes in its totality a sort of timeless and eternal world image. (par. 729)

If we agree that the collective unconscious is the storehouse of countless millions of years' atavistic experiences, if we place this statement in an evolutionary perspective, and if we remember that Jung did not reject the Freudian unconscious as the seat of personal repression and forgetting, then we can conclude that the collective unconscious is also the seat of repression and forgetting, but of a phylogenetic order. That is, we can hypothesize that the personal unconscious is the seat of ontogenetic forgotten memory, whereas the collective unconscious is the seat of phylogenetic forgotten memory.

The idea that the contents of the collective unconscious manifest themselves as a priori becomes understandable if we accept the principle that ontogenesis recapitulates phylogenesis. Along the linear path of development, critical times occur cyclically. These times appear novel to the individual involved, but to the species they form part of the historical ebb and flow.

The evolutionary usefulness of forgetting may be an intrinsic tendency of organisms which leads them to more complex levels of organization. To avoid being accused of Lamarckism we can place forgetting among the mechanisms of natural selection.

If we remember that humans are social animals, Romano and Trevi's (1985) statements are pertinent: "The necessity for a rule, and therefore a system of commands and prohibitions running counter to and limiting instinctive needs, is inherent in the very functioning of social life which, in turn, is an indispensable condition for human survival" (p. 59). Thus, for the purposes of adjustment, it is important to forget or repress natural processes, which are stored in the unconscious so that socialization and the "mind" become more and more developed.

2. *The archetypes correspond to "role" behavior which is conceived and established by society; they are comparable to biological entities and subject to cultural evolution.*

"The archetype is pure, uninvited nature, and it is nature that causes man to utter words and perform actions whose meaning is unconscious to him, so unconscious that he no longer gives it a thought" (CW8, par. 412). These are Jung's words in an essay "On the Nature of the Psyche," which was first published in

1946, later revised and republished in 1954. This was a mature Jung, therefore, who had already elaborated upon his basic concept of the archetype and distinguished it from archetypal images.

The relationship between the archetype and the instinct is indisputable in practical terms. Thus his statement "the archetype is pure, uninvited nature" would by necessity find its true place in an evolutionary perspective. Evolutionary adjustment compels us to consider natural biological events as having the goal of individual survival and successful reproduction. As a corollary, one could make the banal statement: What has conditioned the repetition of certain behavior patterns in the human species and has caused them to become habitual, to the point of becoming archetypes, is their optimum response to the necessity for adjustment.

There is another equally banal consideration that seems fitting here: Ever since primordial times, perhaps more than any other species, humans have been social animals. Therefore, archetypes, as "natural behavior patterns" (Progoff, 1973) represent each individual's physiological maturation states, from birth to death. But above all, these stages and behavior patterns are necessary for the survival of the individual as a social being—for relation to other individuals, the organization of social groups, and relating to other groups.

Indeed, in their studies of socialization ethologists have found use for concepts derived from human social sciences, particularly the concept of roles. A role may be defined as the interface between an individual and the social group. A society is composed of a complex system of roles which make up the social system; it maintains its structure to the extent that individuals conform to the roles expected of them. Viewed in a more specifically Jungian perspective, a role has the quality and the valence of the persona, the "mask" which the individual wears during daily social exchanges.

On closer examination, however, the role as the manifest behavior of a state of being can be extended to include the concept of the archetype in general. And so we find ourselves back where we started, with Jung's words stating that the archetype is pure, uninvited nature. The archetype/role equation appears particularly tenable in view of the fact that the collective unconscious, seat of the archetypes, expresses itself in the structure of the brain and the sympathetic nervous system. Because humans are basically social animals, their experience over millions of years has concerned mainly their relations to other members of the species. From these relations the roles are designated.

The perception of a cyclic, cosmological time, before it was transformed into linear, eschatological time, was probably very relevant and instrumental in crystallizing those primitive experiences into acquired and hereditary patterns. Among these is the archetype.

Jung seemed exasperated at times when trying to clarify the shadow concept. Von Franz (1974) reported that after a long debate on the subject, he once exclaimed, "All this diatribe is nonsense! The Shadow is simply *the whole unconscious*" (p. 5). As we have seen, the unconscious may be considered the seat of forgotten memory, both ontogenetic and phylogenetic, personal and collective. Therefore the shadow contains everything that appears contrary to the ego ideal or to one's ego identity.

3. *In order to be actualized the archetypes must come into contact with personal experience and thus become integrated into perceptive awareness which is the origin of every scientific model and knowledge of reality* (Merleau-Ponty, 1945).

Research in hemispheric disconnection has demonstrated the existence of two kinds of perceptive awareness. What are the consequences? In the biological world in general we find a high degree of correlation between specific predispositions and specific aspects of the environment. Similarly, psychic predispositions are not isolated inner factors which can be separated from the outside world. Indeed, archetypal determinants appear only when they are actualized by a suitable environmental occasion. Whitmont (1969) wrote, "Integration [of the archetypes] requires the assimilation of both the specifically personal and the general religious or mythological dimension" (p. 137). Thus, to make the unconscious conscious and integrate its contents means to use the cerebral structures which allow for the various psychic functions. Because we are speaking of consciousness, we mean a higher, unitary, unique level of intellectual activity, as unique as each individual.

Since the 1960s these matters have become a little more complicated. In 1962, a group of researchers led by Sperry (1968) administered some neurophysiological behavioral tests to a young patient, seriously affected with epilepsy, who had undergone surgical resection of the corpus callosum to prevent the epileptic seizures from spreading to the other hemisphere. The researchers discovered that each hemisphere of the brain functioned quite independently of the other. This hemispheric disconnection syndrome demonstrated that "each hemisphere seems to have its own private, separate sensations, its own perceptions, its own thoughts, and its own impulses for action with their corresponding volitional, cognitive, and learning experiences. After such intervention each hemisphere also has its own separate series of memories, inaccessible to the mnemonic processes of the other hemisphere" (p. 727).

It was a Jungian colleague, Rossi (1977), who first emphasized the correlations between the specialized function of the hemispheres and the meta-psychological constructs used in Analytical Psychology. To the left hemisphere he attributed extraversion, the thinking and sensation functions, ego processes, causal relationships and analysis—in short, rationality. To the right hemisphere he attributed introversion, the feeling and intuition functions, the archetypal processes including the Self, acausal relationships (synchronicity)—in short, irrationality. The existence of two functionally separate hemispheres is an established fact by now. How can we consider this fact in relation to our interests, and to the shadow in particular?

I became interested in the functions of the corpus callosum, investigating the structural changes that take place in schizophrenia (Fiumara, 1985). Among the data I considered, one element is worth mentioning here. In humans, the posterior part of the corpus callosum constitutes a window through which each hemisphere exchanges sensorial and motor information with the other side; the frontal part appears to be a cognitive window. This window is therefore used for transmitting information coming from a higher level of abstraction. The result is that inhibition in conveying information at this level can be considered as the functional basis of repression.

4. *Culture is the consequence of the differentiated functioning of the left and right hemispheres.*

Culture can be understood as acquired knowledge which is passed from one generation to the next. Any discussion on culture contains a paradox: Although culture is the product of evolution and therefore of nature, this nature is expressed through symbols, which are the opposite of what is natural.

We can find some common variables within various cultures and social structures if we take culture back to its most specific production machine – the brain – and examine correlations to its functioning. According to Turner's (1969) theory, there are two broad models of social inter-relations alternating with each other. The first deals with society as a structure, where differences in position and role are established according to sex, age and hierarchical placing. The second model shows a very rudimentary structure, or none; individuals are undifferentiated and equal in every way. This model is necessarily transitory. Every experience in life may be expressed in relation to society as a structure, regulated according to logical and analytical thinking, or with society as a community, regulated according to egalitarian, magical-synthetic thought. Thus we find a correlation with the differentiated functioning of the right hemisphere – magical, synthetic thought – and of the left hemisphere – scientific, analytic thought. Turner discovered these two basic models in Zambia, but the theory can be applied on a much wider scale, wherever human groups are to be found. I would also emphasize the complementarity of these two models. Just as in Gestalt psychology figure and ground correspond to each other and are determined by each other, so also communitas and structure cannot exist without each other.

In his paper "On Psychic Energy" (CW8) Jung stated, "Over against the polymorphism of the primitive's instinctual nature there stands the regulating principle of individuation. . . . Together they form a pair of opposites necessary for self-regulation, often spoken of as nature and spirit" (par. 96). In this same paper, he stated that culture does not really oppose the instincts, but transforms them and channels them into practical and socially useful forms. I propose that the terms "spirit" and "culture" are equivalent.

If we accept the statement that culture is the product of the cerebral hemispheres, then perhaps we can admit that humans, from the church founders to the philosophers and psychologists, have worked out certain models which are specific to their own points of view. They have used these models to define the phenomenon of intersubjectivity of inter-human relations. Thus, terms such as spirit, culture and collective unconscious, have been used with different meanings, but in connection with basically the same phenomena of inter-human communication; we propose considering them as equivalent.

5. *As a model, our split world corresponds to a brain with a functional split between the two hemispheres; for this split to be overcome, we must restore the balanced functioning of these structures and thus bring back to light the forgotten contents which were placed in the shadow.*

As Jung said, the shadow is homologous to the whole unconscious. The split world, therefore, could be compared to a syndrome of hemispheric disconnection. What can this model be used for? This is a heuristic model; its usefulness lies above all in its capacity for activating research and systematizing the resultant data. But I think we can put it to immediate practical use. For example, by submitting to critical examination something we all believe in: the unity of the human person. This unitary conception and the wish for supremacy seems to be inherent in all of us; the wish is reflected in Adler's "will to power." Perhaps more basic is the necessity to safeguard a cohesive, coherent sense of personal identity. Inevitably, competitive polarizations arise: standing on principles which can fall into aboslute categories and change into strategies for keeping at a distance and fighting against anything that appears different.

Coming back to our own points of reference we could say that, in the human race's coming to awareness the identity complex has been activated, but there has been a price to pay; what Jaynes (1976) called the "breakdown" of the bicameral mind. A further step forward in both individual and collective awareness is the recognition that, just as there are two cerebral hemispheres, a duality exists in the unity of consciousness. The atom, which had been considered indivisible, revealed what immense energy it contained only after it had been split. Similarly, the brain can begin to reveal its immense potential when its divided nature is recognized.

Translated from Italian by
Valery Cockburn

386   Fiumara

REFERENCES

Corradi Fiumara, G. (1980). Funzione simbolica e filosofia del linguaggio. Torino: Boringhieri.

Fiumara, R. (1985). Psicologia Analitica ed etologia. Atti XXXVI, Congresso Nazionale Società Italiana di Psichiatria, 21–27.

Fiumara, R.; D'Angelo, C.; Lorini, T.; Morocutti, C. (1985). Attuali vedute suile alterazioni strutturali del corpo calloso nella schizofrenia. Atti IV Congresso Nazionale Società Italiana di Psichiatria Biologica, Pavia, 19–20.

Jaynes, J. (1976) *The origins of consciousness in the breakdown of the bicameral mind*. Princeton, NJ: Princeton University Press.

Merleau-Ponty, M. (1945). *La phénoménologie de la perception*. Paris: Payot.

Neumann, E. (1970). *The origins and history of consciousness*. Princeton, NJ: Princeton University Press.

Progoff, I. (1973). *Jung's psychology and its social meaning*. New York: Anchor Books.

Romano, A. & Trevi, M. (1985). *Studi sull'ombra*. Rome: Marsilio.

Rossi, E. (1977). The cerebral hemispheres in Analytical Psychology. *Journal of Analytical Psychology, 21–1*, 32–51.

Sperry, R. (1968). Hemispheric disconnection and unity in conscious awareness. *American Psychologist, 22–5*, 723–33.

Turner, V. (1969). *The ritual process: Structure and anti-structure*. Chicago: Aldine.

von Franz, M.-L. (1974). *Shadow and evil in fairy tales*. Dallas: Spring Publications.

Whitmont, E. (1969). *The symbolic quest*. New York: Putnam's

Kinship Libido: Shadow in Marriage and Family

Louis Stewart (San Francisco)

The fate of the libido is the decisive issue in life and in the process of individuation. It makes all the difference in the world whether libido is freely available for the tasks of life and for the realization of the Self. Marriage and family and the future generations depend upon a zest for life that is fully realized in imaginative playfulness and divine curiosity. From this perspective the clarity and comprehensiveness of our understanding of the nature and vagaries of the libido assume a high priority. But is there anything essential about the concept of libido that is not already well understood? It would seem that the question—what is libido?—had been answered satisfactorily long ago, in the controversy between Freud and Jung.

Jung's concept of psychic energy offered a broad, all-encompassing solution which, for him, appeared to lay the question to rest. Yet late in his life he introduced the apparently new concept of *kinship libido*, which he had acquired from the anthropologist Layard (1972). What seemed to interest Jung most about this concept was the link it provided between marriage, family, and society, on the one hand, and the transference situation of psychotherapy, on the other. For whatever reasons, kinship libido came to hold an important position in his late works, and he took pains to introduce it into *Symbols of Transformation* (CW5) when he thoroughly revised that book in 1952.

Another issue which is, or at least has been, inseparable from the question of libido is its relationship to incest. From early on in Freud's theory of sexuality, libido and incest were, of course,

intimately entwined. Although Jung offered a psychological definition of incest, he never denied that the relationships between
family members were inevitably tinged with sexuality and hence,
incest. It is not surprising, then, that he came to speak of incest
as kinship libido.

> Incest, as an endogamous relationship, is an expression of the li-
> bido which serves to hold the family together. One could therefore
> define it as "kinship libido," a kind of instinct which, like a sheep-
> dog, keeps the family group intact. This form of libido is the dia-
> metrical opposite of the exogamous form. (CW16, par. 431)

If we are to ask once again what libido is, it appears that we
need to ask: What is incest? Is it to be understood as "family ties,"
and as the projections of the syzygy, in the analytic transference?
Do these "intra-psychic" conceptions provide an adequate understanding of the all-too-frequent occurrences of actual incest in
family life, which are recognized now as sexual abuse of children? These questions, also, were addressed long ago. As we
know, Freud originally understood incest in the conventional
sense as sexual relationships between members of the immediate
family. His women patients told him that their fathers or
brothers had taken sexual liberties with them as children and
adolescents; Freud reasoned that this was the traumatic source
of their neurotic symptoms. Later, as we know, he was persuaded by indignant fathers who denied such behavior, that it
was a mistake to believe these stories. Freud then recanted and
proposed instead that his patients were telling him their childhood fantasies. Thus, the Oedipus complex became the cornerstone of his theory of neurosis.

This decision turns out to have been a double-edged sword.
On the one hand there was an apparent psychological gain in this
shift from trauma as experience to trauma as a function of fantasy; it focused attention on the role of fantasy in the psychic life
of the individual. But there was an unfortunate legacy from this
way of thinking. It haunts us still today in the tortured lives of
children who are sexually abused by family members, but whose
stories often are not believed and are dismissed as the fantasies
of the child's "normal" libidinous and seductive nature (Russell,
1986). It would appear that many cases of schizophrenia in chil-

dren and young adults result from this incestuous rupture of the family temenos and the intense humiliation it engenders. As Masson (1983) has shown, Freud was right in the first place to believe what his patients told him. In fact, incest in families was common, although publicly unacknowledged then as now.

Jung's contribution to this controversy was to move even further in the psychological direction. Although acknowledging actual incest as an infrequent psychopathological variant, Jung focused primarily on the spiritual aspects of incest as the prerogative of the gods and their representatives, kings and priests; and on the archetype of incest which appears in myths and religious symbolism as the hierosgamos, the royal marriage (CW14, pars. 106–107). From this perspective Jung concluded that incest was to be understood psychologically as a clinging to the mother to avoid the difficulties of adaptation, as in the puer and puella symbolism, or as regression to the mother, which has as its goal not actual incest, but rather a return to the original, pre-creation, unitary state of being, experienced in the primal relationship with the mother. The outcome of such a regression is naturally problematic and may lead to the "stuckness" of neurotic or psychotic symptomatology. On the other hand, if it is successful, it may achieve its goal of promoting individuation through a psychological rebirth and renewal in the acquisition of a new spiritual attitude (CW5, par. 654). This was a position that Jung held throughout his life. Nevertheless in his last works (CW16, CW9–II, CW14) where Jung sought a synthesis of the gnostic, alchemical and Christian symbolism as the historical foundations of his theory of Analytical Psychology, the concept of kinship libido holds an important position. But the question remains whether this concept was ever integrated with the original and broad conception of libido as psychic energy, and what implications this might hold for a conceptual understanding of incest.

This brief summary of the concept of libido and its relationship to incest in Analytical Psychology raises the following critical questions. First: What is the relationship of kinship libido to the broader conception of libido as psychic energy? What does it mean, for example, to speak of an endogamous form that is instinctive and turns to the family, and an exogamous form which appears to be a function of the incest taboo, and hence more conscious? And second, perhaps the more significant question:

What is the all-encompassing definition of incest and its relation-ship to libido?

The purpose of this paper is to seek answers to the foregoing questions. I will refer to my recent studies of affects and arche-types, which have given me a new perspective on the nature of the libido in its energic and transformative aspects. This develop-ing perspective requires a review of the relationship between cer-tain aspects of Jung's theory such as the "two kinds of thinking" (CW5, pars. 4–46), the syzygy (anima and animus), and the coniunctio; these ideas are not integrated with his concept of li-bido and should be. First I shall summarize briefly the salient fea-tures of my studies of what I have now come to speak of as the archetypal affects of the innate, primordial Self. This discussion will be focused on the nature and function of the archetypal affects in relation to the archetypes and the differentiated func-tions of the psyche. I shall focus also on the implications of these studies for our understanding of libido and incest.

The Archetypal Affects

When we turn to the affects we approach that mysterious realm of the interface between mind and body, spirit and nature. The constellation of an affect is also a complex intermeshing of world and Self. Hillman's (1961) comprehensive definition used Aristotle's fourfold theory of causation:

> Emotion is "symbol," "energy," "psyche" and "transforma-tion." . . . *Each emotion has: its own pattern of behaviour and quality of experience which is always a total attitude of the whole psyche* (causa formalis); *its own distribution and intensity of energy in the field of the human body situation* (causa materialis); *its own symbolic stimulus which is partly conscious and partly not presented to consciousness* (causa efficiens); *its own achieved transformation which has some survival value and is some improvement compared with non-emotional states* (causa fina-lis). These four causes correspond with each other. The quality and pattern of an emotion is only that quality and pattern given by a specific symbol which in turn corresponds with the specific organi-zation and intensity of energy and a specific kind of transformation. What makes an emotion "joy" and not "disgust" or "shame" always depends upon the specific constellation of the four causes. . . .

> Each emotion has its own peculiar characteristics of expression
> which accord with the purposeful result being achieved. (p. 286)

Jung has referred to an affect as a brief psychosis; it could be called as well a spiritual crisis. According to Hillman (1961), emotion is the place of spirit; acceptance of all emotion is required, since any rejection of emotion would be a refusal of the spirit. Following up the consequences of this point of view he recognized that this could lead to an identity of the two, although he was of the opinion that a criterion for distinguishing spirit from emotion undoubtedly would appear in a phenomenology of the spirit. Nevertheless, in this context the distinctions appear less relevant than is the possibility of a primal identity. This identity would seem to consist mainly in the experience of being moved.

> We might attempt to account for this "mover," this *pneuma*, in the light of things already said about emotion. . . . From the point of view of the phenomenology of the psyche, the ego is passive only to dominants greater than it, in particular to the psyche as a whole. If emotion is a massive, total event setting the whole individual in action, . . . then it is to this wholeness that the ego is passive during inspiration. . . . Spirit could be conceived as the dynamis of the whole person; the quality and intensity of it depending upon the complexity and differentiation of this wholeness. . . . We are led to conclude that it is through emotion, the most convenient way to suffer the helplessness of the ego, that the individual can encounter his wholeness and thereby have access to the grace and might of spirit. (Hillman, 1961, pp. 238–39)

We may well ask of what ultimate significance is it that the affects are the bridge between mind and body, spirit and nature? Is it a prefiguring in the psyche of that other critical bridge between conscious and unconscious, namely the imagination? Or are they perhaps two aspects of the same process? This latter is the conclusion that is more persuasive when we examine closely the relationship of the affects to play and the imagination. I found myself drawn to this question through my work with sandplay and other forms of active imagination. The affects are enmeshed with play and imagination in several ways which are representative of two fundamental aspects of the psyche, namely energy and transformation. For example, children play for the fun of it; we can say that play is energized by the affect of joy. On the other hand, children's play, and imagination in all its forms—pretend, symbolic play, reverie and active imagination—are about feelings and emotions that are not always joyful, such as sadness, fear, anger and shame. In these instances, perhaps in all instances of play and imagination, the function of play/imagination is compensatory and transformative. This we recognize as the fundamental compensatory relationship between consciousness and unconsciousness. The relationship between play/imagination and the affects emerges as a complex one of energy and transformation. During the early period of these studies I was fortunate to have as collaborator my brother Charles T. Stewart, a child psychiatrist. (See L. Stewart and C. Stewart, 1981.) It is now sometimes difficult to sort out his contributions from my own, but I take full responsibility for the form in which these ideas appear here.

The role of play/imagination in relation to the affects is a paradigm for all of the other affects and dynamisms with which we are familiar. For example, the dynamism of curiosity/exploration is the twin or mirror image of play/imagination. Everything the child becomes curious about and explores ends up being played with, and vice versa: Everything the child plays with leads to new possibilities about which it becomes curious and explores. The affect that energizes curiosity/exploration is interest: We become curious enough to explore those things which constellate interest.

There is a natural division in the human emotions between those that lead us into life and enhance life, and those that we find troubling and painful. Clearly the innate affects of joy and interest fall into the first category, while the innate affects of sadness, fear, anger and contempt/shame, fall into the more problematic category. There is, however, one other innate affect, surprise, that is essentially neutral and serves the functions of centering and orienting. In these studies I have benefited greatly from Tomkins' (1962, 1963) seminal research. (Unfortunately the limitations of this paper do not allow for a discussion of the myriad other emotions with which we are all familiar. It is my belief, however, that these other emotions, as well as the sensitive matrix of human feelings, are transformations in the alchemical vessel of the family of the seven innate affects described above).

The positive emotions, joy and interest, are readily identified with the libido in its aspect as an appetite. We can hardly be mistaken in recognizing an expression of the life instinct in these affects; they have that quality of non-specific psychic energy which can be invested in any aspect of life. Of course, the more problematic innate affects—fear, sadness, anger and contempt/shame, as well as surprise—also are expressive of psychic energy, but of specific kinds, related to specific contents and aims. They appear to have evolved as a kind of self-protective system which sensitizes the psyche to the fundamental spiritual crises of life, namely: loss of a loved one (sadness); the unknown (fear); threat to autonomy (anger); rejection (contempt/shame); and the unexpected (surprise). The affects of joy and interest are, of course, constellated by the experience of life's basic polarity, the famliar (joy) and the novel (interest).

The foregoing is a bare-bones outline of what I have come to term the archetypal affective system, which may be thought of as the basis of the primordial Self. The seven archetypal affects discussed above fall into three pairs of opposites: the two archetypal affects of the libido, joy and interest; and the four archetypal affects of the protective system of the Self—sadness and fear; anger and contempt/shame. The seventh archetypal affect, surprise, in its centering and orienting functions, is the opposite of all the other affects. For survival purposes, in the face of the "unexpected," it must instantaneously control all of them, as well as the motility or any expressive response of the organism, to achieve a rapid re-orientation.

This brief sketch of the archetypal affective system must suffice for this paper, since our primary focus is on the archetypal affects joy and interest, and their dynamisms play/imagination and curiosity/exploration. The interested reader may refer to other, more comprehensive presentations (Stewart, 1985, 1986, 1987, in press).

Libido as Psychic Energy

We are arriving by now at a conception of libido which may appear to be a revision of Jung's basic concept. As I see it this is not so; it is a matter of bringing together aspects of Jung's concept which he hinted at, or discussed in one context but not another, or which he made quite explicit but never gave a terminology which allows for immediate recognition. For example, Jung spoke of the splitting of the libido in regression; his concept of kinship libido is of an instinct that has two forms, an endogamous form that turns to the family and an exogamous form that leads out of the family. Then there is his discussion of the two ways of thinking, that is, fantasy/mythical thinking and directed/language thinking. When all these apparently disparate statements are brought together, along with others not mentioned here, a picture develops of libido as having two forms which are yet united in a whole through a dialectical relationship.

This view leads to the hypothesis that the energy of psychic energy is the emotions or at least is expressed through the emotions. Of course, an emotion in the unconscious is not representable; we know it only in the process of its becoming conscious and in the forms it then takes. Finally it must be presumed that the archetypal affective system has evolved in the mammalian species as a more flexible system of instinctive response which replaced the more ancient system of programmed instincts. From this perspective it is apparent that the innate, primal archetypal affects of joy and interest, as expressions of the life instinct, have evolved to insure that young mammals, particularly humans, enter this world with joy in living and divine curiosity. The other innate archetypal affects have evolved presumably as the source and protection of those highest spiritual values: the beautiful, the holy, the true and the good, as they manifest themselves in the fourfold forms of the imagination. They find expression, respectively, in Henderson's (1984) cultural attitudes: the esthetic, religious, philosophic, and social.

Kinship Libido and Incest

The questions now are whether kinship libido is a particular variant of psychic energy or whether, as Jung and Layard seem to say, it is an instinct unto itself which appears in two forms, endogamous and exogamous; Or is it, purely and simply, incest, as Jung stated in the definition at the beginning of this paper? Some of the apparent confusion is due to the terminology that Jung borrowed from Layard, a mix of anthropological and psychological terms. Endogamy and exogamy are anthropological terms for marriage within the family or marriage out of the family; libido is a psychological term, and refers to psychic energy. Incest in its ordinary definition is "sexual union between two persons who are so closely related that their marriage is illegal or forbidden" (American Heritage Dictionary, 1976). Incest in its psychological meanings ranges from the Oedipus complex, which for Freud implied sexual desire on the part of a child for the parent of the opposite sex, to Jung's thoroughly psychological definition of incest: a fixation or regression of libido to the mother imago, to avoid the difficulties of adaptation to life, or as a return to the pre-creation state of unity with oneself as an end point in the individuation process.

The complexity of the definition of incest was faced by Jung in the introduction to "The Psychology of the Transference" (CW16).

> The contents which enter into the transference were as a rule originally projected upon the parents or other members of the family. Owing to the fact that these contents seldom or never lack an erotic aspect or are genuinely sexual in substance, . . . an incestuous character does undoubtedly attach to them, and this has given rise to the Freudian theory of incest. Their exogamous transference to the doctor does not alter the situation. He is merely drawn into the peculiar atmosphere of family incest through the projection. . . . But the interpretation of this fact is, in the very nature of the case, highly controversial. Is it a genuine incestuous instinct or a pathological variation? Or is the incest one of the "arrangements" (Adler) of the will to power? Or is it regression of normal libido to the infantile level, from fear of an apparently impossible task in life? [Footnote: The reader will know that I do not understand *libido* in the original Freudian sense as *appetitus sexualis*, but as an *appetitus* which can be defined as psychic energy.] Or is all incest-fantasy purely symbolical, and thus a re-activation of the incest archetype, which plays such an important part in the history of the human mind? (par. 368).

Thus, Jung covered the range of possible definitions of incest while giving some clues as to his own views. His comments about the experience of the transference, as a projection upon the analyst of contents which were originally projected upon the parents and other family members, are pertinent here. These contents can be interpreted, as they were by Jung, as symptoms of neurosis, which spring from complexes. They could perhaps best be thought of, then, as the family unconscious. But what about libido as psychic energy? Could we not say that kinship libido appears to have two connotations? It either refers to the complexes that have resulted from the child's interpersonal relationships within the family, or it refers to the psychic energy, the libido, which is invested during childhood in the relationships with family members. One meaning refers to the end result, the complexes; the other meaning refers to the process whereby the complexes are created. If the context makes it clear which meaning is intended there is no problem, but confusion would be dispelled if the term kinship libido were reserved for the process of investing libido in family relationships. The complexes might be referred to as "kinship complexes."

The terminology adopted by Jung from Layard raises some further questions as to whether kinship libido is a special instinct, as Jung seemed to suggest, or whether it is just a form or manifestation of libido in its broad definition as psychic energy. There seems to be no evidence that it is a separate instinct, and considerable evidence that it is but a form of libido in general. Even though Jung made the statement that kinship libido is an instinct that has two forms, the endogamous and the exogamous, a careful reading of all that he had to say on the subject shows that he qualified that statement. Mainly he tended to speak of the endogamous form as instinctual, and the exogamous form as a more conscious effect of the incest taboo. However, this too is qualified by his argument that the incest taboo is not the cause of cultural developments; he saw those as primarily due to the human instinct of spiritual development.

My conclusion is that kinship libido is a term which refers to the psychic energy invested in family relationships as a natural consequence of being a family member. The so-called exogamous form of kinship libido, in my estimation, refers to a natural function of libido in general, in its progression and regression, perhaps better stated as an alternation between adaptation to the world and to the Self. In my view this interpretation is supported by Jung's wider writings on the subject of libido; they are grounded in a genetic theory which is supported by contemporary psychological studies of development (Piaget, 1962; Roberts & Sutton-Smith, 1962).

The application of this concept of the libido—the two archetypal affects, joy and interest, with their twin dynamisms, play/imagination and curiosity/exploration—to the family and the child's development is fairly self-evident. One need only observe a healthy infant with its mother to see what joy the child gets from its relationship with the mother, and how playful the child is. In addition one sees how the child's curiosity is also constantly stirred by even the slightest new aspect of the mother's face, or hair, or smell, or anything at all, and how seriously the child will observe this novelty and finger it and put it in its mouth if possible. In this continual absorption in the primal relationship with the mother, the child will play and explore, and explore and play, in ever-widening circles of experience which will lead it further and further from the mother, though at first never leaving sight or sound of her, and often looking over for a comforting familiar smile. Here we see the way in which libido is gradually drawn away from the mother into the wider world of father, siblings, toys, and nature, everything within the child's possible sphere of movement. Eventually one sees the struggle begin between being drawn away into the exciting new outer world, and being drawn back to the comforting familiar world of the mother and the family.

Depending on what parents do at these critical developmental stages the child will either become more and more independent and self-sufficient, while still maintaining its satisfying relationships with family, or it will become fearful of the world and cling to the family. We can see that the normal development is for the child's curiosity to lead it out from the familiar atmosphere of the family into the new and novel world. This is what Jung speaks of as the exogamous form of libido. In our view, it is the normal course of the movement of the libido from the familiar to the novel; this novel aspect of the outer world will become familiar, and will then be played with. This normal development does not mean that the kinship relationships within the family will be given up because of this outward movement, but they will be reevaluated in terms of the needs of adaptation to the outer world, which life demands. On the other hand, if the parental attitudes and behavior create a family atmosphere which undermines the child's normal interest in the outer world, then there may develop that kind of clinging to the family ties which Jung spoke of as psychological incest.

Conclusion

The foregoing is not a definitive evaluation of all the issues of this important and complex subject. However, I believe I have identified some important questions, have begun the exploration of their boundaries, and have shared the new perspectives gleaned from these peregrinations. My hope is that this may spark a challenging dialogue.

Nonetheless, I wish to express my advocacy of the working hypothesis that has been formulated in this paper: that libido, as the instinct of life or the life force—psychic energy—is primarily experienced through the innate archetypal affects of joy and interest, and their twin dynamisms, play/imagination and curiosity/exploration. Further I suggest that these innate, primal affects and their dynamisms, come to represent in their ultimate realized forms, what is meant by the cosmogonic principles, eros and logos or yin and yang. It seems to me that this conception of libido as the intertwining of two primal affects with their dialectical dynamisms, gives some psychological grounding to the archetypal images of incest: the hierosgamos of the gods and that third and final stage of the alchemical process, the chymical marriage.

REFERENCES

Henderson, J. (1984). *Cultural attitudes in psychological perspective*. Toronto: Inner City Books.

Hillman, J. (1961). *Emotion: A comprehensive phenomenology of theories and their meanings for therapy*. Evanston, IL: Northwestern University Press.

Layard, J. (1972). The incest taboo and the virgin archetype. In *The virgin archetype*, pp. 254–307. Zurich: Spring Publications.

Masson, J. (1983). *The assault on truth: Freud's suppression of the seduction theory*. New York: Penguin.

Piaget, J. (1962). *Play, dreams and imitation in childhood*. New York: W. W. Norton.

Roberts, J.; Sutton-Smith, B. (1962). Child training and game involvement. *Ethnology, 1*, 166–85.

Russell, D. (1986). *The secret trauma: Incest in the lives of girls and women*. New York: Basic Books.

Stewart, L. (1985). Affect and archetype: A contribution to a comprehensive theory of the structure of the psyche. In *Proceedings of the 1985 California Spring Conference*, pp. 89–120. San Francisco: C. G. Jung Institute.

Stewart, L. (1986). Work in progress: Affect and archetype; A contribution to a comprehensive theory of the structure of the psyche. In N. Schwartz-Salant & M. Stein (Eds.). *The body in analysis*, pp. 183–203. Wilmette, IL: Chiron.

Stewart, L. (1987). A brief report: Affect and archetype. *Journal of Analytical Psychology, 32-1*, 35–46.

Stewart, L. (in press). Affect and archetype in analysis. In N. Schwartz-Salant M. Stein (Eds.), *The archetypes in clinical practice*. Wilmette, IL: Chiron.

Stewart, L.; Stewart, C. (1981). Play, games and affects: A contribution toward a comprehensive theory of play. In *Play as context*, A. T. Cheska (Ed.), pp. 42–52. Westpoint, NY: Leisure Press.

Tomkins, S. (1962). *Affect imagery consciousness, Volume I: The positive affects*. New York: Springer.

Tomkins, S. (1963). *Affect imagery consciousness, Volume II: The negative affects*. New York: Springer.

The Shadow and Analytic Training

Paolo Aite (Rome)
Concetta Gullotta (Rome)
Antonio Lo Cascio (Rome)
Piergiacomo Migliorati (Rome)
Maria Teresa Rufini (Rome)

This paper deals with the shadow aspects of analytic training, as reflected in the admission evaluation of candidates for the Italian Association for the Study of Analytical Psychology (AIPA; Associazione Italiana per lo studio della Psicologia Analitica). The statement is the result of collaboration among members of the Executive Committee of AIPA. We have worked together as a study team to evaluate the outcome of experiences over a decade with certain aspects of training. Ten years ago, after encountering various problems, we were forced to modify our norms for the training of analyst-candidates. It had become clear that the Admissions Committee had been accepting candidates on the basis of the evaluation given by the candidate's personal analyst and even on the basis of the esteem in which that analyst was held by his or her colleagues. Thus, the committee was not expressing an objective judgment on the candidates themselves but rather was deferring to the analysts who presented them. In addition, those who were refused admission could—as a result of the dynamics of association—become instruments for an unacknowledged aggressiveness. Consequently, errors of evaluation were occurring with some regularity, accompanied by suffering for everyone involved.

In order to correct this situation, we decided that the personal analyst might no longer "present" the applicant, nor was the analyst to express judgments regarding the applicant's maturity. Rather, the applicant, from that point on, was to make his or her own application, at the end of a minimum number of hours of personal analysis, the number set by statutory norms.

Yet it was necessary to maintain a channel for critical evaluation as to the suitability of the prospective analyst. We decided, therefore, to institute a specific analytical realm expressly for this purpose. In this way, what we have termed "propaedeutical analysis" was born; this is a second analysis, carried out by a training analyst other than the individual's first analyst. This second analyst was to provide the evaluation which the Association needed.

This solution has produced two effects. On the one hand we found that the problems were reduced, because the necessary freedom was restored to the personal analysis. On the other hand, as we had foreseen, all of the problems of the shadow and persona which we had noticed previously were concentrated in the propaedeutical analysis. Thus, the difficulty had not been eliminated but only moved to another place. We felt that it was useful, however, to continue with this new methodology, as a lesser evil than the old system.

Nevertheless, we were not satisfied with the negative justification of the "lesser evil," which is dangerous in many ways. In reflecting further on the experiences of these last ten years, we noticed that the concentration of the problems of the shadow and of the personal in the propaedeutical analysis opened new theoretical considerations and gave a scientific significance to the technical procedure chosen. At the heart of these considerations is the relationship between the dynamics of collective consciousness and the analytical-symbolic process. Our position is this: The propaedeutical analysis, which our regulations have instituted within the training program, supplies us with an analytical field particularly suitable for the integration of the various shadow areas connected with analytic training. Three aspects of the shadow illustrate this affirmation; each of these aspects parallels important changes in the field of psychology that have taken place in the last few years.

Pathology as the Archetypal Shadow of the Analyst

Pathology has undergone changes, so that analysis is taking on the disturbing aspect of interminability. Research within the sphere of depth psychology has thrown light on new fields, new abysses, new pathologies. The integration of the unconscious is not a task to be accomplished in a definite period of time but is a long-term process. As a result, even if an analysis is carried out well (or rather, especially when carried out well), the basic psycho-pathological structures of the analyst with those of the analysand converge. This phenomenon may constitute the essential aspect of the transference/countertransference dynamics. Thus, the shadow of the analytic relationship is made up of the basic pathologies of the analyst and analysand.

The goal of every analysis is substantially that of leading one to the irreducible aspect of one's own shadow, through the acceptance of one's own history. At the same time, any sort of judgment is impossible within the framework of a personal analysis. One cannot judge and, simultaneously, be within the situation that is being judged. The difference between the first analysis and the propaedeutical analysis rests in the fact that, in the second analysis, the partners bring with them awareness of their basic pathologies, an awareness gained during previous analytic experience, more complete in the analyst and yet present in the student.

In the second analysis it is possible to evaluate the maturity reached during the first analysis. What will be evaluated is the ability of the student to withstand the continual tension between the conscious and the unconscious, between well-being and pathology, and the availability of the analysand continually to call into question the balance achieved during the first analysis. We agree with Fordham (1970) "that recognition of the irreducible psychopathology of the analyst, as an aspect of his shadow, is important for the maintenance of good enough relations between colleagues besides providing the main motivation for conducting psychotherapy" (p. 70).

The instituting, within the training program, of a specific analytic field able to produce this level of consciousness is an important contribution. Within this field, the level of integration of the shadow takes on a meaning that goes beyond what was possible in the first analysis. The meaning consists of the consciousness of an interminable sense of mourning. It is interminable, not so much because the analysand, if admitted to the Association, will meet his or her own analyst, but because there is the intention to carry out, in the future, this same professional activity. The propaedeutical analysis must help the analysand put up with an endless sense of mourning. Here we find the irreducible shadow; it has, as its only richness and treasure, a constant state of openness to the infinite dimensions of the possible. This openness will be activated repeatedly by future analytic encounters and will make of the student a candidate and of the candidate an analyst.

The Shaman/Trickster Dialectic as the Shadow of the Power Relationship between Training Analyst and Student

The social situation, which is in a state of rapid change, has a bearing on the motivations involved in the desire to become an analyst. Today in Italy the profession of psychotherapy, and of analysis in particular, is continually expanding. This expansion derives in part from the opening of new degree courses in psychology. These courses are furthered by the emphasis on "professional image" or demonized by dwelling on scandals. Because there is no clear regulation regarding this profession, there are many self-appointed therapists who often damage their patients. This situation activates the archetypal image of the trickster and its shamanic counterpart.

A young person who decides to become an analyst may be grasped by the shadow of the trickster. During the training, the candidate must try to acquire the technical means for self-defense against this shadow. This insistence on technique becomes a barrier against the superficiality, arrogance, and omnipotence that are present in certain collective ways of entering the world of the psyche.

In the training analyst, the image of the shaman tends to be activated. This figure opens the doors of knowledge and of health. "There is something of the trickster in the character of the shaman and of the medicine-man," affirmed Jung, "for he too often plays malicious jokes on people, only to fall in his turn to the vengeance of those whom he has injured" (CW9-I, par. 457). Thus, in the training analysis, the relationship falls into the collective power dimension, which can be resolved only through the process of interpreting the transference and countertransference.

The propaedeutical analysis has proved to be the most suitable place for confrontation with this specific shadow. As a part of the training program, it allows for close observation of all the shadows connected with the desire to become an analyst. It focuses on the external values which this desire evokes in one. Thus, the propaedeutical analysis opens possibilities for a confrontation with the darkest personal aspects which have given life to this fantasy. This analytic experience, which hopes to circumscribe these problems within a specific arena, has the task of integrating these aspects and of giving back to them the deep symbolic significance linked to the professional shadow. The future analyst must learn to recognize the human propensity to avoid those responses which grow out of the darkest roots within ourselves and to realize when a defense mechanism has been activated. At the same time, the truest personal nuclei of our relationship with the unconscious may be seen in these responses.

The Law/Transgression Dialectic as Shadow of the Association

The third aspect that we found of the shadow of analytic training is concerned with the relationship between authority and freedom, perhaps one of the hottest issues of collective consciousness today. Analytical associations are not immune to the resultant social and political tensions. The question of freedom must be raised because our Association requires personal analysis of all those who wish to become analysts. This requirement creates an obligation which appears to be in contradiction to the freedom that is necessary to analysis. In addition to this obligation, an evaluation must be made outside the analytic relationship. The propaedeutical analysis institutionalizes this anomalous situation, which represents perhaps the most disturbing problem of the second analysis.

At this level, also, we encounter a vast shadow area: transgression of the law. Qualifications of a candidate must fulfill the norms of the Association, but the judgment of suitability may be subject also to the law. Every law constellates various complex situations of transgressions and every type of transformation comes about through the continuous dialectic of the relationship between law and freedom, between imposition and transgression.

The primary difficulty consists in the fact that the judgment must be public and that this same judgment brings with it possibilities of transgression, a shadow that must be brought to light. However, we find here a possibility for individuation through the training process. Transgression marks a moment of growth and progress only when it comes out of its secretiveness and becomes a challenge to the father's authority. The confrontation between the desire to transgress and the unavoidable need to belong produces a personality which is free within the structure, not outside it. Indeed, the powerful impact of reality on the analytic field characterizes the special setting of this second analysis. Within this field a person may live this reality but limit it to its concrete level. Consequently, the transgression is against the responsibility to search for the symbolic dimension of reality.

We might apply to this potentiality for transgression the myth of Lucifer as the image of the transgressor/light-bringer. But that image may confirm the strong resistance that the introduction of this new technique has met. Law and transgression are constellations which activate each other. We come to discover, then, not only the shadows of those on whom the law is imposed, but also the authors and representatives of the law. For example, the father can react to the son's transgression with collusion. Such a situation can represent the shadow of every associative structure and of the analytical associations in particular. At the same time, the statutory rule, which requires that the shadow of the Association be exposed to the light, is a norm that fertilizes and enriches itself. When the Association (and the training analyst acting on its behalf) accepts the task of training a candidate, the Association itself enters its own training. Just as every analyst grows through analytic work with each patient, the Association grows through the didactic training relationship with its students.

Conclusion

The methodology with which the AIPA began to experiment 10 years ago has proved to be a fruitful area of work and research, despite aspects which require more clarification and elaboration. The introduction of this modification, within the framework of our old regulations, may be seen as part of the renewal witnessed within the field of psychology over the last few years. In addition, it represents a response to the desire to join analytic training more closely with the contradictory and tumultuous socio-cultural development of the latter part of the twentieth century. Our evaluation's being provisional and fragmentary is due to the relatively short period of observation and the limited number of cases that we have followed.

This paper is the synthesis of an arduous journey. During it we have tried not to lose sight of those constant factors that qualify us as Analytical Psychologists, while taking into account a multiplicity of trends and tendencies: the quickening evolution of the empirical practice of psychology, the inter-twining of the history of Analytical Psychology in Italy with post-modern tendencies and, of course, the influence of individual typology. Our procedure occupies a balanced position between attempts at renewal – based on a somewhat rigid orthodoxy – and other experiences which are based on a desire for originality and creativity. Out of these experiences we have made changes that threaten to distort the substance of our work to a degree that we wonder what is the connection to what we call analysis.

From the considerations presented here, we have concluded that the continuation of our new methodology is justified, subject to modifications as needed. The methodology seems to be particularly suitable to the demands of the difficult task of training a new analyst.

Translated from Italian by
Robert Mercurio

REFERENCE

Fordham, M. (1970). Reflections on training analysis. *Journal of Analytical Psychology, 15*-1, 59-71.

Sandplay Workshop
What Makes It Work?

Katherine Bradway (San Francisco)

What is there about sandplay that contributes to its being experienced by patient and therapist alike as having such — as people say — power. What is there about sand in a 19½ by 28½ inch tray with blue base and sides, a supply of water and a collection of miniatures with the instructions to "Do what you want in the sand" that is experienced as so effective in promoting healing and growth? Sandplay is a form of active imagination, but the images are concrete. In comparison with dreams, sandplay is immediate rather than reported. It is, of course, play; but unlike spontaneous play it occurs within time and space boundaries.

To introduce the exploration of what contributes to the power of sandplay, I want to describe a particular sandplay session. A few days before I left for a month's vacation, a young man I had been seeing for several months came in and went directly into the sandplay room and started to make an oval center by putting his fingers into the sand down to the blue base and circling in the largest oval the rectangular box permitted. He ended up with an oval island. He piled the sand in the center from the edges and proceeded to pat the sand down, hard, adding water occasionally, and stroking and restroking the sand into a smooth, and smoother, hard surface. He said nothing until about half the time was up and then he asked me how much more time he had. When I told him, he heaved a sigh of relief and "settled in." He spent the rest of the time smoothing and patting the oval island, sometimes with one hand and sometimes with both hands, circling with his finger or fingers, and clearing the sand away from the blue so that it was a clear blue around the hard and harder oval center. I found myself relaxing with the rhythm of his movements. I had been feeling harassed with last minute preparations and this hour put me in a centered space. He also seemed to enter a new place. I silently thanked this man. Later I learned that for him, too, this had been a healing experience and had prepared him for the interruption of his therapy. And words did not have to be spoken. No amplification, no interpretation, no verbal exchanges were necessary.

In contrast to the healing potential of a single tray is the healing and growth function of a series of trays. The analysis of a series of sand scenes which have a common main element with seemingly only minor changes can show how the changes promote healing. This was true for Ida, a 40-year-old woman, who repeatedly formed a central pool—a "sacred pool"—nearly identical from tray to tray, but with small significant changes. She gradually developed sufficient confidence in her inner feminine to withstand the assault of a required hysterectomy (Bradway, 1981). Often a series of sand scenes includes the transcendence of opposites, sometimes with the use of a bridge which connects opposing parts of one's psyche presented in the tray. Demonstration of the transcendence may be found in the centering shown in a next following tray (Bradway, 1985).

While I was reading Edinger's (1985) book on alchemical symbolism, I realized more strongly than before, the extent to which sandplay has parallels in the alchemical process, which we know Jung found so helpful in describing the individuation process. The chaotic placement of a multitude of objects which often appears in beginning sandplay scenes parallels the *prima materia* of alchemy. As described by Edinger, it "provides a glimpse of the . . . chaos prior to the operation of the world-creating Logos" (p. 12). The chaos, the prima materia, is the connection to the shadow. In a sandplay process one can see order emerging from the chaos in subsequent trays.

The alchemical operations of calcinatio and solutio come first in Edinger's presentation of the sequence of operations. In the process of calcinatio, the matter that has remained is in the form of powder. I liken this to the sand—even the whiteness of it. Edinger referred to the "white earth" as corresponding "to the ash that has survived calcinatio." And, of course, solutio refers to water. But the process that most alerted me to the parallel between sandplay and alchemy was Edinger's description of coaglutio: "Concepts and abstractions don't coagulate. . . . The images of dreams and active imagination do coagulate. They connect the outer world with the inner world . . . and thus coagulate soul-stuff. Moods and affects toss us about wildly until they coagulate into something visible and tangible; then we can relate to them objectively" (p. 100). I see sandplay as offering an opportunity for such coagulation. Emotions and moods are concretized by the use of sand and water with, or even without, miniatures.

It is not just the expression of one's emotions, but the experiencing of their concretization that sandplay is all about. Dieckmann (1986) wrote that it is not the individual who is concerned only with knowing *that* it is (which I relate to finding ways to express oneself), but the individual who is concerned with experiencing *what* it is who attempts to give form to the unformed. To me, sandplay clearly shows this: It is the experiencing of molding the sand, of adding water in sprinkles or by cupfuls; of placing the objects; of burying them; of letting something happen, be it felt as creative or destructive; and of honoring whatever process takes over. In watching patients work, I sometimes feel that they enter a near-trance state.

The sandplay therapist typically avoids intruding upon the patient's experience of the concretization, or coagulation if you will. It is out there in front, to be seen, to be felt with the hands, to be changed with the hands. Although therapists do not overtly enter into the process while it is in progress, they provide the container or temenos. I think Kalff's (1980) phrase, "free and protected space," describes it best. The co-transference, a term I like to use for transference/counter transference, is always there. It is an essential part of therapy. Both negative and positive transference may be depicted in the sand scenes. Sometimes a figure is specifically identified by the patient as the therapist. This is more likely to happen in early scenes. As the sandplay progresses, it tends to be accompanied by reduced consciousness, often verbalized by such remarks as "I don't know what I am making" or "I don't know why I am putting this in." It is at this time that archetypal symbolism is most likely to be used.

The question arises of amplification and when and how to interpret. I think all sandplay therapists agree that interpretation should not be intrusive. When does one go over with the patient the photographs taken of the sandplay scenes? To such a query in my early training, Kalff replied that one goes over them when the patient and therapist feel it is time to go over them. Recently she has talked about the necessity of waiting for one, two—or ten years. She proposes that the daily living has to catch up with the process that takes place in sandplay before any detailed interpretation of the sand pictures is advisable. Then, bringing the process to the level of cognitive understanding can be done safely and is valuable.

Weinrib (1983) wrote of "delayed interpretation" in sandplay and discussed why both the delay of interpretation and its eventual inclusion are essential.

In my experience the mutuality of interpretation is important, as well as the mutuality in deciding when a series of sand scenes should be reviewed. I also find that it is valuable, frequently, to go over a series of scenes more than once—perhaps several times. Each time may yield new insights—new "aha" experiences: "So that's what was happening!"

Research done at the Mount Zion Psychiatric Center in San Francisco offers data that are particularly relevant here. Four of their psychoanalysts designed a study (Gassner, et al., 1982) to investigate Freud's early theory which assumed that analysts' interpretations of their patients' repressed mental contents were essential to making those contents conscious. What they found did not support this theory. Repressed contents typically emerged without the analysts' having made any prior interpretations that were relevant to the repressed contents. I think these findings are valuable to us in that they coincide with the contention that interpretation is not necessary while a sandplay process is occurring.

The Mount Zion group found, however, that the lifting of the defenses against the repressed contents depended upon the therapist's having passed what is called the "transference test," that is, that the patient feels safe in trusting the therapist—with all that this implies. Or we might say that the patient feels held in a safe temenos. Or we might say that the patient experiences being in a "free and protected space."

I think that "free and protected space" is akin to what Goodheart (1980) referred to as "secured-symbolizing field." He saw this field as one of three that occur in therapy, and described it as the one in which the therapist is aligned with the unconscious forces within both the therapist and the patient. Searles (1965), in discussing his version of this field, which he called "therapeutic symbiosis," referred to the therapist's having a feeling orientation which is felt to be awesome in its power, at the same time that a mutual spirit of childhood playfulness obtains. Winnicott (1971) in turn referred to "transitional play space" (p. 95). I find the discussion of these authors and that of Robert Langs about this field or space closely allied to what we find in sandplay therapy. Goodheart's phrase, "respect for the patient" can be translated into "giving the patient freedom to do what he or she wants to do" in sandplay, and his "secure container" can be translated into "protected"—it is the free and protected space of sandplay therapy. It is when there is respect and security, or freedom and protection, that the symbol is constellated in images or concretized within the sandtray and its transformative healing powers experienced. These writers have recognized the need for such a therapeutic space. Goodheart, for example, stated that the therapist's most important job is to provide for and maintain such a space. They also appreciate the hazards of the therapist's intruding into this space. In this connection, Langs (1981) put silence as the primary form of intervention.

Delaying or avoiding amplification and interpretation does not lessen the sandplay therapist's responsibility to become familiar with the cultural and archetypal dimensions of the available objects, and to try to understand both through feeling and thinking what is going on as the process unfolds. Understanding and empathy are essential, but they need not be voiced. As O'Connell (1986) wrote, "Silent amplification nourishes and expands the container. . . . There is meaning in the not-saying, in the conscious use of silent incubation, an inner witnessing" (p. 123). With the witnessing, sandplay therapists often find themselves deeply moved.

In conclusion, for me the power of sandplay has to do with using the coagulative potential of sand and water and miniatures with freedom to do what one wants to do with these media while feeling protected by a non-intruding, wise therapist whom one trusts. It seems so simple: a combination of sand and water, shelves of miniatures, and freedom and protection. But this combination holds the potential for healing and transformation.

REFERENCES

Bradway, K. (1981). A woman's individuation through sandplay. In G. Hill, (Ed.), *Sandplay studies: Origins, theory and practice*. San Francisco: C. G. Jung Institute.

Bradway, K. (1985). *Sandplay bridges and the transcendent function*. San Francisco: C. G. Jung Institute.

Dieckmann, H. (1986). *Twice-told tales: The psychological use of fairy tales*. Wilmette, IL: Chiron.

Edinger, E. (1985). *Anatomy of the psyche: Alchemical symbolism in psychotherapy*. La Salle, IL: Open Court.

Gassner, S.; Sampson, H.; Weiss, J.; Brumer, S. (1982). The Emergence of warded-off contents. *Psychoanalysis and Contemporary Thought, 5–1*.

Goodheart, W. (1980). Review of Langs' and Searles' books. *The San Francisco Jung Institute Library Journal, 1–4*, 2–39.

Kalff, D. (1980). *Sandplay: A psychotherapeutic approach to the psyche*. Boston: Sigo.

Langs, R. (1981). *Resistances and interventions*. New York: Jason Aronson.

O'Connell, C. (1986). *Amplification in context: The interactional significance of amplification in the secured-symbolizing context-plus field*. Unpublished doctoral dissertation, California Institute for Clinical Social Work.

Searles, H. (1965). *Collected papers on schizophrenia and related subjects*. New York: International Universities Press.

Weinrib, E. (1983). *Images of the Self: The sandplay therapy process*. Boston: Sigo.

Winnicott, D. (1971). *Playing and reality*. New York: Basic Books.

Sandplay Workshop
The Shadow and The Cross

Estelle Weinrib (New York)

Dora Kalff's version of sandplay therapy provides concrete visual evidence of the validity of Jung's theory of the structure and dynamics of the human psyche. Jung postulated the Self as a goal-directed, autonomous, self-organizing factor in the psyche.

In sandplay therapy one can see reflected in the sand pictures a recognizable inner developmental process; this process occurs without the analyst's guidance; interpretation of the sand pictures is delayed until critical stages of the process are completed. Sandplay also provides visual support of Jung's theory of the universality and power of archetypal images. Pictures from three cases will illustrate the ubiquity and the power of one of these images, the cross.

At a certain stage in the sandplay process the appearance of a cross in the sand pictures of these patients—some Christian, some not—indicates that they are experiencing the psychological equivalent of crucifixion. By crucifixion I mean psychological suspension between irreconcilable drives and values, resulting in prolonged emotional anguish which can end in profound change and a new stage in the life of the individual. In effect, the cross represents a rite of passage.

The cross as a ritual object pre-dates Christianity. Some early cave drawings consisted of a cross or a cross and circle; ancient burial grounds have yielded crosses from the Bronze and Iron ages; three-day Egyptian mysteries of initiation included the ankh as a symbol of life, rebirth and immortality. Crosses also appeared in Middle Eastern cultures and religions, and in Africa,

Mesopotamia, Sardinia and in Central and South America. The Aztecs used ritual crosses in the worship of the Goddess of Rain. In Europe, druids shaped trees into crosses for their ritual ceremonies.

Human beings were crucified to the glory of pre-Christian gods. Many pre-Christian gods were themselves hanged on cross-shaped trees and became symbols of death and resurrection or rebirth: Odin, Attis, Adonis, Mithra, Dionysus and Osiris. Krishna in India was variously reported to have been killed by an arrow or crucified on a tree.

Jung said of the structure of the cross, "Its meaning is that of a central point defined by the crossing of two straight lines. . . . The cross signifies order as opposed to . . . disorderly chaos. . . . In psychological processes it functions as an organizing center and in states of psychic disorder caused by an invasion of unconscious contents, it appears as a mandala divided into four" (CW11, pars. 432–33). Jung also said the cross symbol suggests that "the limits of the universe are not to be found in a nonexistent periphery but in its centre" (CW11, par. 434). In other words, the critical element of the cross is how well the center holds together. It seems evident that dismemberment is implicit in the structure of the cross, for once the arms have left the center, the force is centrifugal and it is the strength of the center that determines whether or not the structure is wrenched apart.

In my experience, the cross tends to appear in sand pictures well into the sandplay process when a strong center has been coagulated; when there has been some constellation of the Self so that the ego feels supported and sufficiently developed to withstand prolonged tension, that is, tension created between powerful opposing personal values. Or it appears when there has been an intense invasion by the shadow that challenges the ego's position, creating a powerful polarity that demands synthesis. By shadow I mean everything that one has not lived or cannot accept about oneself, plus subliminal perceptions that are not strong enough to reach consciousness; as Jung put it: "contents that are not yet ripe" (CW7, par. 103).

Before the appearance of the cross in the sandtray the patient has usually differentiated opposing personal values and realized there is a moral issue to resolve. The patient feels an urgent need to make a moral or ethical decision that will reflect his or her sense of personal integrity, whether or not the decision accords with contemporary collective social values. The patient realizes that the dilemma may not be soluble by personal resources; there is a willingness to wait and endure, to trust life and/or God. Jung described the situation when he said "anybody who finds himself on the road to wholeness can expect the characteristic suspension that is the meaning of crucifixion" (CW16, par. 470).

One factor that may enable a patient to sustain long periods of suspended uncertainty in service to the Self may be Kalff's "free and protected space," a space which would include a secure transference/countertransference situation. A second enabling factor may be the patient's innate strength of character or life force. The following are excerpts of three cases to illustrate or substantiate what I believe are present-day crucifixions.

The first case is not my own. For these pictures (1 and 2) I am indebted to Yasuhiro Yamanaka, a colleague who lives and works in Japan. He has generously allowed me to use these pictures because they illustrate the appearance of the cross at a time of crisis in the life of a Japanese Buddhist woman.

The patient was a 25-year-old woman, a social worker suffering from a sense of depersonalization. During the course of treatment, she developed an intense erotic transference. The sand pictures herein presented are only two of several created by the patient during the stressful work that brought about the successful resolution of the transference. Yamanaka reported that the entire process was concluded in 14 months and that the patient subsequently married and is the mother of three children. The intensity of emotion depicted in these images speaks for itself.

The second case is that of a Protestant middle-aged man who wanted to be a Jungian analyst. This career change would entail selling a prosperous business he had painfully and single-handedly created with his considerable artistic and creative capacities. Although he was very intelligent, he had learning disabilities, including a form of dyslexia. These disabilities had forced him to give up academic effort at an early age. Coming from a highly educated family, he had been deeply humiliated by his educational failures; during his youth there had been no real knowledge about such learning problems. He was simply judged as "slow" or "stupid."

At a certain point he had gone into Jungian analysis. It gave him a sense of meaning and, as so often happens, he decided he wanted to become an analyst. Somehow he overcame enough of his reading disability to read Jung and he achieved a solid understanding of Jungian theory. Married, with two of four children still at home, selling the business would put him and his family at financial risk.

Unable to resolve the problem with a verbal analysis, he tried sandplay. As with everything he did, he brought intelligence and dedication to the work. At the deepest point of inner conflict, a cross appeared in his sand pictures (3 and 4) and he became aware of the depth of his anguish. He struggled on and eventually decided not to sell his business at that time. Shortly thereafter, synchronistically I believe, his two grown children returned and went to work in the business, freeing him to pursue other creative interests. The issue of becoming an analyst and his obsessive reading of Jung faded.

The third case is that of a middle-aged Jewish man who had lived most of his life as a bi-sexual. Although he loved his wife and had been completely faithful to her in his heterosexual life and had four children with her, he had engaged in secret homosexual activity throughout his life, starting as a teenager long before his marriage.

At a certain point in his analysis, he came to the conclusion that he could no longer endure his secret life. He felt his strongest drive was homosexual and that, as a matter of integrity, he should "come out of the closet" and live his sexual preference openly. He was deterred by his fear that he would lose his hetereosexual friends of a lifetime and that he would have difficulty adjusting to life in the homosexual world.

Most painful was a deep fear that his children would reject him. He lived for a year in great unresolved tension and made dozens of sand pictures with a wooden cross prominently featured. They were especially striking because he had a firm Jewish identity and could not understand why he felt impelled repeatedly to place the cross in his sand pictures. The impasse was finally resolved for him when his children inadvertently found out about his "awful secret" from a third party and assured him that they would care for him whatever course he chose. His wife subsequently left him. He came to the conclusion that the gender of his next partner would not be the deciding factor, so much as the quality of relatedness that could be achieved.

This kind of resolution can happen in sandplay because it is a kind of concrete active imagination where the opposites, consciousness and the unconscious, meet in the transcendent function.

When a person makes a sand picture, whether molding the sand or choosing and placing figures, that person is concretizing unconscious impulses, thereby merging idea and reality, uniting the inner and outer worlds. This union may indeed facilitate transcendence to a new stage in development, another level of consciousness.

Picture 1.

Picture 2.

Picture 3.

Picture 4.

Picture 5.

Picture 6.

Picture 7.

Picture 8.

Voice Dialogue and Holocaust (Workshop)

Gustav Dreifuss (Haifa)

Voice dialogue is a form of active imagination with inner figures; it was developed by Hal Stone (Stone & Winkelman, 1985). It can be applied to improve communication in psychotherapy and elsewhere. The therapist or facilitator speaks directly to the complexes or subpersonalities of the patient. This method is applicable in all psychoanalytic schools but, because of its connection to the theory of complexes, it seems to be especially suitable for Jungians. Voice dialogue also includes elements of Gestalt, psychodrama and Transactional Analysis. It is hardly possible to learn voice dialogue through a lecture; it has to be experienced. An example follows.

Eli took part in a one-day workshop and in several evenings of voice dialogue. As we sat together with other participants and I was forming the groups with two other facilitators, I felt that Eli wanted to be facilitated by me. I asked him about this and he confirmed my feeling. As there were few people that evening I worked with him alone, that is, without an observer.

When we sat opposite each other in another room, I asked him what he would like to work on. He said unhesitatingly, "On a dream I dreamt a few days ago." This is the dream: *I went with a list of things I wanted to buy to a supermarket, but did not find anything. So I went to the information desk where the girl in charge said that there is a special room for VIPs where one sees all the goods listed on a television screen. One has to press a button every time there appears an item on the screen one wants. All the merchandise ordered will be delivered upon leaving the supermarket. I then went into the room, lay*

down on a chair like a dentist chair and suddenly found myself to be na-
ked. I saw staff in white coats walking about. I heard a voice from behind
me asking if I was ready. Then I pressed the button and the chair started
to shake badly and I woke up trembling in fear.

Voice Dialogue on the Dream

Facilitator (F): May I talk to that part that was trembling in fear?
(Eli moves to another chair.)

F: You are that part of Eli who trembled in fear in the dream. Try to be there again, feel it, lie in the chair as in the dream. (After some time of silence, the expression in the face changes, there is fear and eventually trembling.)

F: I would like to hear when you first appeared in Eli's life. (After some moments of silence the facilitator feels that an early experience comes back.) How old are you?

Trembler (T): About 8 years old. I stand at the window of our living room in our apartment in a Polish town. A terrible noise of planes, detonations, fire-war broke out and the Germans bomb our town. (The trembling reappears. Some time passes.)

F: When did you come again to Eli?

T: I am 10 years old, in the apartment. Some KGB agents enter and fetch us to be deported — mother, sister, me.

F: Go into this experience in your fantasy, be there! (Eli trembles.) When did you come to Eli again?

T: I am now in Sibir. I stand at the bedside of my mother, who is very ill. I hold hands with my sister.

F: Yes, be totally there, re-experience the scene.

T: A woman standing next to me says: Your mother is dead. (Trembling, silence.) But now, mother opens her eyes. . . . She is not dead.

F: When were you again with Eli?

T: I see myself, my mother and my sister walking behind a fully loaded cart, all our belongings. The

coachman walks with us. We are on the way to
another town in Sibir. We walk for hours in the
snow. It is cold. It is evening. We are all tired, ex-
hausted. My mother asks the coachman to stop in
order to spend the night at a ranch on the way.
The coachman refuses. Mother begs him again
and again. Now he gives in. We enter the ranch.
They close the gates behind us. Suddenly I hear
ravening wolves attacking the ranch. I hear the
scratching of their claws, without end. (Trembling.) . . . If the wolves enter the ranch . . . If
we had continued the journey without entering
the ranch?

F: When were you again with Eli?

T: I don't think I was with him any more till the night
of the dream.

F: I want to talk now to the part in you which feels
very important; it is the VIP. He sits over there.
(Eli moves to another chair.)

F: Shalom! You are the VIP part of Eli. Tell me, what
do you think of him?

VIP: Well, not bad, but he could give me still more
space. He has it in himself. Look how important
he has become. He is important in his profession,
president of the professional organization, lecturer at the university, he writes papers in his
profession which are very well received. I am
really very important.

F: Thank you. I am glad to have met you and to
know you. Please, move now back to the ego-
chair, and now stand behind the chair.

After having repeated to the awareness level the main content
of what the two sub-personalities, the Trembler and the VIP had
said, Eli was asked to sit on the ego-chair. We discussed what
had happened and I explained to Eli that the VIP part was connected with the trembler; that is, the VIP was an inner aggressor,
a victimizer, an ambitious part. This inner victimizer can constellate the victim who is connected with the trembler. An inner tension between these two sub-personalities exists.

But why did he have this dream now? What happened? Why

was he afraid, trembling in the dream? I asked what happened to his father. Eli told me that after the Blitzkrieg (1939) in Poland was over, his father learned that a group of Jews had succeeded in chartering a Soviet plane and flying to Japan, to freedom. His father was away from town to find out particulars and maybe organize a similar flight for his family, when they were deported to Sibir in 1941. Therefore, the father remained in the territory occupied by the Germans. Later, Eli found out that his father had come back to their apartment and found it empty. He was later deported by the Germans, and murdered in Treblinka. Treblinka: just a week ago, "Ivan the terrible," the murderer of Treblinka, was brought to Israel. This was the trigger of the dream.

Voice Dialogue: Discussion

This dream clearly was evoked by bringing the "butcher of Treblinka" to Israel. Memories of being the victim of the circumstances of war and of being a Jew were evoked. The aggressors or victimizers were Nazis or Russians, that is, human beings who, under an ideology, victimized the Jews. In the awareness of the victims are not only the childhood experiences but also possible new situations of being victimized again. This awareness connects with the existential fears that catastrophes, by nature or by humans, may occur at any time. But, next to these facts which are valid for all humankind, is there an inner, personal victimizer at work as well?

The dream brings up the secretary who knows that Eli is a VIP. In the voice dialogue it became apparent that the VIP part of Eli was very much connected with the ambitious part. This part wants Eli to succeed; it has succeeded in furthering Eli in his professional career. He is very successful in many fields and has a happy family. But, what is the price for his success? Through voice dialogue it became clear that there is an inner aggressor or victimizer in Eli which is also responsible for his fears.

The awareness of these sub-personalities may help to take some energy from the pusher-aggressor and help Eli to live eventually a more relaxed life-style, thus reducing fears.

REFERENCE

Stone, H.; Winkelman, S. (1985). *Embracing ourselves: Voice dialogue manual*. Marina del Ray, CA: Devorss.

The Singer-Loomis Inventory of Personality: An Update on the Measurement of Jung's Typology (Workshop)

June Singer (San Francisco)

Mary Loomis (Detroit)

"Give up all you have ever believed,
and then perhaps you will discover something new."

C. G. Jung

This quotation could well have been the guiding motif of the work on psychological types in which we have been engaged over the past dozen years. It will surely serve as a theme for the statements that follow. We ask you to put aside some of the assumptions that you may have held about the measurement of Jung's typology, and to be open to considering the new perspective offered by the Singer-Loomis Inventory of Personality (SLIP).

Many people have been attracted to Jung because of his remarkable ability to deal with paradox in this world where not everything follows the rules of logic and linearity. A statement attributed to Jung is, "Whatever we say is true; the opposite is also true."

Jung recognized the paradox of his own personality or, rather, his two personalities—the historical personality and the personality that bridged the ages. This dual personality structure, with its temporal and eternal aspects, was not Jung's alone, but may be generalized to all individuals. The historical personality, ruled by the ego, is basically conscious, practical, and functional. It carries on the person's everyday affairs. The timeless personality is ruled by the Self; this is the essential personality, from which the ego emerges and to which it ultimately returns. The corpus of Jung's writings suggests that we cannot have a "psychology of consciousness" as opposed to a "psychology of the unconscious." It is not a matter of either/or, but of both/and. Therefore it would seem that a psychology of typology must come to terms with both the psychology of consciousness and the psychology of the unconscious.

Every one of the eight cognitive modes described by Jung (introverted thinking, introverted feeling, introverted sensation, introverted intuition, extraverted thinking, extraverted feeling, extraverted sensation, and extraverted intuition), whether conscious or unconscious, is a functioning part of the psychological resources of each individual. At any given time, certain cognitive modes are preferred as ways of dealing with oneself and the world. These become well-developed and the individual ego feels confident in using them. Other cognitive modes remain relatively unconscious and are used more or less by default when the ego's control is diminished or when the leading cognitive modes are not available or not appropriate in a particular situation. To recognize and reflect the immense flexibility of the psyche in choosing which of the eight cognitive modes and possible interactions best serve the individual at a certain time or in a certain circumstance, any inventory that purports to measure Jung's typology can best serve the individual by measuring each cognitive mode independently. This is not to suggest that one should overlook the possibility that opposite cognitive modes (for example, introverted thinking and extraverted feeling) might tend to be mutually exclusive, but it does open the way to working toward an integration of the opposites and to recognizing when this integration occurs.

Jung's work with typology stems from his observations while he was a member of the Freudian circle, between 1907 and 1913. He noted the individual differences in approaches to case material, as exemplified by Freud's eros theory and Adler's "will to power." Jung saw these approaches as opposites, a view which eventuated in the opposing "attitudes," extraversion and introversion. In his book *Psychological Types* (CW6), he stated that the functions consist of pairs of opposites that are mutually exclusive. According to that book, the mutual exclusivity theory was based upon Jung's observations drawn from his reading in classical and medieval literature: such writings as those of Schiller, Jordan, Spitteler and William James, and from his experiences of personality conflicts in the Freudian circle. He scarcely referred to any clinical material in support of the bipolarity assumption, much less to the psychology of so-called normal people. Nor were there any reports of objective research either supporting or invalidating this assumption.

Of the general attitudinal types, Jung wrote, "It is a fundamental contrast, sometimes quite clear, sometimes obscure but always apparent when one is dealing with individuals whose personality is in any way pronounced" (CW6, par. 555). This statement leaves open the possibility that, in individuals whose personality is not so pronounced, the fundamental opposition may not prevail. Although Jung hinted at this possibility in his descriptions of types, he never investigated it. He moved on to other interests and left the subject of typology in a relatively undeveloped state. When asked to talk about typology later in his life, for example in the 1935 Tavistock Lectures (CW18), he summarized his earlier findings and gave no indication of having done additional research.

Toward the end of his life, 40 years after his statements about the mutual exclusivity of the types, Jung's main thrust was in the direction of harmonizing the opposites. He made this clear in *Mysterium Coniunctionis* (CW14). His work on anima and animus had also moved in the direction of bringing the opposites together as an important part of the work on individuation. But those individuals involved in psychological type research ignored Jung's later writings concerning the integration of the opposites. They continued their work on the basis of Jung's 1921 assumptions about the bipolarity of type and function. What Jung had put forth as a somewhat tentative assumption became the cornerstone of the work on typology for many years.

When we began the research leading to the development of the SLIP, we questioned Jung's bipolarity assumption. The results of our initial investigation surprised us, as we noted earlier (Loomis

& Singer, 1980). We used two Jungian type inventories in this study, the *Jungian Type Survey* (GW; Gray & Wheelwright, 1942) and the *Myers-Briggs Type Indicator* (MBTI; Myers, 1962). We created a revised version of each inventory, rewriting the items to eliminate the forced-choice format. For example, a single item such as "At a party, I like to: a) talk b) listen" was rewritten into two statements: "At a party, I like to talk," and "At a party, I like to listen." The two new statements were constructed to be evaluated independently on a scale from zero ("never") to four ("always"). Subjects completed both the original and the revised version of one of the inventories. We reasoned that, if Jung's bipolarity assumption was valid, changing the construction of the items from forced choice to free response would have no effect on a person's typology; the typology profile obtained from the revised version would be identical to the profile determined by the original inventory.

We found that the superior function for over half the subjects changed when they responded freely; 72 percent of the people who took the GW and 36 percent of the people who took the MBTI had a different superior function on our revised inventories. In examining the profiles from the revised inventories, we also found that in almost half of the subjects the inferior function was not the opposite of the superior function (55% on the GW and 29% on the MBTI). We concluded that a free response inventory was needed, one that would allow the measurement of typological functioning without imposing a forced bipolarity.

As we continued our research, designing and refining the SLIP, we found increasing evidence to support our position. Other people were also questioning the validity of Jung's bipolarity assumption (Metzner, et al., 1981; Mahlberg, 1982) and some had undertaken empirical research. For example, Mahlberg (1982) investigated bipolarity using a Q-sort technique with the MBTI. He found a number of subjects whose typology did not conform to the bipolar distribution. The proportional incidence of these subjects was almost identical to what we had found with our SLIP research.

More recently, Mahlberg (1987) used the SLIP in a study investigating the validity of Sheldrake's morphogenetic field hypothesis. He discovered that individuals who have introverted feeling more highly developed than extraverted feeling in their cognitive styles, were more likely to show the effects of cognitive resonance in learning a pseudo Morse code. That is, successive groups of people whose cognitive styles had that particular factor were learning the code with increasing speed. Mahlberg speculated that it is through introverted feeling that we are connected to collective memory. Introverted feeling did not have to be the most highly developed cognitive mode, nor did feeling have to be the most highly developed function. What mattered in the individual's cognitive style was for introverted feeling to be more highly developed than extraverted feeling. Mahlberg was of the opinion that this finding would not have emerged if he had used another instrument to measure typology.

Because the SLIP measures the eight cognitive modes independently, it does not impose any particular dynamic on an individual's cognitive style profile. It does not exclude or eliminate profiles that exhibit the bipolar development of the functions. The SLIP shows bipolar development in an individual's typology when it exists. In fact, an analysis of SLIP profiles of Michigan State University students by Mosher (1985) found that most of them had cognitive styles which conformed to Jung's hypothesis. This finding is not surprising. It is known that young adults are striving to adjust to society's demands. To do this, they need to rely on their most highly developed cognitive modes. For most young adults this means a bipolar development of their typology. Generally it is not until individuals are working to become conscious that they transcend the bipolar development of their typology. This change is likely to occur after 35 years of age, when the demands of society usually have been met.

A further analysis of Mosher's subjects was undertaken by Hurley and Cosgro (1986). They analyzed the relation between the SLIP scales and the subjects' responses to the Interpersonal Check List (ICL) of LaForge and Suczek (1955). One result that they said was surprising to them was that the love-hate dimension on the ICL did not correlate with any scale on the SLIP. If the love-hate dimension involved strong emotions, however, we would not expect it to correlate with the SLIP scales; cognitive styles based on Jung's typology are independent of emotions. It is true that the feeling function is often confused with emotions but, as Jung stated, feeling is an evaluative, rational, judging process. Emotions may be connected to poorly developed functions, but not necessarily so. The significant correlations between the eight cognitive modes and the ICL sectors appear to provide some support for the validity of the SLIP scales. For example, extraverted thinking and introverted thinking were both negatively correlated with rebelliousness; this correlation may suggest that thinking is more deliberate and independent than reactionary and conforming. Similarly, extraverted feeling is positively correlated with the self-effacing sector. We have interpreted extraverted feeling as the quality of valuing the group more highly than the individual. Thus, putting one's self down, being self-effacing, would be expected when extraverted feeling is functioning. Significant correlations for all eight cognitive modes suggested to Hurley and Cosgro that the SLIP may have some utility as an interpersonal measure.

Suppport for certain of the SLIP scales has been given by other research. In particular, a study investigating the relationship between cognitive styles and religious beliefs, undertaken by Evans (1985), provided support for the validity of introverted sensation, introverted feeling, extraverted feeling, and extraverted thinking. An interesting finding by Evans, one substantiated by other research, was that extraverts appear to place more importance on dreams than introverts do. His interpretation is that introverts, being more aligned with their inner world, may be attuned to active imagination and meditation as well as to their dreams. Extraverts, on the other hand, being more aligned with the physical, outer world, mainly connect to their inner lives through their dreams. Evans' data also supported the SLIP research, reported in the SLIP Manual (Singer & Loomis, 1983b) in showing that women are more likely to have thinking well developed in their cognitive styles than men are. We have noted—and this is an anecdotal observation, not an empirical study—that if a woman is a professional and has a career, it is likely that she will have thinking as a dominant function.

Research on the SLIP, ours and others', has provided support for the validity of this instrument. Support for some of the scales is greater than for others. Research has been useful also in pointing out where we need to make adjustments in the Inventory. For example, statistical measures described in the Manual, such as the standard error of measurement, are based upon averages and do not take into account the variations in raw score totals brought about by differences in response sets. Some individuals respond to the SLIP items primarily with 1's or 2's and an occasional 3. Other individuals respond with the higher end of the scale, assigning 4's and 5's to most of the items. The people in the first group will have scale scores totalling somewhere around 200 or 250. Those in the latter group could have a grand total approximating 400. We think, as do our publishers, that having only one set of statistical measures of error, based upon the average raw score totals is not accurate enough. We plan to compute standard error of measurement statistics for two distributions, to accommodate the variability in raw score totals caused by these response sets. We plan to make these computations, using a data bank of computer-scored profiles that we are accumulating.

As a prelude to the implementation of a computer-generated interpretation of the SLIP, we undertook a validity study of the SLIP Interpretative Guide (1983a) during 1985 and the early part of 1986. The subjects in this research were participants in SLIP workshops in different localities. These subjects described themselves by agreeing or disagreeing with a set of statements abstracted from the SLIP Interpretive Guide and then completing the SLIP itself. Their self-descriptions were compared to scale scores derived from their SLIP profiles to determine the degree of congruence between them. The congruence between the two self-reports—the self-descriptions and the SLIP scale scores— was taken as a measure of the Interpretative Guide's validity in regard to interpreting SLIP profiles. The greater the congruence, the higher the validity.

The overall validity of the Interpretative Guide was 74 percent, which means that the statements drawn from the Guide were congruent with the SLIP scale scores three out of four times. Agreement ranged from a high of 88 percent for the intuition statement, to a low of 59 percent for the perceiving statement. The variability among the locality groups was not as extreme, ranging from a high of 79 percent to a low of 72 percent. It is interesting that the lowest average agreement occurred for a Zurich group of individuals training to become Jungian analysts. These participants were typologically sophisticated. They had studied Jung's theory of psychological types in a setting where bipolarity had been stressed as the dynamic underlying typology. On the other hand, the group with the highest agreement was composed of individuals from Grosse Pointe, Michigan, who had little or no previous knowledge or information about Jung's theory of typology.

Why did the highest agreement occur for the least knowledgeable group? Why did the most knowledgeable group have the lowest agreement? Perhaps subjects with prior experience of Jung's typology — either through a study of Jung's theory of typology or through having taken the GW or the MBTI — might have approached this study with a mind set that could have influenced their self-descriptions. It could be, also, that individuals had a mind set based on social desirability — what they had been told was of greatest value. Jungians traditionally value intuition over sensation. If the analyst-candidates at the Zurich Institute held this view, most of them would want to be intuitives as well as perceivers rather than judgers.

Similarly, we thought, an individual who had been typed on the MBTI as being introverted, intuitive, feeling, and perceiving might mark the self-descriptive statements in a way that was congruent with that typing, without examining carefully what the statements actually were saying.

In looking at the results for the Zurich group, there was high congruence in regard to intuition: 16 of the 17 had described themselves as intuitives and indeed had intuition scores higher than sensation scores on the SLIP. But in describing themselves as perceivers rather than judgers, their congruence fell to less than 50 percent. There was agreement for only eight of the 17. The less knowledgeable people in the Grosse Pointe group were not constrained in their self-descriptions by an adherence to Jung's hypothesis of bipolarity. Indeed, many had not heard of the bipolar dynamic. They were as likely to describe themselves as having both intuition and sensation highly developed as they were to describe themselves with one highly developed and the other poorly developed. Similarly, they could describe themselves as being judging while also being intuitive. The congruence for them on intuition was 84 percent (16 out of 19) and on judging it was 79 percent (15 out of 19).

Predetermined mind sets could probably account for some of our findings. But some of these people were attempting to be open-minded. How are we to account for them? Could it be that these Zurich analysts in training had a mental image of how bipolarity worked, but lacked an image of the independent development of the functions? Thus, try as they might, were they unable to envision the possibility of having both intuition and sensation well developed? Perhaps we need a new image of how typology works.

It may not have been true in Jung's time, but today almost everyone who has studied typology has encountered the drawing of a cross formed by the four functions. On the vertical axis, thinking and feeling are in opposition, with thinking at the top and feeling at the bottom. Sensation and intuition are in opposition on the horizontal axis. Usually, sensation is to the left, and intuition to the right. The axes are equal in length and the cross implies that energy flows in one direction or the other, but not both. The assumption, in line with Jung's writings, is that thinking and feeling are inversely related, as are sensation and intuition.

Many experiences do not conform to logic. To be true to life we need to follow Jung's lead and strive for a both/and instead of an either/or orientation. We need an alternative for the cross model of typological functioning.

Perhaps the new image symbolizing how psychological types function will be provided by someone in another field. For example Bruwer (1987), using Buckminster Fuller's synergetic geometry, envisioned typology as a tetrahedron. Bruwer argued for the validity of the SLIP's multi-axial approach to measuring typology. A simpler model might be provided by the Native American medicine wheel. According to this model, standing in the center of one's circle, free from the limitations imposed by a particular frame of reference, characterizes the individual who is integrating the opposites. In Jungian terms, this integration would mean, for instance, using thinking and feeling simultaneously to make decisions, or perceiving through a blend of sensation and intuition.

Although Jung did not discuss the integration of the opposing functions, for example, thinking and feeling, in his volume on *Psychological Types* (CW6), he did write about this integration in later works. Moreover, he implied this process from the very beginning, as the full title of the first edition of his volume on typology attests. The complete title was *Psychological Types: The Psychology of Individuation*.

Individuation is the process of expanding the personality to include both opposites of a pair. The transcendent function can be born when one is willing to stand in the center of one's circle typologically and bear the tension of developing an inferior function. Jung wrote:

> This change of personality is naturally not an alteration of the original hereditary disposition, but rather a transformation of the general attitude. Those sharp cleavages and antagonisms between conscious and unconscious, such as we see so clearly in the endless conflicts of neurotic natures, nearly always rest on a noticeable one-sidedness of the conscious attitude, which gives absolute precedence to one or two functions, while the others are unjustly thrust into the background. Conscious realization and experience of fantasies assimilates the unconscious inferior functions to the conscious mind—a process which is naturally not without far-reaching effects on the conscious attitude. . . . I have called this change, which is the aim of our analysis of the unconscious, the transcendent function. This remarkable capacity of the psyche for change, expressed in the transcendent function, is the principal object of late medieval alchemical philosophy. . . . The secret of alchemy was in fact the transcendent function, the transformation of personality through blending and fusion of the noble with the base components, of the differentiated with the inferior functions, of the conscious with the unconscious. (CW7, pars. 359–60)

The SLIP is an effective clinical tool for assessing the subtle shifting in the blending and fusion of attitude and function. It is also useful for those individuals who are struggling with the tension of opposites, who want to know where their growth potential lies, and want to evaluate the degree of progress they are making.

Table I.

Validity of the SLIP Interpretive Guide as determined by the congruence between self descriptions and SLIP scale scores.

N = 140	I	E	J	P	T	F	S	N	AGREEMENT	
PA = 13	11/13	11/12	10/13	6/13	10/13	11/13	8/13	9/13	76/10	73%
GP = 19	16/19	17/19	15/19	12/19	15/19	16/19	13/19	16/19	120/152	79%
CH = 11	10/11	8/11	6/11	7/11	9/11	10/11	7/11	10/11	67/88	76%
RO = 23	19/23	16/23	14/23	13/23	15/23	17/23	20/23	19/23	133/184	72%
NY = 57	44/57	41/57	41/57	36/57	38/57	43/57	37/57	53/57	333/456	73%
ZU = 17	15/17	10/17	11/17	8/17	12/17	15/17	11/17	16/17	98/136	72%
TOTALS	115/	103/	97/	82/	99/	112/	96/	123/	827/	
	140	139	140	140	140	140	140	140	1119	
	82%	74%	69%	59%	71%	80%	69%	88%	74%	

I = Introversion, E = Extraversion, J = Judging, P = Perceiving
T = Thinking, F = Feeling, S = Sensation, N = Intuition

The first numeral represents agreements, the second numeral equals the number of subjects

PA = Palo Alto, GP = Grosse Pointe, CH = Chicago, RO = Royal Oak, NY = New York, ZU = Zurich

REFERENCES

Bruwer, M. (1987). Buckminster Fuller's synergetic geometry in support of the Singer-Loomis Inventory of Personality. *The San Francisco Jung Institute Library Journal*, 7–1, 1–11.

Evans, C. (1985). Religion and cognitive style: An exploration of Jung's typology among A.R.E. study group members. Unpublished doctoral dissertation, University of Michigan, Ann Arbor.

Gray, H.; Wheelwright, J. B. (1942). *Jungian Type Survey*. San Francisco: C. G. Jung Institute.

Hurley, J.; Cosgro, M. (1986). An interpersonal-Jungian interface: Links of divergent personality measures. *Journal of Clinical Psychology*, 42, 469–74.

LaForge, R.; Suczek, R. (1955). The interpersonal dimensions of personality: An interpersonal check list. *Journal of Personality, 24*, 94–112.

Loomis, M.; Singer, J. (1980). Testing the bipolar assumption in Jung's typology. *Journal of Analytical Psychology, 25-4*, 351–56.

Mahlberg, A. (1982). *Bipolar versus independent ordering of the psychological functions in Jung's personality theory.* Doctoral dissertation, University Microfilms International, No. 8225858.

Mahlberg, A. (1987). Evidence of collective memory: A test of Sheldrake's theory. *Journal of Analytical Psychology, 32-1*, 23–34.

Metzner, R.; Burney, C.; Mahlberg, A. (1981). Towards a reformulation of the typology of functions. *Journal of Analytical Psychology, 26-1*, 33–47.

Mosher, D. (1985). Hemisphericity and Jungian typology. Unpublished master's thesis, Michigan State University, East Lansing.

Myers, I. (1962). *The Myers-Briggs Type Indicator.* Palo Alto, CA: Consulting Psychologists Press.

Singer, J.; Loomis, M. (1983a). Interpretive guide for the Singer-Loomis inventory of personality. Palo Alto, CA: Consulting Psychologists Press.

Singer, J.; Loomis, M. (1983b). *Singer-Loomis inventory of personality manual.* Palo Alto, CA: Consulting Psychologists Press.

Singer, J.; Loomis, M. (1984). *The Singer-Loomis inventory of personality (SLIP).* Palo Alto, CA: Consulting Psychologists Press.

Also from DAIMON ZÜRICH

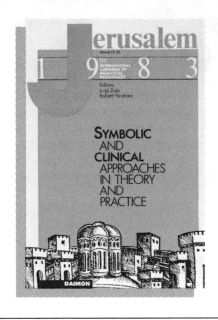

Symbolic and Clinical Approaches in Theory and Practice – the Proceedings of the Ninth International Congress of Analytical Psychology, edited by Luigi Zoja and Robert Hinshaw – is now available in a hardbound volume of 370 pages. Twenty-five contributors from around the globe address a controversial issue and reveal that their approaches to the soul are often highly individual, if not directly contradictory.

ISBN 3-85630-504-1

Meetings with Jung is the first publication of personal diary entries made by British psychiatrist E. A. Bennet during his frequent visits in the household of Swiss analyst C. G. Jung during the last years of Jung's life, 1946–1961. The notes are at once deep, lively, serious and entertaining; an ideal introduction to Jung for the casual beginner, a warm and intimate addition to more scholarly works for advanced students of Jung.

ISBN 3-85630-501-7

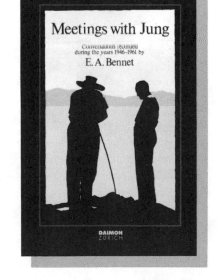

A Testament to the Wilderness consists of ten international responses to a highly original paper by Swiss psychiatrist C. A. Meier. This colorful collection of authors views wilderness within and without, psychologically and ecologically, presenting a wealth of perspectives on an ancient – and at the same time eminently relevant – phenomenon.

Published with The Lapis Press.

ISBN 3-85630-503-3

The Myth of Meaning is a classic work by the well-known co-author of C. G. Jung's «Memories, Dreams, Reflections». Still working and writing in the tradition of Jung today, Aniela Jaffé here elaborates on the vital role played by meaning – or its absence – in every human life. This book can help us to more awareness of our own – collective as well as personal – myths of meaning.

ISBN 3-85630-500-9

German Language Editions from Daimon Verlag:

C. G. Jung im Gespräch – Interviews, Talks, Encounters. In this handsome hard-bound edition of 340 pages, numerous transcripts and reports, most of them previously untranslated, are published in the German language for the very first time. C. G. Jung shows himself to be at once a deep clear thinker and also a humorous and warm human being, with a far-reaching range of interests, knowledge and concern.

ISBN 3-85630-022-8

- **Die Engel erlebt**
  Gitta Mallasz

- **Psyche und Erlösung**
  Siegmund Hurwitz

- **Lilith – die erste Eva**
  Siegmund Hurwitz

- **Von Freud zu Jung**
  Liliane Frey-Rohn

- **Der Heilige und
  das Schwein**
  Regina Abt-Baechi

- **Selbstmord und
  seelische Wandlung**
  James Hillman

- **Jenseits der Werte
  seiner Zeit**
  Liliane Frey-Rohn

- **Der Mythus vom Sinn**
  Aniela Jaffé

- **Themen bei C. G. Jung**
  Aniela Jaffé

- **Der Traum als Medizin**
  C. A. Meier

- **Die Suche nach innen**
  James Hillman

- **Aufsätze zur Psychologie
  C. G. Jungs**
  Aniela Jaffé

- **Religiöser Wahn und
  Schwarze Magie**
  Aniela Jaffé

- **Studien zu
  C. G. Jungs Psychologie**
  Toni Wolff

- **Im Umkreis des Todes**
  von Franz · Frey-Rohn · Jaffé

- **Weltenmorgen**
  Gitta Mallasz

- **Die Passion der Perpetua**
  Eine Frau zwischen zwei
  Gottesbildern
  Marie-Louise von Franz

- **Die Psychologie C. G. Jungs
  und die Psychiatrie**
  Heinrich Karl Fierz

- **Kunst und schöpferisches
  Unbewusstes**
  Erich Neumann